Hebrews, the General Epistles, and Revelation

Hebrews, the General Epistles, and Revelation

FORTRESS COMMENTARY ON THE BIBLE STUDY EDITION

Margaret Aymer
Cynthia Briggs Kittredge
David A. Sánchez
Editors

Fortress Press
Minneapolis

HEBREWS, THE GENERAL EPISTLES, AND REVELATION
Fortress Commentary on the Bible Study Edition

Copyright © 2016 Fortress Press. All rights reserved. Except for brief quotations in critical articles and reviews, no part of this book may be reproduced in any manner without prior written permission from the publisher. Visit http://www.augsburgfortress.org/copyrights/contact.asp
or write to Permissions, Augsburg Fortress, Box 1209, Minneapolis, MN 55440.

Unless otherwise noted, Scripture quotations are from New Revised Standard Version Bible, copyright © 1989 by the Division of Education of the National Council of Churches of Christ in the United States of America.

Excerpted from the *Fortress Commentary on the Bible: The New Testament*
(Minneapolis: Fortress Press, 2014); Margaret Aymer, Cynthia Briggs Kittredge, David A. Sánchez, volume editors.

Fortress Press Publication Staff:
Neil Elliott and Scott Tunseth, Project Editors
Marissa Wold, Production Manager
Laurie Ingram, Cover Design.

Copyeditor: Jeffrey A. Reimer

Typesetter: PerfecType, Nashville, TN

Proofreader: David Cottingham and Linda Maloney

Library of Congress Cataloging-in-Publication data is available

ISBN: 978-1-5064-1593-2

eISBN: 978-1-5064-1594-9

The paper used in this publication meets the minimum requirements of American National Standard for Information Sciences—Permanence of Paper for Printed Library Materials, ANSI Z329, 48-1984. Manufactured in the U.S.A.

CONTENTS

Publisher's Note about Fortress Commentary on the Bible Study Editions   vii
Abbreviations   ix
Series Introduction   1

Reading the Christian New Testament in the Contemporary World
    Kwok Pui-lan   5

Negotiating the Jewish Heritage of Early Christianity
    Lawrence M. Wills   31

Rootlessness and Community in Contexts of Diaspora
    Margaret Aymer   47

The Apocalyptic Legacy of Early Christianity
    David A. Sánchez   63

Introduction to Hebrews, the General Epistles, and Revelation   *Neil Elliott*   621
    Hebrews   *David A. deSilva*   625
    James   *Timothy B. Cargal*   655
    1 Peter   *David L. Bartlett*   667
    2 Peter   *Pheme Perkins*   685
    1, 2, 3 John   *Jaime Clark-Soles*   691
    Jude   *Pheme Perkins*   711
    Revelation   *Barbara R. Rossing*   715

PUBLISHER'S NOTE

About the Fortress Commentary on the Bible Study Editions

In 2014 Fortress Press released the two-volume *Fortress Commentary on the Bible*. See the Series Introduction (pp. 1–3) for a look inside the creation and design of the Old Testament/Apocrypha and New Testament volumes. While each comprehensive commentary volume can easily be used in classroom settings, we also recognized that dividing the larger commentaries into smaller volumes featuring key sections of Scripture may be especially helpful for use in corresponding biblical studies courses. To help facilitate such classroom use, we have broken the two-volume commentary into eight study editions.

Please note that in this study edition the page numbers match the page numbers of the larger Fortress Commentary on the Bible volume in which it first appeared. We have intentionally retained the same page numbering to facilitate use of the study editions and larger volumes side by side.

Hebrews, the General Epistles, and Revelation was first published in Fortress Commentary on the Bible: The New Testament.

ABBREVIATIONS

General

AT	Alpha Text (of the Greek text of Esther)
BOI	Book of Isaiah
Chr	Chronicler
DH	Deuteronomistic History
DI	Deutero-Isaiah
Dtr	Deuteronomist
Gk.	Greek
H	Holiness Code
Heb.	Hebrew
JPS	Jewish Publication Society
LXX	The Septuagint
LXX B	Vaticanus Text of the Septuagint
MP	Mode of production
MT	Masoretic Text
NIV	New International Version
NRSV	New Revised Standard Version
OAN	Oracles against Nations (in Jeremiah)
P.	papyrus/papyri
P	Priestly source
PE	Pastoral Epistles
RSV	Revised Standard Version
TI	Trito-Isaiah

Books of the Bible (NT, OT, Apocrypha)

Old Testament/Hebrew Bible

Gen.	Genesis
Exod.	Exodus
Lev.	Leviticus
Num.	Numbers
Deut.	Deuteronomy

Josh.	Joshua
Judg.	Judges
Ruth	Ruth
1 Sam.	1 Samuel
2 Sam.	2 Samuel
1 Kgs.	1 Kings
2 Kgs.	2 Kings
1 Chron.	1 Chronicles
2 Chron.	2 Chronicles
Ezra	Ezra
Neh.	Nehemiah
Esther	Esther
Job	Job
Ps. (Pss.)	Psalms
Prov.	Proverbs
Eccles.	Ecclesiastes
Song.	Song of Songs
Isa.	Isaiah
Jer.	Jeremiah
Lam.	Lamentations
Ezek.	Ezekiel
Dan.	Daniel
Hosea	Hosea
Joel	Joel
Amos	Amos
Obad.	Obadiah
Jon.	Jonah
Mic.	Micah
Nah.	Nahum
Hab.	Habakkuk
Zeph.	Zephaniah
Hag.	Haggai
Zech.	Zechariah
Mal.	Malachi

Apocrypha

Tob.	Tobit
Jth.	Judith
Gk. Esther	Greek Additions to Esther
Sir.	Sirach (Ecclesiasticus)

Bar.	Baruch
Let. Jer.	Letter of Jeremiah
Add Dan.	Additions to Daniel
Pr. Azar.	Prayer of Azariah
Sg. Three.	Song of the Three Young Men (or Three Jews)
Sus.	Susanna
Bel	Bel and the Dragon
1 Macc.	1 Maccabees
2 Macc.	2 Maccabees
1 Esd.	1 Esdras
Pr. of Man.	Prayer of Manasseh
2 Esd.	2 Esdras
Wis.	Wisdom of Solomon
3 Macc.	3 Maccabees
4 Macc.	4 Maccabees

New Testament

Matt.	Matthew
Mark	Mark
Luke	Luke
John	John
Acts	Acts of the Apostles
Rom.	Romans
1 Cor.	1 Corinthians
2 Cor.	2 Corinthians
Gal.	Galatians
Eph.	Ephesians
Phil.	Philippians
Col.	Colossians
1 Thess.	1 Thessalonians
2 Thess.	2 Thessalonians
1 Tim.	1 Timothy
2 Tim.	2 Timothy
Titus	Titus
Philem.	Philemon
Heb.	Hebrews
James	James
1 Pet.	1 Peter
2 Pet.	2 Peter
1 John	1 John

2 John	2 John
3 John	3 John
Jude	Jude
Rev.	Revelation (Apocalypse)

Journals, Series, Reference Works

ABD	*Anchor Bible Dictionary.* Edited by David Noel Freedman. 6 vols. New York: Doubleday, 1992.
ACNT	Augsburg Commentaries on the New Testament
AJA	*American Journal of Archaeology*
AJT	*Asia Journal of Theology*
ANET	*Ancient Near Eastern Texts Relating to the Old Testament.* Edited by J. B. Pritchard. 3rd ed. Princeton: Princeton University Press, 1969.
ANF	*The Ante-Nicene Fathers.* Edited by Alexander Roberts and James Donaldson. 1885–1887. 10 vols. Repr., Peabody, MA: Hendrickson, 1994.
ANRW	*Aufstieg und Niedergang der römischen Welt: Geschichte und Kultur Roms im Spiegel der neueren Forschung.* Edited by Hildegard Temporini and Wolfgang Haase. Berlin: de Gruyter, 1972–.
ANTC	Abingdon New Testament Commentaries
AOAT	Alter Orient und Altes Testament
AbOTC	Abingdon Old Testament Commentary
AOTC	Apollos Old Testament Commentary
A(Y)B	Anchor (Yale) Bible
BA	*Biblical Archaeologist*
BAR	*Biblical Archaeology Review*
BDAG	Bauer, W., F. W. Danker, W. F. Arndt, and F. W. Gingrich. *Greek-English Lexicon of the New Testament and Other Early Christian Literature.* 3rd ed. Chicago: University of Chicago Press, 1999.
BEATAJ	Beiträge zur Erforschung des Alten Testaments und des Antiken Judentum
Bib	*Biblica*
BibInt	*Biblical Interpretation*
BJRL	*Bulletin of the John Rylands University Library of Manchester*
BJS	Brown Judaic Studies
BNTC	Black's New Testament Commentaries
BR	*Biblical Research*
BRev	*Bible Review*
BSac	*Bibliotheca sacra*
BTB	*Biblical Theology Bulletin*
BZAW	Beihefte zur Zeitschrift für die alttestamentliche Wissenschaft
CAT	Commentaire de l'Ancien Testament

CBC	Cambridge Bible Commentary
CBQMS	Catholic Biblical Quarterly Monograph Series
CC	Continental Commentaries
CH	*Church History*
CHJ	*Cambridge History of Judaism*. Edited by W. D. Davies and Louis Finkelstein. Cambridge: Cambridge University Press, 1984–.
ConBNT	Coniectanea biblica: New Testament Series
ConBOT	Coniectanea biblica: Old Testament Series
CS	Cistercian Studies
CTAED	*Canaanite Toponyms in Ancient Egyptian Documents*. S. Ahituv. Jerusalem: Magnes, 1984.
CTQ	*Concordia Theological Quarterly*
CurTM	*Currents in Theology and Mission*
ExpTim	*Expository Times*
ETL	*Ephemerides Theologicae Lovanienses*
ExAud	*Ex auditu*
FAT	Forschungen zum Alten Testament
FC	Fathers of the Church
FRLANT	Forschungen zur Religion und Literatur des Alten und Neuen Testaments
HAT	Handbuch zum Alten Testament
HBT	*Horizons in Biblical Theology*
HNTC	Harper's New Testament Commentaries
HR	*History of Religions*
HSM	Harvard Semitic Monographs
HTKAT	Herders Theologischer Kommentar zum Alten Testament
HTR	*Harvard Theological Review*
HTS	Harvard Theological Studies
HUCA	*Hebrew Union College Annual*
HUCM	Monographs of the Hebrew Union College
HUT	Hermeneutische Untersuchungen zur Theologie
IBC	Interpretation: A Bible Commentary for Teaching and Preaching
ICC	International Critical Commentary
Int	*Interpretation*
JAAR	*Journal of the American Academy of Religion*
JAOS	*Journal of the American Oriental Society*
JBL	*Journal of Biblical Literature*
JBQ	*Jewish Bible Quarterly*
JECS	*Journal of Early Christian Studies*
JJS	*Journal of Jewish Studies*
JNES	*Journal of Near Eastern Studies*

JNSL	*Journal of Northwest Semitic Languages*
JQR	*Jewish Quarterly Review*
JRS	*Journal of Roman Studies*
JSem	*Journal of Semitics*
JSJ	*Journal for the Study of Judaism in the Persian, Hellenistic, and Roman Periods*
JSNT	*Journal for the Study of the New Testament*
JSOT	*Journal for the Study of the Old Testament*
JSOTSup	Journal for the Study of the Old Testament Supplement Series
JSQ	*Jewish Studies Quarterly*
JSS	*Journal of Semitic Studies*
JTI	*Journal of Theological Interpretation*
JTS	*Journal of Theological Studies*
JTSA	*Journal of Theology for Southern Africa*
KTU	*Die keilalphabetischen Texte aus Ugarit.* Edited by M. Dietrich, O. Loretz, and J. Sanmartín. AOAT 24/1. Neukirchen-Vluyn: Neukirchener, 1976.
LCC	Loeb Classical Library
LEC	Library of Early Christianity
LHB/OTS	Library of the Hebrew Bible/Old Testament Studies
LW	*Luther's Works.* Edited by Jaroslav Pelikan and Helmut T. Lehmann. 55 vols. St. Louis: Concordia; Philadelphia: Fortress Press, 1958–1986.
NAC	New American Commentary
NCB	New Century Bible
NCBC	New Cambridge Bible Commentary
NedTT	*Nederlands theologisch tijdschrift*
Neot	*Neotestamentica*
NICNT	New International Commentary on the New Testament
NICOT	New International Commentary on the Old Testament
NIGTC	New International Greek Testament Commentary
NovT	*Novum Testamentum*
NPNF[1]	*The Nicene and Post-Nicene Fathers*, Series 1. Edited by Philip Schaff. 14 vols. 1886–1889. Repr., Grand Rapids: Eerdmans, 1956.
NTL	New Testament Library
NTS	*New Testament Studies*
OBT	Overtures to Biblical Theology
OTE	*Old Testament Essays*
OTG	Old Testament Guides
OTL	Old Testament Library
OTM	Old Testament Message
PEQ	*Palestine Exploration Quarterly*
PG	Patrologia graeca [= Patrologiae cursus completus: Series graeca]. Edited by J.-P. Migne. 162 vols. Paris, 1857–1886.

PL	John Milton, *Paradise Lost*
PL	Patrologia latina [= Patrologiae cursus completus: Series latina]. Edited by J.-P. Migne. 217 vols. Paris, 1844–1864.
PRSt	*Perspectives in Religious Studies*
QR	*Quarterly Review*
RevExp	*Review and Expositor*
RevQ	*Revue de Qumran*
SBLABS	Society of Biblical Literature Archaeology and Biblical Studies
SBLAIL	Society of Biblical Literature Ancient Israel and Its Literature
SBLDS	Society of Biblical Literature Dissertation Series
SBLEJL	Society of Biblical Literature Early Judaism and Its Literature
SBLMS	Society of Biblical Literature Monograph Series
SBLRBS	Society of Biblical Literature Resources for Biblical Study
SBLSCS	Society of Biblical Literature Septuagint and Cognate Studies
SBLSP	*Society of Biblical Literature Seminar Papers*
SBLSymS	Society of Biblical Literature Symposium Series
SBLWAW	SBL Writings from the Ancient World
SemeiaSt	Semeia Studies
SJT	*Scottish Journal of Theology*
SNTSMS	Society for New Testament Studies Monograph Series
SO	Symbolae osloenses
SR	*Studies in Religion*
ST	*Studia Theologica*
StABH	Studies in American Biblical Hermeneutics
TD	*Theology Digest*
TAD	*Textbook of Aramaic Documents from Ancient Egypt*. Vol. 1: *Letters*. Bezalel Porten and Ada Yardeni. Winona Lake, IN: Eisenbrauns, 1986.
TDOT	*Theological Dictionary of the Old Testament*. 15 vols. Edited by G. Johannes Botterweck, Helmer Ringgren, and Heinz-Josef Fabry. Translated by David E. Green and Douglas W. Stott. Grand Rapids: Eerdmans, 1974–1995.
TJT	*Toronto Journal of Theology*
TNTC	Tyndale New Testament Commentaries
TOTC	Tyndale Old Testament Commentaries
TS	*Theological Studies*
TZ	*Theologische Zeitschrift*
VE	*Vox evangelica*
VT	*Vetus Testamentum*
VTSup	Supplements to Vetus Testamentum
WBC	Word Biblical Commentary
WSA	Works of St. Augustine: A Translation for the Twenty-First Century
WUANT	Wissenschaftliche Untersuchungen zum Alten und Neuen Testament

WUNT	Wissenschaftliche Untersuchungen zum Neuen Testament
WW	*Word and World*
ZAW	*Zeitschrift für die alttestamentliche Wissenschaft*
ZBK	Zürcher Bibelkommentare
ZNW	*Zeitschrift für die neutestamentliche Wissenschaft und die Kunde der älteren Kirche*

Ancient Authors and Texts

1 Clem.	*1 Clement*
2 Clem.	*2 Clement*
1 En.	*1 Enoch*
2 Bar.	*2 Baruch*
Abot R. Nat.	*Abot de Rabbi Nathan*
Ambrose	
Paen.	*De paenitentia*
Aristotle	
Ath. Pol.	*Athēnaīn politeia*
Nic. Eth.	*Nicomachean Ethics*
Pol.	*Politics*
Rhet.	*Rhetoric*
Augustine	
FC 79	*Tractates on the Gospel of John, 11–27.* Translated by John W. Rettig. Fathers of the Church 79. Washington, DC: Catholic University of America Press, 1988.
Tract. Ev. Jo.	*In Evangelium Johannis tractatus*
Bede, Venerable	
CS 117	*Commentary on the Acts of the Apostles.* Translated by Lawrence T. Martin. Cistercian Studies 117. Kalamazoo, MI: Cistercian Publications, 1989.
Barn.	*Barnabas*
CD	Cairo Genizah copy of the Damascus Document
Cicero	
De or.	*De oratore*
Tusc.	*Tusculanae disputationes*
Clement of Alexandria	
Paed.	*Paedogogus*
Strom.	*Stromata*
Cyril of Jerusalem	
Cat. Lect.	*Catechetical Lectures*
Dio Cassius	
Hist.	*Roman History*

Dio Chrysostom
    Or.   *Orations*
Diog. Diognetus
Dionysius of Halicarnassus
    Thuc.   *De Thucydide*
Epictetus
    Diatr.   *Diatribai (Dissertationes)*
    Ench.   *Enchiridion*
Epiphanius
    Pan.   *Panarion (Adversus Haereses)*
Eusebius of Caesarea
    Hist. eccl.   *Historia ecclesiastica*
Gos. Thom.   *Gospel of Thomas*
Herodotus
    Hist.   *Historiae*
Hermas, *Shepherd*
    Mand.   *Mandates*
    Sim.   *Similitudes*
Homer
    Il.   *Iliad*
    Od.   *Odyssey*
Ignatius of Antioch
    Eph.   *To the Ephesians*
    Smyr.   *To the Smyrnaeans*
Irenaeus
    Adv. haer.   *Adversus haereses*
Jerome
    Vir. ill.   *De viris illustribus*
John Chrysostom
    Hom. 1 Cor.   *Homiliae in epistulam i ad Corinthios*
    Hom. Act.   *Homiliae in Acta apostolorum*
    Hom. Heb.   *Homiliae in epistulam ad Hebraeos*
Josephus
    Ant.   *Jewish Antiquities*
    Ag. Ap.   *Against Apion*
    J.W.   *Jewish War*
Jub.   *Jubilees*
Justin Martyr
    Dial.   *Dialogue with Trypho*
    1 Apol.   *First Apology*

L.A.E.	*Life of Adam and Eve*
Liv. Pro.	*Lives of the Prophets*

Lucian
Alex.	*Alexander (Pseudomantis)*
Phal.	*Phalaris*
Mart. Pol.	*Martyrdom of Polycarp*

Novatian
Trin.	*De trinitate*

Origen
C. Cels.	*Contra Celsum*
Comm. Jo.	*Commentarii in evangelium Joannis*
De princ.	*De principiis*
Hom. Exod.	*Homiliae in Exodum*
Hom. Jer.	*Homiliae in Jeremiam*
Hom. Josh.	*Homilies on Joshua*

Pausanias
Descr.	*Description of Greece*

Philo
Cher.	*De cherubim*
Decal.	*De decalogo*
Dreams	*On Dreams*
Embassy	*On the Embassy to Gaius (= Legat.)*
Fug.	*De fuga et inventione*
Leg.	*Legum allegoriae*
Legat.	*Legatio ad Gaium*
Migr.	*De migratione Abrahami*
Mos.	*De vita Mosis*
Opif.	*De opificio mundi*
Post.	*De posteritate Caini*
Prob.	*Quod omnis probus liber sit*
QE	*Quaestiones et solutiones in Exodum*
QG	*Quaestiones et solutiones in Genesin*
Spec. Laws	*On the Special Laws*

Plato
Gorg.	*Gorgias*

Plutarch
Mor.	*Moralia*
Mulier. virt.	*Mulierum virtutes*

Polycarp
Phil.	*To the Philippians*

Ps.-Clem. Rec.	*Pseudo-Clementine Recognitions*
Pss. Sol.	*Psalms of Solomon*
Pseudo-Philo	
L.A.B.	*Liber antiquitatum biblicarum*
Seneca	
Ben.	*De beneficiis*
Strabo	
Geog.	*Geographica*
Tatian	
Ad gr.	*Oratio ad Graecos*
Tertullian	
Praescr.	*De praescriptione haereticorum*
Prax.	*Adversus Praxean*
Bapt.	*De baptismo*
De an.	*De anima*
Pud.	*De pudicitia*
Virg.	*De virginibus velandis*
Virgil	
Aen.	*Aeneid*
Xenophon	
Oec.	*Oeconomicus*

Mishnah, Talmud, Targum

b. B. Bat.	*Babylonian Talmudic tractate Baba Batra*
b. Ber.	*Babylonian Talmudic tractate Berakhot*
b Erub.	*Babylonian Talmudic tractate Erubim*
b. Ketub.	*Babylonian Talmudic tractate Ketubbot*
b. Mak.	*Babylonian Talmudic tractate Makkot*
b. Meg.	*Babylonian Talmudic tractate Megillah*
b. Ned.	*Babylonian Talmudic tractate Nedarim*
b. Naz.	*Babylonian Talmudic tractate Nazir*
b. Sanh.	*Babylonian Talmudic tractate Sanhedrin*
b. Shab.	*Babylonian Talmudic tractate Shabbat*
b. Sotah	*Babylonian Talmudic tractate Sotah*
b. Ta'an.	*Babylonian Talmudic tractate Ta'anit*
b. Yev.	*Babylonian Talmudic tractate Yevamot*
b. Yoma	*Babylonian Talmudic tractate Yoma*
Eccl. Rab.	*Ecclesiastes Rabbah*
Exod. Rab.	*Exodus Rabbah*
Gen. Rab.	*Genesis Rabbah*

Lam. Rab.	*Lamentations Rabbah*
Lev. R(ab).	*Leviticus Rabbah*
m. Abot	*Mishnah tractate Abot*
m. Bik.	*Mishnah tractate Bikkurim*
m. Demai	*Mishnah tractate Demai*
m. 'Ed.	*Mishnah tractate 'Eduyyot*
m. Git.	*Mishnah tractate Gittin*
m. Pesaḥ	*Mishnah tractate Pesaḥim*
m. Šeqal.	*Mishnah tractate Šeqalim (Shekalim)*
m. Shab.	*Mishnah tractate Shabbat*
m. Sotah	*Mishnah tractate Sotah*
m. Ta'an.	*Mishnah tractate Ta'anit*
m. Tamid	*Mishnah tractate Tamid*
m. Yad.	*Mishnah tractate Yadayim*
m. Yebam.	*Mishnah tractate Yebamot*
m. Yoma	*Mishnah tractate Yoma*
Num. Rab.	*Numbers Rabbah*
Pesiq. Rab.	*Pesiqta Rabbati*
Pesiq. Rab Kah.	*Pesiqta Rab Kahana*
S. 'Olam Rab.	*Seder 'Olam Rabbah*
Song Rab.	*Song of Songs Rabbah*
t. Hul.	*Tosefta tractate Hullin*
Tg. Onq.	*Targum Onqelos*
Tg. Jer.	*Targum Jeremiah*
y. Hag.	*Jerusalem Talmudic tractate Hagiga*
y. Pesaḥ	*Jerusalem Talmudic tractate Pesaḥim*
y. Sanh.	*Jerusalem Talmudic tractate Sanhedrin*

Dead Sea Scrolls

1QapGen	*Genesis apocryphon* (Excavated frags. from cave)
1QM	*War Scroll*
1QpHab	*Pesher Habakkuk*
1QS	*Rule of the Community*
1QSb	*Rule of the Blessings* (Appendix b to 1QS)
1Q21	*T. Levi*, aramaic
4Q184	Wiles of the Wicked Woman
4Q214	Levi^d ar (*olim* part of Levi^b)
4Q214b	Levi^f ar (*olim* part of Levi^b)
4Q226	psJub^b (4Q *pseudo-Jubilees*)
4Q274	Tohorot A

4Q277	Tohorot B^b (*olim* B^c)
4Q525	*Beatitudes*
4QMMT	*Miqsat Ma'aśê ha-Torah*
4QpNah/4Q169	4Q Pesher Nahum
4Q82	*The Greek Minor Prophets Scroll*

Old Testament Pseudepigrapha

1 En.	*1 Enoch*
2 En.	*2 Enoch*
Odes Sol.	*Odes of Solomon*
Syr. Men.	*Sentences of the Syriac Menander*
T. Levi	*Testament of Levi*
T. Mos.	*Testament of Moses*
T. Sim.	*Testament of Simeon*

INTRODUCTION

The *Fortress Commentary on the Bible*, presented in two volumes, seeks to invite study and conversation about an ancient text that is both complex and compelling. As biblical scholars, we wish students of the Bible to gain a respect for the antiquity and cultural remoteness of the biblical texts and to grapple for themselves with the variety of their possible meanings; to fathom a long history of interpretation in which the Bible has been wielded for causes both beneficial and harmful; and to develop their own skills and voices as responsible interpreters, aware of their own social locations in relationships of privilege and power. With this in mind, the *Fortress Commentary on the Bible* offers general readers an informed and accessible resource for understanding the biblical writings in their ancient contexts; for recognizing how the texts have come down to us through the mediation of different interpretive traditions; and for engaging current discussion of the Bible's sometimes perplexing, sometimes ambivalent, but always influential legacy in the contemporary world. The commentary is designed not only to inform but also to invite and empower readers as active interpreters of the Bible in their own right.

The editors and contributors to these volumes are scholars and teachers who are committed to helping students engage the Bible in the classroom. Many also work as leaders, both lay and ordained, in religious communities, and wish this commentary to prove useful for informing congregational life in clear, meaningful, and respectful ways. We also understand the work of biblical interpretation as a responsibility far wider than the bounds of any religious community. In this regard, we participate in many and diverse identities and social locations, yet we all are conscious of reading, studying, and hearing the Bible today as citizens of a complex and interconnected world. We recognize in the Bible one of the most important legacies of human culture; its historical and literary interpretation is of profound interest to religious and nonreligious people alike.

Often, the academic interpretation of the Bible has moved from close study of the remote ancient world to the rarefied controversy of scholarly debate, with only occasional attention to the ways biblical texts are actually heard and lived out in the world around us. The commentary seeks to provide students with diverse materials on the ways in which these texts have been interpreted through the course of history, as well as helping students understand the texts' relevance for today's globalized world. It recognizes the complexities that are involved with being an engaged reader of the Bible, providing a powerful tool for exploring the Bible's multilayered meanings in both their ancient and modern contexts. The commentary seeks to address contemporary issues that are raised by biblical passages. It aspires to be keenly aware of how the contemporary world and its issues and perspectives influence the interpretation of the Bible. Many of the most important insights of contemporary biblical scholarship not only have come from expertise in the world of antiquity but have also been forged in modern struggles for dignity, for equality, for sheer survival, and out of respect for those who have died without seeing justice done. Gaining familiarity with the original contexts in which the biblical writings were produced is essential, but not sufficient, for encouraging competent and discerning interpretation of the Bible's themes today.

Inside the Commentary

Both volumes of *The Fortress Commentary on the Bible* are organized in a similar way. In the beginning of each volume, **Topical Articles** set the stage on which interpretation takes place, naming the issues and concerns that have shaped historical and theological scholarship down to the present. Articles in the *Fortress Commentary on the Old Testament* attend, for example, to the issues that arise when two different religious communities claim the same body of writings as their Scripture, though interpreting those writings quite differently. Articles in the *Fortress Commentary on the New Testament* address the consequences of Christianity's historic claim to appropriate Jewish Scripture and to supplement it with a second collection of writings, the experience of rootlessness and diaspora, and the legacy of apocalypticism. Articles in both volumes reflect on the historical intertwining of Christianity with imperial and colonial power and with indexes of racial and socioeconomic privilege.

Section Introductions in the Old Testament volume provide background to the writings included in the Torah, Historical Writings, Wisdom, Prophetic Writings, and a general introduction to the Apocrypha. The New Testament volume includes articles introducing the Gospels, Acts, the letters associated with Paul, Hebrews, the General Epistles, and Revelation. These articles will address the literary and historical matters, as well as theological themes, that the books in these collections hold in common.

Commentary Entries present accessible and judicious discussion of each biblical book, beginning with an introduction to current thinking regarding the writing's original context and its significance in different reading communities down to the present day. A three-level commentary then follows for each sense division of the book. In some cases these follow the chapter divisions of a biblical book, but more often contributors have discerned other outlines, depending on matters of genre, movement, or argument.

The three levels of commentary are the most distinctive organizational feature of these volumes. The first level, "The Text in Its Ancient Context," addresses relevant lexical, exegetical, and literary aspects of the text, along with cultural and archaeological information that may provide additional insight into the historical context. This level of the commentary describes consensus views where these exist in current scholarship and introduces issues of debate clearly and fairly. Our intent here is to convey some sense of the historical and cultural distance between the text's original context and the contemporary reader.

The second level, "The Text in the Interpretive Tradition," discusses themes including Jewish and Christian tradition as well as other religious, literary, and artistic traditions where the biblical texts have attracted interest. This level is shaped by our conviction that we do not apprehend these texts immediately or innocently; rather, even the plain meaning we may regard as self-evident may have been shaped by centuries of appropriation and argument to which we are heirs.

The third level, "The Text in Contemporary Discussion," follows the history of interpretation into the present, drawing brief attention to a range of issues. Our aim here is not to deliver a single answer—"what the text means"—to the contemporary reader, but to highlight unique challenges and interpretive questions. We pay special attention to occasions of dissonance: aspects of the text or of its interpretation that have become questionable, injurious, or even intolerable to some readers today. Our goal is not to provoke a referendum on the value of the text but to stimulate reflection and discussion and, in this way, to empower the reader to reach his or her own judgments about the text.

The approach of this commentary articulates a particular understanding of the work of responsible biblical interpretation. We seek through this commentary to promote intelligent and mature engagement with the Bible, in religious communities and in academic classrooms alike, among pastors, theologians, and ethicists, but also and especially among nonspecialists. Our work together has given us a new appreciation for the vocation of the biblical scholar, as custodians of a treasure of accumulated wisdom from our predecessors; as stewards at a table to which an ever-expanding circle is invited; as neighbors and fellow citizens called to common cause, regardless of our different professions of faith. If the result of our work here is increased curiosity about the Bible, new questions about its import, and new occasions for mutual understanding among its readers, our work will be a success.

Fortress Commentary on the Old Testament

Gale A. Yee
Episcopal Divinity School

Hugh R. Page Jr.
University of Notre Dame

Matthew J. M. Coomber
St. Ambrose University

Fortress Commentary on the New Testament

Margaret Aymer
Interdenominational Theological Center

Cynthia Briggs Kittredge
Seminary of the Southwest

David A. Sánchez
Loyola Marymount University

Reading the Christian New Testament in the Contemporary World

Kwok Pui-lan

On Ascension Sunday in May 2012, the faculty and students of my school who were taking part in a travel seminar to China attended the worship service at the Shanghai Community Church. We arrived half an hour before the service began, and the church, which can accommodate about two thousand people, was already filled to capacity. Another two thousand people who could not get into the sanctuary watched the worship service on closed-circuit TV in other rooms in the church building. Through this experience and while visiting churches in other cities, we learned about and encountered the phenomenal growth of the Chinese churches in the past twenty-five years. The official statistics put the number of Chinese Christians at around 30 million, but unofficial figures range from 50 to 100 million, if those who belong to the unregistered house churches are counted. China is poised to become the country with the highest number of Christians, and China has already become the largest printer and user of the Bible in the world. In 2012, the Amity Printing Company in Nanjing celebrated the publishing of 100 million Bibles since its inception in 1987 (United Bible Societies 2012).

Besides China, sub-Saharan Africa has also experienced rapid church growth, especially among the African Independent Churches, Pentecostal churches, and Roman Catholic churches. By 2025, Africa will be the continent with the greatest number of Christians, at more than 670 million. At the turn of the twentieth century, 70 percent of the world's Christians were European. By 2000, that number had dropped to 28 percent (Flatow). The shift of Christian demographics to the South and the prospect of Christianity becoming a non-Western religion have attracted the attention of scholars and popular media (Sanneh 2003; Jenkins; Johnson and Ross). According to the *World Christian Encyclopedia*, almost two-thirds of the readers of the Bible are Christians from Africa, Asia, Latin America, and Oceania (around 1.178 billion) as compared to Europe and America (around 661 million) and Orthodox Eastern Europe (around 158 million) (Patte, xxi).

These changing Christian demographics have significant implications for reading the Bible as global citizens in the contemporary world. To promote global and intercultural understanding, we can no longer read the Bible in a narrow and parochial way, without being aware of how Christians in other parts of the world are reading it in diverse linguistic, cultural, and social contexts. In the past decade, biblical scholars have increasingly paid attention to global perspectives on the Bible to prepare Christians to live in our complex, pluralistic, and transnational world (Patte; Wicker, Miller, and Dube; Roncace and Weaver). For those of us living in the Global North, it is important to pay attention to liberative readings from the Global South and to the voices from the majority world. Today, the field of biblical studies has been enlivened and broadened by scholars from many social locations and culturally and religiously diverse contexts.

The New Testament in Global Perspectives

The New Testament touches on many themes highly relevant for our times, such as racial and ethnic relations, religious pluralism, social and political domination, gender oppression, and religious movements for resistance. The early followers of Jesus were Jews and gentiles living in the Hellenistic world under the rule of the Roman Empire. Christianity developed largely in urban cities in which men and women from different linguistic, cultural, and religious backgrounds interacted and commingled with one another (Theissen; Meeks). Christians in the early centuries lived among Jews and people devoted to emperor cults, Greek religion, and other indigenous traditions in the ancient Near East. Jesus and his disciples spoke Aramaic, the common language of Palestine. The New Testament was written in Koine Greek, the lingua franca of much of the Mediterranean region and the Middle East since the conquest of Alexander the Great. Living under the shadow of the Roman Empire, early Christians had to adapt to the cultures and social structures of empire, as well as resist the domination of imperial rule.

From its beginning in Palestine and the Mediterranean, Christianity spread to other parts of the Roman Empire and became the dominant religion during Constantine's time. Some of the notable early theologians hailed from northern Africa: Origen (c. 185–254) and Athanasius (c. 300–373) from Alexandria, Tertullian (160–225) from Carthage, and Augustine (354–431) of Hippo. While Christianity was persecuted in the Roman Empire prior to 313, it found its way to the regions east of the Tigris River possibly as early as the beginning of the second century. Following ancient trade routes, merchants and missionaries brought Christianity from the Mediterranean to the Persian Gulf and across central Asia all the way to China (Baum and Winkler, 8). In the early modern period, Christianity was brought to the Americas and other parts of the world, with the help of the political and military power of colonizing empires. Even though Christianity was a world religion, the study of church history in the past tended to focus on Europe and North America and to marginalize the histories in other parts of the world. Today, scholars of world Christianity have contested such Eurocentric biases. They have produced comprehensive accounts that restore the peoples of Africa, the Near East, and Asia to their rightful place in the rich and multilayered Christian tradition (Hastings; Irvin and Sunquist 2001; 2012; Sanneh 2007).

The translation of the Bible, especially the New Testament, into the native and vernacular languages of different peoples was and remains an important strategy of Christian missions. The United Bible Societies (2013) report that the complete Bible has been translated into at least 451 languages and the New Testament into some 1,185. The Bible is the most translated collection of texts in the world. There are now 2,370 languages in which at least one book of the Bible has been produced. Although this figure represents less than half of some 6,000 languages and dialects presently in use in the world, it includes the primary means of communication of well over 90 percent of the world's population.

Most Christians are more familiar with the New Testament than the Hebrew Bible. The New Testament is read and preached throughout the world in liturgical settings and worship services, taught in seminaries and church Sunday schools, studied in private devotions, and discussed in Bible study groups, women's fellowships, college campuses, and grassroots religious organizations and movements. Christians, Jews, Muslims, and atheists debate the meaning of Jesus and the gospel in books, mass media, and on the Internet. The life and the story of Jesus Christ have been depicted and interpreted in popular culture, such as films, songs, music videos, fiction, blogs, websites, photographs, paintings, sculpture, and other forms of art. The study of the New Testament is not limited to the study of the biblical text, but includes how the text is used in concrete contexts in Christian communities, popular media, and public spheres.

The Bible is taken to mean many things in our contemporary world. Christian communities regard the Bible as *Scripture*, and many Christians think that it has authority over their beliefs and moral behavior. In the academy, the Bible is treated more as a *historical document*, to be studied by rigorous historical criticism. Increasingly, the Bible is also seen as a *cultural product*, embedded in the sociocultural and ideological assumptions of its time. The meaning of the Bible is not fixed but is continually produced as readers interact with it in different contexts. The diverse understanding of what the Bible is often creates a clash of opinions. For example, Christians may think Lady Gaga's "Judas" video (2011) has gone too far in deviating from orthodox teaching. There is also a wide gap in the ways the Bible is read in the church and academy. The experts' reading may challenge the beliefs of those sitting in the pews.

In the field of biblical studies, Fernando F. Segovia (34–52) delineates three stages in the development of academic biblical criticism in the twentieth century. The historical-critical method has been the dominant mode of interpretation in academia since the middle of the nineteenth century. The meaning of the text is seen as residing *behind* the text—in the world that shaped the text, in the author's intention, or both. The second stage is literary criticism, which emerged in the middle of 1970s in dialogue with literary and psychoanalytic theory. The literary critics emphasize the meaning *in* the text and focus on genre, plot, structure, rhetoric, levels of narration, and characterization as depicted in the world of the text. The third stage is cultural studies or ideological criticism of the Bible, which developed also in the 1970s, when critics from the two-thirds world, feminist theologians, and racial and ethnic minority scholars in North America began to increase their numbers in the guild. They have increasingly paid attention to the flesh-and-blood readers *in front of* the text, who employ different methods, such as storytelling and reader-response criticism, in their interaction with the text to construct meaning in response to concerns arising from their communities.

The shift to the flesh-and-blood reader contests the assumption that there is a "universal" reader and an "objective" interpretation applicable to all times and places. The claim of an "objective" and "scientific" reading is based on a positivistic understanding of historiography, which presumes that historical facts can be objectively reconstructed, following established criteria in Western academia. But the historical-critical method is only one of the many methods and should not be taken as the "universal" norm for judging other methodologies. Its dominance is the result of the colonial legacy as well as the continued hegemony of Eurocentric knowledge and cultural production of our time. Nowadays, many methods are available, and biblical critics have increasingly used interdisciplinary approaches and a combination of theories and methods, such as postmodern theory, postcolonial theory, and queer studies, for interpretation (Crossley; Moore 2010).

What this means is the democratization of the study of the Bible, because no one group of people has a monopoly over the meaning of the Bible and no single method can exhaust its "truths." To understand the richness of the biblical tradition, we have to learn to listen to the voices of people from multiple locations and senses of belonging. Eleazar S. Fernandez (140) points out, "real flesh-and-blood readers assume a variety of positions—in relation to time, geography, geopolitics, diaspora location, social location, religion, ethnicity, gender, sexuality, and so on—in the power-knowledge nexus that inform their readings and cultural or religious discursive productions in the global market." Interpreting the Bible in global perspectives requires us to pay attention to the contextual character of reading and the relationships and tensions between the global and the local.

Reading the New Testament in Diverse Contexts

The shift from the author and the text to the reader means that we need to understand the ways the Bible functions in diverse sociolingusitic contexts (Blount 1995). Our critical task must go further than analyzing the text and the processes for production and interpretation, to include the cultural and social conditions that influence the history of reception. Let us go back to the examples of reading the Bible in the Chinese and African contexts. When Christianity arrived in China, the Chinese had a long hermeneutical tradition of interpreting Confucian, Buddhist, and Daoist texts. The missionaries and biblical translators had to borrow from indigenous religious ideas to translate biblical terminologies, such as God, heaven, and hell. The rapid social and political changes in modern China affected how the Bible is read by Christians living in a Communist society (Eber, Wan, and Walf). When the Bible was introduced to the African continent, it encountered a rich and complex language world of oral narratives, legends, proverbs, and folktales. The interpretation of oral texts is different from that of written ones. In some instances, the translation of the Bible into the vernacular languages has changed the oral cultures into written cultures, with both positive and negative effects on social development (Sanneh 1989). And if we examine the history of translation and reception of the English Bible, we will see how the processes have been affected by the rise of nationalism, colonial expansion, and the diverse forms of English used in the English-speaking world (Sugirtharajah 2002, 127–54).

Some Christians may feel uneasy about the fact that the Bible is read in so many different ways. For the fundamentalists who believe in biblical inerrancy and literal interpretation, multiple ways of reading undermine biblical authority. Even liberals might wonder if the diversity of readings will open the doors to relativism. But as James Barr has pointed out, the appeal to the Bible as authority for all doctrinal matters and the assumption that its meaning is fixed cannot be verified by the Bible itself. Both Jesus and Paul took the liberty to repudiate, criticize, and reinterpret parts of the Hebrew Bible (Barr, 12–19). Moreover, as Mary Ann Tolbert has noted, since the Reformation, when the doctrine of *sola scriptura* was brought to the forefront, the invocation of biblical authority by various ecclesiastical bodies has generally been negative and exclusive. "It has been used most often to *exclude* certain groups or people, to *pass judgment* on various disapproved activities, and to *justify* morally or historically debatable positions [such as slavery]" (1998, 142). The doctrinal appeal to biblical authority and the insistence on monocultural reading often mask power dynamics, which allow some groups of people to exercise control over others who have less power, including women, poor people, racial and ethnic minorities, and gay people and lesbians.

Multiple readings and plurality of meaning do not necessarily lead to relativism, but can foster deeper awareness of our own interpretive assumptions and broaden our horizons. In his introduction to the *Global Bible Commentary*, Daniel Patte (xxi–xxxii) offers some helpful suggestions. (1) We have to acknowledge the contextual character of our interpretation. There is no context-free reading, whether in the past or in the present. (2) We have to stop and listen to the voices of biblical readers who have long been silenced in each context. (3) We have to learn the reading strategies and critical tradition developed in other parts of the world, such as enculturation, liberation, and inter(con)textuality. Contextual readings do not mean anything goes or that interpreters may proceed without self-critique. (4) We have to respect other people's readings and assume responsibility for our own interpretation. (5) Other people's readings often lead us to see our blind spots, and invite us to notice aspects of the Bible we have overlooked. (6) We have to learn to read *with* others in community, rather than reading *for* or *to* them, assuming our reading is superior to others.

We can use the different readings of the story of the Syrophoenician woman (Matt. 15:21-28; Mark 7:24-30) to illustrate this point. Many Christians have been taught that the story is about Jesus' mission to the gentiles, because Jesus went to the border place of Tyre and Sidon and healed the gentile woman's daughter and praised her faith. Japanese biblical scholar Hisako Kinukawa (51–65), however, does not emphasize gentile mission but Jesus' crossing ethnic boundaries to accept others. She places the story in the cultic purity and ethnic exclusion of first-century Palestine and draws parallels to the discrimination of Koreans as minorities living in Japan. We shall see that the generalization of first-century culture may be problematic. Nevertheless, Kinukawa argues that the gentile woman changed Jesus' attitude from rejection to affirmation and created an opportunity for Jesus to cross the boundary. Jesus has set an example, she says, for Japanese people to challenge their assumptions of a homogeneous race, to overcome their prejudice toward ethnic minorities, and to respect other peoples' dignity and human rights.

On the African continent, Musa W. Dube, from Botswana, emphasizes the importance of *reading with* ordinary readers. She set out to find out how women in the African Independent Churches in Botswana read the Matthean version of the story (2000, 187–90). She found that some of the women emphasized that Jesus was testing the woman's faith. They said the meaning of the word "dog" should not be taken literally, as Jesus often spoke in parables. Several women did not read the story as if Jesus had insulted the woman by comparing the Canaanites as "dogs" to the Israelites as children. Instead, they saw the Canaanite woman as one of the children because of her faith, and the "dogs" referred to the demonic spirits. This must be understood in the context of the belief in spirits in the African religious worldview. The women interpreted the woman's answer to Jesus, that even the dogs eat the crumbs from the master's table (Matt. 15:27), to mean that no one is permanently and totally undeserving. The women believed that Jesus had come for all people, without regard for race and ethnicities.

These two examples show how social and cultural backgrounds affect the interpretation of the story and the lessons drawn for today. The majority of interpreters, whether scholars or ordinary readers, have focused on the interaction between Jesus and the woman. I would like to cite two other readings that bring to the forefront other details of the text that have been overlooked. Laura E. Donaldson reads the story from a postcolonial Native American perspective and places the "demon-possessed" daughter at the center of her critical analysis. In the text, the daughter does not speak, and her illness is considered taboo and stigmatizing. Donaldson challenges our complicity in such a reading and employs the insights of disabilities studies to demystify the construction of "able" and "disabled" persons. She then points out that the Canaanites were the indigenous people of the land, and the daughter might not be suffering from an illness pejoratively identified as "demon possession" by the Christian text. Instead, the daughter may be in an altered state of consciousness, which is a powerful form of knowing in many indigenous spiritual traditions. For Donaldson, the daughter may "signify a trace of the indigenous," who has the power to access other sites of knowledge (104–5).

While many commentators have noted the lowly position of dogs in ancient Mediterranean and Near East culture, Stephen D. Moore, who grew up in Ireland and teaches in the United States, looks at the Matthean story through the prism of human-animal relations. He contrasts the construction of the son of man with the dog-woman in Matthew. While the son of man is not an animal and asserts power, sovereignty, and self-control, following the elite Greco-Roman concept of masculinity, the dog-woman of Canaan embodies the categories of savages, women, and beasts. Jesus said that he was sent to the lost sheep of the house of Israel and it was not fair to take the children's food and throw it to the dogs. The problem of the dog-woman is that she is not a sheep woman. The image of Canaan as heathen, savage, and less than human justified the colonization of non-Christian people in Africa, the Americas, and other regions. Moore notes that the image of "heathens" in nineteenth- and twentieth-century biblical commentary conjured up the reality of "unsaved" dark-skinned people in need of Christ and in need of civilizing, and hence in need of colonizing (Moore 2013, 63). Moore's reading points out that mission to the gentiles may not be benign, and might mask colonial impulses.

These diverse interpretations of the Syrophoenician woman's story illustrate how reading with other people can radically expand our imagination. We can see how a certain part of the story is emphasized or reinterpreted by different readers to address particular concerns. Sensitivity to contextual and cross-cultural interpretation helps us to live in a pluralistic world in which people have different worldviews and assumptions. Through genuine dialogue and listening to others, we can enrich ourselves and work with others to create a better world.

Interpretation for Liberation

In the second half of the twentieth century, people's popular movements and protests led to the development of liberation theologies in various parts of the world. In Africa and Asia, anticolonial struggles resulted in political independence and people's demand for cultural autonomy. In Latin America, theologians and activists criticized the dependence theory of development, which continues to keep poor countries dependent on rich countries because of unequal global economic structures. Women from all over the globe, racial and ethnic minorities, and lesbian, gay, bisexual, and transgender people have also begun to articulate their theologies. People who are multiply oppressed began to read the Bible through the intersection of gender, race, class, sexuality, religion, and colonialism. I focus on liberative readings from the Global South here.

Following Vatican II (1962–1965), Latin American liberation theology began to develop in the 1960s and focused on social and economic oppression and the disparity between the rich and the poor. Using Marxist analysis as a critical tool, liberation theologians in Latin America argued that the poor are the subjects of history and that God has a preferential option for the poor. They insisted that theology is a reflection of social praxis, which seeks to change the oppressive situation that the majority of the people find themselves in. Juan Luis Segundo (9) developed a hermeneutical circle that consists of four steps: (1) our way of experiencing reality leads to ideological suspicion, (2) which we apply to the whole ideological superstructure, and especially theology, (3) being aware of how prevailing interpretation of the Bible does not take important data into account, resulting in (4) the development of a new hermeneutic.

Latin American theologians contested the formulation of traditional Christology and presented Christ as the liberator. The gospel of Jesus Christ is not about saving individual souls, without import for our concrete lives. In *A Theology of Liberation*, Gustavo Gutiérrez (102–5) argues that Christ is the liberator who opts for the poor. Jesus' death and resurrection liberates us from sin. Sin, however, is not private, but a social, historical fact. It is the absence of fellowship of love in relationship among persons and the breach of relationship with God. Christ offers us the gift of radical liberation and enables us to enter into communion with God and with others. Liberation, for Gutiérrez, has three levels: political liberation, liberation in the course of history, and liberation from sin and into communion with God.

Latin American women theologians have criticized their male colleagues' lack of attention to women's issues and *machismo* in Latin American culture. Elsa Tamez, from Mexico, is a leading scholar who has published extensively on reading the New Testament from a Latin American feminist perspective (2001; 2007). She has raised questions about Jesus' relation with women in the Gospels and the class difference between rich and poor women in the early Christian movement. The discussion of the Bible in the base Christian communities and women's groups helped spread the ideas of liberation theology among the populace. A collection of discussions of the gospel by Nicaraguan peasants who belonged to the Christian community of Solentiname was published as *The Gospel in Solentiname* (Cardenal). The peasants approached the Bible from their life situation of extreme poverty, and they connected with Jesus' revolutionary work in solidarity with the poor of his time. Some of the peasants also painted the scenes from the Gospels and identified biblical events with events leading to the 1979 Sandinista revolution (Scharper and Scharper). In response to the liberation movement, which had spread to the whole continent, the Vatican criticized liberation theology and replaced progressive bishops with conservative ones. But second-generation liberation theologians continue the work of their pioneers and expand the liberation theological project to include race, gender, sexuality, migration, and popular religions (Petrella).

Unlike in Latin America, where Christians are the majority of the population, Christians in many parts of Africa and Asia live among people of other faith traditions. Here, interpretation of the Bible follows two broad approaches. The liberation approach focuses on sociopolitical dimensions, such as the fight over poverty, dictatorship, apartheid, and other social injustice. The enculturation or the indigenization approach brings the Bible into dialogue with the African or Asian worldviews, popular religion, and cultural idiom. The two approaches are not mutually exclusive, and a holistic transformation of society must deal with changing the sociopolitical structures as well as the culture and mind-sets of people.

One of the key questions for those who read the Bible in religiously pluralistic contexts is how to honor others who have different religious identities and cultures. Some of the passages in the New Testament have been used to support an exclusive attitude toward other religions. For example, Jesus said that he is the way and no one comes to the Father except through him (John 14:6) and charged his followers with the Great Commission, to "make disciples of all nations" (Matt. 28:19). But as Wesley Ariarajah (1989) has said, the universality of Christ supports the spirit of openness, mutual understanding, and interfaith dialogue with others. In Acts 10:9-16, Peter is challenged in a vision to consider nothing unclean that God has made clean. He crosses the boundary that separates Jews and gentiles and meets with Cornelius, the Roman centurion, which leads to his conversion. When Paul speaks to the Athenians, he says that they are extremely religious, and he employs a religious language different from that when he speaks to the Jews (Acts 17:22-31). Ariarajah argues that openness to others and dialogue does not contradict Christian witness.

In their protests against political oppression and dictatorship, Asian Christians have reread the Bible to empower them to fight for human rights and dignity. *Minjung* theology arose in South Korea during the 1970s against the dictatorship of the Park Chung Hee government. The word *minjung* comes from two Chinese characters meaning the masses of people. New Testament scholar Ahn Byung Mu points out that in the Gospel of Mark, the *ochlos* ("crowd or multitude") follows Jesus from place to place, listens to his teachings, and witnesses his miracles. They form the background of Jesus' activities. They stand on Jesus' side, against the rulers of Jerusalem, who criticize and challenge Jesus (Mark 2:4-7; 3:2-22; 11:8; 11:27; 11:32). Jesus has "compassion for them, because they were like sheep without a shepherd" (6:34). Jesus proclaims to them "the kingdom of God has come near" (1:15). He identifies with the suffering *minjung* and offers them a new hope and new life. *Minjung* theology developed a political hermeneutics not for the elite but for the people, and spoke to the Korean reality at the time.

In India, the caste system has subjected the Dalits—the "untouchables"—to the lowest rank of society. Dalits are the oppressed and the broken. They are discriminated against in terms of education, occupation, social interaction, and social mobility. The prejudice against the Dalits is so deep-seated that they face a great deal of discrimination even in Indian churches. Dalit theology emerged because of the insensitivity of the Indian churches to the plight of the Dalits and to give voice to Dalits' struggle for justice. In constructing a Dalit Christology, Peniel Rajkumar (115–26) finds Jesus' healing stories particularly relevant to the Dalit situation. Jesus touches and heals the leper (Mark 1:40-45), and transcends the social norms regarding purity and pollution. Afterward, Jesus asks the man to show his body to the priest (Mark 1:44) to bear witness that he has been healed and to confront the ideological purity system that alienates him. Jesus is angry at the system that maintains ritual purity to alienate and classify people. In coming to ask for healing, the leper also shows his faith through his willingness to break the cultural norm of purity. Again, we will find that the generalization of Jewish culture and purity taboo may be open to criticism. Jesus' anger toward injustice and his partnership with the leper to create a new social reality would help Dalits in their present struggles. The emphasis of Jesus' crossing boundaries is a recurrent theme in other Dalit readings (Nelavala). Many of the Dalit women from poor rural and urban areas are illiterate and do not have access to the written text of the Bible. The use of methods such as storytelling and role-play has helped them gain insights into biblical stories (Melanchthon).

In Africa, biblical scholars have addressed poverty, apartheid, religious and ethnic strife, HIV and AIDS, and political oppression, all of which have wreaked havoc in the continent. During apartheid in South Africa, a black theology of liberation was developed to challenge the Western and white outlook of the Christian church and to galvanize people to fight against apartheid. Itumeleng J. Mosala developed a historical-materialist reading of the Bible based on black history and culture. Mosala and his colleagues from Africa have asserted that Latin American liberation hermeneutics has not taken seriously the history of the blacks and Indians. His reading of Luke 1 and 2 brings out the material condition of the text, focusing on the colonial occupation of Palestine by Rome and the imperial extraction from peasants and the poor. He then uses the history, culture, and struggle of black people as a hermeneutical tool to lay bare the ideological assumptions in Luke's Gospel, showing it to be speaking for the class interest of the rich and eclipsing the experiences of the poor. He charges that some of the black theologians have continued to use Western and white hermeneutics even as they oppose the white, dominant groups. What is necessary is a new hermeneutics based on a black working-class perspective, which raises new questions in the interpretative process and enables a mutual interrogation between the text and situation.

In order to develop this kind of hermeneutics, biblical scholars must be socially engaged and read the Bible from the underside. With whom one is reading the Bible becomes both an epistemological and an ethical question. Several African biblical scholars emphasize the need for socially engaged scholars to read the Bible with ordinary poor and marginalized "readers." Gerald O. West maintains that if liberation theology begins with the experience of the poor and the oppressed, then these persons must be invited and included in the dialogical process of doing theology and reading the Bible. He describes the process of contextual Bible study among the poor, the roles of engaged biblical scholars, and lessons gleaned from the process. In the contextual reading of Luke 4:16-22, for instance, the women living around Pietermaritzburg and Durban related the meaning of setting the prisoners free, healing of the blind, and the relief of debts to their society. They discussed what they could do following the insights from the story to organize their community and create social change.

The Circle of Concerned African Women Theologians, formed in 1989, has encouraged Christian women from the African continent to produce and publish biblical and contextual hermeneutics. Some of the contributions have been published in *Other Ways of Reading: African Women and the Bible* (Dube 2001). The authors discuss storytelling methods, reading with and from nonacademic readers, toward a postapartheid black feminist reading, and the divination method of interpretation. The volume demystifies the notion of biblical canon, showing how women of the African continent have read the Bible with the canon of various African oral cultures. Aspects of African cultures serve as theories for analyzing the Bible. The volume is also conversant with feminist readings from other parts of the world, and in particular with African American women's hermeneutical approaches.

The HIV and AIDS epidemic brings enormous loss of life and suffering in the African continent, and the virus has spread mostly among heterosexual people. There is an increasing concern that in the sub-Saharan region, HIV infects more women than men. Musa Dube has played a key role in helping the African churches and theological institutions in addressing HIV and AIDS issues. In *The HIV and AIDS Bible* (Dube 2008), she implores scholars to develop biblical scholarship that is prophetic and healing. She challenges patriarchy and gender justice, and urges the churches to move beyond their comfort zone to respond to people affected by the virus. The church is HIV positive, she claims. Reading with people living with AIDS allows her to see the potential of the Bible to liberate and heal. She brings new insights to reading the miracles and healing stories of Jesus, such as the healing of Jairus's daughter (Mark 5:21-45). Her reading breaks the stigma and silence around HIV and AIDS while calling for adequate and compassionate care, and placing the HIV and AIDS epidemic within the larger context of other social discrimination.

The biblical readings from the Global South contribute to a global scholarship that takes into account other religious texts and classics in what is called intercultural and cross-textual reading (Lee). It is also interpreted through the lens of oral texts and retold and performed through storytelling, role-play, and skits. The exploration of these methods decentralizes Eurocentric modes of thinking that have gripped biblical studies for so long. It allows us to see the Bible and the world with fresh perspectives and new insights.

Contemporary Approaches to the New Testament

Books that introduce the wide array of contemporary methods used to interpret the New Testament are readily available (Anderson and Moore; Crossley). I have selected a few approaches that have global significance, as scholars from both the Global North and the Global South have used them and commented on them to illustrate current discussions shaping biblical scholarship. We will look at feminist approaches, social scientific approaches, racial and ethnic minority approaches, and postcolonial approaches.

Feminist Approaches

The New Testament was written by authors who lived in a patriarchal world with androcentric values and mind-sets. For a long time, churches have used parts of the Bible to deny women's full participation and treat them as second-class citizens in church and society. For example, churches have denied women's ordination based on the argument that all of Jesus' disciples were male. People have also cited the household codes (Col. 3:18—4:1; Eph. 5:21—6:9; 1 Peter 2:18—3:7) to support wives' submission to their husbands. Paul's teaching that women should be silent in the church (1 Cor. 14:34-35) has often been used to deny women's religious leadership. It is little wonder that some Western feminists have concluded that the Bible is irredeemably sexist and have become post-Christian. But feminist interpreters around the globe have developed ingenious ways to read against the grain and to find the Bible's liberating potential.

Christian feminists in many parts of the world have focused on stories about women in the Gospels. They have shown that women followed Jesus, listened to his preaching, and were healed because of their faith. Even when the disciples deserted Jesus at the cross, women steadfastly showed their faith. Scholars have drawn from some of these Gospel stories of women to illuminate how the gospel may speak to women's liberation of our time (Kinukawa; Tamez 2001). Christian women have also reclaimed and retold these stories, imagining dialogues, and supplying different endings. For example, I have heard from Christian women that the ending of Mary and Martha's story (Luke 10:38-42) should not end in Jesus' praising Mary over Martha, but the sisters' inviting Jesus to help in the kitchen so that all could continue the dialogue.

Other scholars find that the focus on biblical women is rather limited, for it does not provide a comprehensive framework to interpret the whole New Testament and still gives primacy and authority to the biblical text. Elisabeth Schüssler Fiorenza's influential book *In Memory of Her* (1983) presents a feminist historical-reconstructionist model, which places women at the center of the reconstruction of the Jesus movement and early Christianity. She shows that women were apostles, prophets, missionaries, as well as founders of household churches. She suggests that the radical vision of Jesus' movement was the praxis of inclusive wholeness and "discipleship of equals" (105–59). But women's leadership was increasingly marginalized in the second century, as patriarchalization set in when the church became more institutionalized. Schüssler Fiorenza's feminist model of critical interpretation insists that women should have the authority to judge whether a particular text is liberating or oppressive in the context of its reception.

Another approach is to use historical data and social theories to investigate the social world of early Christianity and to present a feminist social history. These studies look at women's marriage, status in the family, work and occupation, slave women and widows, and women's resistance in the Roman Empire (Schottroff; Yamaguchi). The parable of the leaven, for instance, makes visible women's work and uses a woman baking bread to describe the kingdom of God (Matt. 13:33; Luke 13:20-21). These works examine the impact of Roman persecution on women, the exploitative economic system, and Jewish resistance movements to provide a wider context to read the New Testament. Influenced by liberation theology, Elsa Tamez (2007) employs class analysis to study the Pastoral Letters. She describes how the rich people had challenged the leadership of the elders and presbyters in the church to which 1 Timothy was addressed. The injunction that women should be silent and submissive (1 Tim. 2:11-12) targeted the rich women, who used their power and status to cause troubles in the church.

Feminist scholars have also used literary and rhetorical approaches. For example, Ingrid Rosa Kitzberger uses a literary approach to examine the women in the Gospel of John, paying attention to the characterization of the Samaritan woman, Mary Magdalene, Mary and Martha, and the mother of Jesus, the intention of the narrator, narrative devices and rhetorical strategies, and the sequential perception of the reader in the reading process. Her goal is to present a reading against the grain—a feminist hermeneutics that empowers women. Antoinette Clark Wire reconstructs a picture of the women prophets in the church of first-century Corinth by analyzing Paul's rhetoric in 1 Corinthians. She suggests that the Corinthian women prophets claim direct access to resurrected life in Christ through the Spirit. These women sometimes conflicted with Paul, but they were known for proclaiming God's thought in prophecy and responding for the people to God (11:5; 14:1-38). Others use rhetorical criticism not to reconstruct historical reality but to focus on the persuasive power of the text to motivate action and shape the values and ethos of the community. Schüssler Fiorenza (1992, 40–50) has suggested a rhetorical approach that unmasks the interlocking system of oppression because of racism, classism, sexism, and colonialism. She coins the term *kyriarchy* (from *kyrios*, the Greek word for "lord" or "master") to describe these multiple systems of domination and subordination, involving more than gender oppression. Her goal is to create an alternative rhetorical space that respects the equality and dignity of women and is defined by the logic of radical democracy. She uses the term *ekklēsia gynaikōn* or "wo/men church" to denote this political hermeneutical space. The Greek term *ekklēsia* means the democratic assembly, and "wo/men" signifies not the feminine gender (as ladies, wives, mothers, etc.) but full decision-making political subjects. She argues that "one can theorize *ekklēsia* of wo/men not only as a virtual utopian space but also as an already partially realized space of radical equality, as a site of feminist struggles to transform social and religious institutions and discourses" (2007, 73). Feminist biblical scholars have also begun to unpack the structures of masculinity in the ancient world and how they were embedded in the biblical text (Moore and Anderson).

Social-Scientific Approaches

As mentioned above, biblical interpreters have used social sciences to learn about the social and cultural world of New Testament texts. One of the early important figures is Gerd Theissen, who studied the sociology of early Palestinian Christianity by focusing on the three roles of the Jesus movement: the wandering charismatics, their supporters in local communities, and the bearers of revelation. The use of social scientific methods has broadened the scope and sources of the third quest or newest quest of the historical Jesus since the 1980s. Billed as interdisciplinary research, scholars claim to possess at their disposal the latest archaeological knowledge, sociological analysis, cultural anthropology, and other newest social-scientific tools. Scholars have employed theories from the study of millennial movements, Mary Douglas's theory of purity and pollution, and non-Western medicine, magic, and charismatic religion to scrutinize the Jesus movement (e.g., Gager; Crossan 1991; Borg).

Schüssler Fiorenza has criticized the social-scientific quest of Jesus. She notes that the emergence of this third quest coincided with conservative politics of the Reagan and Thatcher era and with growing right-wing fundamentalist movements. She chastises the restoration of historical positivism as corresponding to political conservatism and the proliferation of the historical Jesus books as feeding "into literalist fundamentalism by reasserting disinterested scientific positivism in order to shore up the scholarly authority and universal truth of their research portrayal of Jesus" (2000, 46). While these Jesus books are written for popular consumption with their authors featured in mass media, the works of feminist scholars are sidelined and dismissed as being too "political" and not "objective" enough.

From a South African perspective, Mosala asks whether the social-scientific approaches to the Bible are "one step forward, two steps back" (43). On the one hand, the social-scientific approaches are useful, he says, because they help us to see biblical texts as ideological products of social systems and power relations. Far too often, middle-class Christians have the tendency to psychologize or use an individualist lens while reading the Bible. On the other hand, the social-scientific approaches as practiced in the white, liberal, North American and European academy often reflect bourgeois interests. Many scholars, for example, have adapted interpretive sociology and structural-functionalist analysis to study the social world of the New Testament. The structural-functionalist approach looks at how social systems are related to one another so that society can function as a whole. Focusing more on integration, stability, and unity, it is less prone to analyze social confrontation and conflict. Using Theissen's study of Palestinian Christianity as an example, Mosala points out that Theissen fails to provide an adequate structural location of the Jesus movement in the political economy of the Roman Empire and does not deal with the real economic and political contradictions of the time (64–65). As such, Theissen's study will be of limited use for the black South Africans struggling against apartheid and other social oppression. Mosala challenges biblical scholars to be open about their own class interest and the limitations of their methods.

One of the important dimensions of social-scientific criticism is the introduction of models from social and cultural anthropology. In addition to the ancient Jewish, Hellenistic, and Roman cultures that biblical scholars have been studying, Bruce J. Malina, Jerome H. Neyrey, and others suggest a pan-Mediterranean culture, with values and ethos markedly different from those in North American culture. The pivotal characteristics of Mediterranean culture in the first century included honor and shame, patronage and clientele, dyadic personality, and rules of purity. They apply the study of Mediterranean culture to interpret the group development of the Jesus movement and Paul's Letters. Scholars have questioned whether it is appropriate to impose models of contemporary societies onto the ancient Mediterranean. They remain doubtful whether the pivotal values of honor and shame are so different from the values in North American and northern European cultures. James G. Crossley also notes that "the Mediterranean frequently blurs into the contemporary Arab world, an area of renewed interest in American and European politics and media in the past forty years" (27).

As a discipline, anthropology emerged during the colonial time and often served the interests of empire. The hypothesis of a distinct Mediterranean culture and personality as contrasted with those in Western society reinforces a binary construction of the colonizers and the colonized. Malina and others have imported twentieth-century anthropological studies to the study of first-century Galilean and Judean society, assuming that Mediterranean cultures had remained unchanged over the years. Furthermore, the honor and shame code is attributed to a strong division of sexual and gender roles in the region and to the anxiety of Mediterranean men over their manhood. Female scholars such as Marianne Sawicki have voiced concerns that the study of honor and shame has largely followed a masculinist script and that women's experiences are overlooked and different. She suggests that the honor-shame sensibility might simply be an ethnocentric projection of the Euro-American male researchers onto the people they are studying (77).

R. S. Sugirtharajah, from Sri Lanka, has criticized Orientalism in the work of biblical scholars who use social-scientific methods. In *Orientalism*, Edward W. Said questions the representation of the Middle East as inferior, exotic, and stagnant in Western scholarship. Sugirtharajah notes prevalent Orientalist tendencies and the recycling of Orientalist practices in biblical scholarship, especially in the study of the social and cultural world of Jesus. He surmises that designations such as "Israel," "Judah," "the Holy Land," "Mediterranean," "world of Jesus," and "cultural world of Jesus" are "ideologically charged rhetoric and markers of Eurocentric and Christian-centric conceptualizations of that part of the world" (2012, 103). New Testament scholars have reinscribed Orientalist messages by suggesting the idea of a static Orient, by generalizing and reducing complex Mediterranean cultures to a few essentials, by gender stereotyping, and by highlighting the contrast between the East and the West. Jesus is depicted as one who is secure in his culture and yet critical of it through redefining honor culture and rearranging Mediterranean values. Since the publication of Said's work, many disciplines have become cautious about Orientalist methods and tendencies. But such methods have resurfaced in biblical studies and books that display Orientalist biases. Sugirtharajah points out that some of them have even become best sellers in mainstream culture (102–18).

Racial and Ethnic Minority Approaches

Racial and ethnic minorities in the United States began to develop their hermeneutical approaches to the Bible during the struggles of the civil rights movement in the 1960s. The development of black theology, Hispanic/Latino theology, and Asian American theology in the United States could not be separated from the ferment and protest against imperialism and apartheid in the Global South. Tat-siong Benny Liew (2013) characterizes racial and ethnic minority readings of the New Testament as "border crossing"—transcending the border of theology and biblical studies and the border between biblical studies and other disciplines. He also succinctly delineates the different stages of the development of such readings. In the first stage, racial and ethnic minority theologians and biblical scholars interpreted the biblical message through their social realities and experiences. For example, James Cone's black theology (1969; 1973) relates the gospel of Jesus to black power and freedom and argues that Christ is black, because Christ identifies with the powerless in society. Mexican American theologian Virgilio Elizondo relates the story of the marginalized Galilean

Jesus who came from the borderland area of Galilee to the story of Hispanic/Latino people as a new *mestizo* people. Asian American Chan-Hie Kim sees parallels between the Cornelius story in Acts 10–11 and Asian immigrant experience because both Cornelius and Kim are outsiders. Other scholars began to find minority subjects in the Bible and presented positive images of them or more complex pictures, such as the Ethiopian eunuch in Acts 8:26-40 (C. J. Martin 1989), and discussed slavery in early Christianity and modern interpretations (Lewis; Martin 1991).

In the current, second stage, racial and ethnic minority scholars do not simply employ different methods of biblical criticism with a racial inflection; they are more thoroughly informed by scholarship in ethnic studies and cultural studies. Their interpretation of the New Testament no longer begins with the biblical texts but with their experience as racial and ethnic minorities living in the United States. Liew characterizes this shift of emphasis as the move from "reading Scripture reading race" to "reading race reading Scripture" (2013, 183). Instead of finding "race" in the biblical text, new frameworks and paradigms of engaging with the Bible are sought. This shift can clearly be seen in *African Americans and the Bible* (Wimbush), which considers the Bible in contemporary African American culture, including poetry, aesthetics of sacred space, gospel music and spirituals, rap music, folk oratory, and many other contexts. Liew's own volume *What Is Asian American Biblical Hermeneutics?* (2008) reads all the major genres of the New Testament with Asian American literature, ethnic studies, and current events. David A. Sánchez's study of Revelation includes significant resources from Latino/a studies and Chicana/o studies.

Another significant development in the second stage is the move beyond a unified and essentialized notion of race to an acknowledgment of internal diversity within each racial and ethnic minority group. African American women articulate the issues of womanist interpretation of the Bible, placing gender at the intersection of race, class, and other anthropological referents. Demetrius K. Williams examines the biblical foundation of understanding of gender in black churches, while Rachel Annette Saint Clair presents a womanist reading of Mark's Gospel. Within the Asian American community, heterogeneity can be seen not only in the addition of women's voices but also in readings by diverse ethnic groups, intergenerational interpretations, and readings by Asian American adoptees and queer people (Foskett and Kuan; Cheng). Likewise, the diversity of the Hispanic/Latino people has been highlighted, and notions of borderland and *mestizaje* differ among different ethnic groups. Manuel Villalobos has combined the insights from feminist and queer theories to read the Ethiopian eunuch in Acts to bring hope and affirmation to Latino queer bodies.

Moving into the third stage, racial and ethnic minority theologians and biblical scholars have begun collaboration across minority groups. The move from articulating minority experience vis-à-vis the white dominant culture to conversing with other racial and ethnic minorities signals a new awareness, which is much needed to prepare for 2040, when, if current trends continue, there will be no racial and ethnic majority in the United States. An important example of such endeavor is the volume *They Were All Together in One Place? Toward Minority Criticism*, coedited by African, Asian, and Hispanic Americans (Bailey, Liew, and Segovia). This collaboration shows a desire for mutual learning and communication across color lines. In the future, more attention needs to be paid both to engaging Native American readings and, given our transnational world, to linking minority criticism with readings in the Global South.

Postcolonial Approaches

Emerging in the late 1970s, postcolonial studies has had significant influence in the fields of the humanities and social sciences. The prefix *post-* does not simply signify the period after colonialism in a chronological sense, but also refers to reading and social practices that aim at contesting colonialism and lifting up the voices of the suppressed and formerly colonized. Postcolonial criticism has drawn from many disciplines and was introduced to biblical studies in the 1990s, particularly through the works and encouragement of R. S. Sugirtharajah (1998; 2002). Other scholars have included a postcolonial optic in the study of the New Testament; for example, Tat-siong Benny Liew (1999), Fernando F. Segovia, Musa W. Dube (2000), Laura D. Donaldson, Stephen D. Moore (2006), and me (2005).

During Jesus' time, Galilee was under Roman imperial occupation and ruled by Herod Antipas (4 BCE–39 CE), and the early Christian communities lived under the whims of empire. Postcolonial critics of the New Testament share common interests with those contributing to the emerging subfield of "empire studies," promoted enthusiastically by Richard A. Horsley (1997; 2002) and other scholars (e.g., Carter; Crossan 2007). This subfield consists of books and articles with the recurrent words *empire* or *imperial* in their titles and with the intention of using the theme of empire to reframe New Testament interpretation. While the authors of works in empire studies are interested in the ancient imperial contexts, and some have related their work to contemporary contexts, they may or may not use postcolonial studies to aid their research and few have shown particular interest in affixing the label "postcolonial" to their works (Moore 2006, 14–19).

Postcolonial critics emphasize that biblical texts are not innocent. Sugirtharajah, for instance, understands postcolonial criticism as "scrutinizing and exposing colonial domination and power as these are embodied in biblical texts and in interpretations, and as searching for alternative hermeneutics while thus overturning and dismantling colonial perspectives" (1998, 16). Postcolonial criticism shares similarities with liberation hermeneutics, but also diverges from it because postcolonial critics are more suspicious of the historical-critical method that many liberation critics use. Postcolonial critics see biblical texts as more complex and multilayered and do not construct rich/poor, colonizer/colonized, and oppressor/oppressed in binary and dichotomous ways, as some liberation theologians do. Liberation theologians from Latin America tend to be Christocentric, while postcolonial critics engage more fully with religious pluralism and popular religions (Sugirtharajah 2002, 103–23).

Applying postcolonial criticism to the Gospels, Sugirtharajah (2002, 86–91) finds that there is no mention of Jesus' explicit resistance against the colonial occupiers. Yet Jesus' critique of local profiteers who colluded with the Romans and some of his sayings about earthly rulers (Matt. 11:8; Luke 7:25; 13:32) suggest that his alternative vision was against those in power. Horsley (2002) takes a stronger stance that Jesus was against empire. He places the Jesus movement within the context of popular resistance movements in Judea and Galilee, and says that the anti-imperial nature of Jesus' movement can provide a basis for theological critique of the Roman Empire in the past and the American empire in the present. Postcolonial studies of Paul's letters have also appeared; for example, Joseph A. Marchal applies feminist and postcolonial theories to the study of Philippians. The 2011 volume *The Colonized Apostle: Paul through Postcolonial Eyes* (Stanley) is the most comprehensive study to date, discussing Pauline agency, Paul's supposed social conservatism, hybrid identity and ethnicity, gender and colonialism, and Paul's relation to struggles in South Korea and the Philippines, among other topics. Moore (2006) uses postcolonial theorist Homi Bhabha to read apocalypse in Mark and John and the book of Revelation and argues that these texts mimic to a certain extent Roman imperial ideology, even when resisting and eroding it. *A Postcolonial Commentary on the New Testament Writings* (Segovia and Sugirtharajah), published in 2007, showcases the diversity of approaches and is an invaluable resource for further studies.

Postcolonial feminist interpretation challenges white male and female metropolitan readings for ignoring the issues of colonialism and imperialism and shows how their readings might collude with empire (Dube 2000). As we have discussed, Dube has lifted up the readings of ordinary female readers in African Independent Churches. Other critical concerns of postcolonial feminist criticism include the investigation of how the deployment of gender and symbolization of women relate to class interests and colonial domination in the Bible and studying women in the contact zones and the borderlands, such as Rahab, Ruth, and the Syrophoenician woman (Kwok, 81–85).

The publication of *Postcolonial Perspectives in African Biblical Interpretations* (Dube, Mbuvi, and Mbuwayesango) in 2012 pushes the envelope of postcolonial criticism even further. It raises the possibilities of "unthinking Eurocentrism" in biblical studies and developing Afrocentric criticism. The volume discusses the politics of translation of the Bible, the Bible as read in and through African creative writings, the relation of the Bible and "the scramble of Africa," HIV and AIDS, and the roles of socially engaged biblical scholars. The volume offers much insight and food for thought for interpreters in other parts of the Global South as well as in metropolitan areas who want to decolonize their minds and their methods when approaching the Bible.

Contemporary Issues

In this final section, I would like to take up some contemporary issues to see how they have led to new readings of the New Testament from fresh angles. First, the Holocaust has prompted many scholars to be conscious of the long history of anti-Jewish and antisemitic biases in the history of biblical interpretation. Scholars have proposed new ways to interpret New Testament texts so that they will not be construed as anti-Jewish. Second, the vigorous debates on same-sex marriage in the United States and elsewhere require us to reexamine the teachings on marriage, family, and same-gender relationships in the New Testament. Third, the study of "Gnosticism" and other writings in early Christianity has made us keenly aware of the politics of inclusion and exclusion surrounding the New Testament canon. A group of scholars has produced a new version of the New Testament combining both traditional and newly discovered texts.

Anti-Judaism and Antisemitism

Anti-Jewish attitudes and prejudices have contributed to antisemitism and the tragic genocide in modern times of Jewish people in Europe. Jews have been blamed for killing Jesus. Jesus' accusations against the scribes and Pharisees as hypocrites and his polemical sayings about the Jews in

John's Gospel have been used to cast Jewish people as the other, who did not accept the good news of Jesus Christ. Jesus has been seen as the founder of a new religion, separate from his Jewish background. Paul's contrast of law and gospel has been taken as the foundational difference between the covenant of the old and the new. Christianity has often been hailed as a universal religion, accepting gentiles into its mix, while Judaism has been cast in a negative light as a religion belonging to a particular group. Many Christians continue to harbor a supersessionist viewpoint, believing that Christianity ultimately triumphs over Judaism.

Interpreters sensitive to the charges of anti-Judaism and antisemitism have presented alternative views and interpretations different from those often taught in Christian churches. New Testament scholars have emphasized Jesus' Jewishness and interpreted Jesus' movement as a movement *within* Judaism. For example, Géza Vermes regards Jesus as a Jewish Galilean charismatic, while E. P. Sanders sees Jesus as an eschatological prophet who believed that the promises to Israel would soon be fulfilled and restoration would be at hand. Jewish New Testament scholar Amy-Jill Levine (2011) calls Jesus "the misunderstood Jew," and her work helps Jews and Christians understand the Jewish context of the first century. In *The Jewish Gospels*, Daniel Boyarin, a professor of talmudic culture, argues that Jesus' teachings can be found in the long-standing Jewish tradition and the coming of the Messiah was imagined in many Jewish texts. Many also point out that Jesus' arguments with the Pharisees and Jewish leaders were not conflicts between Christian and Jews, but intra-Jewish arguments (Wills, 101–32).

Jewish scholars such as Judith Plaskow and Levine (2000) have cautioned against the blanket generalizations of Jewish culture as misogynist in order to construct Jesus as a feminist over against his cultural background. Sometimes, Christian feminists have used Jesus' critique of his culture to support their challenge of patriarchy in their own cultures. To heed these scholars' call, we must avoid generalization and not imagine "the Jews" as the same transhistorically and transculturally. Some of the characterizations of "purity" discussed earlier would seem to fall under this criticism. More attention must be paid to local practices, regional history, and religious views and political ideologies of different groups and factions in first-century Judaism. Levine also suggests reading in community so that we can be exposed to our biases and blind spots in our reading.

An exciting development is the publication of the volume *The Jewish Annotated New Testament* (Levine and Brettler) in 2011, a collaborative effort of an international team of fifty Jewish scholars, which presents Jewish history, beliefs, and practices for understanding the New Testament. The New Testament is interpreted within the context of the Hebrew Bible and rabbinic literature. Each book of the New Testament is annotated with references, and the volume includes thirty essays covering a wide range of topics, including the synagogue, the law, food and table fellowship, messianic movements, Jewish miracle workers, Jewish family life, divine beings, and afterlife and resurrection. It also addresses Jewish responses to the New Testament and contemporary Jewish-Christian relations. The book will facilitate Jewish-Christian dialogue because it helps Christians better understand the Jewish roots of the New Testament and offers Jews a way to understand the New Testament that does not proselytize Christianity or cast Judaism in a negative light.

It should be pointed out that there is a difference between antisemitism and the critique of the policies of the state of Israel and its unequal treatment of Palestinians. Some Jewish thinkers and leaders, such as Judith Butler and Rabbi Michael Lerner, have criticized political Zionism, the dispossession of land, and hard-line policies of the Israeli state. Palestinian liberation theologian Naim Stifan Ateek has challenged Christian Zionism, adherents of which believe that the Jews must return to the Holy Land as a prerequisite for the second coming of Christ. Ateek draws from the example of Jesus to discuss the relation between justice and peace, nonviolent resistance, and the peacekeeping imperatives of the church.

Same-Sex Marriage

Debates on same-sex marriage in United States, Europe, Latin America, and Asia saw both supporters and opponents citing the Bible to support their positions. In the United States, the influential conservative Christian leader James Dobson defends what he calls the biblical definition of marriage, and blames homosexuality and gay marriage for all kinds of social decline. A cursory search on the Internet can find numerous posts citing biblical passages to defend heterosexual marriage and label homosexual passions and acts as unnatural, shameful, and contrary to God's will. These posts usually cite the creation of Adam and Eve in Genesis and the views of Jesus and Paul on marriage and sexuality as support.

Many Christians believe that the modern nuclear family represents the Christian ideal, but the current focus on heterosexual nuclear family dates back only to the 1950s. Dale B. Martin argues that there are more sources in the New Testament to criticize the modern family than to support it. Jesus was not a family man, and the Gospels present Jesus as living in alternative communities that shared his vision of divinely constituted family. He refused to identify with his natural family, saying, "Whoever does the will of God is my brother and sister and mother" (Mark 3:35; cf. Matt. 12:50; Luke 8:21). Jesus forbade divorce, even though Mosaic law allowed it (Matt. 19:4-9; Mark 10:6-12). But Matthew follows this with the saying about those who have "made themselves eunuchs for the sake of the kingdom of heaven" (Matt. 19:12), which might imply that the avoidance of marriage and of procreation is preferable. Jesus also says in the Gospels that in the resurrection, marriage will be obsolete (Matt. 22:30; Mark 12:26).

Paul in 1 Corinthians 7 did not promote marriage or traditional family and preferred Christians to follow his example and remain single and celibate. He thought that marriage would become a distraction from the life of faith "in Christ." But he allowed marriage for those who were weak and could not control their passions, saying "it is better to marry than to be aflame with passion" (1 Cor. 7:9). In Paul's time, passion and sexual desires were associated with the body and had to be put under severe control. The letters to the Colossians and Ephesians contain the household codes, which propose the hierarchy and order of a patriarchal family. But these letters are generally considered deuteropauline and were written during the increasing patriarchal institutionalization of the church.

Opponents to same-sex marriage often cite Rom. 1:23-27 to support their claims that homosexual acts are unnatural. Scholars have offered different explanations of the context of this text to argue that it is not against homosexual relations as we have come to know them in the present day (Goss, 198–202). Some suggest that homosexual acts were considered part of unclean gentile culture and were condemned by Paul for that reason. Others claim that Paul was not speaking about adult homosexual relations but pederasty in the Greco-Roman world. Some even proffer that Paul might have in mind oral or anal sex as unnatural sexual intercourse, among opposite-sex partners as well. Bernadette J. Brooten comments that Paul's injunction against female homosexual relations was due to his understanding of gender roles. Paul did not want women to exchange their supposedly passive and subordinate desire for an active role (216). Feminist scholars have challenged the androcentric mind-set and patriarchal ideologies of Pauline and other New Testament writings.

The New Testament thus cannot be easily enlisted to support a reductionistic understanding of "Christian marriage" or "family values," as if these have not changed over time. While same-sex marriage has become a rallying cry for marriage equality and recognition of human rights, some lesbians and gay men have also expressed concerns that the legislation of marriage would give too much power to the state, which can legitimize one form of sexual relationship while excluding others. Dale B. Martin belongs to this latter group and encourages queer Christians to expand their imaginations to "allow scripture and tradition to inspire new visions of Christian community free from the constraints of the modern, heterosexual, nuclear family" (39). Tolbert (2006) adds that same-sex couples can find the ideals of friendship in the New Testament supportive of their relationship. In John, Jesus told the disciples that they were his friends and shared with them his deepest knowledge of God. The New Testament, Tolbert says, does not promote marriage, heterosexual or not, as the bedrock of Christian community, but rather values friendship; as Jesus says, "No one has greater love than this, to lay down one's life for one's friends" (John 15:13). Even though the notion of friendship in the ancient world might be quite different from ours, the shift from promoting marriage to friendship opens new horizons.

A "New" New Testament

In 1945, local peasants in Nag Hammadi in Egypt discovered papyrus codices in a clay sealed jar consisting of fifty-two gnostic writings that were previously unknown. Though the papyrus dated back to the fourth century, some of the texts in the manuscripts can be traced back to as early as the first or second century. The Nag Hammadi library contains texts such as the *Gospel of Thomas*, the *Gospel of Philip*, the *Gospel of Truth*, and writings attributed to Jesus' followers, such as the *Secret Book of James*, the *Apocalypse of Paul*, and the *Apocalypse of Peter* (Pagels). The discovery of these texts greatly expanded our knowledge of religious writings in the early centuries.

Just as Jewish scholars have challenged us to reexamine our assumptions about Christian origins and the Jewish roots of Christianity, the discovery and study of the Nag Hammadi library raised new issues about the conceptualization of the history of the early church. Before the discovery, all we knew about "Gnosticism" was that the orthodox heresiologists, especially Irenaeus and Tertullian, vilified it. Karen L. King (2003) argues that these polemicists had constructed the category "heresy" as part of their project of identity formation and to exclude Jews and pagans as outsiders. The Nag Hammadi writings show what scholars have called "Gnosticism" as highly pluralistic and the boundary between Christianity and "Gnosticism" as more permeable than previously assumed. Both the so-called orthodox and the heretical writings belonged to a common body of tradition and represented "distinct varieties of Christianity developed in different geographical areas, at a time when the boundaries of orthodox and heresy were not at all fixed" (152). Moreover, certain texts were excluded from the

New Testament canon because of ideological reasons, such as to marginalize women's authority and leadership. For example, the *Gospel of Mary*, which was excluded, depicts Mary Magdalene as having received special knowledge from Jesus and serving as a leader among the disciples after Jesus' resurrection. This portrait of Mary should be considered together with the depiction of her as one of Jesus' followers and a key witness to his resurrection in the New Testament (King 1998).

In addition to the Nag Hammadi library, other texts have been discovered in the nineteenth and twentieth centuries and scientifically verified to be almost as old as the manuscripts of the traditional New Testament. A group of scholars, pastors, and church leaders under the leadership of Hal Taussig have produced a New Testament for the twenty-first century that includes with the established canon a selection of some of the texts outside the canon and called it "a new New Testament." The newly added documents include ten books, two prayers, and the *Odes of Solomon*, which consists mostly of prayers. Now, within the same volume, we can read about Mary Magdalene in the traditional Gospels as well as in the *Gospel of Mary*. In contrast to the traditional book of Revelation, the *Secret Revelation of John* offers a different picture of how Christ rescues the world, not through apocalyptic battles, but by teaching about God's light and compassion. Taussig hopes that this new New Testament can offer readers a chance to form new opinions about the earliest traditions of Christianity and be inspired by the teachings, songs, prayers, letters, and meditations of Jesus' early followers (xviii–xix).

Conclusion

The New Testament has shaped human cultures for millennia and is read by Christians, people of other religious traditions, and secular people in different tongues, cultural backgrounds, social contexts, and life circumstances. As global citizens living in the twenty-first century, we have to remember how the gospel of Jesus Christ has been misused to oppress and construct the other, whether the other is Jewish people, women, racial and ethnic minorities, colonized people, or queer people, so that history will not be repeated. The availability of so many new resources and methods in New Testament studies and the addition of underrepresented voices from all over the world are cause for celebration. New Testament reading in the contemporary world has become more global, multicentered, and plurivocal, and contributes to interreligious understanding. The interpretation of the New Testament has also been brought to the public square, as people look for insights from the Bible to address problems of our day. I hope that those among the younger generation who profess that they are "spiritual but not religious" will also appreciate the wisdom in the New Testament, as one of the most fascinating and influential religious and spiritual literatures of humankind.

Works Cited

Ahn, Byung Mu. 1981. "Jesus and the Minjung in the Gospel of Mark." In *Minjung Theology: People as the Subjects of History*, edited by Kim Yong Bock, 136–52. Singapore: Commission of Theological Concerns, Christian Conference of Asia.

Anderson, Janice Capel, and Stephen D. Moore, eds. 2008. *Mark and Method: New Approaches in Biblical Studies*. 2nd ed. Minneapolis: Fortress Press.

Ariarajah, Wesley. 1989. *The Bible and People of Other Faiths*. Maryknoll, NY: Orbis.

Ateek, Naim Stefan. 1989. *Justice, and Only Justice: A Palestinian Theology of Liberation*. Maryknoll, NY: Orbis.

Bailey, Randall C., Tat-siong Benny Liew, and Fernando F. Segovia, eds. 2009. *They Were All Together in One Place? Toward Minority Biblical Criticism*. Atlanta: Society of Biblical Literature.

Barr, James. 1983. *Holy Scripture: Canon, Authority, Criticism*. Oxford: Clarendon.

Baum, Wilhelm, and Dietmar W. Winkler. 2003. *The Church of the East: A Concise History*. London: RoutledgeCurzon.

Blount, Brian K. 1995. *Cultural Interpretation: Reorienting New Testament Criticism*. Minneapolis: Fortress Press.

Borg, Marcus J. 1994. *Jesus in Contemporary Scholarship*. Valley Forge, PA: Trinity Press International.

Boyarin, Daniel. 2012. *The Jewish Gospels: The Story of the Jewish Christ*. New York: New Press.

Brooten, Bernadette J. 1996. *Love between Women: Early Christian Responses to Female Homoeroticism*. Chicago: University of Chicago Press.

Butler, Judith. 2012. *Parting Ways: Jewishness and the Critique of Zionism*. New York: Columbia University Press.

Cardenal, Ernesto. 1976–1982. *The Gospel in Solentiname*. Translated by Donald D. Walsh. 4 vols. Maryknoll, NY: Orbis.

Carter, Warren. 2001. *Matthew and Empire: Initial Explorations*. Harrisburg, PA: Trinity Press International.

Cheng, Patrick S. 2002. "Multiplicity and Judges 19: Constructing a Queer Asian Pacific American Biblical Hermeneutic." *Semeia* 90–91:119–33.

Cone, James H. 1969. *Black Theology and Black Power*. New York: Seabury.

———. 1975. *God of the Oppressed*. New York: Seabury.

Crossan, John Dominic. 1991. *The Historical Jesus: The Life of a Mediterranean Jewish Peasant*. San Francisco: HarperSanFrancisco.

———. 2007. *God and Empire: Jesus against Rome, Then and Now*. New York: HarperCollins.

Crossley, James G. 2010. *Reading the New Testament: Contemporary Approaches*. London: Routledge.

Dobson, James C. 2004. *Marriage under Fire: Why We Must Win This War*. Sisters, OR: Multnomah.

Donaldson, Laura E. 2006. "Gospel Hauntings: The Postcolonial Demons of New Testament Criticism." In *Postcolonial Biblical Criticism: Interdisciplinary Intersections*, edited by Fernando F. Segovia and Stephen D. Moore, 97–113. London: Continuum.

Dube, Musa W. 2000. *Postcolonial Feminist Interpretation of the Bible*. St. Louis: Chalice.

———, ed. 2001. *Other Ways of Reading: African Women and the Bible*. Atlanta: Society of Biblical Literature.

———. 2008. *The HIV and AIDS Bible: Selected Essays*. Scranton, PA: University of Scranton Press.

Dube, Musa, Andrew M. Mbuvi, and Dora R. Mbuwayesango, eds. 2012. *Postcolonial Perspectives in African Biblical Interpretations*. Atlanta: Society of Biblical Literature.

Eber, Irene, Sze-kar Wan, and Knut Walf, eds. 1999. *The Bible in Modern China*. Nettetal, Germany: Steyler.

Elizondo, Virgilio. 1983. *Galilean Journey: The Mexican-American Promise*. Maryknoll, NY: Orbis.

Fernandez, Eleazar S. 2013. "Multiple Locations-Belongings and Power Differentials: Lenses for Liberating Biblical Hermeneutic." In *Soundings in Cultural Criticism: Perspectives and Methods in Culture, Power, and Identity in the New Testament*, edited by Francisco Lozada Jr. and Greg Carey, 139–49. Minneapolis: Fortress Press.

Flatow, Sheryl. 2009. "Christianity on the Move." *Bostonia*. http://www.bu.edu/bostonia/fall09/christianity.

Foskett, Mary F., and Jeffrey Kah-Jin Kuan, eds. 2006. *Ways of Being, Ways of Reading: Asian American Biblical Interpretation*. St. Louis: Chalice.
Gager, John G. 1975. *Kingdom and Community: The Social World of Early Community*. Englewood Cliffs, NJ: Prentice-Hall.
Goss, Robert E. 2002. *Queering Christ: Beyond Jesus Acted Up*. Cleveland: Pilgrim.
Gutiérrez, Gustavo. 1988. *A Theology of Liberation: History, Politics, and Salvation*. Translated by Caridad Inda and John Eagleson. Rev. ed. Maryknoll, NY: Orbis.
Hastings, Adrian, ed. 1999. *A World History of Christianity*. Grand Rapids: Eerdmans.
Horsley, Richard A., ed. 1997. *Paul and Empire: Religion and Power in Roman Imperial Society*. Harrisburg, PA: Trinity Press International.
———. 2002. *Jesus and Empire: The Kingdom of God and the New World Disorder*. Minneapolis: Fortress Press.
Irvin, Dale T., and Scott W. Sunquist. 2001. *History of the World Christian Movement*. Vol. 1, *Earliest Christianity to 1453*. Maryknoll, NY: Orbis.
———. 2012. *History of the World Christian Movement*. Vol. 2, *Modern Christianity from 1454 to 1800*. Maryknoll, NY: Orbis.
Jenkins, Philip. 2007. *The Next Christendom: The Coming of Global Christianity*. Rev. ed. New York: Oxford University Press.
Johnson, Todd M., and Kenneth R. Ross. 2009. *Atlas of Global Christianity, 1910–2010*. Edinburgh: Edinburgh University Press.
Kim, Chan-Hie. 1995. "Reading the Cornelius Story from an Asian Immigrant Perspective." In *Reading from This Place*. Vol. 1, *Social Location and Biblical Interpretation in the United States*, edited by Fernando F. Segovia and Mary Ann Tolbert, 165–74. Minneapolis: Fortress Press.
Kinukawa, Hisako. 1994. *Women and Jesus in Mark: A Japanese Feminist Perspective*. Maryknoll, NY: Orbis.
King, Karen L. 1998. "Canonization and Marginalization: Mary of Magdala." In *Women's Sacred Scriptures*, edited by Kwok Pui-lan and Elisabeth Schüssler Fiorenza, 29–36. London: SCM.
———. 2003. *What Is Gnosticism?* Cambridge, MA: Harvard University Press.
Kitzberger, Ingrid Rosa. 1998. "How Can This Be? (John 3:9): A Feminist Theological Re-Reading of the Gospel of John." In *What Is John?* Vol. 2, *Literary and Social Readings of the Fourth Gospel*, edited by Fernando F. Segovia, 19–41. Atlanta: Society of Biblical Literature.
Kwok Pui-lan. 2005. *Postcolonial Imagination and Feminist Theology*. Louisville: Westminster John Knox.
Lady Gaga. 2011. "Judas." Posted on May 3. http://www.ladygaga.com/media/?meid=6765.
Lee, Archie C. C. 1998. "Cross-Textual Interpretation and Its Implications for Biblical Studies." In *Teaching the Bible: The Discourses and Politics of Biblical Pedagogy*, edited by Fernando F. Segovia and Mary Ann Tolbert, 247–54. Maryknoll, NY: Orbis.
Levine, Amy-Jill. 2000. "Lilies of the Field and Wandering Jews: Biblical Scholarship, Women's Roles, and Social Location." In *Transforming Encounters: Jesus and Women Re-viewed*, edited by Ingrid Rosa Kitzberger, 329–52. Leiden: Brill.
———. 2006. *The Misunderstood Jew: The Church and the Scandal of the Jewish Jesus*. San Francisco: HarperSanFrancisco.
Levine, Amy-Jill, and Marc Z. Brettler, eds. 2011. *The Jewish Annotated New Testament*. New York: Oxford University Press.
Lewis, Lloyd A. 1991. "An African American Appraisal of the Philemon-Paul-Onesimus Triangle." In *Stony the Road We Trod: African American Biblical Interpretation*, edited by Cain Hope Felder, 232–46. Minneapolis: Fortress Press.

Liew, Tat-siong Benny. 1999. *The Politics of Parousia: Reading Mark Inter(con)textually.* Leiden: Brill.

———. 2008. *What Is Asian American Biblical Hermeneutics?* Honolulu: University of Hawai'i Press.

———. 2013. "Colorful Readings: Racial/Ethnic Minority Readings of the New Testament in the United States." In *Soundings in Cultural Criticism: Perspectives and Methods in Culture, Power, and Identity in the New Testament*, edited by Francisco Lozado Jr. and Greg Carey, 177–89, Minneapolis: Fortress Press.

Malina, Bruce J. 1981. *The New Testament World: Insights from Cultural Anthropology.* Atlanta: John Knox Press.

Marchal, Joseph A. 2008. *The Politics of Heaven: Women, Gender, and Empire in the Study of Paul.* Minneapolis: Fortress Press.

Martin, Clarice J. 1989. "A Chamberlain's Journey and the Challenge of Interpretation for Liberation." *Semeia* 47:105–35.

———. 1991. "The *Haustafeln* (Household Codes) in African American Interpretation: 'Free Slaves' and 'Subordinate Women.'" In *Stony the Road We Trod: African American Biblical Interpretation*, edited by Cain Hope Felder, 206–31. Minneapolis: Fortress Press.

Martin, Dale B. 2006. "Familiar Idolatry and the Christian Case against Marriage." In *Authorizing Marriage? Canon, Tradition, and Critique in the Blessing of Same-sex Unions*, edited by Mark D. Jordan, 17–40. Princeton: Princeton University Press.

Meeks, Wayne A. 1983. *The First Urban Christians: The Social World of the Apostle Paul.* New Haven: Yale University Press.

Melanchthon, Monica Jyotsna. 2010. "Dalit Women and the Bible: Hermeneutical and Methodological Reflections." In *Hope Abundant: Third World and Indigenous Women's Theology*, edited by Kwok Pui-lan, 103–22, Maryknoll, NY: Orbis.

Moore, Stephen D. 2006. *Empire and Apocalypse: Postcolonialism and the New Testament.* Sheffield: Sheffield Phoenix Press.

———. 2010. *The Bible in Theory: Critical and Postcritical Essays.* Atlanta: Society of Biblical Literature.

———. 2013. "The Dog-Woman of Canaan and Other Animal Tales from the Gospel of Matthew." In *Soundings in Cultural Criticism: Perspectives and Methods in Culture, Power, and Identity in the New Testament*, edited by Francisco Lozada Jr. and Greg Carey, 57–71. Minneapolis: Fortress Press.

Moore, Stephen D., and Janice Capel Anderson, eds. 2003. *New Testament Masculinities.* Atlanta: Society of Biblical Literature.

Mosala, Itumeleng J. 1989. *Biblical Hermeneutics and Black Theology in South Africa.* Grand Rapids: Eerdmans.

Nelavala, Surekha. 2006. "Smart Syrophoenician Woman: A Dalit Feminist Reading of Mark 7:24-31." *ExpTim* 118, no. 2: 64–69.

Neyrey, Jerome H. 1990. *Paul, in Other Words: A Cultural Reading of His Letters.* Louisville: Westminster John Knox.

Pagels, Elaine. 1979. *The Gnostic Gospels.* New York: Random House.

Patte, Daniel. 2004. Introduction to *Global Bible Commentary*, edited by Daniel Patte, xxi–xxxii. Nashville: Abingdon.

Petrella, Ivan. 2005. *Latin American Liberation Theology: The Next Generation.* Maryknoll, NY: Orbis.

Plaskow, Judith. 1980. "Blaming the Jews for the Birth of Patriarchy." *Lilith* 7:11–12, 14–17.

Rajkumar, Peniel. 2010. *Dalit Theology and Dalit Liberation: Problems, Paradigms, and Possibilities.* Burlington, VT: Ashgate.

Roncace, Mark, and Joseph Weaver, eds. 2013. *Global Perspectives on the Bible.* Upper Saddle River, NJ: Pearson.

Said, Edward W. 1978. *Orientalism.* New York: Pantheon.

Saint Clair, Rachel Annette. 2008. *Call and Consequences: A Womanist Reading of Mark*. Minneapolis: Fortress Press.
Sánchez, David A. 2008. *From Patmos to the Barrio: Subverting Imperial Myths*. Minneapolis: Fortress Press.
Sanders, E. P. 1985. *Jesus and Judaism*. Philadelphia: Fortress Press.
Sanneh, Lamin O. 1989. *Translating the Message: The Missionary Impact on Culture*. Maryknoll, NY: Orbis.
———. 2003. *Whose Religion Is Christianity? The Gospel beyond the West*. Grand Rapids: Eerdmans.
———. 2007. *Disciples of All Nations: Pillars of World Christianity*. New York: Oxford University Press.
Sawicki, Marianne. 2000. *Crossing Galilee: Architectures of Contact in the Occupied Land of Jesus*. Harrisburg, PA: Trinity Press International.
Scharper, Philip, and Sally Scharper, eds. 1984. *Gospel in Art by the Peasants of Solentiname*. Maryknoll, NY: Orbis.
Schottroff, Luise. 1995. *Lydia's Impatient Sisters: A Feminist Social History of Early Christianity*. Translated by Barbara Rumscheidt and Martin Rumscheidt. Louisville: Westminster John Knox.
Schüssler Fiorenza, Elisabeth. 1983. *In Memory of Her: A Feminist Theological Reconstruction of Christian Origins*. New York: Crossroad.
———. 1992. *But She Said: Feminist Practices of Biblical Interpretation*. Boston: Beacon.
———. 2000. *Jesus and the Politics of Interpretation*. New York: Continuum.
———. 2002. "The Ethos of Biblical Interpretation: Biblical Studies in a Postmodern and Postcolonial Context." In *Theological Literacy for the Twenty-First Century*, edited by Rodney L. Petersen, 211–28. Grand Rapids: Eerdmans.
———. 2007. *The Power of the Word: Scripture and the Rhetoric of Empire*. Minneapolis: Fortress Press.
Segovia, Fernando F. 2000. *Decolonizing Biblical Studies: A View from the Margins*. Maryknoll, NY: Orbis.
Segovia, Fernando F., and R. S. Sugirtharajah, eds. 2007. *A Postcolonial Commentary on the New Testament Writings*, New York: T&T Clark.
Segundo, Juan Luis. 1976. *Liberation of Theology*. Translated by John Drury. Maryknoll, NY: Orbis.
Stanley, Christopher D., ed. 2011. *The Colonized Apostle: Paul through Postcolonial Eyes*. Minneapolis: Fortress Press.
Sugirtharajah, R. S. 1999. *Asian Biblical Hermeneutics and Postcolonial Criticism: Contesting the Interpretations*. Maryknoll, NY: Orbis.
———. 2002. *Postcolonial Criticism and Biblical Interpretation*. Oxford: Oxford University Press.
———. 2012. *Exploring Postcolonial Biblical Criticism: History, Method, Practice*. Malden, MA: Wiley-Blackwell.
———, ed. 1998. "Biblical Studies after the Empire: From a Colonial to a Postcolonial Mode of Interpretation." In *The Postcolonial Bible*, edited by R. S. Sugirtharajah. Sheffield: Sheffield Academic Press.
Tamez, Elsa. 2001. *Jesus and Courageous Women*. New York: Women's Division, General Board of Global Ministries, United Methodist Church.
———. 2007. *Struggles for Power in Early Christianity: A Study of the First Letter to Timothy*. Translated by Gloria Kinsler. Maryknoll, NY: Orbis.
Taussig, Hal, ed. 2013. *A New New Testament: A Bible for the Twenty-First Century Combining Traditional and Newly Discovered Texts*. Boston: Houghton Mifflin Harcourt.
Theissen, Gerd. 1978. *Sociology of Early Palestinian Christianity*. Translated by John Bowden. Philadelphia: Fortress Press.
Tolbert, Mary Ann. 1998. "Reading the Bible with Authority: Feminist Interrogation of the Canon." In *Escaping Eden: New Feminist Perspectives on the Bible*, edited by Harold C. Washington, Susan Lochrie Graham, and Pamela Thimmes, 141–62. Sheffield: Sheffield Academic Press.

———. 2006. "Marriage and Friendship in the Christian New Testament: Ancient Resources for Contemporary Same-Sex Unions." In *Authorizing Marriage? Canon, Tradition, and Critique in the Blessing of Same-Sex Unions*, edited by Mark D. Jordan, 41–51. Princeton: Princeton University Press.

United Bible Societies. 2012. "Celebrating 100 Millions Bibles printed in China!" November 12. http://www.unitedBiblesocieties.org/news/2902-celebrating-100-million-Bibles-printed-in-china.

———. 2013 "About UBS Translation Work." http://www.ubs-translations.org/about_us.

Vermes, Géza. 1973. *Jesus the Jew: A Historian's Reading of the Gospels*. London: Collins.

Villalobos, Manuel. 2011. "Bodies *Del Otro Lado* Finding Hope in the Borderland: Gloria Anzaldúa, the Ethiopian Eunuch of Acts 8:26–40, *y Yo*." In *Bible Trouble: Queer Reading at the Boundaries of Biblical Scholarship*, edited by Teresa Hornby and Ken Stone, 191–221. Atlanta: Society of Biblical Literature.

West, Gerald O. 1999. *The Academy of the Poor: Towards a Dialogical Reading of the Bible*. Sheffield: Sheffield Academic Press.

Wicker, Kathleen O'Brien, Althea Spencer Miller, and Musa W. Dube, eds. 2005. *Feminist New Testament Studies: Global and Future Perspectives*. New York: Palgrave Macmillan.

Williams, Demetrius K. 2004. *An End to This Strife: The Politics of Gender in the African American Churches*. Minneapolis: Fortress Press.

Wills, Lawrence M. 2008. *Not God's People: Insiders and Outsiders in the Biblical World*. Lanham, MD: Rowman & Littlefield.

Wimbush, Vincent L., ed. 2000. *African Americans and the Bible: Sacred Texts and Social Textures*. New York: Continuum.

Wire, Antoinette Clark. 1990. *The Corinthian Women Prophets: A Reconstruction through Paul's Rhetoric*. Minneapolis: Fortress Press.

Yamaguchi, Satoko. 2002. *Mary and Martha: Women in the World of Jesus*. Maryknoll, NY: Orbis.

Negotiating the Jewish Heritage of Early Christianity

Lawrence M. Wills

Any discussion of the dialogue between Jews and Christians in the twenty-first century must begin with some historical perspective as to what the traditional Christian view has been concerning the relations of Jews and followers of Jesus in the first century. In the first half of the twentieth century, for instance, the dominant Christian view was the following: on the one hand, there was one clear Judaism—viewed through the lens of Paul's critique of the law and represented by the Pharisees as depicted in Matthew—and on the other hand, one clear Christianity as a new entity that had separated from Judaism. If there was any disagreement among the first Christians, it was only that between the "correct" party—those who followed Paul—and the "incorrect" party—those who followed James in retaining Jewish law. How the divorce between Judaism and Christianity took place is treated in the book of Acts, which was taken as a historically accurate record of the intransigence of Jews in the face of Paul's preaching of the message of Christ. True, there were ambiguous passages throughout the Gospels, such as:

> When Jesus saw that he [the scribe] answered wisely, he said to him, "You are not far from the kingdom of God." (Mark 12:34)
>
> Jesus said to them, "The scribes and the Pharisees sit on Moses' seat; therefore, do whatever they teach you and follow it." (Matt. 23:2-3)

But these could be explained away by interpreting them in light of Paul's letters and Acts.

Over the last century, scholars have moved away from this simple view of the relation of ancient Judaism and early Christianity to a much more complex view, questioning almost every part of the description above. In the first half of the twentieth century, some Christian scholars argued that the variety of early Christian groups did not evolve out of one unified body of followers of Jesus, or even from the two divergent paths of "Paul Christians" and "James Christians." Rather, from the earliest period, there were already widely divergent practices and beliefs, without any clear sense of an agreed-on center. This challenge to a trunk-with-branches view of early Christian groups gave more weight to the "branches," groups formerly regarded as smaller, marginal, too Eastern, or heretical. Walter Bauer was a leading figure in this development; more recent scholars who exemplify this approach include James Robinson and Helmut Koester; Jack Sanders; and Stephen Wilson.

For instance, whereas it was traditionally assumed that the four Gospels were narrative depictions of a Jesus who taught essentially what Paul said in his letters using different language, now one had to take seriously the differences among the authors and audiences of these texts. The varied emphases that were found among the four Gospels, or between Paul's letters and Revelation, or between Acts and Jude, or between canonical texts and early Christian texts from outside the canon, came to be seen as reflective of widely divergent movements and eddies in this new religious movement. Scholars might retain the theological preferences of their own traditions, but in colleges and universities, and even in seminaries, the historical narrative no longer seemed like a tree with a clear trunk and branches, but followed the pattern of tubers and vines—widely propagating members with little clear order or lines of development.

In this process, Christian texts from outside the New Testament canon, even those that had been considered "heretical," came to be viewed as having an equal claim in the *historical* reconstruction of early Christianity, regardless of their theology. There was a larger and larger patchwork of groups, and a clear history of origins and development became ever more difficult to reconstruct. Very basic questions about the history of Judaism and Christianity were also introduced: Has the early Eastern history of Judaism and Christianity, all the way from Syria to India and later to China, been ignored as a result of the Western focus of much of the Christian church and of Judaism? To be sure, the Eastern church also included Paul in its canon, but was the relation between eastern Christians and Jews vastly different from that of their Western counterparts (Foltz)?

But another, parallel shift was also underway. In the last half of the twentieth century, scholars proposed a similar proliferation in the number of Jewish groups as well. Before about 1960, many scholars would have described Judaism in the first century as divided into three parties—Sadducees, Pharisees, and Essenes—based on a description of Judaism by the first-century Jewish historian Josephus (*J.W.* 2.117–66). But the discovery of the Dead Sea Scrolls, a new appreciation for the differences among the many Jewish texts of the period, and a growing realization that early rabbinic views were not authoritative for all Jews compelled scholars to recognize the wide variety of Jewish groups, beliefs, and practices (see Cohen 2006; J. J. Collins; Nickelsburg). The classic nineteenth-century history of the Judaism of this period by Emil Schürer (1886–1890) was enlarged in each of the many subsequent editions by the inclusion of more variety in terms of texts, theology, and practices.

Jewish scholars were also motivated by a desire to participate fully in the public discourse on the nature of religions. Judaism, they argued, should be studied in our colleges and universities as an important religious tradition alongside Christianity and other world religions. After World War II and the Shoah, or Holocaust—the genocide of six million Jews—there was an added motivation for both Jews and Christians: a more searching engagement about the origins of Jewish-Christian relations in the ancient world. If the historical assumptions behind a presumed Christian superiority could be challenged, then Christians, Jews, and others would have a chance of living in peace in the twentieth century and afterward without the corrosive effects of stereotypes derived from a misreading of ancient evidence.

Corresponding to the recognition of ancient variety was a new variety among the modern scholars who were studying it as well. During the twentieth century, there arose a full participation of Christian scholars in the study of Judaism and Jewish scholars in the study of Christianity—along with scholars from other religious backgrounds or with no religious affiliation at all. By the second half of the twentieth century, it came to be quite expected that New Testament scholars would know something about rabbinic literature and that Jewish historians of the Roman period would know something about the New Testament and early church. By the end of the twentieth century, there was not just one or two but a number of important studies on the New Testament by Jewish scholars and a number of important studies on rabbinic Judaism by Christians.

The situation at the end of the twentieth century, then, was drastically different from that at the beginning. Influenced by challenges in the social sciences, philosophy, and literary criticism, new issues came to be raised that only made the comparison more complicated, but in many cases, more interesting to modern audiences. Formerly, scholars compared Judaism and Christianity as two clearly defined bodies of people with separate identities, but increasingly many scholars realized that more elite voices within Judaism—for instance, the chief priests, Josephus, or Philo—were being unfairly compared to the less elite forms of Christianity—Mark or the sayings source of Matthew and Luke. The nonelite layers of the Christian movement seemed more revolutionary when compared with the aristocratic voices within Judaism, yet a comparison of Jewish prophetic movements (such as those reported in Josephus) to more elite Christian texts like Hebrews would look very different. Which is the "proper" comparison? Should popular movements among Christians be compared with popular movements among Jews, and more elite texts among Christians with elite Jewish authors, say, Hebrews with Philo? And further, would a female Christian who was the slave of a Christian master have had more in common with her master, or with a Jewish woman who was the slave of a Jewish master, or a female worshiper of Isis who was the slave of a master who worshiped Isis? The effects of geographical distance were also relevant, as both Jews and followers of Jesus were found in communities stretching well over a thousand miles, from Spain to the East, assimilating in each case to vastly different local customs. It was becoming increasingly difficult to define clearly separate bodies of "Jews" and "Christians."

The earlier consensus, then, might have compared the "three parties" of Judaism—Sadducees, Pharisees, and Essenes—and the "two parties" within Christianity—Pauline Christians and "Jewish Christians"—a comparison that could be depicted in this way:

| Jewish groups: | 1 1 1 |
| Followers of Jesus: | 1 1 |

But by the end of the twentieth century, in recognition of the great variety of subgroups, the comparison would appear more like this:

| Jewish groups: | 1 1 1 1 1 1 1 1 1 1 1 1 1 |
| Followers of Jesus: | 1 1 1 1 1 1 1 1 1 1 |

If many Jewish groups maintained strict observance of Torah, so did many followers of Jesus. If many followers of Jesus believed that the end of time was near, so did many Jewish groups. If many followers of Jesus believed that the community of believers was bathed in the holiness of God in a way that made the Jewish temple superfluous, so did some Jews. And finally: If the death of Jesus was the theological affirmation that supposedly separated Christians from Jews, what do we make of the fact that some followers of Jesus did not emphasize his death and some Jewish texts (for example, 4 Maccabees) did emphasize the death of Jewish heroes? Similarities and differences among the groups in *both* rows above introduced new challenges for comparing "Judaism" and "Christianity." The Gospel of Matthew, for instance, was clearly critical of Pharisees—*one* of the Jewish groups in the row above—but was it possible that Matthew was actually more similar to Pharisees than he was to Paul? The simple question of the relation of "Jews" and "Christians" could no longer be answered without pressing a more specific question: *Which* Jews? *Which* Christians?

Incorporating this new consensus concerning a variety of groups among Christians and among Jews, some scholars toward the end of the twentieth century began charting the history of the "partings of the ways" or the "divorce" between Judaism and Christianity (e.g., Dunn 1991; Townsend). A title that exemplified the new consensus of variety was James D. G. Dunn's *The Partings of the Ways* (1991), but challenges to the "new consensus" were, of course, inevitable. Dunn's title was countered by a collection of conference papers called *The Ways That Never Parted* (Becker and Reed; see also Boyarin). This volume asked: At what point were the followers of Jesus thoroughly parted from "Judaism" or "Israel"? True, differences among Jewish or Christian subgroups could be discerned, but could the line above of Christian subgroups really be clearly distinguished from the Jewish line? Thus it is somewhat ironic that, after a century of new studies emphasizing the distinctions among different Jewish groups and different Christian groups, some of the heirs of that consensus would amend it by deemphasizing the boundary line *between* Judaism and Christianity. As more and more subgroups were divided off, they began to fill out the *overall* circle of "Judaism and Christianity" approximately equally. It is even suggested that texts that seem at first to affirm a clear, separate identity are in some cases overstating the distinction, or even creating the illusion of separation, imposing distinctions that may barely exist, in order to instill a clearer sense of identity. (This may be true, for example, of Matthew.) As we learn from modern identity studies, the strongest assertions of difference, or the strongest assertions of a good "We" and an evil "Other," often appear between groups that are similar to each other, and almost indistinguishable by outsiders (Wills). Although this newest development appears at first to undo the previous consensus about variety and difference, it actually carries it forward by demonstrating that there is a wide, overlapping spectrum of beliefs and practices among Jews *and* followers of Jesus, and yet the differences that we perceive among groups and subgroups does not result in one clear line *between* Jews and followers of Jesus. Some Christian groups would admittedly be more clearly separated from Judaism—for example, the implied audience of the Letter to the Hebrews—but others would be more ambiguous in their separation than once thought. Again, it is as if the two lines of groups above should be merged into one indistinct set.

The Continuing Demand for Comparison, Despite the Complexity of the Data

While recognizing all of these challenging new questions, the effort to draw general conclusions about the relations of Jews and Christians continues, and is indeed necessary for a dialogue between Jews and Christians in the twenty-first century. The demands of modern Jews and Christians for dialogue have required some general observations about the first century in order to proceed. Some of the older conclusions still inform the present, more complex discussions among Jews, Christians, and others, and can be used as starting points.

Douglas R. A. Hare, for instance, divided the different assessments of Judaism found in the New Testament into three types. Some polemic in the Gospels is simply a critique of Jewish institutions by people who were, after all, also Jews. This he termed "prophetic anti-Judaism," the critique by a prophetic figure of his or her own institutions. (Even this use of the term *anti-Judaism* seems to separate the prophet from the people and imply that the prophet is *not* Jewish; it is tantamount to referring to Martin Luther King's "anti-Americanism." George Michael Smiga [12–13] tried to address this terminological problem.) According to Hare, Jesus himself would have fit in this category, and might be compared to figures such as Socrates, who, although he criticized his fellow Athenians, was not "un-Greek" or "anti-Greek." Nor did his students suggest that they must create a new entity in which to explore his philosophy (though Plato did eventually leave Athens to advise the king of Syracuse in a failed experiment to establish a "philosopher's state"). Other polemic in the New Testament, however, became progressively harsher, and pronounced a final condemnation on those Jews who did not accept Jesus as the Messiah. Hare termed this "Jewish-Christian anti-Judaism." Unlike the previous category, this type represents a division of groups within Judaism that is at the point of divorce, and the polemical language reflects the tension of being "mid-divorce" (Townsend). A third type is "gentilizing anti-Judaism," and is truly postdivorce: the critique of Judaism as a whole by gentile Christians (Wilson, 110–42, 258–84). Authors in this category are no longer realistically concerned with the conversion of Israel. It can be debated which texts of the New Testament or the early church would fall into these categories, but many scholars would consider the Gospel of Matthew as the first type, a prophetic critique of some (or even most) Jews from within Judaism; the Acts of the Apostles as a text of the second type, which condemns Jews for not accepting the message of Jesus as Messiah; and the Epistle to the Hebrews as an example of gentilizing anti-Judaism. But any of these might be and have been debated. Only if we could interrogate the authors could we be sure where they stood on key questions of the relations of the subgroups in a constantly differentiated Judaism.

In addition to historians and biblical scholars, theologians also entered into the dialogue and introduced terminology to define the various positions that Christians have taken in regard to their relation to Judaism. "Supersessionism" describes the traditional Christian view that in Jesus and Paul we find the belief that Judaism was superseded by God's new dispensation in Christ and the church. (Some New Testament scholars use the compound term rejection-replacement.) But even a doctrine of supersessionism can be more or less negative about the validity of the Jewish covenant. Does the old covenant have any continuing role in God's dispensation, or is it simply the precursor to Christianity (Novak; see also Soulen)? A so-called dual-covenant theology has arisen among liberal Christians, which is the notion that God's new dispensation in Christ did not cancel out the existing covenant with Jews. In this view, there are still two covenants operative, and thus there is no supersessionism, but rather a continuing coexistence of parallel covenants. Some passages from early Christian authors might be adduced in support of this position (see below concerning Paul).

Yet this overture only calls forth new questions. Even if Christians developed a benign view of the continuing validity of God's covenant with Jews, that does not begin to address the relations of Christians with religions other than Judaism. Jewish-Christian dialogue is an important beginning, but only a beginning, to dialogues with other faiths, and this should not be forgotten in discussions of the history of Jewish-Christian relations. Although it is understandable that Jewish leaders have often engaged in dialogue with Christian leaders in order to ameliorate the effects of antisemitism, for many Jews it would be unacceptable to achieve a recognition of God's continuing covenant with Jews if other religions still remained in a less favored status. In the twenty-first century, a broader notion of religious acceptance, beyond a "dual-covenant theology," has often arisen.

With these and similar analyses in mind, in the late twentieth century, scholars of the New Testament, including many Jewish scholars, proposed sweeping changes in regard to how the New Testament texts themselves evaluated Judaism. Vermes, Fredriksen, and Levine (17–52) returned to the Gospel accounts and Acts and argued that recoverable evidence about the historical Jesus depicts a teacher who may have *argued* about Jewish law—not surprising for a Jewish teacher—but who probably remained fairly observant to the end. A great deal of consensus has gathered around this view. If Jesus did reject certain aspects of Jewish law that were advocated by others, such as the Pharisees—again, not surprising for any non-Pharisaic Jew—he never made a blanket rejection of the markers of Judaism. Otherwise, why would Paul have been forced to argue so strongly with the disciples who actually knew Jesus (Galatians 1–2)? Some of Jesus' claims in the Gospels might actually constitute a *stricter* than usual observance of Jewish law, an "ultraorthodox" position! (These cases are sometimes ambiguous, and identifying something or someone as more or less orthodox is always a relative question—who defined the norm? Yet Jesus' rejection of divorce in Mark 10:2-12, or his constraints on accepted Jewish law in Matt. 5:17-48, could be considered a stricter "fence around the Torah" than that which became the norm in rabbinic literature. See also Vermes [80–81], and on the apparent exception in Mark 7:19, see below.)

It is likely that any observer in the year 30 CE would not have considered Jesus a "Reform" Jew (admittedly an anachronistic term), but more probably, a "strict" or "pious" Jew. As noted above, a compelling argument was also made that the Gospel of Matthew, although formerly viewed as "anti-Jewish" ("Scribes and Pharisees, hypocrites!" Matt. 23:13), was actually more anti-*Pharisaic* (Harrington, 1–3; Wills, 101–32). That is, Matthew does not perceive the movement of the followers of Jesus as opposing Judaism, but as opposing some within Judaism, especially Pharisees. To be sure, it is stated in Matthew that at the end, the gentiles will come in (28:19), but that is true of many Jewish texts as well. Matthew does not betray a "Pauline" critique of Jewish law and remains observant to the end.

Even if Jesus and the Gospel of Matthew assumed a continuing adherence to Jewish law, it has been assumed that Paul had irrevocably altered this situation by instituting a mission to gentiles without the law. But now this assumption as well has come in for a major reevaluation. The so-called new perspective on Paul has questioned the chasm that Christians have traditionally perceived between this apostle and the Judaism of his day (Dunn 1983). For the new-perspective scholars, Paul was more a missionary theologian than an abstract theologian or a psychologist of the human condition, and was rarely setting up an opposition between "Jews" and those in Christ. Rather than critiquing and rejecting Judaism as a form of legalism and "works righteousness" at odds with God's plan, almost all of Paul's apparent references to "Jews" are more likely referring to those *in the Jesus movement*, whether originally Jewish or gentile, who oppose his mission to gentiles without the law. This raises a challenging question: If gentiles had been allowed to enter freely into his churches without adhering to Jewish law, would Paul have voiced any reservations about the law for Jews at all?

The debate over the new perspective has been significant. The new perspective represents a direct challenge to strongly held tradition, and yet has achieved a large following. Still, conservative Protestant theologians have opposed it, and even those scholars who have self-identified as part of the new perspective can be divided into two groups, a moderate new perspective and a radical new perspective (Wills, 179–82). The distinction is based on how far they would push the questioning of the older consensus. The moderate new-perspective scholars hold that Paul was much less critical of Judaism than once thought. Says E. P. Sanders (552), whom we might consider a moderate new-perspective scholar: "In short, this is what Paul finds wrong in Judaism: it is not Christianity." That is, God (in Paul's view) is not "displeased" with Jews, Judaism, or Jewish law, but has simply, by the death of Christ, created a new door for all, both Jews and gentiles, to enter into the graces of God. The *discontinuity* between Judaism and Christianity is thus drastically reduced. This shift alone unsettled much Protestant tradition.

But the radical new-perspective scholars go further and argue a version of the dual-covenant theology mentioned above. For Paul, the death of Christ did indeed open a new door of access for gentiles that did not require Jewish law, but the old door for Jews remained open as well—without Christ and with the law still in effect! God was not closing one door to open a new one, but was opening an option for gentiles parallel to the one for Jews (Eisenbaum). Paul's letters are ultimately unclear on this question, but Eisenbaum's conclusions may be correct. However, as above with dual-covenant theology, the same demurral still applies: even if Paul envisioned a two-door access, for gentiles in Christ without the law and for Jews with the law only, he is quite explicit that gentile religion (apart from belief in Christ) is degraded and alienated from God (Rom. 1:2; Gal. 4:8; see

Wills, 179–82). There is no "newer perspective" on Paul that could soften his condemnation of the gentile religions, and in the twenty-first century this becomes a fundamental challenge for interfaith dialogue. (It would be speculative to try to imagine what Paul's views of Islam might have been, although the parallels to Paul's theology are significant. In Islam, Jesus is the Messiah of God, born of a virgin, who performed miracles, and the revelation in Islam came to a prophet who was also "last of all, as to one untimely born" [cf. 1 Cor. 15:8]. But even if, continuing this imaginative exercise on the analogy of the "two-covenant" understanding described above, we were to imagine Paul countenancing a third covenant, with Islam, what would we say of the status of other religions?)

Now, many passages in Paul, especially in Romans, would appear to fly in the face of the radical new-perspective scholars, but in each case an alternative interpretation is possible that would at least make this dual-covenant reading a plausible option. Consider the much-discussed case of Rom. 10:4: "For Christ is the end [*telos*] of the law so that there may be righteousness for everyone who believes." Like the English "end," *telos* can be translated as either "point of cessation" or "goal"; does Paul mean that Christ will bring the covenant of law to an end, or that Christ will constitute the goal of that law *for gentiles*? The interpretation of individual passages sometimes also comes down to whether Paul is speaking principally about Christ or God. For example, in Rom. 9:33, Paul quotes Isa. 8:14-15; 28:16.

> See, I am laying in Zion a stone that will make people stumble, a rock that will make them fall, and whoever believes in him will not be put to shame.

Is Paul referring here to Christ, as Christian tradition has generally held, or, like the Isaiah passages he quotes, to *God's* role in establishing Jerusalem? Note here that the Greek pronoun for "him" could equally be "*it*," that is, the stone (a masculine noun in Greek). Which is the center of Paul's vision, Christ or God? Is it necessary for Jews to have faith *in Christ*, or faith *in the promises of God for gentiles*? The radical new-perspective scholars point out that in Romans, Paul speaks of both.

Quite often, we see that the debate narrows to a microanalysis of individual verses. Indeed, interpretation can only proceed one passage at a time, and yet, if at each stop alternative understandings are possible, then the decision about the whole becomes more difficult to adjudicate. But for this, as for any important and difficult issue, the positions of scholars and of laypeople will likely not be based on "decoding" one or two passages, but rather on general dispositions to the texts. However, it is possible that the undisputed letters of Paul, really only about seventy-five pages in the English translations, simply do not unambiguously reveal Paul's view on this question. That in itself would still be news. If the supersessionist position were really so central to Paul's theology, should it not be easy to establish it in the letters without question? If the overall impression of ambiguity is sustained, does that not at least suggest that the assurance with which earlier interpreters spoke of Paul in supersessionist ways was unwarranted? If one sets aside the *later* Christian tradition on supersessionism, does the same view disappear in Paul's letters?

The issues found in the Gospel of John have also come under scrutiny. Unlike Matthew, which focuses its polemic stridently on the Pharisees, John equally insistently refers to opponents as "Jews"—*Ioudaioi* in Greek—which can also be translated "Judeans" (that is, those from Judea, where

Jerusalem was located). How does one explain the intense anti-Judaism of John, where it is stated that *Ioudaioi* are the "children of the devil" (8:44)? Was the audience of John an "introversionist sect," which turned the promise of salvation inward to a small group of followers who no longer identified with the *Ioudaioi*, meaning Jews who revered the temple authorities in Judea (Wills, 133–66; Reinhartz, 25; Kittredge, 49–63)? Or is the Galilean origin of the Gospel of John at play here, and should *Ioudaioi* be translated not as "Jews" but as "Judeans," those members of Israel who lived in Judea and exercised some control over the members of Israel (which may include Samaritans) who lived in Galilee and Samaria? Whatever sociological theory is asserted to explain the *Ioudaioi* in the Gospel of John, the text seems to express a polemical separation that is different from Matthew on one hand or Paul on the other. The distinction between good and bad people, or even good and evil people, is even stronger in John than in Paul or Matthew.

For twenty-first-century audiences, it is difficult to come to terms with the strong polemics voiced in our sacred texts. Should modern readers, both Christian and Jewish, simply conclude that the ancient writers of the now-sacred texts took group identity too far? Consider a passage from the Hebrew Bible and a passage from the New Testament.

> When the LORD your God brings you into the land that you are about to enter ... and he clears away ... the Hittites, the Girgashites, the Amorites, the Canaanites, the Perizzites, the Hivites, and the Jebusites, ... then you must utterly destroy them. (Deut. 7:1-2)

> You [Jews] are from your father the devil, and you choose to do your father's desires. He was a murderer from the beginning and does not stand in the truth. ... He is a liar and the father of lies. (John 8:44, referred to above)

One can imagine asking, "If you knew a Hittite well (or a Jew well), would you say that?" (On the ambiguity of these designations, see Wills, 21–51, 133–66.) But the many varieties of early followers of Jesus means that *different* lines were being drawn in the sand to differentiate groups, and while they defined the fissures between most Jews and followers of Jesus, they also defined serious breaches among different followers of Jesus. Would Paul, Matthew, or John have placed *each other* among the saved, or among the damned?

The Gospel of Mark as a Test Case

At the same time that bold new assessments were being raised in regard to the relations of Jews and followers of Jesus in Matthew, Paul, and John, there was relatively little rethinking of the situation in the Gospel of Mark, and this Gospel could become a test case for the *old* view. It has long been assumed that, *regardless of the original meaning of Paul's letters*, Mark understood Paul as Paul's followers did. The following assumptions seemed secure:

1. Mark was influenced by Paul and inherited a Pauline doctrine of faith.
2. Mark reflected a mission that was like Paul's; in Mark, Jesus moved into gentile territory to demonstrate an openness to gentile converts (Mark 7–9).

3. Mark must have been a gentile, because there are inaccuracies in regard to Jewish practice in the passion narratives and elsewhere, and Mark explains basic Jewish practices, often inaccurately (7:3-4).
4. Jesus is depicted as rejecting kosher laws across the board (7:19).

Now, however, these conclusions have also been challenged. First, it is not at all clear that Mark knew Paul's theology of faith *in contrast to law*. Faith was a constant element in the Hebrew Bible and also in the Jewish discourse of the period. The Hebrew word *'aman* ("to believe, have faith") and its related forms (in Aramaic as well) can be found behind the use of "amen" in liturgy and are related to the word truth (*'emet*, derived from *'aman*), and to the "faithful ones" (*ne'emanim*) among the Pharisees (*m. Demai* 4:6). In Neh. 9:38, the restored community in Jerusalem joins in a "faith covenant" (*'amanah*). The use of this root by Jews speaking Hebrew or Aramaic, and of the *pist-* root by those speaking Greek, only increases in the Hellenistic period. Thus, although the use of the language of "faith" and "believing" in Mark is pronounced, *it was also common in Judaism*, a fact that is almost totally ignored in assessments of Jewish-Christian relations in the first century. Further, the language of "faith" and "believing" in Mark is not explicitly contrasted with law as Paul would have it; it is used in the same way as other Jews were using it. (Parallels between Mark and Paul are often listed, but the Pauline passages are almost all found in Romans. Were Paul's words in this letter carefully chosen to respond to the *Jewish* discourse on faith in which that community would have been schooled?)

Second, although in Mark, Jesus does move into territories occupied by gentiles, these were also (with one exception, 7:1) part of the ancient borders of Israel. The Maccabees and their descendants had already conquered these lands in order to reestablish the boundaries of ancient Israel; so might we regard Jesus' itinerary in Mark as also reconstituting "Israel"? Jesus also heals gentiles, but so had the prophet Elisha (2 Kings 5); was the latter also "gentilizing" Israel? Third, Mark's Gospel does seem to include many *apparent* inaccuracies concerning Jewish practices, but these, too numerous to mention, are in some cases found in other Jewish texts or taken over in the "Jewish" Gospel Matthew, and other cases are much less clear than once thought (A. Y. Collins).

Last, we come to the argument that has often seemed conclusive: Mark's apparent cancellation of all kosher laws in Jesus' debate with the Pharisees and scribes at 7:1-23. The relevant verses are displayed here side by side with the equivalent section of Matthew. The parallel columns allow one to read Mark's words closely while at the same time noting the differences found in Matthew's treatment of this important issue. (Luke and John do not include this passage.)

Mark 7:1-23 (in part)	**Matthew 15:1-20** (in part)
[1] When the Pharisees and some of the scribes who had come from Jerusalem gathered around him, [2] they noticed that some of his disciples were eating with defiled hands, that is, without washing them. [3] For the Pharisees, and all the Jews, do not eat unless they thoroughly wash their hands, thus observing the tradition of the elders; [4] and they do not eat anything from the market unless they wash it; and there are also many other traditions that they observe, the washing of cups, pots, and bronze kettles. [5] So the Pharisees and the scribes asked him, "Why do your disciples not live according to the tradition of the elders, but eat with defiled hands?" [Several scriptural and legal arguments follow here.] [14] He called the people to him again and said, [15] "There is nothing outside a person which by going in can defile, but the things which come out are what defile. [18] Do you not see that whatever goes into a person from outside cannot defile, [19] since it enters not the heart, but the stomach, and goes out into the sewer?" Thus he declared all foods clean [literally, "Thus he cleansed all foods"]. [20] And he said, "It is what comes out of a person that defiles. [21] For it is from within, from the human heart, that evil intentions come: fornication, theft, murder, [22] adultery, avarice, wickedness, deceit, licentiousness, envy, slander, pride, folly. [23] All these evil things come from within, and they defile a person."	[1] Then Pharisees and scribes came to Jesus from Jerusalem, and said, [2] "Why do your disciples break the tradition of the elders? For they do not wash their hands before they eat?" [Several scriptural and legal arguments follow here.] [10] He called the people to him and said, [11] "It is not what goes into the mouth that defiles a person, but what comes out of the mouth, this defiles. [17] Do you not see that whatever goes into the mouth enters the stomach, and goes out into the sewer? [18] But what comes out of the mouth proceeds from the heart, and this is what defiles. [19] For out of the heart come evil intentions, murder, adultery, fornication, theft, false witness, slander. [20] These are what defile a person, but to eat with unwashed hands does not defile."

Mark's words here are traditionally interpreted in a "Pauline" way, that is, that Jewish law now no longer applies among the followers of Jesus. However, challenges to that interpretation of this passage have also arisen. Jesus' debate with Pharisees about eating food with unwashed hands may not be a rejection of Jewish law but a debate *within* Judaism. Mark here may actually have Jesus endorse the majority Jewish position against the stricter Pharisees. Was the view Mark attributes to Jesus actually more typical of Jewish practice in the first century than the Pharisees'? One also notices that the run-on sentence in 7:3-4 may have resulted from the combination of a simple, and accurate, statement about Pharisees and additional comments about practices of "all the Jews" that were added later. (Note that these verses are not present in Matthew.) But Mark's explanation of Jewish customs may also not be as out of place in Jewish discourse as once thought (A. Y. Collins, 345; Regev 2000, 180–81, 188–89). To be sure, the passage indicates (if it was not inserted later in its entirety) that Mark is including gentiles in the audience of the Gospel, but it does not necessarily reveal a gentile *author*. Mark's reference to the practices of "all the Jews" certainly seems to distance himself from them, but we encounter here a hidden problem with English that affects interpretation. An English-speaking Jew might say, "All Jews do such-and-such," but not "All *the* Jews do such-and-such." The English definite article has the power in this construction to separate off the group in question and to distance the speaker from the group. In Greek, however, usage of the definite article is often quite different from English, and it is not clear that it would distance the speaker in this way. Did Mark mean, "All Jews wash their hands"—which could include Mark—or "All *the* Jews wash their hands"—which seems to distance the Markan Jesus from the Jews?

The last half of this passage has also been reassessed. The central statement—"There is nothing outside a person which by going in can defile, but the things which come out are what defile"—may not be a rejection of purity concerns, as long supposed, but simply an insistence that *moral* purity is as important, or even more important, than *ritual* purity. The prioritizing of moral motives over observance was well known in the Jewish background (Mic. 6:6-8, Hosea 6:6), but the insistence that Jewish observance remains in effect as well is also found in New Testament texts: "You Pharisees tithe mint and rue and herbs of all kinds, and neglect justice and the love of God. It is these you ought to have practiced, *without neglecting the others*" (Luke 11:42; Klawans, 147–48).

But Mark also broadens the discussion by the insertion of 7:19c, "thus he declared all foods clean" (*katharizōn panta ta brōmata*). This awkward and intrusive phrase, which does not appear in Matthew (the section as a whole, as noted, is lacking in Luke and John), may have been inserted later in the textual history of Mark (Booth, 49–50, 62–65), but even if these were Mark's own words, it is also possible that this clause has an entirely different meaning. The Greek literally says, "Jesus *cleansed* all foods," but translators, stumped by what that would mean, have chosen a paraphrasing translation that made perfect sense in the twentieth-century consensus: "Jesus declared all foods clean." This translation means that the "Pauline" Jesus was instituting a new policy canceling all kosher laws. However, in the ancient period, it was sometimes stated, in both Jewish and Christian texts, that at the end of time, for the special, saved community, there would be a *cleansing* of foods, vessels, or people. From Ezekiel (36:22-31) to Zechariah (14:16, 20-21) to *1 Enoch* (10:17—11:2) to Qumran (1QS 4:20-21), there are discussions of a shower of purity on the saved community, however that community is described (see also *Jub.* 1:17, 23; 4:26; 50:5; *Abot R. Nat.* B 42; *b. Erub.*

100b; Regev 2000; 2004). Indeed, with this notion in mind, one may look at other passages in Mark as well. Consider Jesus' healing of a leper, phrased in terms of "cleansing" (the *kathar* root in Greek).

> A leper came to him begging him, and kneeling he said to him, "If you choose, you can cleanse me [*katharisai*, cf. 7:19, discussed above]." Moved with pity, Jesus stretched out his hand and touched him, and said to him, "I do choose. Be cleansed [*katharisthēti*]!" Immediately the leprosy left him, and he was cleansed [*ekatharisthē*]. After sternly warning him he sent him away at once, saying to him, "See that you say nothing to anyone; but go, show yourself to the priest, and offer for your cleansing [*katharismos*] what Moses commanded, as a testimony to them." (Mark 1:40-44)

Although this passage is often understood, from the perspective of *later* Christianity, as the rejection of purity laws about leprosy, a close reading reveals that Jesus miraculously returns the leper to a state of being clean, but does nothing to alter the Jewish laws concerning purity. In fact, the man is instructed to go to the temple to make the offering that Moses commanded (Leviticus 14). The point is important. Technically, in Jewish law, a leper is not pure until after the temple offering is made, but the point of Mark's story is that purity is now made miraculously available as an eschatological event (see Regev 2000; 2004). In the similar but not identical case in the Hebrew Bible mentioned above (2 Kings 5), the prophet heals Naaman the Syrian from his leprosy. But just as it is not generally suggested in Jewish or Christian tradition that Elisha is opening Israel to gentiles, it is also not suggested that he is canceling Jewish purity laws concerning leprosy. And Mark is not the only Christian text to describe an end-time cleansing of the saints; in an otherwise puzzling passage, Paul finds a new cleansing in the community members themselves; note the juxtaposition of "cleansing" with holiness language (the *hag-* root in Greek):

> The unbelieving husband is made holy [*hēgiastai*] through his wife, and the unbelieving wife is made holy through her husband. Otherwise, your children would be unclean [*akatharta*], but as it is, they are holy [*hagia*]. (1 Cor. 7:14; see Johnson Hodge)

So just as the leper in Mark 1:40-45 is *cleansed*—purity rules are *not* abrogated—and in 1 Corinthians 7 an unbelieving spouse is made holy and the children cleansed, so in Mark 7 it is likely that in anticipation of an eschatological change, Jesus *cleanses* foods, as the Greek actually states. Thus, even if this verse was in Mark's original text, it may not have meant that Jewish kosher laws were being rejected, but that for this community, there is at the end of time a dispensation of purity that overwhelms impurity, and also defeats "impure spirits," Mark's more Jewish term for "demons." If, as Zech. 14:20 says, all vessels can be rendered pure at the end of time, and if, as 1 Corinthians 7 says, spouses can be rendered holy, why not lepers in the community, and foods? At the end of time, all heaven breaks loose, but only on the holy community, the *hagioi* ("saints"). There is a division of humanity for a simultaneous cleansing and judgment. The canceling of Jewish food laws, which is how Acts 10, for instance, has been traditionally interpreted, has been too hastily read back into Mark (see also Rom. 14:20).

This passage, then, which had been treated by scholars as a clear confirmation of the Pauline theology at the center of Mark, is much more ambiguous than was once supposed. Paul's letters were often used to justify a gentile mission and identity, but was Mark part of that development (as were Luke and Acts), or was it, like Matthew, part of that segment of the movement, perhaps the larger part, that had not abrogated Jewish law? What was once considered unlikely in regard to Mark now seems quite possible.

Conclusion

A common theme here is that Matthew, Paul, John, and Mark were likely much more rooted in Jewish tradition than Christians have generally assumed. The net effect of these newer investigations is to make discussions among Jews, Christians, and others much more unsettled, but also much richer. Much uncertainty has arisen about each old consensus, and this may seem daunting to contemporary audiences. But there is now a possibility of a wholly *new* dialogue, one that goes back to both the Jewish and Christian sources and asks again what the texts might have meant and what the relations were—both within each body and between the two bodies. The seeds of modern anti-Judaism and the Holocaust can still be seen in some of the ancient texts, but the varied relations also reveal the truth that the story is complex, and it includes many alternative visions of how religious subgroups could respond to each other. There is not just one blueprint for "the relations of Judaism and Christianity" in the first century.

Works Cited

Bauer, Walter. 1934. *Rechtgläubigkeit und Ketzerei im ältesten Christentum*. Tübingen: Mohr. Translated as *Orthodoxy and Heresy in Earliest Christianity*. Philadelphia: Fortress Press, 1979.
Becker, Adam H., and Annette Yoshiko Reed, eds. 2007. *The Ways That Never Parted: Jews and Christians in Late Antiquity and the Early Middle Ages*. Minneapolis: Fortress Press.
Booth, Roger P. 1986. *Jesus and the Laws of Purity: Tradition History and Legal History in Mark 7*. Sheffield: JSOT Press.
Boyarin, Daniel. 2004. *Border Lines: The Partition of Judaeo-Christianity*. Philadelphia: University of Pennsylvania Press.
Cohen, Shaye J. D. 2006. *From the Maccabees to the Mishnah*. 2nd ed. Louisville: Westminster John Knox.
Collins, Adela Yarbro. 2007. *Mark: A Commentary*. Hermeneia. Minneapolis: Fortress Press.
Collins, John J. 2000. *Between Athens and Jerusalem: Jewish Identity in the Hellenistic Diaspora*. 2nd ed. Grand Rapids: Eerdmans.
Dunn, James D. G. 1983. "The New Perspective on Paul." *BJRL* 65:95–122.
———. 1991. *The Partings of the Ways: Between Christianity and Judaism and Their Significance for the Character of Christianity*. London: SCM.
Eisenbaum, Pamela. 2009. *Paul Was Not a Christian: The Real Message of a Misunderstood Apostle*. New York: HarperOne.
Foltz, Richard. 2010. *Religions of the Silk Road: Premodern Patterns of Globalization*. 2nd ed. New York: Palgrave Macmillan.
Fredriksen, Paula. 1995. "Did Jesus Oppose Purity Laws?" *BR* 11:18–25, 42–48.
Hare, Douglas R. A. 1967. *The Theme of Jewish Persecution of Christians in the Gospel according to St. Matthew*. Cambridge: Cambridge University Press.

Harrington, Daniel J. 1991. *The Gospel of Matthew*. Sacra pagina. Collegeville, MN: Liturgical Press.

Johnson Hodge, Caroline. 2007. *If Sons, then Heirs: A Study of Kinship and Ethnicity in the Letters of Paul*. Oxford: Oxford University Press.

———. 2010. "Married to an Unbeliever: Households, Hierarchies, and Holiness in 1 Corinthians 7:12-16." *HTR* 103:1–25.

Kittredge, Cynthia Briggs. 2007. *Conversations with Scripture: The Gospel of John*. Harrisburg, PA: Morehouse.

Klawans, Jonathan. 2000. *Impurity and Sin in Ancient Judaism*. Oxford: Oxford University Press.

Levine, Amy-Jill. 2006. *The Misunderstood Jew: The Church and the Scandal of the Jewish Jesus*. San Francisco: HarperSanFrancisco.

Nickelsburg, George W. E. 2005. *Jewish Literature between the Bible and the Mishnah: A Historical and Literary Introduction*. 2nd ed. Minneapolis: Fortress Press.

Novak, David. 2004. "The Covenant in Rabbinic Thought." In *Two Faiths, One Covenant? Jewish and Christian Identity in the Presence of the Other*, edited by Eugene B. Korn, 65–80. Lanham, MD: Rowman & Littlefield.

Regev, Eyal. 2000. "Pure Individualism: The Idea of Non-Priestly Purity in Ancient Judaism." *JSJ* 31:176–202.

———. 2004. "Moral Impurity and the Temple in Early Christianity in Light of Ancient Greek Practice and Qumranic Ideology." *HTR* 97:377–402.

Reinhartz, Adele. 2001. *Befriending the Beloved Disciple: A Jewish Reading of the Gospel of John*. New York: Continuum.

Robinson, James M., and Helmut Koester. 1971. *Trajectories through Early Christianity*. Philadelphia: Fortress Press.

Sanders, E. P. 1977. *Paul and Palestinian Judaism: A Comparison of Patterns of Religion*. Philadelphia: Fortress Press.

Sanders, Jack T. 1993. *Schismatics, Sectarians, Dissidents, Deviants: The First One Hundred Years of Jewish-Christian Relations*. London: SCM.

Schürer, Emil. 1886–1890. *Geschichte des jüdischen Volkes im Zeitalter Jesu Christi*. 2 vols. Leipzig: Hinrichs.

Smiga, George Michael. 1992. *Pain and Polemic: Anti-Judaism in the Gospels*. Mahwah, NJ: Paulist.

Soulen, R. Kendall. 1996. *The God of Israel and Christian Theology*. Minneapolis: Fortress Press.

Townsend, John. 1979. "The Gospel of John and the Jews: The Story of a Religious Divorce." In *Antisemitism and the Foundations of Christianity*, edited by Alan T. Davies, 72–97. New York: Paulist.

Vermes, Géza. 1991. *Jesus the Jew: A Historian's Reading of the Gospels*. Philadelphia: Fortress Press.

Wills, Lawrence M. 2008. *Not God's People: Insiders and Outsiders in the Biblical World*. Lanham, MD: Rowman & Littlefield.

Wilson, Stephen G. 1995. *Related Strangers: Jews and Christians, 70–170 C.E.* Minneapolis: Fortress Press.

Rootlessness and Community in Contexts of Diaspora

Margaret Aymer

Rootlessness wanders through Christian imagination today as it has for thousands of years. Even today, hymns proclaiming "this world is not my home," and "I am a poor pilgrim of sorrow, I'm lost in this wide world alone," are sung by women and men whose families can trace their ancestry on any given land mass back multiple generations. Often, the Hebrew Scriptures are credited as the origin of themes of rootlessness, wandering, pilgrimage, and dispersion. However, the New Testament also contains themes of rootlessness and of the creation of community in times of diaspora.

Perhaps it takes an uprooted soul to notice these themes, this ongoing trope in the New Testament. Perhaps it takes the eyes of a woman between cultures, not fully American, and unquestionably not Caribbean—except when I unquestionably am—who emigrated as a child and has functioned as an interpreter of cultures for both my home and host cultures. Some Asian Americans call this the phenomenon of being "the 1.5 generation," the generation that stands between the deep memory of the first-generation immigrant who grew to adulthood in the country of origin and the deep acculturation of the second generation, born in the country of migration. As 1.5-generation people, we stand between homelands, always on a journey, negotiating when possible, turning away when endangered, forging a third way when necessary, and always being in the midst of creating and re-creating culture in ways that are at once rooted in the old, transplanted into a strange land, and bearing hybrid, sometimes nourishing fruit that may at times be unrecognizable as the result of transplantation.

I often read the New Testament with 1.5-generation eyes, eyes not only of an immigrant but also of an immigrant of color. And when I do, I notice that many of these New Testament texts bear marks of migration: evidence of negotiating one's way between home and host cultures, and of the work of forging culture and making meaning in the midst of displacement.

(Re)Considering the History and Rhetoric of New Testament Writings

To argue that the New Testament writings bear marks of migration is to make both a historical and a rhetorical argument. The historical argument is grounded in the accepted historical reconstruction of the creation of these writings by the majority of scholars. The rhetorical argument is grounded in the way in which the authors describe their displacement, their own rootlessness, and that of their community; and how they use that rhetoric to construct strategies of interaction with the wider world. Take, for example, the general consensus that Mark is the oldest canonical Gospel, written after the siege of Jerusalem (of which Mark 13 is understood as description after the fact rather than foretelling), and that it was not written in Judea or Galilee. Already that history suggests displacement, the Gospel narrative written in migration. This would not be the case if the story were an invention out of the imagination of "Mark" the Gospel writer. But if, as biblical scholars have claimed, "Mark" uses oral sources as well as written ones to construct a narrative that he believes to be factually true at least in part, then the ultimate origin of those oral sources would have had to be persons from Judea or Galilee whose bodies, or stories, had migrated to Mark's location. Thus we know with some certainty that at the very least, the stories are migratory.

Mark gives us more clues to suggest that the cultural home of his narrative is not his current audience. He includes and, of even more importance, he *translates* a number of Aramaic sayings of Jesus, among them *Talitha kum* (5:41), *Ephphatha* (7:34), and the cry from the cross, *Eloi, Eloi, lama sabachthani* (15:34). That there is Aramaic in Mark should come as no surprise. After all, Aramaic was one of the languages of Judea and the Galilee. The surprise is Mark's need to translate the Aramaic. This suggests, first, that either Mark or his oral source knows Aramaic, for the short passages are translated correctly. This makes Mark at least bilingual; the Gospel of Mark was composed in Greek. Second, it suggests that Mark is writing to an audience that is, at most, only partially literate in Aramaic.

All of these are traces, hints of the possible origins of the Gospel of Mark, which are, in reality, largely lost. However, these traces suggest a Gospel written in displacement and a writer bridging the distance between a story perhaps told in Aramaic and one written in Greek with Aramaic traces, translating the first generation to the second generation. If this is the case, Mark's Gospel not only tells the good news of Jesus Christ but also, like the older exilic writings of the Hebrew Scriptures, tells a story about a homeland and a home culture no longer accessible to a generation that may be in danger of forgetting. It is an immigrant's tale, a tale of which, if Mark 16:8 can be believed, Mark alone is the only faithful teller.

The other Gospels and the Acts of the Apostles might take issue with Mark's monopoly on faithful discipleship. As second- and third-generation readers (see Luke 1:1-2), they take the traditions of the migrants and rework them for their contemporaries, not unlike the transformation of English plum pudding into Caribbean Christmas cake or the twenty-first-century hip-hop recensions of Bob Marley's twentieth-century reggae hits. Some translation still needs to take place. Some original language still remains in place. And depending on the nature of the community, more of the home culture (Matthew) or more of the host culture (Luke) is emphasized. But the history remains the same: communities of persons outside of Judea and Galilee, and distant from the events of Jesus' life, inheriting a story told and retold in migration, a story possibly even recounted and written by migrants.

With the writings of Paul, one can demonstrate a case for their historical marks of migration much more simply. Paul is, after all, a wandering preacher writing to assemblies in cities and villages outside of his natal Tarsus. This alone is enough to make these writings migrant writings. But Paul, too, is engaging in translation: in this case, not translation from Aramaic to Greek, but the cultural work of translating a primarily Jerusalem-based, Jewish sect into an assembly that denies the distinctiveness between Jew and Greek, slave and free, perhaps even man and woman (Galatians 3). This is an assembly not just for gentiles, but even more powerfully for Diaspora Jews, those who for generations have lived away from but never completely separated from Jerusalem and Galilee. This group would have maintained some traditions and let others go, particularly others that would have made them peculiar or abhorrent to their majority-gentile neighbors. Indeed, by the time he writes to Philippi, Paul radically begins to imagine these assemblies not merely as bodies of believers gathered to pray but also as political entities in which those assembled had status, citizenship, and inheritance (Phil. 3:20). Paul's writing bears marks not only of his own migrant life but also of the diasporic migrant lives of his communities, and of a migrant imagination that forms new communities of migrants—persons living in one place with their citizenship in another.

Paul's interpreters, those who wrote the deuteropauline and Pastoral Epistles, are similarly involved in a work of translation: translation as cultural accommodation of the majority culture. Once Paul's apocalyptic insistence on the imminent return of Christ proves to be premature, these interpreters, perhaps a generation removed from Paul's migrant fervor, use their second-generation status to re-create a Christianity less dangerous to the empire in which it must survive.

Like Paul, John of Patmos seems to be a migrant, perhaps an involuntary migrant, if we take his self-description in Revelation 1:9 as evidence that he is in exile. His epistolary apocalypse then takes on the work of migrant writing, a writing both in migration (he is on Patmos) and to migrant communities. The letter does what John can no longer do, moving from place to place encouraging communities to hold fast and to remember that their final dwelling place is not the place where they currently abide and that their allegiances are not to the beasts of land and sea or to the dragon who gives them power. Rather, their allegiances are to the lion/slaughtered lamb on the throne and their true home is the new Jerusalem, which will come down from the new heaven on the new earth. They are thus to live as citizens of "an-other" place, as migrants in an evil world, waiting, like the souls under the altar, until all is accomplished and their nomadic God migrates to the new Jerusalem and pitches the divine tent among them (Rev. 21:3).

The writings attributed to John the Gospel writer and his community (the Gospel and the three pseudonymous epistles) betray a similar orientation to the world in which the community lives.

John 9, famously, has been held up by Raymond Brown and others as a narrative of the community's forced exile, its forced (e)migration from its community of origin (the synagogue/formative Judaisms) to an-other place, a location somehow outside of both "world" and "home" (John 1). Those who leave this other place are castigated in the first of the Johannine Epistles as antichrists. Within the Johannine community, forced migration on the basis of belief is virtuous; voluntary migration out of the community is satanic.

Migration as an underlying physical and/or rhetorical concern is thus evident in many of the New Testament writings. However, only two make it explicit: James and 1 Peter. James may well be a letter to, rather than by, migrant communities. Indeed, James's letter, addressed "to the twelve tribes in the Diaspora," strongly resembles other such Jerusalem-to-Diaspora missives sent by the Sanhedrin contemporary with this writing (Bauckham, 19–20). James's sermon-in-a-letter, or homiletic epistle, reminds those outside of the immediate influence of Jerusalem of the particular ethics expected of those who gather in synagogues (James 2), claim to follow the "royal law" (2:8), and consider themselves to be followers of the Lord Jesus Christ (2:1). Primarily, these communities should not resemble the stain of the world, but should be separate entities marked by an ethical concern for the workers, the widows and orphans, and the poor (1:27). However, they are not to consider their status permanent. They will continue in their involuntary migration only until the Parousia of the Lord (5:7). At that time, the injustices experienced in their exile will be adjudicated by the Lord of Sabaoth (5:4).

First Peter takes a similar tack. Writing specifically to those Diasporan exiles in Asia Minor, the advice of 1 Peter to these migrant communities is twofold. First, the author insists on the identity of these migrants as displaced royalty, exiled priests, and a people belonging to God (1 Peter 2). Their dispersal does not change their identity. Rather, it requires prudent interaction with the dominating culture of their exile until they can regain their inheritance as heirs to the kingdom of God. Second, the author requires that the migrant congregation act in ways that would be considered blameless during the time of their exile. For this author, this means that the community of faith must adopt even the norms of the kyriarchy of their community of exile. "Kyriarchy," a neologism coined by Elisabeth Schüssler Fiorenza, describes "the rule of the emperor, lord, slave master, husband, or the elite freeborn, propertied, educated gentleman to whom disenfranchised men and all wo/men were subordinated" (Schüssler Fiorenza, 9). Acceptance of such norms moved 1 Peter's Christian community away from less hierarchical structures such as those intimated by Galatians 3 and toward the more accommodationist stance of the second generation of the Pauline school. It was, among other things, a way for these migrants to "fit in." This kyriarchy-as-camouflage was, of course, counseled uncritically by a member of the literate class (or at least one who could pay for an amanuensis). Those who bore its burden most profoundly were the migrant community's least powerful members: women, children, and slaves.

Other New Testament writings give us far fewer clues about their migrant status. Yet even these reference comings, goings, and their impact on community identity. The pseudonymous letters of 2 Peter and Jude, for example, are unlikely to be of Galilean or Judean origin, although this is impossible to know. As such, they would also be migrant writings, strictly speaking. However, their discourse focuses less on the community's migrant nature and more on the danger of the immigration of other people—with other ideas about Christian identity—into their communities (2 Pet. 2:3; Jude 4). Even without a specific focus on the community's movement or clear evidence of displacement, these writings seek to create and strengthen communities that are outside the general population (e.g., not pagan, not Jewish, not licit), and there is still a sense of migration about them.

Hebrews, of course, stands as the New Testament enigma, giving its readers very few clues about authorship, dating, placement, or any other historical data. Yet even if one argues for Hebrews as an early Judean or Galilean document (as does DeSilva in this volume), there is still an overlay of migration in its rhetoric. For even if one depicts Hebrews as a letter/sermon written to, by, and in Judea or the Galilee, one cannot escape the trope of community-as-migrants and the rhetorical journey toward rest that wends its way through the homiletics of the unknown preacher. Hebrews too, although less explicit, bears the marks of migration.

Thus a phenomenon often overlooked marks at least a significant plurality of New Testament literature. The bulk of it, and perhaps all of it, could be categorized as migrant writing. As a result, although rootlessness is most frequently considered a concern of James and 1 Peter, and perhaps to a lesser extent of the rhetorics of Hebrews and Philippians, in truth, underlying all of the New Testament canon is a sense of rootlessness, of dispersion, and of the need to survive in a place that is not home, whether physically or culturally. The rest of this essay seeks to explore the implications of this underlying rootlessness, both in the New Testament writings and for those who appropriate these writings as Scriptures.

New Testament Writings as Diaspora Spaces

What difference might it make if the New Testament writings were considered to be migrant writings? Here, a brief consideration of theory about "diaspora spaces" might be helpful. Sociologist Avtar Brah proposes that diaspora space is that place

> where multiple subject positions are juxtaposed, contested, proclaimed or disavowed; where the permitted and the prohibited perpetually interrogate; and where the accepted and the transgressive imperceptibly mingle even while these syncretic forms may be disclaimed in the name of purity and tradition. [It is a space where] *tradition is itself continually invented even as it may be hailed as originating from the mists of time.* (Brah, 208, emphasis added)

This thick description reflects the struggle and promise of diaspora spaces, those spaces where migrants and host communities enter into the never-ending dance of self-definition. But what does it have to do with the New Testament? Simply this: If the New Testament writings are, indeed, migrant writings, these migrant rhetorics might be expected to create texts that are diaspora spaces, texts/spaces in which migrant writers and migrant communities struggle with the nature of faithfulness to their understanding of the new Christian movements while living in a majority-pagan world.

So, if the New Testament writings are migrant writings, one might expect to note the juxtaposition, contestation, proclamation, and/or disavowal of multiple subject positions (Brah, 208). Perhaps the quintessential example of such struggle is bound up in the person and history of Saul/Paul of Tarsus. He names himself a Jew, born of the tribe of Benjamin, circumcised and a Pharisee (Phil. 3:5). However, he is also named a citizen of the pagan, primarily Greek-speaking Roman Empire, and claims that status by birth rather than through financial or military transaction (Acts 22:25-28). He is Saul, named after the first king of Judea, but without fanfare becomes Paul as he begins his gentile evangelism, no doubt because his Hebrew name is transliterated *saulos* in Greek (Acts 13:9), and *saulos* is an adjective that describes "the *loose, wanton* gait of courtesans or Bacchantes" (Liddell and Scott, s.v. "*saulos*"). This is a person who claims to himself and to his entire community, Jew and Greek, the promises of the particularly Jewish Abrahamic covenant (Gal. 3:1-9). This same person claims to become "all things to all people" for the sake of his Christian evangelism (1 Cor. 9:22).

Of course, Paul is not alone in this place of juxtaposition, of negotiation between cultures. Other characters carry two names, two identities: consider Tabitha/Dorcas and John/Mark (Acts 9; 12). Neither is Paul alone is standing between cultures and negotiating different subject positions: consider Joanna, the wife of Chuza, Herod's steward, who stands between Roman client privilege in Herod's household and her support of Jesus—who would, no doubt, have been understood as a wandering Jewish prophet and social critic, and who was killed for sedition against the Roman Empire (Luke 8). However, not every New Testament figure makes the same choices that Paul makes when faced with this negotiation between cultures. The author of the Epistle of James, for instance, in his counsel to the "twelve tribes of the diaspora" (James 1:1), calls for withdrawal and self-preservation (1:27). Similarly, the seer on Patmos island, echoing the prophet's jeremiad, calls his people to "come out" of Babylon (Rev. 18:4, cf. Jer. 51:45). In a different response to the same question of positionality with respect to one's own culture and to "the world," John's Gospel suggests a third way, a way that is neither of the world nor of the home culture of the migrant outsiders. This way is signified by the Johannine phrase, "sons of God," and represents the formation of an-other position in society (John 1).

In addition to matters of the subject's positionality, New Testament writings also reveal the ongoing interrogation of permitted and prohibited, the mingling of accepted and transgressive, and ultimately the creation of syncretic forms that Brah describes as characteristics of diaspora space. Perhaps the most obvious New Testament example of the interrogation of the permitted and prohibited is the conflict regarding the inclusion of gentiles into the early churches without requiring of them the rite of circumcision. This early church-dividing conflict emerges in many of the undisputed Pauline writings, and differently in the Acts of the Apostles. Paul is usually the anticircumcision champion in his own writings; but the author of Luke-Acts makes Peter the standard-bearer after a theophany and an encounter with a gentile named Cornelius (Acts 10; 15). However, circumcision is not the only New Testament example of the interrogation and re-creation of traditions and forms. The "healing on the Sabbath" crisis seen in many of the Gospels is also part of this ongoing interrogation of what is and is not permitted to be done by faithful people during the Sabbath rest. Table fellowship is yet another example of the New Testament interrogation of permitted and prohibited: not merely who was admitted to the table (thus the Syrophoenician woman's protest in Mark 7) but even more the question of whether meat was to be served (1 Corinthians 8; Revelation 2). After all, meat was almost always sacrificed to the gods, whom Christians and Jews saw as idols. Should, then, Christians eat meat at their symposia, or was this a tacit acceptance of idolatry

(Taussig)? These discussions and debates about the interaction between the permitted and transgressive likely preceded the advent of Christianity among the Jewish migrants in Diaspora around the greater Mediterranean world. However, a new urgency in response to these questions would have been felt after the Roman destruction of the Jerusalem temple in 70 CE. After this destruction of the ritual and political center of Judaism, all claimants to the traditions of Abraham and Moses were in ongoing debates regarding what it might mean to be Jewish in a post-temple diasporic reality. This was not specific to the Gospel writers—or even to Christian writers. The rabbis, too, were beginning to argue about the nature of faithfulness after the fall of the temple.

Circumcision, Sabbath observance, and table fellowship were some of the more blatant ways in which this kind of cultural interrogation between permitted and transgressive took place. Other questions also arose, even if they were more subtly addressed. Should slavery persist in the Christian community, and how could one argue for slavery and yet argue that all have one master (see Col. 3:22-23)? What is the appropriate role of women, particularly of wives, in the early church and how might that intersect with the wider society's understanding of Christians (1 Cor. 7:12-13)? The answers are not straightforward. There are clear moves, particularly among the later Christian writings, to preserve kyriarchy, but the rationale for it is often a subtle rebuke of the dominating structures of the society, even if that rebuke does nothing to alleviate the distress of women, children, or slaves. In Colossians, for example, the command that slaves should obey their masters is followed by counsel to these slaves to perform their tasks "as for the Lord and not for your masters" and a promise that "the wrongdoer will be paid back for whatever wrong has been done" (3:23-25). When there is no rebuke, often there is a call for kyriarchal structuring of society as a mark of purity of the church, purity that makes the otherwise illicit church gathering unassailable by the pagan majority. Thus in 1 Timothy, slaves are told to obey their masters "so that the name of God and the teaching may not be blasphemed" (6:1).

Ultimately, as Brah posits, these ancient migrant writings represent the invention of a new tradition, a tradition we have come to call Christianity. For an example of this, one need look no further than to the name given to this ancient collection of writings: "New Testament." New Testament is an appropriation of the language of the Christian meal found in 1 Cor. 11:25 and Matt. 26:28. While most contemporary translations present this as a "new covenant," the Greek word *diathēkē* can be used either for "covenant" or "testament" (as in "last will and testament," see Galatians 3). So, "New Testament" also means "new covenant," and this in turn cannot be understood without reference to the "old covenant," as the early Christians would have understood it.

For many of these migrant groups, the "old" or Abrahamic covenant between God and God's people functioned not only as tradition but also as a fundamental identifier of the people (*ethnos*—the basis for the concept "ethnic group"). This identifier was traced primarily through the Abrahamic bloodline but could be extended to those who adhered to the identity markers of the covenant, among which were circumcision and the keeping of *kashrut*. So, when Paul and the Gospel writers, quoting the oral tradition that both trace to Jesus, speak of the table meal of the early church as a "new covenant" or "new testament," they are not only relating an important story in the birth of the church but also reinventing tradition, reinventing, not exorcising it. To speak of these stories and letters as a "new *diathēkē*" is both to invent a new way of being a covenant people in the world and to appropriate to the church—made increasingly of people from outside of the Abrahamic bloodline and covenant practices—the ancient *diathēkē* of the Abrahamic era.

Paul and the author of Luke-Acts do not explicitly value the new covenant as superior to the old covenant. However, for the writer to the Hebrews, the "new covenant" or "new testament" clearly supersedes the older. As the author of Hebrews argues, "if that first covenant had been faultless, there would have been no need to look for a second one" (Heb. 8:7). Yet even this assertion is premised on a reinterpretation of the received Scriptures of the people, the "Old Testament." The author to the Hebrews would probably not be claiming to invent tradition any more than would Paul or the author of Luke-Acts. Instead, he would assert that this new covenant is the real, heavenly variety—and thus ultimately more ancient than the human copy. And yet he, like Paul and Luke-Acts, is engaging in that diaspora-space activity of inventing, and claiming ancient provenance for, traditions (Brah).

All of this briefly suggests that, as a collection of primarily migrant writings, the writings of the New Testament can be shown to be diaspora space. The examples above are intended to be representative rather than exhaustive, and self-evident rather than nuanced. The struggle with subject positionality, juxtaposition of the permitted and transgressive, and (re)invention of tradition all appear in some of the most important theological discussions in the collection: discussions around identity, around who and what these Christians will be. However, to say that the New Testament writings constitute a kind of literary diaspora space is not to claim some uniformity of migrant reaction to their host cultures or their home culture. Rather, in the next section, four such possible migrant reactions will be explored, both for their presence or absence within the New Testament canon of writings and for their implications for the migrants who hold them.

New Testament Migrant Strategies

Just because one can argue that the New Testament writings constitute a kind of literary diaspora space, this does not mean that their migrant strategies for life as Christians in migration were identical. Psychologist John Berry's work proves helpful for unpacking these strategies. Berry outlines four migrants' strategies for interacting in their places of migration. He calls these four categories marginalization, separation, assimilation, and integration (Berry, 619).

Three of these strategies are readily observable in the New Testament writings. However, the strategy of assimilation is absent. Assimilation requires that migrants reject their home culture in favor of the host culture in which they find themselves. In twenty-first-century terms, this is the immigrant who intentionally loses her accent, forgets her native language, and claims only the nationality and culture of the nation in which she finds herself. Such assimilation does not exist in the New Testament canon; for, if it did, the writings would be pagan, extolling the virtues of the goddess Roma or the God Zeus/Jupiter. Indeed, an assimilationist of this time would have been found marching with the silversmiths of Ephesus crying out, "Great is Artemis of the Ephesians" (Acts 19:28).

In retaining their monotheistic theologies, both Jews and Christians set themselves apart from the majority-pagan polytheism of the ancient world in ways that were seen as misanthropic by their neighbors, regardless of how much else they mimicked the cultural norms of their host country. There seem to have been some Christians who did aspire to assimilate. To do so, they claimed a higher knowledge that allowed them to participate in pagan religiosity in all of its forms (including eating meat sacrificed to pagan gods) while at the same time claiming the faith of the early Christian church (see 1 Corinthians 7; Revelation 2). Such practices were condemned by those whose writings are preserved in the New Testament as misguided at best and satanic at worst. In fact, no New Testament writing counsels migrant assimilation; none offers a theology of assimilation. In the face of migration, each of the New Testament writings, regardless of how much they appear to mimic the greater society, preserves some separation from that society.

Liminal, or as Berry calls them, "marginalized" migrants take as their response to migration the rejection of both their home culture and their host culture. To determine that a migrant writing counsels such a stance for its audience, one must show *both* its rejection of the home culture, which in the case of early Christianity is Judaism and/or temple culture, *and* its rejection of the host culture in which it finds itself, which in many New Testament writings is simply called "the world." The Gospel according to John contains both of these kinds of counsel for its audience. Consider first this quotation:

> Then Jesus said to the Jews/Judeans who had believed in him, "If you continue in my word, you are truly my disciples; and you will know the truth, and the truth will make you free." They answered him, "We are descendants of Abraham and have never been slaves to anyone....
>
> ... Jesus said to them, "If you were Abraham's children, you would be doing what Abraham did, but now you are trying to kill me, a man who has told you the truth that I heard from God. This is not what Abraham did. You are indeed doing what your father does." They said to him, "We are not illegitimate children; we have one father, God himself." Jesus said to them, "If God were your Father, you would love me, for I came from God and now I am here.... You are from your father the devil, and you choose to do your father's desires." (John 8:31-33a, 39b-42b, 44a)

In this quotation, part of Jesus' longer diatribe against the "Jews" or the "Judeans," the author of John's Gospel, through Jesus, is disavowing any cultural consonance with those who would seem to be his own people, his home culture. There is no plea, here, that those who self-identify as Jews/Judeans are of the same family tree as the community to which John is writing. Raymond Brown posits that John's community has been forcibly removed from the synagogue worship out of which it sprang because of its assertion of the messianic nature of Jesus. This seems to suggest that the audience of John's Gospel has separated itself from its home culture.

However, in turning from its home culture, John's audience has not uncritically embraced its host culture. To the contrary. As part of the symposium dialogue in the fifteenth chapter, the Gospel of John records the following teaching of Jesus:

> If the world hates you, be aware that it hated me before it hated you. If you belonged to the world, the world would love you as its own. Because you do not belong to the world, but I have chosen you out of the world—therefore the world hates you. (John 15:18-19)

Here, John's Gospel is depicting Jesus, and through Jesus, his community, as rejected by its host culture, "the world."

In all fairness, a careful reader of John realizes this at the very outset of the Gospel. In the first chapter, John describes the incarnate Word (*logos*) and the community of those who accepted him this way:

> He [the Word/*logos*] was in the world, and the world came into being through him; yet the world did not know him. He came to what was his own, and his own people did not accept him. But to all who received him, who believed in his name, he gave power to become children of God, who were born, not of blood or of the will of the flesh or of the will of man, but of God. (John 1:10-13)

Perhaps no verse better illustrates John's liminality, the stance of a community leader—and thus of a community—rejected both by the world (host culture) and by his own people (home culture). The audience shaped by John's Gospel reflects such a liminality, neither being part of the world nor part of the home culture, a stance that requires the community of faith to strike out into unknown territory, creating an ostensibly brand-new culture apart from either of these cultural anchors.

The Gospel according to John is joined by the Johannine Epistles (1, 2, and 3 John) and possibly the Gospel according to Mark in this liminal stance. However, most New Testament writings do not use this migrant strategy to interact with their home and host cultures. The Epistle of James is illustrative of a more popular strategy: separation. Consider the following:

> Religion that is pure and undefiled before God, the Father, is this: to care for orphans and widows in their distress, and *to keep oneself unstained by the world*. (James 1:27, emphasis added)

and

> Those conflicts and disputes among you, where do they come from? Do they not come from your cravings that are at war within you? You want something and do not have it; so you commit murder. And you covet something and cannot obtain it; so you engage in disputes and conflicts. You do not have, because you do not ask. You ask and do not receive, because you ask wrongly, in order to spend what you get on your pleasures. [Adulterous women]! Do you not know that *friendship with the world is enmity with God?* Therefore whoever wishes to be a friend of the world becomes an enemy of God. (James 4:1-4, emphasis added)

Like the Gospel of John, the Epistle of James stands firm in its dismissal of the world. As in the Gospel of John, so here also the host culture is rejected. However, unlike John, James also says this:

> Do not speak evil against one another, brothers and sisters. Whoever speaks evil against another or judges another, speaks evil against the law and judges the law; but if you judge the law, you are not a doer of the law but a judge. (James 4:11)

Law, in this case, must be understood as Torah, the law of James's own people and community. James thus is not advocating a liminal migrant strategy. Instead, James is advocating a strategy of separation.

Luke Timothy Johnson has demonstrated that James is very possibly a letter written from the earliest Christians in Jerusalem, through the brother of Jesus, to the earliest diasporic communities of Jews/Judeans who have accepted Jesus as the Christ and son of God. From Jerusalem, James writes to migrant Christ-communities still worshiping in synagogues (James 2). He counsels the earliest believers to adopt a migrant strategy of separation: not to adopt gentile ways in their time of migration. Rather, they are to continue their adherence to the law, to be wary of accepting worldly ways, and to keep themselves unstained from the world.

The Epistle of James is not alone in this counsel. The Gospel of Matthew provides a similar strategy to its readers, almost until the Great Commission at the end; and even that commission is less about befriending the world and more about recruiting it to the "home culture" (Matthew 28). Likewise, the enigmatic book Hebrews, with its focus on Christian endurance, seems to counsel separation from the things of the world in favor of the "race that is set before us" (Hebrews 12). Jude, the often overlooked polemic toward the end of the canon, embraces this sort of strategy; and it is central to the theology of the Revelation to John with its admonition to "come out of" Babylon (Revelation 18). In each of these cases, the migrant strategy of separation calls the community of faith back to its roots and away from the world.

Liminality and separation define strategies in some of the more pivotal New Testament writings. However, the predominant migrant strategy within the literary diaspora space called the New Testament is accommodation. Consider, for example, these quotations from the writings of Paul of Tarsus:

> As many of you as were baptized into Christ have clothed yourselves with Christ. There is no longer Jew or Greek, there is no longer slave or free, there is no longer male and female; for all of you are one in Christ Jesus. And if you belong to Christ, then you are Abraham's offspring, heirs according to the promise. (Gal. 3:27-29)

and

> To the Jews I became as a Jew, in order to win Jews. To those under the law I became as one under the law (though I myself am not under the law) so that I might win those under the law. To those outside the law I became as one outside the law (though I am not free from God's law but am under Christ's law) so that I might win those outside the law. To the weak I became weak, so that I might win the weak. I have become all things to all people, that I might by all means save some. (1 Cor. 9:20-22)

These writings indicate a shift in strategy. Paul's overt inclusion of persons both from within and outside his own migrant culture, and his willingness to accommodate gentile inclusion in his ministry, suggests that he does not advocate a total avoidance of the gentile world. However, Paul simultaneously claims that his mixed community of Jews/Judeans and gentiles, a community comprising migrant Jesus-believers, somehow inherits the benefits reserved specifically for the Jews/Judeans: the covenant blessings of Abraham (Galatians 3). Paul thus not only invites "the world" in but also continues to embrace some of his home culture, a culture steeped in the Abrahamic covenant and the Mosaic law.

This Pauline migrant strategy I have termed accommodation, following sociologist Margaret Gibson, rather than using Berry's term *integration* (Berry, 618; Gibson, 20). According to Gibson, accommodation is marked by "the deliberate preservation of the homeland culture, albeit in an adapted form more suitable to life in the host country" (Gibson, 20–21). To argue that Paul is engaged in accommodation and not integration is to argue that he has deliberately preserved the Jewish narrative while adapting it so that faith communities may include gentiles. The result is an uneasy tension of a migrant strategy that both accepts and critiques home and host cultures. This uneasy tension is most clearly evident in Romans 12 and 13. In chapter 12, Paul famously counsels, "Do not be conformed to this world, but be transformed by the renewing of your minds, so that you may discern what is the will of God—what is good and acceptable and perfect" (Rom. 12:2). However, in Romans 13, this same Paul calls for a certain amount of conformity to the world *as a way to fully comply with the requirements of the Mosaic law*. Here, I quote Paul at length:

> Let every person be subject to the governing authorities; for there is no authority except from God, and those authorities that exist have been instituted by God. Therefore whoever resists authority resists what God has appointed, and those who resist will incur judgment. For rulers are not a terror to good conduct, but to bad. Do you wish to have no fear of the authority? Then do what is good, and you will receive its approval; for it is God's servant for your good. But if you do what is wrong, you should be afraid, for the authority does not bear the sword in vain! It is the servant of God to execute wrath on the wrongdoer. Therefore one must be subject, not only because of wrath but also because of conscience. For the same reason you also pay taxes, for the authorities are God's servants, busy with this very thing. Pay to all what is due them—taxes to whom taxes are due, revenue to whom revenue is due, respect to whom respect is due, honor to whom honor is due. Owe no one anything, except to love one another; for the one who loves another has fulfilled the law. The commandments, "You shall not commit adultery; You shall not murder; You shall not steal; You shall not covet"; and any other commandment, are summed up in this word, "Love your neighbor as yourself." Love does no wrong to a neighbor; therefore, love is the fulfilling of the law. (Rom. 13:1-10)

Despite the counsel in Rom. 12:1-2, one must read Romans 13 as advice to conform to the world—at least in part—even as you also attempt to conform to the law. Here Paul, deliberately holding to the law, counsels the Romans to adapt a form of his adherence better suited to accommodate the host culture in which they find themselves and the home culture to which they must cling.

Paul is not alone in his use of the migrant strategy of accommodation. Along with the thirteen writings written either by him or by imitators of him, this strategy is adopted by the writer of the Gospel of Luke and the Acts of the Apostles, and by the authors of the Petrine letters. This constitutes the majority of the New Testament writings, both by number of writings and by size of corpus.

These three migrant strategies—liminality, separation, and accommodation—reflect three competing New Testament canonical responses to the historical reality of migration and the literary trope of displacement encoded in this canon. It would be a mistake to read this description as though it were intended to denote some kind of progression from "unrealistic" to "realistic"; nor a decline from "purity" to "admixture." Liminality, separation, and accommodation are survival strategies in the face of displacement and dispersion adopted by these different migrant writings. Each adds to the Pentecost-like cacophony (Acts 2) of the diaspora space called the New Testament.

Migrant Writings as Twenty-First-Century Scriptures

Considering the extent to which New Testament writings may also be migrant writings is certainly of interest for the historical study of these texts, as well as for their academic and, perhaps, theological interpretation. But how might this information allow us better to understand the role of these writings in the twenty-first century? To respond, one must first consider the nature of Scriptures themselves: specifically, one must consider what makes certain cultural productions (writings, recitations, songs, etc.) into Scriptures.

Here, the work of Wilfred Cantwell Smith will be a helpful conversation partner. Smith's seminal work *What Is Scripture? A Comparative Analysis* traces the human activity of Scripture-making and Scripture-using across a variety of religious communities and traditions. He finds that

> scripture is a human activity. . . . The quality of being scripture is not an attribute of texts. It is a characteristic of the attitude of persons—groups of persons—to what outsiders perceive as texts. *It denotes a relation between a people and a text.* Yet that too is finally inadequate. . . . at issue is the relation between a people and the universe, in the light of their perception of a given text. (Smith, 18, emphasis added)

Smith's definition makes explicit that those who consider New Testament writings to be Holy Scripture are living in a particular relationship with these ancient texts. This relationship involves more than just a people and their Scripture. The relationship stretches "between a people and the universe, in light of their perception of a given text" (Smith, 18). To use another metaphor, for people of faith, their Scriptures function as a lens through which all things are considered. Scripture helps people of faith to clarify their proper relationships with one another, with the God of their understanding, and with the world.

For the New Testament, an added complication is that not every person of faith has considered every text as equally scriptural, or as scriptural at all. This conflict between what is and is not truly "Scripture" dates as far back as the early second century CE, when Marcion of Sinope rejected those Scriptures he considered "Jewish." Later Christians have had similar reactions to particular books. Reformers like John Calvin and Martin Luther had no love for the Revelation to John and the Epistle of James, respectively. As twentieth-century theologian Howard Thurman revealed, among African Americans descended from US chattel slavery, New Testament writings in favor of slavery were held in low esteem, and even "read out" of the Bible (Thurman, 30–31). In *Jesus and the Disinherited*, Thurman tells a story of his grandmother who would not let him read from the Pauline Epistles, with the exception, on occasion, of 1 Corinthians 13. Thurman recounts:

> What she told me I shall never forget. "During the days of slavery," she said, "the master's minister would occasionally hold services for the slaves. . . . Always the white minister used as his text something from Paul. At least three or four times a year, he used as a text: 'Slaves be obedient to them that are your masters as unto Christ.' Then he would go on to show how it was God's will that we were slaves, and how, if we were good and happy slaves, God would bless us. I promised my Maker that if I ever learned to read and if freedom came, I would not read that part of the Bible." (Thurman, 30–31)

Thurman's grandmother's quite candid assessment of the New Testament caused her to determine not to treat the proslavery writings of the New Testament as Scripture, even if she had to omit almost every word attributed to the apostle Paul. She refused, in so doing, to use the proslavery New Testament writings as Scripture—as lenses to help her negotiate her relationship to the universe.

Like Marcion, Luther, Calvin, and even Thurman's grandmother, Christian practitioners still very often select which among the New Testament writings they will treat as Scripture, although they may not do so consciously. More commonly, even among those who claim inerrant divine inspiration for all of the biblical writings, certain texts are seen as "favorites," or as "the heart of the gospel." As noted above, each of these writings is also a migrant writing. As a result, unsurprisingly, people of faith very often also end up incorporating into their scriptural lenses not only the theological concepts that the texts propose but also the migrant strategies toward home and host cultures embedded in them. Those for whom John's Gospel is paramount might find themselves valuing liminality as the ideal interaction with their world. Those who privilege the Revelation to John might find themselves valuing separation. Those who hold to Paul's letters might find themselves valuing accommodation. These migrant strategies become inseparable from scriptural lenses. As a result, Christians of the dominant culture of a particular country, whose families may not have experienced migration for many generations, may still interact with that culture as though they were migrants in a host culture because of their scriptural lenses.

Within twenty-first-century civic life, this adaptation of migrant strategies may take the form of groups that stay to themselves and are viewed with suspicion because they privilege a separate migrant strategy. In a society in which every detail of human life is readily accessibly through the Internet, the choice of such groups to distance themselves from society at large may be seen as inviting or, by contrast, quite suspicious. Alternatively, it may take the form of groups that vilify both Christian religion as it is typically practiced and the society at large, turning instead to an alternative way of being entirely. Certainly such practices might go unnoticed. On the other hand, when in positions of power, Christians adopting liminal migrant strategies might have profound impact on schools, political parties, and social policy—whether they are found on the left or right wing of the political spectrum. This may seem oxymoronic. However, the liminality in this case is not actual societal power. Rather, these persons adopt a liminal stance toward society because of the Scriptures through which they refract their world, and which counsel them regarding their appropriate interaction with the world.

However, perhaps the migrant strategy that has had the strongest historical stance and still continues to be heard from among Christian practitioners is that of accommodation. In the United States and the Western north, this is in part due to the outsize influence of the writings of Paul in the Protestant churches. It is this strategy that brings us the abolitionist and civil rights movements among African Americans and many other movements for social justice. It is also this strategy that brings us the proslavery movement within the church and the twenty-first-century church's willingness to accommodate unjust policies regarding poverty and human rights. In each of these opposing cases, Christian interaction with the world is governed not only by what the Scriptures say but also by the scriptural stance of holding on to tradition while finding a way to engage the "world," which may appear to be hostile. Thus an abolitionist holds on to one set of scriptural sayings and a slaveholder to another set; however, both take the Pauline tack that both holds to the tradition and engages the society. At stake is the argument over what aspects of the dominant culture shall be accommodated and what resisted. Faithful Christians have, over time, responded very differently to these questions.

Each of these strategies persists today, strengthened by the migrant strategies in these ancient writings that continue to be Scripture for twenty-first-century Christians. As students of these texts, paying attention to these strategies may help us to unpack some of the Christianity-related arguments in our civic commons. Pay attention, also, to the sense of rootlessness that undergirds some of the music and culture, particularly of the United States: the sense that "there's no place like home," but also that "we're not in Kansas anymore" that can emerge in the rhetoric even of people whose families have been resident since the days of European colonialism. For this is not simply a product of changing times; times have always changed. In a culture so steeped in these migrant writings, this literary diaspora space called the New Testament, surely some of that rootlessness, some of those uncritically employed migrant strategies can be traced back to these ancient writings, these migrant Scriptures of the Christian church.

Works Cited

Bauckham, Richard. 1999. *James*. New Testament Readings. New York: Routledge.
Berry, John W. 2001. "A Psychology of Immigration." *Journal of Social Issues* 57, no. 3:615–31.
Brah, Avtar. 1996. *Cartographies of Diaspora: Contesting Identities*. New York: Routledge.
Brown, Raymond. 1979. *The Community of the Beloved Disciple: The Lives, Loves, and Hates of an Individual Church in New Testament Times*. Mahwah, NJ: Paulist.
Gibson, Margaret A. 2001. "Immigrant Adaption and Patterns of Acculturation." *Human Development* 44:19–23.
Johnson, Luke Timothy. 2004. *Brother of Jesus, Friend of God: Studies in the Letter of James*. Grand Rapids: Eerdmans.
Schüssler Fiorenza, Elisabeth. 2009. "Introduction: Exploring the Intersection of Race, Gender, Status, and Ethnicity in Early Christian Studies." In *Prejudice and Christian Beginnings*, edited by Laura Nasrallah and Elisabeth Schüssler Fiorenza. Minneapolis: Fortress Press.
Smith, Wilfred Cantwell. 1993. *What Is Scripture? A Comparative Approach*. Minneapolis: Fortress Press.
Taussig, Hal. 2009. *In the Beginning Was the Meal: Social Experimentation and Early Christianity*. Minneapolis: Fortress Press.
Thurman, Howard. 1976. *Jesus and the Disinherited*. Boston: Beacon.

The Apocalyptic Legacy of Early Christianity

David A. Sánchez

a•poc•a•lyp•tic (adj): of, relating to, or involving terrible violence and destruction: of or relating to the end of the world

leg•a•cy (noun): something transmitted by or received from an ancestor or predecessor or from the past

(*Merriam-Webster Dictionary*, 2003)

Introduction: The Problem of a Suppressed Legacy

We twenty-first-century Christians find ourselves in a strange place in relationship to our apocalyptic biblical inheritance. In many of our churches, apocalyptic literature, especially the Revelation to John, is treated with benign neglect, yet its images continue to fascinate us, as witness the tremendous success of novels like the *Left Behind* series. This is especially true from my perspective as a Roman Catholic: the book of Revelation remains liturgically peripheral in my tradition (with the exception of December 12—the Feast of the Virgin of Guadalupe, when Revelation 12 is a focal reading—and, on occasion, during the Lenten season). Yet Roman Catholics, like most twenty-first-century Christians, remain remarkably vulnerable to conjuring apocalyptic scenarios, under the right circumstances.

Meanwhile, over the last several decades, a great deal of ink has been spilled by scholars attempting to specify matters like the genre, form, and content of those ancient texts that qualify as "apocalyptic" and thus have contributed to this legacy. As one might expect, the book of Revelation has been the most obvious focal point in those conversations. Indeed, according to the most learned biblical specialists, this is the *only* writing in the New Testament that meets the scholarly criteria regarding the form of the genre apocalypse. I, for one, am in total agreement with this assessment, but I remain unsatisfied with the emphases of the scholarly conversation because something tells me, deep in my soul, that there is more to our Christian apocalyptic legacy than is addressed by such formal considerations.

In this essay, I would like to suggest an alternative point of entry, other than the Revelation to John, for discussing our apocalyptic inheritance. I would like initially to consider the Synoptic Gospels, not, however, as we usually read them, conflated together, as if they are telling roughly the same story; that keeps us from seeing something important—that from the very beginning, Christians have struggled with the troubling legacy of a genuinely apocalyptic vision. The Gospel tradition has embedded within it, specifically within the Gospel of Mark, what functions as a genuinely apocalyptic text. By examining how Matthew and Luke altered that text, we see how early Christians negotiated the first apocalyptic legacy in their tradition by altering its eschatological moorings. More precisely, Matthew and Luke demonstrate how a Christian *apocalyptic* moment was turned into an ecclesiastical movement with the alteration to a less imminent expectation of the Parousia of Jesus Christ.

To start with, this less obvious biblical apocalyptic moment serves several purposes. (1) It prevents us from isolating the book of Revelation as if it were the only example of an apocalyptic worldview in the Christian canon, and from sequestering it in the category of prophetically anomalous literature, rendering it so much easier to ignore. (2) It demonstrates that Matthew and Luke believed they needed to domesticate the apocalyptic agenda of the Gospel of Mark in the wake of the delayed return of Jesus Christ. And (3) it challenges us to bring to consciousness, in a cultural-psychoanalytic sense, the way other scriptural sources, in addition to Revelation, are embedded in our psyches and contribute to our perduring fascination with apocalyptic solutions, prompting us to "act out" apocalyptically under the right circumstances.

Apocalypticism

At this point it is critical to be clear how I am employing the term *apocalyptic*, especially because much scholarly ink has been spilled on the contentious question of categorization. I rely on David Aune's summary in an illuminating 2005 article.

> "Apocalyptic eschatology" is the narrative theology, characteristic of apocalypses, centering in the belief that (1) the present world order, regarded as both evil and oppressive, is under temporary control of Satan and his human accomplices, and (2) that the present evil world order will shortly be destroyed by God and replaced by a new and perfect order corresponding to Eden before the fall. During the present evil age, the people of God are an oppressed minority who fervently expect God, or his specially chosen agent the Messiah, to rescue them. The transition between the old and the new ages will be introduced with a final series of battles fought by the people of God

against the human allies of Satan. The outcome is never in question, however, for the enemies of God are predestined for defeat and destruction. (Aune, 236)

What I find most compelling in this definition—for the purposes of this essay and for my own personal relationship to apocalypticism—are the notions of cosmological dualism (with a war of heavenly proportions affecting, and afflicting, human actors), the introduction of the messianic agent (i.e., Jesus Christ), and the sense of temporal urgency. The present world order will be destroyed *soon*. It is this temporal consideration that I find most compelling when looking at an apocalyptic text like the Gospel of Mark—and at the Matthean and Lukan responses to Mark's acute temporality.

Excavating Mark as Another Example of Christian Apocalyptic

With this working definition of apocalypticism in mind, how does the Gospel of Mark function apocalyptically? Our first consideration is the moment in history when the Gospel of Mark was written. The majority of New Testament scholars date the Gospel between 66 and 70 CE, that is, squarely during the Jewish War with Rome, or shortly after the destruction of the Jerusalem temple. Thus Mark was written during a time of *real* political and cultural crisis (cf. Adela Yarbro Collins's language of *perceived* crisis; A. Y. Collins, 84–110) that may have indeed been an impetus for an apocalyptic response. Second, the Christology of the Gospel of Mark foregrounds the messiahship of Jesus. This is made explicit in the very first verse of the Gospel: "The beginning of the gospel of Jesus Christ" (i.e., Messiah). This christological emphasis is maintained throughout the Gospel (e.g., in the messianic secret motif: see the commentary on Mark). The relationship of a messianic figure to different apocalyptic scenarios is still under scholarly debate. I defer to Aune's assessment, noted above, which highlighted the expectation of God's oppressed people that an agent of God would act on their behalf at the critical and ultimate moment.

Other features of the Gospel of Mark that add to its apocalyptic tenor include its explicit cosmological dualism, as represented in the temptation of Jesus, after his baptism, by Satan (1:12-13) and the multiple exorcisms in the Gospel (e.g., 1:21-28; 5:1-20; 9:14-29). In comparison, the Gospel of John, arguably the least apocalyptic of the four canonical Gospels—has not one exorcism.

The Gospel of Mark also maintains a unique relationship to time. It is by far the most compressed of the four Gospels, narrating the ministry of Jesus from baptism to empty tomb. The Gospels of Matthew and Luke each begin with narratives of Jesus' birth, and end with accounts of his ascension into heaven. The Gospel of John goes even further, beginning "in the beginning" and ending with an ascension account. The Gospel of Mark employs the phrase "and immediately" some forty-one times in its narrative, twelve times in the first chapter alone. (The Greek phrase *kai euthys* occurs only nineteen times in the rest of the New Testament.) The phrase gives the reader/hearer the impression of a story moving very rapidly, and may remind the reader, ancient and modern alike, of the initial words uttered by Jesus in the Gospel: "The time is fulfilled, and the kingdom of God has come near" (1:15). Further, aspects of Mark's story reveal aspects of sectarian groups, as identified by modern theory: the requirement of severance of ties with one's biological family (e.g.,

1:16-20; 2:13-14; 10:28), the creation of a new eschatological family (3:31-35), and the mandatory renunciation of personal wealth for the benefit of the group (6:7-13; 10:17-27).

These observations crystallize the argument that Mark has apocalyptic features. This "excavation" goes beyond the usual characterization of Mark 13 as the "Little Apocalypse" to reveal that an apocalyptic character pervades the Gospel, and thus to foreground another apocalyptic moment in early Christian history; the Revelation to John does not stand in isolation. But consider next how both Matthew and Luke, unsatisfied with Mark's apocalyptic moorings some ten to fifteen years after the fact, chose to domesticate Mark when they incorporated his Gospel into their own. By means of this domestication, the legacy of Christian apocalypticism has been canonically offset, if not altogether suppressed, by the consequent conflated readings of the Gospel narratives.

Domesticating Mark: Matthew and Luke-Acts

I often imagine Matthew and Luke separately clinging to their manuscripts of Mark's Gospel and wondering just what on earth they were going to do with such an apocalyptically urgent Gospel. It is a humorous scene in my mind's eye, considering that apocalyptic movements have a short shelf life. How long can a preacher and/or teacher keep saying that deliverance is just around the corner? Thus I imagine Matthew and Luke questioning the validity of Mark's Gospel and how their Christian movements should proceed. In the wake of the delayed Parousia, with its delayed fulfillment of prophecy, do they quit the movement? Weren't the words of imminence placed on the very lips of Jesus himself (see esp. Mark 9:1; 13:30)? Perhaps they should bring about their own apocalypse, as subsequent Christian groups have done throughout the Christian era? Surely even slight provocation of Roman might accomplish that end. Or what if they took Mark's expected imminent Parousia and moved it into the distant future (by what scholars call "reserved eschatology")? If, as I contend here, this last was the option they chose, what were they to do with the rest of Mark, and even more acutely, what were they to do in the interim before the deferred Parousia?

These are fascinating questions that require some parsing. Note, first, that almost 90 percent of the Gospel of Mark is absorbed into Matthew's account. But how could one domesticate so apocalyptic a Gospel while absorbing so much of the original? Perhaps the best approach to this question is to assess how Matthew employed his sources. Arguably, the Gospel of Matthew can be reduced to three source-rich divisions. Chapters 1–2 are composed of material known as special M, biblical material unique to Matthew. This special source includes the (Matthean) birth narrative, the visitation of the magi, and the holy family's escape to Egypt in the wake of Herod's execution of Jewish male infants. This material accomplishes various purposes for Matthew, but most importantly for my point here, it expands the story of Jesus' life by almost three decades. Recall that the Gospel of Mark begins at Jesus' baptism, approximately one year before his death in his early thirties. Thus Matthew expands narrative time.

Matthew also proceeds in a much less rushed manner. The next section of the Gospel is made up primarily of materials gleaned from the sayings source Q. (See the essay on Jesus and the Gospels.) Embedded in this layer is a collection of words and teachings of Jesus apart from his deeds. In this material, we find the Sermon on the Mount, which takes up three chapters of Matthew's Gospel (chapters 5-7), and includes the Beatitudes and the Lord's Prayer. This saturation of Jesus' teachings in the middle of Matthew shifts the focus from Mark's apocalyptic Jesus to a more refined, rabbinic Jesus, one who certainly has much more time to teach and instruct his disciples on how to interact with the world in the interim before the Parousia.

We are finally introduced to the bulk of the Markan material as it is embedded in Matthew 12-28 (esp. after ch. 16). However, we have already been lulled into a more tranquil state of consciousness by the birth narrative and teaching discourse, so already the apocalyptic materials appear much more distant and future. The apocalyptic predictions imported from chapter 13 of the "Markan apocalypse" (Matthew 24) will come to pass (i.e., the destruction of the Jerusalem temple, wars and rumors of wars, persecution of the faithful, the desolating sacrilege, the appearance of false prophets, astronomical chaos, and the return of the son of man), but without the imminent tones of Mark's composition. This is also the case in the Lukan parallel to Mark 13 (Luke 21).

Even more brilliantly, Matthew incorporates ascension materials (28:16-20) to place Jesus back in heaven in the interim, thus overcoming what is, to Matthew, the more than slightly problematic lack of any indication where Jesus is during the interim according to the original ending of Mark (Mark 16:8, which, in my estimation, is a perfect ending for an *apocalyptic* Gospel). By conjoining it to the "Great Commission" in 28:18-20, Matthew has reframed Mark's apocalypticism into a template for a fledgling church movement that has much to accomplish before Christ's return. It is a brilliant piece of editorial work that simultaneously honors the primacy of Mark, by using so much of it as a source, *and* shifts Mark's emphasis from crisis and end-time speculation to an expanded story of the life of Jesus, with an emphasis on Jesus as aphoristic teacher and founder of a church. However, the point must not be overlooked that Matthew also felt the need for a complete eschatological overhaul of the Gospel of Mark, one that would privilege an emerging church. In my view, this was perhaps the most compelling reason for Matthew's privileged position in the New Testament canon. To place Mark at the beginning of the canon—noting its primacy among the Gospels—would have created an apocalyptic inclusio for the New Testament that would begin with Mark and end with the book of Revelation! The rhetorical brilliance of the canon as it now stands, however, is that the apocalypticism of the book of Revelation is now viewed as a futuristic culmination of the age of Matthew's developing and spreading church.

Luke, like his Synoptic cousin Matthew, had to make a tough decision regarding what to do with Mark's Gospel. I have always found it fascinating that both Luke and Matthew chose to retain and employ material from the Gospel of Mark. Surely, one avenue each author could have taken was to ignore the Gospel of Mark altogether and start from scratch. But neither did. Luke, as did Matthew, also employed special materials unique to his own Gospel, identified today as special L, and employed the 235 sayings of Jesus from Q. Unlike Matthew, however, the author of the Gospel of Luke used approximately one-half of the Gospel of Mark in the composition of his own Gospel (a large percentage even in relation to Matthew). Like Matthew, Luke also expanded the narrative time frame by introducing narratives of Jesus' birth and ascension. However, unlike any of his Gospel counterparts, Luke wrote a second contribution that would find its way into the New Testament canon, the Acts of the Apostles, which maps out the earliest years of the post-Easter church and the spread of the gospel from the Jewish world (foregrounding the apostleship of Peter) to the worldwide spread of the gospel to the gentiles (foregrounding the apostleship of Paul). In Lukan terms, this was the interim age of the Holy Spirit. The Parousia was delayed and Luke was prepared to encounter the delay, not as an unfulfilled prophecy, but as an opportunity to spread the gospel to the world. As in Matthew, the Gospel of Mark is relegated to the apocalyptic drama that would occur in the eschaton in the indeterminate future (again, reserved eschatology). Luke even hinted at an eschatology that we find most pronounced in the Gospel of John (that is, realized eschatology) when he hints at the benefits of the Parousia being accessible already, in the present, in Luke 17:20-21.

> Once Jesus was asked by the Pharisees when the kingdom of God was coming, and he answered, "The kingdom of God is not coming with things that can be observed; nor will they say, 'Look here it is!' or 'There it is!' For, in fact, the kingdom of God is among you."

It is evident from this brief analysis of both Matthew and Luke that both Gospel writers thought enough of the tradition of Mark to incorporate it into their literary productions while simultaneously toning down Mark's apocalyptic sensibilities to make it more palatable for Christians living in the 80s or later. Both spent much intellectual energy doing so. Matthew and Luke found themselves at least a decade removed from Mark's imminent apocalyptic prediction. The apocalyptic rhetoric had to shift because you cannot be an imminent apocalyptic preacher or sustain an apocalyptic community year after year after year.

Thus the Gospels present us with this curious combination of competing eschatologies. Because it has been a Christian interpretive practice to conflate our readings of the Gospels, emphasizing their presumed unity, the apocalypticism of Mark has been absorbed into the grander "gospel story." It is lost, or ignored, or projected into the undetermined future. The Markan legacy is a painful one, to be sure, because embedded within it is an unfulfilled prophecy of the imminent second coming of Christ, and so we can understand the energy that wants to avoid or defer it. But the presence of Mark among the Gospels means that even if we sequester the book of Revelation as some sort of apocalyptic anomaly, the intellectual fodder for subsequent apocalyptic movements and imaginings remains. Apocalypticism is embedded in our Gospel tradition itself, right in front of us, even if we choose not to acknowledge it. We may suppress it—and then act entirely surprised when apocalyptic inklings manifest themselves in us, like any other neurosis or psychosis would, given the right circumstances.

Expanding the Apocalyptic Landscape: The Pauline Tradition

Even the Pauline tradition—where scholars have long recognized the strength of apocalyptic influence on the apostle's thought—is not immune from a similar apocalyptic suppression. Paul's response to the church in Thessalonica regarding the fate of deceased Christians is illuminating:

> But we do not want you to be uninformed, brothers and sisters, about those who have died, so that you may not grieve as others do who have no hope. For since we believe that Jesus died and rose again, even so, through Jesus, God will bring with him those who have died. For this we declare to you by the word of the Lord, that we who are alive, who are left until the coming of the Lord, will

> by no means precede those who have died. For the Lord himself, with a cry of command, with the archangel's call and with the sound of God's trumpet, will descend from heaven, and the dead in Christ will rise first. Then we who are alive, who are left, will be caught up in the clouds together with them to meet the Lord in the air; and so we will be with the Lord forever. (1 Thess. 4:13-17)

Here, Paul speaks to the faithful in Thessalonica in no uncertain terms—imminent apocalyptic terms. Paul expects to be at the Parousia of Jesus Christ. And just as we saw in the Synoptic tradition, Paul faced a period of time (approximately five or six years, if we accept the dating of 1 Thessalonians c. 49 CE and Romans c. 55 CE) in which he personally was confronted with the delayed Parousia. Although Romans was written to a different congregation on a completely different set of issues, it is nevertheless surprising how completely lacking are apocalyptic tones in the letter. If we regard Pauline Christianity as an apocalyptic movement like other apocalyptic groups throughout history, we should expect apocalypticism to be the theological lens through which all things are assessed. How could it be otherwise? But then the absence of apocalyptic elements in Romans is altogether curious.

It appears, then, that any assessment of the apocalyptic legacy of early Christianity must begin with an expansion of the scriptural materials we delegate as apocalyptic. To continue to focus our consideration of apocalyptic material solely on the book of Revelation allows us to compartmentalize our assessment of early Christian apocalyptic wholly on the last book of the Christian canon. Thus any subsequent appropriation of apocalyptic worldviews by Christian groups is easily marginalized by placing the hermeneutic blame on simplistic and/or overly literal readings of the book of Revelation. The first step in recovery is acknowledgment: in this case, acknowledgment that our apocalyptic roots run much deeper than the book of Revelation. Therefore, the work of intellectually excavating texts such as the Gospel of Mark and Paul's First Letter to the Thessalonians is a positive first step in parsing how and why Christian apocalypticism has endured over two millennia. It is in our biblical DNA, present in the earliest letter from the apostle Paul and in the first Gospel ever written. And indeed, it is there, in all of its pure genre form, in the book of Revelation. It is more pervasive than we choose to admit, and scholarly discussions on matters of proper form have only distracted us from that fact. But Matthew, Luke, and Paul have left evidence not only of the prevalence of apocalyptic expectation but also of some measure of its unsustainability: that is, evidence that they tried to distance themselves from a perspective that had such a short shelf life. It appears that individuals and communities simply can't be perpetually apocalyptic. Nevertheless, our apocalyptic memories are short, and we Christians find ourselves bouncing to and fro, from postures of apocalyptic fervor to more tranquil, reserved eschatological expectation. It is a rhythmic dance that has played out over two Christian millennia.

The Book of Revelation and the Explicit Legacy of Christian Apocalypticism

Acknowledgment of the comprehensive influence of the book of Revelation on the Western Christian imagination goes unchallenged even with attempts by some denominations to altogether suppress it. It is, according to both form and content, the only true apocalypse in the New Testament (Collins 1979, 9; see the commentary on Revelation). Its rich imagery, full of beasts, martyrs, heavenly interlocutors, plagues, mysterious gematria, natural disasters, whores, and a great descending city is almost too much for the senses to comprehend, yet simultaneously hypersensual enough to draw even the casual reader into a hypnotic state of attention. It is like the car wreck on the highway that simultaneously repels and irresistibly attracts at least a momentary gaze as we cautiously pass by. It has been the source of Christian apocalyptic ambivalence and anxiety for the last two millennia. A summary of that interpretive history will bear out the alternating rhythm described above, in which our collective traditions have tried to come to terms with the last entry in the New Testament.

The apocalyptic legacy of the book of Revelation began early in the second century of the Common Era. According to Robert M. Royalty Jr. and Arthur W. Wainwright, proto-orthodox Christians like Justin Martyr (c. 100–165) and Irenaeus (c. 130–200) represented an interpretive position known as chiliasm (i.e., millenarian, from the Greek *chilia*, "thousand"). Chiliasm, which represented a literal interpretation of the book of Revelation, was theologically "mainstream" in the early second century. This position is best defined as the theological system that "believed literally in the thousand-year reign of the saints in Rev. 20:4 and the actual, physical new Jerusalem in Rev. 21–22" (Royalty, 285). Wainwright argues that "the chiliasts lived in an age of persecution. It was for such an age that they believed the Apocalypse was written. . . . During this period Chiliasm provided an antidote to the fear of persecution. When people are oppressed, they find consolation in dreams of a better life and focus their anger on the institutions and leaders that threaten them" (Wainwright, 22). Thus Wainwright makes the interpretive assumption that the Apocalypse functioned as a rhetorical call for endurance during times of persecution.

One of the first challenges to literal chiliastic readings of the book of Revelation came from Phrygia in Asia Minor. The "New Prophecy" (c. 150–175), or Montanism (as it was called by its opponents), was founded by Montanus, Prisca, and Maximilla. According to the New Prophecy, the new kingdom would be inaugurated by Christ—but in Pepuza, the geographical epicenter of the New Prophecy movement, and not Jerusalem. The New Prophecy thus challenged "normative" chiliastic expectations through a very selective literal approach to the text by its protagonists (including Tertullian, c. 160–220).

The chiliastic certainty of the of the mid-second century was also countered by emerging late second-century and early third-century allegorical interpretations of the book of Revelation forwarded by the likes of Dionysius, bishop of Alexandria (third century), Clement of Alexandria (c. 150–215), and Origen (c. 185–254). These allegorical readings came to full fruition under Augustine of Hippo (ca. 354–430), who himself was first a proponent of chiliasm until his "eschatological conversion" later in his career. Dionysius, Clement, and Origen began to challenge aspects of chiliasm, especially the literal interpretation of the new Jerusalem as a *physical* and earthly place where "the redeemed would eat, drink, marry, have children, and exercise dominion over other people" (Origen, *De princ.* 2.11.2–3). Thus the early challenges to the literal interpretations focused primarily on the location of the new Jerusalem (New Prophecy) and its physical nature, as depicted in Revelation 21–22. These challenges were just enough to begin to dislodge the mainstream chiliastic interpretations that nevertheless prevailed until the reign of Constantine, in the fourth century of the Common Era. That is a fascinatingly long tenure for literal apocalyptic musings. In some ways, the first three centuries of the Christian era mirror the apocalyptic tension that existed in the now emerging canon, representing both movements with apocalyptic sensibilities and those that countered them. Our ambivalence regarding apocalypticism and the variety of divergent interpretive possibilities were beginning to take shape in these earliest Christian centuries.

It could be argued, if one follows the logic of Wainwright, that the fourth century, with the shift in Rome's relationship to Christianity from one of indifference to persecution, then to tolerance and ultimately acceptance, also marked a shift in the Christian rhetorical posture toward apocalyptic literature in general, and the book of Revelation in particular. Violently imaginative and passive-aggressive fantasies of revenge of the Apocalypse were no longer necessary with Christianity's new and prominent relationship to the empire. This was especially the case after 381, when Emperor Theodosius endorsed orthodox Nicene Christianity over Christian Arianism and banned all pagan religious ritual. What was once peripheral was now central, and the Christian relationship to its apocalyptic legacy needed to be reevaluated. On this matter, Royalty notes, "after the Roman emperors moved from tolerance to acceptance and promotion of orthodox Christianity, millenarian views were even more strongly challenged. No imperial ruler, political or ecclesiastical, eagerly anticipated the destruction of the empire they now controlled" (Royalty, 286).

The influence of Augustine's allegorical reading of the Apocalypse was comprehensive and dominated orthodox circles from the fifth through thirteenth centuries of the Common Era. Perhaps the greatest challenge to traditional readings of the Apocalypse was Augustine's hesitance in speculating about the date of the end. Recall that Aune's working definition of apocalypse (see above) identified one of the key elements of literal apocalyptic readings as the expectation of the imminent end. This was not the case for Augustine, however, and in essence, by his very hesitation, he lowered the expectation of what is probably the most important aspect of apocalyptic eschatology: imminence. To challenge literal chiliastic views on the imminent apocalypse, derived from Revelation 20,

> Augustine offered two key interpretive points in the *City of God*, Book 20. First, the thousand year period is symbolic of "the whole duration of the world," the earthly fullness of time. Thus Augustine tried to put an end to speculations about dates and times for this millennium to start and end, a point for which he had plenty of biblical proof texts. Second, this symbolic millennium has already begun in the time of the church for that is what binds Satan until the final end.... And as for the final, *final* end, do not count the days, for the thousand year period is symbolic. (Royalty, 286–87)

Thus, with one powerful, stunning theological gesture, Augustine succeeded in shifting the emphasis from literal readings of the apocalypse to spiritual and nonmillennial readings that would last through the thirteenth century—until a Calabrian abbot named Joachim of Fiore (c. 1135–1202) would once again shift our relationship and understanding of the Apocalypse.

In contrast to Augustine's symbolic reading of the Apocalypse, Joachim of Fiore insisted on what he believed was a historical reading of the text. Joachim alleged that the persecution of Christians in his lifetime was evidence that the signs predicted in the book of Revelation were being realized.

Thus Joachim countered the allegorized reading promoted by Augustine by renewing a historicized reading of the Apocalypse similar to those first endorsed by Justin and Irenaeus. After his spiritual conversion and time spent in the Holy Land on pilgrimage, Joachim returned to Calabria and became a recluse, devoting his study and prayer time to deciphering the book of Revelation. Completely frustrated with his attempt to come to terms with the text, he reported that upon awakening one Easter morning, the meaning of the Apocalypse was revealed to him. Thus, unlike Augustine, Joachim is best understood—like John of Patmos—as an apocalyptic seer.

Joachim's primary contribution as a mystical seer was formulating a system (*concordia*) that divided human history into three historical epochs or states (*status* in Latin). The first *status* was the period from Adam to Jesus Christ, which Joachim called the period of God the Father, corresponding to the Hebrew Scriptures (and to the layperson's church). The *status* from Jesus Christ to 1260 was the period of God the Son and of the Christian Testament (corresponding to the papal church). This was the period in which Joachim himself lived. The third and final *status* began in 1260 and was the period of the Holy Spirit. This third epoch corresponded to the Friars' church. This age, according to Joachim, was the age of the new millennial kingdom:

> [The third epoch] was to be inaugurated by a new Adam or a new Christ who would be the founder of a new monastic order. The transition between the Papal Church of the second age and the Spiritual Church of the third age would be a time of great troubles during which the period of the Papal Church was to endure all the sufferings that corresponded to Christ's passion. The Papal Church would be resurrected as the Spiritual Church in which all men would live the contemplative life, practice apostolic poverty, and enjoy angelic natures. To this level Joachim's ideas were debased and popularized during the thirteenth century by a series of pseudo-Joachimite writings, which probably originated amongst the spiritual Franciscans themselves. St. Francis was identified with the messiah that Joachim prophesied. During the later Middle Ages Joachimism and the Apocalypse preserved their ideological union. (Phelan, 14)

Again, in contrast to Augustine's more domesticating and spiritual reading of the Apocalypse, Joachim revisited subversive interpretations of the text that were more at home in a historical interpretive framework. On this matter, Royalty notes, "Joachim reenergized historicized and potentially politically subversive readings of the Apocalypse, with one result being ideological challenges to ecclesiological and civil authorities in Europe within some monastic and mendicant religious communities" (Royalty, 289). And like the historicized readings of the first century, Joachim employed the powerful rhetoric of persecution. The echoes of his historicized reading reverberated most prominently from the thirteenth through the sixteenth centuries in Western Christendom and, in a few select traditions, are palpable even today (Sánchez).

The Protestant Reformation was also not immune from the perduring legacy of the Apocalypse to John. The onetime Roman Catholic German monk Martin Luther (1483–1546) also had an ambivalent relationship with the book of Revelation. In his early career, Luther remarked,

> I miss more than one thing in this book, and this makes me hold it to be neither apostolic nor prophetic . . . there is one sufficient reason for me not to think highly of it—Christ is neither taught nor known in it. (Luther 1960a, 399)

On a disenchanting trip to Rome, Luther felt betrayed by the "corruption" of the Catholic Church. This initiated an intense search of the Scriptures, which led him to conclude that salvation was a function of his own personal faith rather than derived from any corporate church entity—especially a church that he now found so dismaying. Luther set his own course with the posting of his Ninety-Five Theses in Wittenberg, Saxony, which ultimately led to his excommunication from the Roman Catholic Church.

One of the most significant appropriations of the book of Revelation among Protestant Reformers, including Luther, was the equating of the papacy with the beast(s) of the Apocalypse. Wainwright notes that Luther himself promoted "that . . . the papacy was the beast of the land [Rev. 13:11-18], [and] the empire was the beast of the sea [Rev. 13:1-10]. But the pope, he [i.e., Luther] argued, had control over the empire" (Wainwright, 61). Luther was not the first or the only critic of the papacy who employed negative apocalyptic accusations at Rome: "Some of the sharpest criticism came from Bohemia and England. In Bohemia John Milicz (d. 1374), Mathias of Janow (d. 1394), and John Hus (1369–1415) implied the pope was Antichrist" (Wainwright, 59).

Roman Catholicism in general and the papacy in particular came under a severe Protestant challenge. The need for a swift Catholic response was clear. In some circles, the Catholic response was simply to employ the same apocalyptic polemic against the Protestants. Catholic bishops like Bertold Pürstinger (1463-1543), bishop of Chiemsee (Germany), "explained that the locusts of the sixth trumpet vision [Rev. 9:13-19] were Lutherans. Serafino da Fermo described Luther as the star falling from heaven [Rev. 9:1] and the beast from the land [Rev. 13:11-18]" (Wainwright, 61).

Two other lines of interpretation employed by Catholics against Protestant antipapal interpretations were futurism, championed by the Spanish Jesuit Francisco Ribera (1537-1591), and preterism, developed most fully by the Portuguese Jesuit Luis de Alcazar (1554-1613). "Futurists contended that most of the prophecies in the Apocalypse were still unfulfilled, Preterists argued that most of them had been fulfilled already" (Wainwright, 63). Both methods of interpretation were effective. Futurism was attractive to Catholics, "because it dissociated the pope from Antichrist. It was cogent because it recognized the connection of the beast and the harlot of Rome, although it was a Rome of the future. Futurism challenged both the antipapal interpretation and the assumption that the Apocalypse provided a survey of church history" (Wainwright, 63). Preterism, by arguing that most of the prophecies of the Apocalypse had already been fulfilled, "was congenial to Catholics because it rejected the suggestion that the pope was Antichrist and it gave honor to the Roman Catholic Church" (Wainwright, 63).

One interesting offshoot of the Reformation era was the contemporary emergence of a group known as the Anabaptists. The name Anabaptist was not claimed by the group itself but rather came from other Christian groups opposed to their rejection of infant baptism (a common practice in Roman Catholic circles). The name is derived from the Greek *anabaptismos*, which is loosely translated as "being baptized (over) again." The Anabaptists were part of a movement classified today as the Radical Reformation, and it should be noted that both Protestant and Catholics persecuted Anabaptists. Beyond their baptismal practices, Anabaptists rejected organized religious hierarchies in favor of an idealized theocratic state. This ideology led to a faction of their membership occupying the German city of Münster, which they likened to the new Jerusalem (Revelation 21), to await the return of the heavenly Christ. Within the Anabaptist ranks, a Dutch national named Jan Bockelson declared himself the Messiah of the end times, and coins were minted that referenced the imminent apocalypse. The siege of Münster ended violently in 1535.

In the nineteenth century, three religious movements emerged that also took a historical interpretive approach to the Apocalypse. Those groups are the Church of Jesus Christ of Latter-Day Saints (Mormons) founded by Joseph Smith (c. 1830) shortly after the publication of the Book of Mormon; the Seventh-Day Adventists (Millerites), founded by William Miller (c. 1833); and the Jehovah's Witnesses, founded by Charles Russell (c. 1872). These three US-born movements are relevant for the current discussion because all three movements predicted an imminent apocalypse in their initial years, survived those unrealized predictions, and continue to remain with us today. Therefore, all three movements are interesting examples of how to negotiate an evolving apocalyptic expectation.

Latter-Day Saints (LDS) are an interesting example of a religious group that expanded on the Christian canon by including the Book of Mormon, *The Pearl of Great Price*, and the *Doctrine and Covenants* as church Scripture. LDS members also accept the prophecies of their church leadership as authoritative. (The head of the LDS Church at any given time in its history is recognized as prophet.) This combination of Scriptures and "[prophetic] pronouncement of their leaders has led them to expect both the rebuilding of Jerusalem in the old world and the erection of the New Jerusalem [Revelation 21] in North America. They look forward to the return of Christ to inaugurate his millennial reign over the earth" (Wainwright, 99). This bifurcated manner of dividing the old and new worlds is consistent with the LDS belief that Jesus Christ also visited the Americas shortly after his resurrection, in the first century CE.

Seventh-Day Adventists, like the earliest apocalyptic Christians, also had to deal with their own version of the delay of the Parousia. Their founder, William Miller, predicted that Christ would return in 1843. When his prophecy was not fulfilled, he changed the date to 1844, but that too was not realized. This unrealized prophecy was cause for the earliest Adventists to reconsider and reconfigure their intense apocalyptic hopes. What does an apocalyptic group do when their dated expectation is not realized? As noted above, these groups can abandon their expectations, they can initiate their own (violent) apocalypse (see below for modern examples of this option), or they can adjust the anticipated date—thereby adjusting their imminent expectation much as Matthew and Luke adjusted the Markan apocalyptic time frame. Such was the case with the Adventists; and the denomination still thrives today, some 170 years after the original apocalyptic prophecy. The rhetorical shift they made was to the notion that "another divine event, invisible to human eyes, had occurred in 1844. Christ, they said, had entered the heavenly sanctuary (Heb. 9:24-28)" (Wainwright, 99; cf. Froom, 889–99).

Note that the domesticating of apocalyptic imminence among Adventists did not sway the denomination away from their allegiance to the Apocalypse itself. Wainwright notes, "In arguing for the observance of Saturday as the holy day, they quoted the statement that those who did not keep God's commandments have the mark of the beast (Rev. 14:9-12). The Adventist John Nevis Andrews (1829–83) identified the beast from the land with the United States, whose two horns were civil and religious liberty. The beast from the sea and the whore of Babylon represented the papacy" (Wainwright, 99–100). Thus the continued Adventist appropriation of the Apocalypse shifted away from imminent temporal concerns toward an applied cosmological dualism, a trait common in most apocalyptic literature (as expressed, e.g., in the explicit distinction of insiders from outsiders, saved from unsaved, sinners from righteous).

At the forefront of Jehovah's Witness appropriations of the Apocalypse is their privileging of the 144,000 elect referenced in Revelation 7 and 14. Revelation 7:4-8 reads:

> Then I heard the number of those who were sealed: 144,000 from all the tribes of Israel.
>
> > From the tribe of Judah, 12,000 were sealed,
> > from the tribe of Reuben 12,000,
> > from the tribe of Gad 12,000,
> > from the tribe of Asher 12,000,
> > from the tribe of Naphtali 12,000,
> > from the tribe of Manasseh 12,000,
> > from the tribe of Simeon 12,000,
> > from the tribe of Levi, 12,000,
> > from the tribe of Issachar 12,000,
> > from the tribe of Zebulun 12,000,
> > from the tribe of Joseph 12,000,
> > from the tribe of Benjamin 12,000.

And Rev. 14:1 again refers to the 144,000: "Then I looked, and there before me was the Lamb, standing on Mount Zion, and with him 144,000 who had his name and his Father's name written on their foreheads." According to Jehovah's Witnesses, "the United Nations and the world's religious leaders will be on Satan's side in the Battle of Armageddon. Against them will be ranged the 144,000 and the other sheep, but Christ's heavenly army will actually win the victory, and the only survivors of the battle will be the Jehovah's Witnesses" (Wainwright, 100). This position is consistent with founder Charles Russell's original teaching that the 144,000 will constitute the foundation of God's people during the Christian millennium and will do battle with people marked with the mark of the beast (Wainwright, 100). Again, the acute dualism of this apocalyptic appropriation is evident in this end-time narrative. And like the Adventist Church, Jehovah's Witnesses have survived the crisis of unrealized apocalyptic prophecy.

> Mistaken prophecies have not daunted the Jehovah's Witnesses. Joseph Franklin Rutherford, who succeeded Russell as their leader, predicted that Abraham, Isaac, Jacob and other faithful Israelites would return to earth in 1925. More recent Witnesses have entertained the hope that the millennium might begin about 1975. In spite of the failure of these expectations, the organization continues to thrive. (Wainwright, 101)

The Apocalyptic Legacy Today

Looking back on this succinct review of how the apocalyptic legacy has endured over the Christian centuries, I, for one, am perplexed—yet not surprised—by the apocalyptically saturated culture in which we continue to live today. Over the last several decades, myriad films on the imminent end have been produced. Examples include *The Seventh Seal* (1958), *Fail Safe* (1964), *Planet of the Apes* (1968), *The Omega Man* (1971), *The Omen* (1976), *Apocalypse Now* (1979), *Pale Rider* (1985), *The Seventh Sign* (1988), the *Terminator* series (1984, 1991, 2003, 2009, and possibly a fifth episode in the series in 2015), *Independence Day* (1996), *The Matrix* series (1999, 2003, 2003), *Apocalypto* (2006), *Knowing* (2009), *The Road* (2009), *The Book of Eli* (2010), and *The Colony* (2013). At best, this is just a small representation of the hundreds of films produced in the recent past on an apocalyptic and catastrophic "end."

A great deal of apocalyptic music has also emerged over the same period: *The End*, by the Doors, 1967; *Burn*, by Deep Purple, 1974; *It's the End of the World as We Know It (And I Feel Fine)*, by R.E.M., 1987; *Idioteque*, by Radiohead, 2000; *When the Man Comes Around*, by Johnny Cash, 2002; and *Radioactive*, by Imagine Dragons, 2013.

From the literary world, one need look no further than Hal Lindsey and Carla C. Carlson's best-selling *The Late Great Planet Earth* (1970) and Tim LaHaye and Jerry B. Jenkins's sixteen books in the *Left Behind* series (1995–2007). Both pairs of authors were greatly influenced by another form of futurism known as dispensationalism, a term coined by British author John Nelson Darby (1800–1882) that "refers to the idea that all time can be divided into [seven] separate periods known as dispensations. The present dispensation spans the time between the first and second comings of Christ, and the next great dispensation will be the millennium" (Koester, 275). The reading and composition strategy of Lindsey and Carlson was to cut and paste a series of biblical passages to give the reader a comprehensive view of the end-time scenario. According to Craig Koester, "Hal Lindsey's *Late, Great Planet Earth* . . . linked the biblical text used in Darby's system [esp. Genesis 15; Daniel 9; 1 Thessalonians 4; 2 Thessalonians 2; 1 John 2; and the entirety of Revelation] to current newspaper headlines, giving readers the impression that scripture had predicted the dominant political trends of the Cold War. The *Left Behind* novels . . . present Darby's system through the medium of fiction" (Koester, 275).

Examples of Lindsey and Carlson's interpretation of current events as correlative of apocalyptic biblical scenarios include, but surely are not limited to examples like these:

> The seal visions . . . predict the outbreak of war in the Middle East. . . . They tell of economic distress, shortage of food, and the death of a quarter of the human race as a result of these disasters. . . . The sixth seal vision may describe the beginning of nuclear war, and the trumpet visions may foretell the disasters of that war. . . . The bowl visions describe the fearful punishment that will be inflicted on those who reject the Christian Gospel. (Wainwright, 84)

Unrealized scenarios, in Lindsey and Carlson's schema, are considered "still yet to come" rather than failed. Jack Van Impe, a popular apocalyptic and "historical" dispensationalist preacher on the Trinity Broadcasting Network, is another outstanding example of the ongoing hermeneutic tradition initiated by Darby and executed by Lindsey and Carlson. He too postpones unfulfilled prophetic expectations and continues to look to contemporary events as potential signs of imminent fulfillment.

The *Left Behind* series, as noted above, correlates apocalyptic biblical themes with fictional events (although the narrative can include real-world entities). For example, the first novel

> opens against a context of international food shortages, inflation (Rev. 6.5-6) and conflict (Rev. 6.4) in the Middle East. Amidst the upheaval, the rapture occurs. Children and Christian adults are taken up, but a few of those left behind appreciate what has occurred; most prefer the explanations offered by United Nations Secretary General Nicolae Carpathia, who promises a solution to the world's problems, heads a new ten-member (evoking the "ten crowns" of Rev. 13.2) Security Council, and brokers a peace deal for Israel. Carpathia is hailed as a great leader and replaces the United Nations with a totalitarian Global Community, as nations seeking peace and security willingly surrender their sovereignty. (Rev. 13; Wright, 2009, 81)

The popularity of the *Late Great Planet Earth* and the *Left Behind* series cannot be overstated. Combined sales of the books are well into the tens of millions. These books are, for many Christians, the primary source for their understanding of Christian apocalyptic. As Koester has noted, "The view of the future presented in [*Left Behind*] affirms that God is sovereign despite ominous world conditions.... The novels show that simple believers, who know the biblical script, are far better informed about global developments than the commentators on television" (Koester, 278). An appealing script for the apocalyptically inclined, indeed.

No survey of the apocalyptic legacy of Christian Scripture is complete without an acknowledgment of three of the most sensational and horrific demonstrations of that legacy in recent memory: Jonestown (1978), the Branch Davidians (1993), and Heaven's Gate (1997). As noted in the beginning of this essay, one generalized way to categorize the trajectories of apocalyptic groups is according to their responses when initial prophecies of an imminent event have been delayed. The group in question can disband; they can move the date of the end into the undefined future; or they can initiate a violent end within the parameters of their apocalyptic rhetoric. The three groups just named all chose the last option, under different circumstances. These three groups (and several others like them) pique our imaginations when we discuss modern apocalyptic groups. They represent the most extreme cases.

It may very well be that my own interest in apocalyptic groups began with the images I witnessed, as an eighteen-year-old, of the Jonestown debacle. The photos and film sent over the newswire were shocking: piles of bodies (many of whom were children) stacked up and grouped together in a jungle in Guyana, a dead US Congressman and reporters executed point blank lying on an airstrip, and syringes and vats of cyanide-laced, purple Kool Aid. Over 900 people died on a single day, March 18, 1978.

What we learned about the group and its leaders after the mass suicide was equally sensational. Pastor Jim Jones (1931-1978) had led his flock from its roots in Indianapolis, Indiana, to Redwood Valley, California, then to San Francisco, and ultimately to their final "utopian" location in Jonestown, Guyana. The group's migration to Jonestown began in 1977 and was executed in several stages: survey, development, occupation. Dominant in the group's rhetoric were themes of persecution, suffering, and potential martyrdom for the cause. The echoes of Christian apocalyptic are not difficult to discern in this rhetoric. Jones and his flock were committed to fighting what they perceived as "the injustices of a racist, classist, and capitalistic society" (Moore, 95). Jones believed that the group's new location in the jungles of Guyana would allow for the free exercise of their religion and the development of a socialist utopia.

The utopian beginnings of the relocated group were hounded by reports as early as 1972—the San Francisco years—"when a religion reporter for the *San Francisco Chronicle* wrote that a member wanting to leave the group had died under suspicious circumstances" (Moore, 97). Moore also reports that "the apostate group called the Concerned Relatives publicized an 'accusation of Human Rights Violations,' which detailed abuses that they believed were occurring in Jonestown" (Moore, 97). These accusations were the impetus for the visit of US Congressman Leo Ryan's visit to Jonestown in 1978. These accusations, combined with some current members desiring to leave Jonestown in conjunction with Jones's elevated paranoia (which may have included an increasing dependence on narcotics), fueled the volatile mix of the rhetoric of persecution and suffering and perceived external pressures. The pressure and paranoia became so acute that the infamous "white nights" (actual rehearsals of mass suicide) became more common in the latter stages of the group's existence. The actual performance was executed on the evening of March 18, 1978. In the words of the self-proclaimed messiah Jones, it was an act of "revolutionary suicide," an act no doubt influenced by apocalyptic ideation.

Fifteen years after the events of Jonestown, another apocalyptic group, the Branch Davidians, appeared on our apocalyptic landscape. The forensic analysis of the global press and the emerging World Wide Web allowed us our closest and most detailed look at an apocalyptic group and its violent end. Led by David Koresh (Vernon Howell, born 1959), another self-proclaimed messiah (Koresh is the Hebrew transliteration of Cyrus, a reference to the Persian king proclaimed messiah by the prophet Isaiah in Isa. 45:1), the Branch Davidians—an offshoot of the Seventh-Day Adventists Church—engaged in a lethal gun battle with US federal agents on April 19, 1993, in which their compound was destroyed by fire and seventy-six Davidians lost their lives. The source of the fire is still under debate: the two competing theories are that federal tear-gas canisters started the fire in the compound, or that members of the Davidians started the fire from within.

What is especially fascinating about this group was their explicit employment of the book of Revelation to map out their perceived apocalyptic destiny. Kenneth Newport argues, "The text [i.e., the book of Revelation] was at the very least an important factor . . . in the decision of the Branch Davidians to self-destruct (or 'act out their biblical destiny' as they would more probably have seen it)" (Newport, 213). He continues, "The community read the Book of Revelation (together with numerous other parts of the Bible, especially the Psalms) and what they read there, I suggest, together with the context in which they read it, led to the group's planned for and well executed apocalyptic self-destruction" (Newport, 213). Certainly texts like Rev. 10:7 were used by Koresh to depict himself as the seventh angel of the Apocalypse. The description of a lamblike beast in Rev. 13:11-18 was used to demonize the US government. Such passages were vital to group awareness. Thus, for the Branch Davidians, "the arrival of the ATF and then the FBI on the morning of 28 February, 1993, was highly significant and prophetically charged" (Newport, 219). For the Davidians (especially Koresh), as for Jonestown, all pressures from outside the group were biblically prophesied signs of the apocalyptic times. So when the *Waco Tribune-Herald* began publishing a critical exposé on Koresh, called "The Sinful Messiah," the day before the first day of the siege on the Davidian compound, all signs pointed to their impending end.

An interesting variation on the modern apocalyptic group coming to an abrupt end is Heaven's Gate. Founded in 1972 by Marshall Applewhite (1932–1997) and Bonnie Lu Nettles (1928–1985), the group chose to end their lives via ritualistic suicide by consuming a lethal combination of Phenobarbital (an anticonvulsant barbiturate) mixed with applesauce and chased with vodka. After law-enforcement authorities received an anonymous tip, thirty-nine bodies were discovered in a mansion in Rancho Santa Fe (an affluent suburb of San Diego), twenty-one women and eighteen men of various ages from twenty-six to seventy-two. The ritualistic suicides were performed over several days in 1997: fifteen on March 22, fifteen on March 23, seven on March 24, and the final two somewhere between March 24 and their eventual discovery on March 26.

The bodies (known as "vessels" by Heaven's Gate members) were all dressed in black shirts and trousers, black Nike sneakers, and a purple cloth covered their upper torsos. Each had an armband with the words "Heaven's Gate Away Team" embroidered on the band. The majority of the deceased had in their possession a five-dollar bill and three quarters.

The impetus for this ritualistic suicide is uniquely different from the rhetoric of persecution, suffering, and martyrdom commonplace in Jonestown and in Waco, Texas, among the Branch Davidians. Benjamin Zeller concludes that "while the movement surely experienced a sense of persecution and failure . . . these conditions are not in themselves sufficient to cause self-violence" (Zeller, 175). What motivated this group ritualistically to end their lives was their belief (according to their still-active website: heavensgate.com) that humanity needed to move beyond human existence to their rightful place at the "next level above human," the realm of God. For the members, the imminent timing of this transition was critical because it was their belief that the earth was soon to be "recycled."

It should be noted, however, that ritualistic suicide was not always a part of the group's theology. Rather, "for the first decade of the group's history it flatly rejected the very notion of suicide, arguing instead for the need to transition into the heavens while still embodied" (Zeller, 175). So what mechanism triggered the shift from embodied to disembodied transformation? The matter is still up for debate, but it should be noted that the death of cofounder Bonnie Lu Nettles of liver cancer in 1985 caused some cognitive dissonance among the membership. This period also marked the beginning of the group's devaluation of the body (from this point on, referred to as "vessels") that may have been a first step in their formulation of ritual suicide as spiritual release to the next level above human. This new understanding of the body, in combination with the belief that the earth was soon to be "recycled," played out when the comet Hale-Bopp manifested itself in the late-March skies of 1997. For Applewhite and the members of the Heaven's Gate group, this was *the sign*. A hypothesis was promoted by the group that located behind this comet was a spaceship that would gather the "elect" for the trip to the level above human. Although Zeller argued (as mentioned above) that the experienced sense of persecution and failure was not sufficient to explain the ritualistic violence that the group enacted, members were convinced in the days leading up to their end of "a massive government conspiracy to hide an extraterrestrial flying saucer trailing the comet" (Zeller, 177).

Epilogue

This essay began by questioning whether the book of Revelation was the sole source for the rich apocalyptic legacy in Western Christendom. It is, according to this essay, no doubt a tour de force in that history. Yet the history also reveals that Western Christians have had an ambivalent relationship with Revelation. The post-Augustinian shift from historical to spiritual readings is demonstrative of that point. That shift was, like Matthew and Luke's appropriation of Mark, a domestication of the apocalyptic tradition. And from roughly that point in history, Christians have both foregrounded and retreated from that position based on our interpretive agendas. The biblical tradition and the interpretive legacy have embedded within them *both* potentialities, for historicizing or for spiritualizing readings, and we are their inheritors.

With this inheritance comes great responsibility. History shows how easy it is for those enthusiastic for a final, definitive ending to risk actions that bring about lesser, still devastating ends. Today, however, more is at stake than the welfare of the members of an apocalyptic group. Apocalyptic scripts and a highly weaponized world make for a volatile mixture. As Catherine Wessinger observes, for example,

> In the 1980s Americans learned that President Reagan (Republican, served 1981–1989) had been influenced by [Hal] Lindsey's predictions about the roles of Israel and nuclear war in the final events. Throughout the Reagan administration Americans who did not believe in these apocalyptic prophecies contemplated the danger of having a Dispensationalist President as commander of the American nuclear arsenal. (Wessinger, 428; cf. Boyer, 140–43)

Apocalyptic scripts also make it much too easy to separate the world into sheep and goats, "axes of evil" and "elect nations"—perpetually seeking to identify antichrists for destruction. For example, George W. Bush's war on terror was often framed in the totalizing language of good versus evil. Again, Wessinger notes that the Bush administration's response to the attacks of 9/11 by Islamic jihadists was an act of "apocalyptic mirroring" (see Rosenfeld) in which "the radical dualism of the Bush administration matched that of jihadists, and Bush's apocalyptic war rhetoric mirrored that of bin Laden and colleagues" (Wessinger, 436). In a speech delivered on September 14, 2011, Bush declared that it was America's responsibility "to answer these attacks *and rid the world of evil*" (italics added; see Räisänen, 155). It should also be noted that the lyrics of hymns such as "Onward Christian Soldiers" and "The Battle Hymn of the Republic"—the musical selections for the Day of Prayer and Remembrance for the victims of 9/11 on September 14, 2001—reflect the anticipation of some fully to participate in the apocalypse on their time rather than God's. But all such appropriations are irrational and zealous impositions on the biblical texts—*all* of the texts we have identified as apocalyptic within the Christian canon (Jewett).

Perhaps it is our role as scholars, theologians, ministers, priests, and simply as rational human beings to remind those in our midst of the consequences of such human impositions on our sacred texts. The models of Jonestown, the Branch Davidians, and Heaven's Gate are just a few examples of the potential for disaster when we set the apocalyptic clock on our time. One could readily add other events and groups to an ever-expanding list (e.g., the Manson Family, Aum Shinrikyo, and the Solar Temple). Against the reflex to expedite the apocalyptic clock, we would do well to heed what the biblical texts actually have to say about the time frame of the end; for example, Jesus' words in Mark 13:32: "But about that day or hour no one knows, not even the angels in heaven, nor the Son, but only the Father." What is most tragic, however, is that our self-imposed acceleration of the apocalyptic clock has also accelerated the dangers of which the seer John issues an awesome warning against anyone who adds to his prophecy.

> I warn everyone who hears the words of the prophecy of this scroll: If anyone adds anything to them, God will add to that person the plagues described in this scroll. And if anyone takes words away from this scroll of prophecy, God will take away from that person any share in the tree of life and in the Holy City, which are described in this scroll. (Rev. 22:18-19)

The reflex to accelerate an apocalyptic schedule has actualized the calamities of which John warns. With or without explicit appeal to apocalyptic texts, the effort to determine the course of history through force has already begun to inflict plagues of biblical proportions on our world: the plague of war, the plague of famine, the plague of disease, the plague of a deteriorating ecosystem, and the plague of abject poverty are just a few prime examples. The time has come to stop and recognize the gravity, both explicit and implicit, of the scriptural inheritances that inform our apocalyptic legacy. Only then will we be able to begin to neutralize it.

Works Cited

Aune, David E. 2005. "Understanding Jewish and Christian Apocalyptic." *WW* 25, no. 3:233–45.

Boyer, Paul. 1992. *When Time Shall Be No More: Prophecy Belief in Modern American Culture*. Cambridge, MA: Harvard University Press.

Cameron, Averil, ed. 1989. *History as Text: The Writing of Ancient History*. Chapel Hill: University of North Carolina Press.

Chilton, Bruce. 2013. *Visions of the Apocalypse: Receptions of John's Revelation in Western Imagination*. Waco, TX: Baylor University Press.

Collins, Adela Yarbro. 1984. *Crisis and Catharsis: The Power of the Apocalypse*. Philadelphia: Westminster.

Collins, John J. 1979. "Introduction: Towards the Morphology of a Genre." *Semeia* 14:1–20.

———. 1984. *The Apocalyptic Imagination: An Introduction to Jewish Apocalyptic Literature*. New York: Crossroad.

Froom, LeRoy E. 2009. *The Prophetic Faith of Our Fathers*. Vol. 4. Hagerstown, MD: Review and Herald Publishing Association.

Hanson, Paul. 1979. *The Dawn of Apocalyptic: The Historical and Sociological Roots of Jewish Apocalyptic Eschatology*. Philadelphia: Fortress Press.

Jones, Ken Sundet. 2005. "The Apocalyptic Luther." *WW* 25, no. 3:233–45.

Koester, Craig R. 2005. "Revelation and the *Left Behind* Novels." *WW* 25, no. 3:274–82.

Kovacs, Judith L. 2005. "The Revelation to John: Lessons from the History of the Book's Reception." *WW* 25, no. 3:255–63.

Moore, Rebecca. 2011. "Narratives of Persecution, Suffering, and Martyrdom: Violence in Peoples Temple and Jonestown." In *Violence and New Religious Movements*, edited by J. R. Lewis, 95–111. Oxford: Oxford University Press.

Jewett, Robert. 1973. *The Captain America Complex: The Dilemma of Zealous Nationalism*. Philadelphia: Westminster.

Luther, Martin. 1960a. "Preface to the Revelation of John [I]." In *LW* 35.

———. 1960b. "Preface to the Revelation of John [II]." In *LW* 35.

Newport, Kenneth. 2009. "Be Thou Faithful Unto Death (cf. Rev. 2.10): The Book of Revelation, The Branch Davidians and Apocalyptic (Self-)Destruction." In *The Way the World Ends? The Apocalypse of John in Culture and Ideology*, edited by W. J. Lyons and Jorunn Økland, 211–26. Sheffield: Sheffield Phoenix.

Perkins, Judith. 1995. *The Suffering Self: Pain and Narrative Representation in the Early Christian Era*. London: Routledge.

Phelan, John Leddy. 1970. *The Millennial Kingdom of the Franciscans in the New World*. Berkeley: University of California Press.

Räisänen, Heikki. 2009. "Revelation, Violence, and War: Glimpses of a Dark Side." In *The Way the World Ends? The Apocalypse of John in Culture and Ideology*, edited by W. J. Lyons and Jorunn Økland, 211–26. Sheffield: Sheffield Phoenix.

Rosenfeld, Jean E. 2011. "Nativists Millennialism." In *The Oxford Handbook of Millennialism*, edited by Catherine Wessinger, 89–109. New York: Oxford University Press.

Royalty, Robert M., Jr. 2005. "The Dangers of the Apocalypse." *WW* 25, no. 3:283–93.

Sánchez, David A. 2008. *From Patmos to the Barrio: Subverting Imperial Myths*. Minneapolis: Fortress Press.

Wainwright, Arthur W. 1993. *Mysterious Apocalypse: Interpreting the Book of Revelation*. Nashville: Abingdon.

Wessinger, Catherine. 2014. "Apocalypse and Violence." In *The Oxford Handbook of Apocalyptic Literature*, edited by John J. Collins, 422–40. New York: Oxford University Press.

Wright, Melanie J. 2009. "Every Eye Shall See Him": Revelation and Film. In *The Way the World Ends? The Apocalypse of John in Culture and Ideology*, edited by W. J. Lyons and Jorunn Økland, 76–94. Sheffield: Sheffield Phoenix.

Wright, Stuart A. 2011. "Revisiting the Branch Davidian Mass Suicide Debate." In *Violence and New Religious Movements*, edited by J. R. Lewis, 113–31. Oxford: Oxford University Press.

Zeller, Benjamin E. 2011. "The Euphemization of Violence: The Case of Heaven's Gate." In *Violence and New Religious Movements*, edited by J. R. Lewis, 173–89. Oxford: Oxford University Press.

Introduction to Hebrews, the General Epistles, and Revelation

Neil Elliott

The transition from the Letters of Paul to the "Epistle to the Hebrews" and the General Epistles that follow offers an opportunity to reflect on the organization of writings that we call the New Testament. Although early Bible manuscripts show a number of different ways of organizing the collection, from the fourth century onward the pattern began to take hold in different codices that we see in our current New Testament.

First appear the four Gospels, then the Acts of the Apostles (though this followed the Epistles of Paul in the fourth-century Codex Sinaiticus). Note that the gathering together of Gospels means the separation of the two-volume work Luke and Acts. Then come the Letters of Paul—arranged roughly in order of length, rather than chronology, with 1 and 2 Corinthians and 1 and 2 Thessalonians being put together, and with letters to churches preceding letters apparently written to individuals (though note that Philemon, the last of the Pauline Epistles, is also addressed to a church). Hebrews was often included among Paul's letters, following Romans (for example, already in P[46], c. 200), presumably on the assumption, held for example by Augustine and Jerome, that Paul had written it. Its present position following Paul's letters (as it appears already in Sinaiticus) may be the result of its dislocation from that collection as doubts about its authorship gradually arose. (The third-century theologian Origen quipped that "God only knows" who penned the epistle, but he usually quoted the letter as if it came from Paul, and commended churches who held it to be from the apostle. He also knew of a tradition that the epistle had been written by Clement of Rome: Eusebius *Hist. eccl.* 6.25.)

In the Syriac Peshitta (c. second century CE), the letters appearing under the names of the most prominent of the apostles—James, 1 Peter, and 1 John—appear immediately after Acts, before the Pauline Epistles. Other epistles that appear in our New Testament today—2 Peter, Jude, and 2 and 3 John—gained currency relatively late in the first centuries of Christianity; they were not included in the Peshitta or in early lists of the New Testament writings. The fourth-century Codex Vaticanus arranges all the General Epistles before the Epistles of Paul; Sinaiticus puts Acts and the General Epistles together, but following Paul's letters.

The nomenclature of "General" or "Catholic" Epistles (from the Greek *kath' holikos*, "general" or "universal") was first used by Alexandrian scholars to refer to 1 Peter and 1 John, then by the fourth-century bishop and historian Eusebius to refer to James; 1 and 2 Peter; 1, 2, and 3 John; and Jude—though Eusebius acknowledged that several of these were "disputed" by different churches (*antilegomena*: *Eccl. hist.* 2.23; 3.25.1–3). Referring to these as "Catholic" Epistles implies a distinction from Paul's letters: if Paul wrote to specific congregations, these epistles are written to the church "Catholic" or universal. The distinction cannot be maintained, of course, once we recognize that Paul's letters are also directed to multiple congregations (e.g., the "churches" of Galatia, Gal. 1:2) and consider that early manuscripts of Ephesians do not include the address "in Ephesus" (1:1); indeed, the collection of Paul's letters shows that they were perceived by some Christians, at least, as relevant and useful for churches beyond their original addressees. Colossians 4:16 assumes an interchange of letters between churches. And the probability that some of those letters are pseudepigrapha, created after Paul's death to extend his legacy (or claim his authority) to new audiences, shows a "catholicizing" impulse at work in that collection.

Meanwhile, the Epistle of James and the First Epistle of Peter explicitly address more general audiences ("to the twelve tribes in the Dispersion," James 1:1; "to the exiles of the Dispersion in Pontus, Galatia, Cappadocia, Asia, and Bithynia," 1 Pet. 1:1), but these letters were nonetheless written in specific circumstances with particular goals in mind. Furthermore, the characterization of addressees in terms of "exile" and Diaspora may have a particular rhetorical function. It hardly distinguishes these as the only two writings in our New Testament written to communities of immigrants or "rootless" people, as Margaret Aymer shows in her article in this volume ("Rootlessness and Community in Contexts of Diaspora," 47–61).

Neither should we assume that the reference to Diaspora is evidence that these writings both addressed Jews (see the introductions to each epistle). Similarly, the title "To the Hebrews" may well be secondary; it neither indicates that this "word of exhortation" (Heb. 5:11; 6:1) was intended for Jewish readers or that it enjoyed particular popularity among them. To be sure, the status of the law, the temple, and the covenant with Israel are prominent topics in several of these writings, but as Lawrence M. Wills shows, these were paramount concerns in numerous early churches, over many decades ("Negotiating the Jewish Heritage of Early Christianity," 31–45).

In short, all of these writings give important glimpses into the convictions and concerns of early believers in Jesus. We can well imagine that their authors and intended readers shared particular knowledge and assumptions that are lost to us now. Their collection into a loose and rather ill-fitting category, "General Epistles," may obscure important historical connections (for example, between the Johannine Epistles and the Gospel according to John). At any rate, that category, and the place of these epistles and Hebrews "in between" Paul's letters and the Revelation to John, should not be taken to indicate that their various authors actually aimed these writings at churches "in general." As the introduction to each of the following entries will indicate, we can make reasonable judgments about the specifics of place, time, and situation surrounding each letter. Taken together, they offer us additional glimpses of the diversity, no less than the commonality, of early churches. But their being grouped together in one part of our New Testament labeled "General Epistles" is little more than a matter of organizational convenience, and readers today should not for that reason consider themselves more included in the implied audience of any of these than of any other New Testament writing. The responsibility for how any of us read ourselves "into" these ancient writings, or read them "into" our own time, remains, at last, with us.

HEBREWS

Davld A. deSilva

Introduction

"The Epistle of Paul the Apostle to the Hebrews," as the KJV names this book, is a misnomer in every respect. First, the author does not present this text as an epistle. The opening sentence does not reflect the standard letter-opening formula, but the beginning of a well-crafted oration. He labels his own text a "word of exhortation" (13:22), a term for a "sermon" in early Judaism (see Acts 13:15). Hebrews is best read as an example of early (and expert) Christian preaching. The author closes with the elements of an epistolary postscript (13:18-25), in keeping with the fact that he has, of necessity, had to commit his sermon to writing to be read aloud to the audience by a third party.

The sermon is anonymous. The mention of Timothy (Heb. 13:23) and Paul's reputation as a letter-writer led early scribes to attribute the text to Paul. This is unlikely on several grounds. Paul vehemently insists that he came to faith in Christ without human mediation (Gal. 1:11-17; 1 Cor. 15:3-10), whereas this author came to faith through the preaching of other apostles (Heb. 2:3-4). Paul's undisputed letters exhibit none of the attention to rhetorical ornamentation that one finds in Hebrews. Indeed, Paul avoids rhetorical polish in principle, lest persuasion come through the speaker rather than the Spirit (1 Cor. 2:1-5), a reluctance this author did not share. The author does seem to belong to the large circle of teachers that constitute the Pauline team (Heb. 13:23).

Debates in the early church concerning authorship (Apollos and Barnabas were also suggested) show that it was consistently regarded as Pauline, prior to Jerome's and Augustine's championing of Pauline authorship (in connection with their promoting its canonical status). Although it has become popular to suggest Priscilla as a candidate, the author's use of a self-referential masculine participle in 11:32 argues against this. Arguments that this was intended to hide the author's gender founder on the fact that addressees clearly know the author's identity (13:19, 23) and on the Pauline churches' openness to female leadership (see, e.g., Rom. 16:1-3; Col. 4:15).

The author mastered both the Jewish scriptural heritage and the art of rhetoric, giving the clearest signs of formal training, at least at the level of elementary rhetorical education, of any New Testament author (deSilva 2012, 3–19). He writes Greek like a native speaker and shows a broad familiarity with elements of Greek culture (like athletic practices, philosophy of education, and popular ethics). The text has some connection with Christianity in Italy (Heb. 13:24), though it is unclear whether the author sends greetings from Italy abroad (which seems more likely) or back home to fellow Italian Christians. Clement of Rome's use of the sermon in 95–96 CE confirms some connection with Roman Christianity and also sets the latest possible date of composition. The author's references to the Levitical sacrifices as ongoing (e.g., Heb. 10:2-3) most naturally suggest a date prior to 70 CE, when the temple was destroyed by the Roman armies.

The audience is not made up of "Hebrews," at least as Acts 6:1-6 understands the term. The recipients speak Greek and know the Jewish Scriptures primarily in the Greek translation rather than Hebrew (the author makes several points that rely on details found only in the former). If the audience was part of the Pauline mission, the goal of which was to take the good news to non-Jews and to establish congregations in which Jewish and gentile believers worshiped together, it was likely of mixed ethnicity (Attridge, 10–13; deSilva 2000, 2–7; Eisenbaum, 8–9). The author's extensive use of the Jewish Scriptures is no argument against this, as these were the authoritative oracles of God for both gentile and Jewish Christians.

The text provides three windows into the audience's past: their initial conversion, in which a new experience of divine power cemented their commitment to a new group (2:1-4); their socialization into the worldview of the Christian group, in which they learned some of the foundational convictions on which the author will build throughout his sermon (6:1-3); and their experience of rejection by their neighbors, who used a variety of tactics to shame them into abandoning their new way of life and returning to a more acceptable one (10:32-34). While they had successfully resisted those pressures in the past, their current behavior suggests that the loss of status and honor had begun to make some disciples, at least, question whether God's nonmaterializing promises were worth enduring continued alienation from the way of life and social networks of support they once enjoyed. Some individuals have already ceased to associate openly with the Christian group (10:25).

The author perceives that others may be in danger of doing the same (hence the recurring warnings in 2:1, 3; 3:12; 4:11; 6:4-6; 10:26-31; 12:15) and writes to stave off any such course of action. He seeks to confirm the hearers in their commitment to persevere in their Christian practice and to invest in one another's perseverance as well, countering society's negative pressures (3:6, 14; 4:11; 6:9-12; 10:23-25, 35-36, 39; 12:1, 3, 12-13; 13:12-14). He pursues several strategies to advance this agenda. He "normalizes" the experience of rejection and disgrace and turns endurance of the same into an opportunity for honor in God's sight. He taps into the foundational social codes of reciprocity, presenting Jesus as a supremely generous mediator of God's patronage and setting before the audience's eyes the insuperable advantages of continuing to nurture this relationship through appropriate loyalty and gratitude (rather than incurring divine wrath through ingratitude). He uses the authoritative Scriptures and the basic convictions of the Christian community (for example, final judgment, the passing away of the present age, and the imminence of God's kingdom) to locate the audience on the very threshold of encountering Jesus at his return and entering into God's unshakable realm, thus promoting consideration of the "eternal" over the "temporal" by stressing the former's imminence.

The sermon alternates between exposition and exhortation, the former consistently providing the warrant for the latter. Scholars formerly questioned whether chapter 13, with its relatively brief and practical instructions, was originally a part of the sermon, but Floyd Filson's study effectively ended the debate in favor of the text's unity.

Clement of Rome and Justin Martyr used and valued Hebrews, but the book was slow to gain recognition as a canonical authority in the West. It was more widely used and embraced among Eastern Christians. The question of apostolic authorship was important to some early church teachers, but not to others (like Origen, who could accept both the sermon's authority and anonymity). Hebrews provided, nevertheless, an important resource for the development of Christology (e.g., the question of the relationship of Jesus to God as "Son" and the idea of the two natures of Christ) and for reflection on the meaning of Jesus' death and the mechanics of atonement. Its acceptance into the canon of Paul's letters finally facilitated its acceptance into the canon of the New Testament.

Contemporary readers question the appropriateness of the author's interpretation of the Jewish Scriptures, taking these texts almost solely as a witness in some way to the person and work of Jesus, showing no interest in the text's meaning in its own right. While this is integral to the sermon's contribution to the formation of Christology, it also flies in the face of the practice of modern biblical criticism. Closely related to this is the theological problem of supersessionism—the replacement of the Mosaic covenant with the new covenant—that runs throughout the sermon. Other major issues revolve around the author's apparent impositions of limitations on repentance and God's mercy (no less a problem for ancient Christians than modern ones) and his sublimation of a brutal execution through the language of sacrifice and atonement. On the other hand, there is a growing appreciation for the anti-imperial rhetoric in Hebrews and its function as resistance literature (both sociopolitically and culturally).

Hebrews 1:1-14: The Ultimate Revelation in God's Son

The Text in Its Ancient Context

In an artfully crafted antithesis, the author opens by emphasizing the ultimacy, completeness, and finality of the word spoken by God in the Son, the word around which his hearers were shaped into a new community. This opening sentence sounds the "indicative" that underscores every "imperative" to keep giving this word its due weight and to continue to respond properly to this announcement (e.g., 2:1-4; 3:7-8, 14-15; 5:11; 12:25-29). The Son's exalted status remains an important datum throughout the sermon, underscoring both the value of remaining connected with Jesus and the danger of dishonoring such a being. Locating the hearers "in the later part of these days" (1:2, my translation) heightens the importance of responding well. The imminence of the end, portending eternal deliverance for the Son's loyal clients and eternal judgment for the Son's enemies (1:13-14), intensifies the importance of the choices made in the present moment. The author's use of Ps. 110:1 (1:3) foreshadows the author's use of the Jewish Scriptures throughout: these texts are so completely a witness to the Son, Jesus, that they can be read to speak of events in his story prior to his birth and after his ascension (events for which there could be no human witnesses).

Hebrews 1:5-14 provides a sampling of how the author sees the "many pieces" (*polymerōs*, 1:1) of God's prior words spoken through prophets (here including David, the traditional author of royal psalms such as Pss. 2; 45; and 110; see Heb. 1:5, 8, 13) coming together in the revelation of the Son. The true significance of those many "pieces" emerges as they are read as though spoken *to*, *about*, or even *by* the Son. The author's focus on the Son's superiority to angels has given rise to the mistaken view that the author addressed some heresy involving an inferior view of Christ or a strange fascination with angels. The rhetorical questions of 1:5, 14, however, presuppose agreement between the author and the recipients on these points. Angels were seen as mediators and messengers: as intercessors in the heavenly temple (*T. Levi* 3:4-8; Tob. 12:12, 15; Matt. 18:10; Rev. 8:3-4) and also as the couriers who brought the law to Israel (see *Jub.* 1:27-29; 2:1; Acts 7:38, 53; Gal. 3:19). The Son will be presented throughout the sermon as a superior mediator and superior messenger, thus more to be held on to and heeded than any previous ones (see the comparisons with Moses and with the Levitical priesthood). Here, the scriptural "proof" of Jesus' superiority to angels (1:5-14) serves to establish the premise (1:4) on which the hortatory conclusion drawn in 2:1-3a will depend.

A second major point is the unchangeableness—the constancy—of the Son vis-à-vis the mutable angels and the temporary material creation (1:7-12). The latter introduces us to the author's cosmology, which is of great importance to the whole of his sermon. The cosmos is divided into two principal parts: the visible, material earth and heavens (skies, stars, etc.) and the invisible realm beyond creation ("heaven itself," 9:24). The first is transitory and will eventually be removed (1:10-12; 12:26-28). The second existed prior to creation and will last forever. Everything belonging to God's realm, therefore, is of infinitely greater quality and value than anything in the material realm—hence, "better," because "lasting" (thematic words in the sermon). This cosmology undergirds the author's exhortations to act with a view to keeping hold of the invisible, eternal goods that God has promised, and not to sacrifice these for short-lived relief in the present age.

Christ's exaltation to God's right hand carries both promise and menace (1:13-14). The author strategically frames the hearers' consideration of their presenting challenges with the "larger" challenge: How should they respond to this Son so as to remain in his favor rather than return to the ranks of his enemies (2:1-4)?

The Text in the Interpretive Tradition

The author ascribed attributes of Wisdom known from Proverbs 8 and Wisdom of Solomon 7–9 (see especially 7:22, 26-27; 8:1; 9:9) to the preincarnate Son, who gives Wisdom a new face. Hebrews 1:1-14 thus became an important resource for early Christian reflection on the relationship of Jesus to God. The analogy of the relationship of "radiance" to "glory" figured prominently in discussions of the Son's sharing in the essence of the Father (Origen, Athanasius, against Arius) and his coexisting with God for eternity: to declare that there was a time when the "radiance" was not would imply that there was a time when the "glory" was not (Gregory of Nyssa).

The comparison of the Son with the angels fed early Christian fascination with the latter. Early theologians were also concerned with how each of these statements applied to each of the two natures of Christ: the divine nature was unchanging and unending in every way; the human nature could experience exaltation to God's right hand (Theodoret of Cyr). These readers accepted without question the Christ-centered interpretation applied to the Hebrew scriptural texts recited by the author, a mode of interpretation they embraced completely (patristic commentary on Hebrews has been conveniently compiled in Heen and Kray 2005).

■ The Text in Contemporary Discussion

Questions abound about the integrity of biblical interpretation in the early church such as Hebrews exhibits. The author does not ground his interpretations in a consideration of the "original meaning" of many of the texts he uses and has therefore been accused of co-opting them for his own group-forming and ideology-sustaining agenda. It is worth noting, however, that his reading also reflects an implicit criticism of his own tradition. For example, his reading transcends the nationalism and the legitimation of a particular system of domination (the Davidic monarchy) inherent in the context of the royal psalms' composition.

The author's cosmology also raises questions. Is it, as many since Bultmann would aver, a relic of a more primitive stage in human thinking? Or does it represent, conversely, a persistent and needful challenge to contemporary philosophical materialism, as well as its practical manifestations in contemporary priorities and practices?

There are strong trends in contemporary scholarship that resist making Jesus more than human. This author's assertions about the "Son" and his place at God's right hand could again seem to reflect a more mythologically driven understanding of the man Jesus. The author will go on to speak about Jesus' complete humanness with the same energy as he speaks of Jesus' proximity to the divine. The fundamental connection between reflecting God's image and being truly human (Gen. 1:26-27; Heb. 1:3) may lead Christians to reexamine the author's language from the point of view that Jesus is *the* Human One (the "son of man") par excellence, the one in whom the image of God is seen fully and without distortion. Jesus reminds his followers of what it means to be human and to show God's image in one's being and doing, as well as revealing something important about the character and commitments of God. Readers may also appreciate the politically subversive overtones of speaking of Jesus as "Son of God" in an environment in which the emperor Tiberius, for example, was named "son of the deified Augustus." The author again is seen to address and oppose the sort of mythic language that legitimated domination systems in favor of an alternative vision of how the divine reaches into and nurtures human community.

Hebrews 2:1-18: God's Son and the Many Sons and Daughters

■ The Text in Its Ancient Context

Hebrews 2:1-4 presents the argumentative point toward which Heb. 1:1-4 and 1:5-14 have been leading. God has spoken a definitive word in the Son (1:1-4); the Son's honor is greater than that of the angels (1:5-14); therefore, since God expected the earlier message articulated through angels (the Torah) to be obeyed and enforced this with the death penalty, the hearers would do well to respond to the Word they heard from the Son with even greater diligence and commitment (2:1-4). The author strategically presents as "drifting away" the course of action that the Christians' neighbors would have urged as "getting back on course," namely, dissociation from the Christian gospel and the group that promoted it. This is the first of several such calls to keep responding to the gospel in a manner befitting the supreme dignity of the Son who enacted and announced it (see also 4:1-11; 6:4-8; 10:26-31; 12:25-29). The author's specific recommendations concerning *how* to keep responding appropriately center mostly on ongoing investment in the lives of one's fellow disciples and ongoing witness—through both speech and action—to the value of Jesus' friendship and God's promises.

The author recalls the hearers' experience of the presence of the supernatural as a divine confirmation of the truth of the gospel, reminding them how their new way of life brought them in line and in contact with God. The description resembles Paul's own reminiscences about his congregations' experiences of conversion (see 1 Cor. 2:1-5; Gal. 3:1-5). Religious experience was an important element in the hearers' process of converting to this new faith.

The discussion returns to the person of the Son, this time focusing on his complete sharing in human nature and experience (2:5-18). The author recites Ps. 8:4-6, called to mind perhaps by the shared interest between this text and Ps. 110:1 in the subjection of "enemies" or "all things" under someone's "feet." While the divine realm (designated by the author as the *oikoumenē* at 1:6; 2:5, informed perhaps by the opposition of the shakable "earth," *gē*, to the unshakable *oikoumenē* in, e.g., Ps. 96:9-10) has been subjected to the Son, not all things have yet been brought under his dominion. But the story *is* unfolding as God indicated: the disciples have witnessed Jesus' humiliation in his incarnation and death and his exaltation, so the remainder must just be a matter of time. The author may show awareness of the fact that the psalm was originally a text about humanity in general. What we "see" in Jesus is the foretaste of what we will yet see when the many sons and daughters share in the glory and honor that the Son now enjoys (2:10).

The author interjects that suffering death on behalf of others, as a manifestation of God's favor (2:9), was the precondition to exaltation. Such costly beneficence supports the author's call for costly gratitude on the hearers' part (see, e.g., 13:12-14). Moreover, the course of Jesus' life through suffering to glory was the result of God's forethought for the hearers in the struggles that God knew *they* would have to endure on *their* journey to lay hold of God's promises. It was "fitting" for God to "perfect" the pioneer—that is, to bring him to the appointed goal of his own journey—through sufferings because God knew that the many sons and daughters would have to journey through sufferings themselves (see, e.g., 10:32-34). Thus God charted out Jesus' path specifically so that he would become fully sympathetic with his followers, and thus be fully committed to helping them in their own struggles to respond faithfully to God, as Jesus had (2:16-18). Speaking of the hearers' experience of rejection as "trials" or "tests" is also strategic: their neighbors' hostility becomes an opportunity to prove themselves, and yielding to such hostility means failing the test (2:18).

Jesus' solidarity with his followers is also exhibited using a string of Scripture citations (2:11-13; see Ps. 22:23; Isa. 8:17-18), where, once again, the author finds the ancient texts' meaning by referring them to—or even placing them on the lips of—Jesus himself. The fact that such an exalted figure (1:1-14) would associate himself so closely and confidently with the marginalized disciples should bolster their own self-respect and repair their esteem.

■ The Text in the Interpretive Tradition

Discussing the nature of the "salvation" or "deliverance" provided through the Son (2:1-4), early theologians focused their readers' expectations not on deliverance from temporal ills or enjoyment of earthly rewards, but rather on deliverance from the power of death and the devil over human beings in this life and the next (John Chrysostom). They were also sensitive to the warning given in this passage, reading it as a stern admonition to be watchful over one's own heart and life, so as not to throw away Jesus' deliverance (Origen, John Chrysostom).

These theologians were also interested in the text's focus on the two natures of Christ who, as God, was always superior to the angels but, as a human being, lived for a short while below them in the order of being (Theodoret of Cyr, Theodore of Mopsuestia)—and that *genuinely* as a human being, against docetist claims to the contrary (Cyril of Alexandria). The fact that not everything was yet subjected to Christ explained the ongoing suffering of his followers: both Christ's own experience of suffering and the promise of his eventual triumph over all things provided encouragement to the many sons and daughters (John Chrysostom).

■ The Text in Contemporary Discussion

Contemporary readers might find themselves alienated from the author's assumption of a future visitation of divine judgment, from which "deliverance" is needed (2:1-3a). On the other hand, many people still believe in some kind of accountability beyond death and hope for "deliverance" resulting in a better postmortem existence (2:10). A belief in divine judgment is often an important ideological prop for continued resistance to cultural and religious imperialism, such as the Christian group experienced at the hands of the dominant Roman culture and the better-empowered Jewish culture.

In an era in which theological violence (inscribed, for example, in satisfaction or substitutionary theories of atonement) has become more highly problematic than in centuries past, the author's interpretation of the cross as Jesus' confronting and destroying the power of death to distort and constrain human life (2:14-15; this was also of interest to early theologians) can provide a constructive alternate model. The fear of death remains a basic datum of the human psyche (Becker, 11–24). It threatens to distort life by driving people to finding ways to "make their mark," to prioritizing their own enjoyment of this brief span over the concerns of others, to avoiding confrontations with the powers that be on behalf of the oppressed, and to more obvious neuroses. The promise of "deliverance" from its power is a great desideratum.

The passage challenges the modern Western allergy to suffering, whether one's own or another person's, making suffering the focal point of God's interest, Jesus' experience, and the experience of humanity, as well as the locus for encountering Jesus' help. The robust theology of the incarnation promoted by the author of Hebrews challenges Western Christians (in particular) not to embrace their culture's avoidance of suffering, but to look more bravely at the plight of the suffering and allow that vision to transform their priorities and practices. On the other hand, many in the Western and in the majority world cannot escape suffering, marginalization, and deprivation. The author of Hebrews holds out a vision in which the God of the universe took a particular interest in them and others like them, conforming the experience of the Son of God to their experience, indeed making people in their plight the chief focal point of the divine redemptive intervention. While this perspective never legitimates the infliction of deprivation or suffering, it lends an empowering dignity to the experience of the same that may assist both endurance and resistance.

Hebrews 3:1-19: The Dangers of Responding with Distrust

The Text in Its Ancient Context

First Samuel 2:35 spoke of God's raising up "a faithful priest" *and* "a faithful house," which may account for the author's transition from the former (2:18) to the latter (3:1-6). The author compares Jesus favorably now with Moses: while the latter was faithful in God's house (see Num. 12:7) as a servant (like the angels, 1:7, 14), the former was faithful *over* God's house as a Son. Both possess the positive virtue of reliability, but Jesus' proximity to God remains closer and his status greater (Attridge, 105). Moses, like the angels, was regarded as a mediator figure (see Exod. 32:7-14, 30-34; *T. Mos.* 11.17; Pseudo-Philo, *L.A.B.* 19.11). The hearers have in Jesus the best-placed mediator of God's favor and promises possible, and should for no reason relinquish that relationship. Their continuing place in God's household depends on it (3:6).

Repeating the pattern of 1:1—2:4, this comparison leads to an exhortation to heed the word spoken by the Son, comparing the audience's situation with that of Moses' generation (3:7-19). The author uses Ps. 95:7-11, with its summons to listen for and heed the divine voice, as a principal scriptural resource. While the original Hebrew recalls three separate incidents of failure to respond well to God's voice (at Massah, Meribah, and Kadesh-barnea), the Greek version focuses only on the episode in Numbers 14, which is essential background for this chapter. With the exceptions of Caleb and Joshua, the exodus generation gave more weight to the hostility and power of the Canaanites than to the promise and power of God, with the result that they disobeyed God's command to take Canaan and were condemned to wander in the desert till they dropped dead (3:8-11, 15-19). The author places his audience in an analogous situation, standing on the very threshold of the greater promised land of the divine realm. Hostile people stand in their way (see, e.g., 10:32-34), but God has given God's assurance of victory and possession. They should, therefore, learn from the exodus generation's example (3:19; 4:11) to persevere in moving forward in trust and obedience to God's call, rather than turn aside (3:12).

The Text in the Interpretive Tradition

Calling Jesus an "apostle" (Heb. 3:1), when many people were called "apostles," seemed not to suit Jesus' unique dignity. Justin Martyr and Theodoret of Cyr read this in terms of the incarnation and Jesus' unique sense of having been "sent" by the Father in the Fourth Gospel. Patristic commentators also recognized that the comparison with Moses stems from the genuine esteem in which the author and audience held Moses (Theodoret of Cyr, John Chrysostom).

While acknowledging the warning inherent in 3:7-19, particularly to the first hearers who found themselves in a situation like that of the wilderness generation (Theodore of Mopsuestia), early commentators also found the emphasis on "Today" to be a source of ongoing encouragement to those who stood in need of repentance. As long as this age lasted, there was hope for the sinner's recovery (John Chrysostom).

The Text in Contemporary Discussion

The author's reading and application of the example of the exodus generation conforms quite closely with modern standards of exegesis, maintaining the distance between the original situation and the situation of application, deriving principles more by analogy than direct application to the new situation. Many modern Christians may have difficulty, however, with the suggestion that belonging to God's household or of remaining Christ's partners is conditional (3:6, 14), because of the theological domination of certain post-Reformation interpretations of *Pauline* texts that negate the contributions of human effort or actions to salvation. Hebrews challenges these interpretations, and could helpfully even raise questions about their correctness in regard to Paul himself.

The text challenges contemporary presuppositions in other important respects. The author presupposes a degree of intimacy and interaction that runs counter to ecclesiastical practices nurtured in a context of Western individualism and of Western conceptualizations of the lines between private and public, insiders and outsiders. The community as a whole is charged with looking out for signs that individuals might be wavering in their commitment and acting to shore up that commitment (3:12-13; see also 4:1; 5:12; 10:24-25; 12:15), as well as investing themselves fully to relieve the pressures that weigh on other members (6:9-10; 13:1-3, 15-16), creating a strong alternative social body (Filson, 69; deSilva 2012, 139–49). Each member of the community bears some responsibility for the perseverance or nonperseverance of the other members. The author does not address his audience as "brothers and sisters" (3:1, 12) because of superficial religious convention, but because he truly expects them to take on the same obligations toward one another (as members of God's household) as they would undertake for their natural family.

This passage is based on a segment of a deeply problematic narrative within the Hebrew Bible, namely, the conquest of the land of Canaan and the genocide that essentially accompanied this conquest. This is a narrative that has repeated itself in the New World in regard to its indigenous peoples as well as within other episodes of colonial conquest throughout the globe. While the author of Hebrews does not explicitly critique this aspect of his own heritage, he offers a delegitimating perspective on the narrative as a call to conquest in the geopolitical sphere of this world. In his understanding, the conquest of Canaan did not accomplish God's purposes for God's people, for Joshua did not, in fact, lead Israel into "God's rest." Similarly, he leaves no room for such a crusade in the visible, material world, for God's people "are seeking a better, that is a heavenly," homeland (11:16). The divine narrative and call is, in his view, not one that invites us into conflict and the quest nation of territory. The history of Western and other colonization, however, has shown the author's reinterpretation not to be influential.

Hebrews 4:1-13: Entering God's "Rest"

■ The Text in Its Ancient Context

"Entering God's rest" is thematic throughout 3:7-19 (see 3:11, 18-19) and becomes even more prominent in 4:1-11 (4:1, 3 [2×], 5, 6 [2×], 10, 11). This drums into the hearers' ears the importance of succeeding in "entering God's rest," drowning out, for the moment at least, other potential agenda items. The author crafts an argument based on Scripture passages related to God's "rest" to establish exactly what this destiny entails. Based on the fact that "David" speaks of a promise to enter God's rest centuries after Joshua led the children of the exodus generation into Canaan (Ps. 95:11; Heb. 4:7-8), the author concludes that the destined "rest" had nothing to do with entry into Canaan. This "rest," furthermore, must exist outside of creation—it was the place where God "rested" after creation, the place where God's full presence dwells eternally (Gen. 2:2; Heb. 4:3-5). Entering God's rest, therefore, speaks of the same reality as the many other images the author uses to speak of the divine realm beyond the visible creation ("glory," 2:10; "the inner side of the curtain," 6:20; "the better, heavenly homeland," 11:16; the "unshakable kingdom," 12:28; the "city that is to come," 13:14). Other texts also conceived of the coming age as an eschatological "sabbatical" (4:9; see *Barn.* 15.3-6; *L.A.E.* 51.2–3). Hebrews 4:10 is an ambiguous verse, but it might be read as an oblique reference to Jesus (Vanhoye, 99–100), who has indeed already entered into God's rest, that is, into "heaven itself," at his ascension (9:12, 24-25) as the forerunner for the hearers (2:10; 6:19-20; 12:2-3).

The author places the hearers at the threshold of this "rest": they "are entering" (3:3a), but still must "make every effort to enter" (4:11; see also 10:19-22, 35-36). The thing to fear is failing to enter, falling into the exodus generation's pattern on the threshold of their own inheritance (4:1, 11). This is a strong ideological move, as some members of the congregation clearly "fear" other losses, which has already led some to defect (10:25). If they accept the author's framing of their position in terms of Numbers 14, they will be more likely to persevere in their commitment to the group and to the cost of continued identification with Jesus in the midst of an unsupportive society.

The passage concludes with a strong warning. Hebrews 4:12 is often quoted as a triumphant testimony to the power of Scripture, but 4:12 and 4:13 together really paint a fearsome image. They compare God's Word, in its power to cut through our psychological defenses and rationalizations, to a two-edged sword—a familiar accoutrement of the omnipresent Roman soldiers that could slice through any part of a human body and send the "soul" to Hades and the "spirit/breath" back to God (4:12). They further compare the hearers to naked victims, whose throats are exposed (Gk. *tetrachēlismena*) to the executioner's blade, awaiting the word from the Judge (4:13). The author's use of wordplay is once again masterful, as he poses the implicit question: What kind of "account" (*logos*, 4:13) will the hearers be able to give in regard to their response to the Word (*logos*, 4:12) announced in the Son?

■ THE TEXT IN THE INTERPRETIVE TRADITION

Patristic- and Reformation-era commentators emphasized the different kinds of "rest" envisioned in Scripture, with the people of faith looking ahead to the perfect tranquility of God's eternal kingdom rather than any earthly kingdom that would always be subject to war and unrest. They were also keenly interested in what 4:12-13 had to say about the power of the Word, usually understood as the Scriptures (with Augustine even relating the double-edged quality to the two testaments), and about the human desire to hide oneself from God's all-searching Word (Ambrose). John Chrysostom and Martin Luther viewed 4:12-13 as a warning concerning the judgment of the ungodly.

■ THE TEXT IN CONTEMPORARY DISCUSSION

More objections could be raised concerning the author's exegesis in 4:1-11 than 3:7-19, most notably the fallacy of claiming that Ps. 95:11 actually speaks of a "rest" other than the one denied the exodus generation at Kadesh-barnea. The psalmist himself uses the Numbers 14 incident to illustrate a poor response to God's word, urging worshipers to be more attentive to God's voice than were their ancestors, and the oath (Ps. 95:11) is just part of that example. Nevertheless, by the canons of first-century biblical interpretation (notably the application of the rule of *gezera shawa*, the use of one verse, like Gen. 2:2, to interpret a second verse, like Ps. 95:11, linked by a common lexical element, like "rest"), the author's argument has integrity. He is also ultimately pointing to a conceptual reality (God's realm) that is amply attested elsewhere, so that his exegesis aligns with his contemporaries' cosmology.

A more pressing question concerns the author's appeals to fear here and elsewhere throughout his sermon. Many contemporary people of faith would not regard fear to be an adequate—or a spiritually mature—motivator of religious commitment. They would critique a theology that incorporated notions of God as a more powerful being willing to exercise that power in violent, punitive ways intending harm—the potential that is prerequisite to "fear." The text might challenge these readers in return, however, asking whether the modern discomfort with "fear" reflects their failure to apprehend the power and holiness of the divine and, thus, the demands placed on their response, if that response is to be appropriate.

Hebrews 4:14—5:10: God's Son as Sympathetic Mediator

■ THE TEXT IN ITS ANCIENT CONTEXT

Arousing particular emotions in an audience was an integral part of the ancient art of persuasion (see, e.g., Aristotle, *Rhet.* 2.1–11). While the author crafted images designed to arouse fear in 4:12-13, he turns immediately in 4:14-16 to craft an appeal designed to instill confidence in the hearers. This pattern recurs throughout the sermon (6:4-8 // 6:9-12; 10:26-31 // 10:32-36), with the author associating cause for fear with drifting away from commitment to the group and its confession, and cause for confidence with perseverance in commitment to Christ and one another.

While the audience endured significant losses as a result of their conversion (10:32-34), the author dwells extensively on what they also now "have" as a result—here the help of Jesus, God's Son, to keep them connected with God and God's favor. The author urges the hearers to deal with the pressures they face not by acquiescing (and thus withdrawing from the group), but by going confidently before God in prayer (and thus drawing closer to the center of the group), seeking God's resources and support to meet any and every challenge to perseverance (4:16).

The concept of a mediator or "broker" whose main gift was providing a connection with a better-placed patron was well known in the Hellenistic-Roman world. Priests were de facto brokers of divine patronage (5:1). Like other priests (ideally), Jesus was sympathetic toward his clients' weaknesses, having experienced the same trials and tests himself (2:14, 17-18; 4:15). Unlike other priests, however, Jesus was not overcome by any of those tests, such that he himself affronted God by transgression and had first to make peace between himself and God before he could secure God's favors for others (4:15; 5:2-3; 7:27). While the author will affirm Jesus' complete identification with the readers in their shared humanity (2:14-18), he also will not allow them to forget his distance from them (both in terms of proximity to God and sinlessness)—a distance that proves, in the end, to be to their ultimate advantage.

The Scriptures provide "proof" of Jesus' legitimate appointment to serve as such a mediator: the author finds this proof in Ps. 110:4, a little further on in the same psalm that spoke of the Son's exaltation (Ps. 110:1; see Heb. 1:13; 8:1; 10:12; 12:2). Again, he discovers the significance of the ancient text by hearing it as if spoken *to* Jesus. The significance of this appointment to serve "in the order of Melchizedek" (5:6, 10) will occupy Heb. 7:1-28.

Readers tend to identify the portrait of Jesus in 5:7-9 with the account of Jesus' agony in Gethsemane (Mark 14:32-42 and parallels), even though the author otherwise shows no signs of familiarity with the Synoptic tradition. The author's portrait also closely aligns with depictions of righteous petitioners and intercessors in other Jewish texts (e.g., 2 Macc. 11:6; 3 Macc. 1:16; 5:7, 25; Attridge, 151). Jesus emerges here more as a model of offering pious, committed prayer. It is unclear whether the phrase "although he was a Son" qualifies what precedes or follows (a question raised as early as the ninth century by Photius of Constantinople). The majority of translations favor reading this in connection with Jesus learning through suffering, as if this should *not* be expected for a "Son." However, in 12:5-11, the author will argue precisely that legitimate sons and daughters *should* expect to experience formative discipline. It may thus be preferable to read the concessive clause ("although he was a Son") as qualifying what precedes: it was Jesus' *piety* that led to his being heard by God, and thus an example of what any pious follower could hope for; it was not a case of preferential treatment.

The language of "perfection" and "being perfected" pervades this sermon. This word group appears generally to speak of a person or thing having arrived at its final state or goal (such that it describes the child who has reached adulthood, or an ordinary person when the rite of consecration to priesthood is complete). Here, Jesus' perfection relates to his having entered God's realm after the completion of his course, from which vantage point he is able to exercise his mediation (deSilva 2000, 194–204).

■ The Text in the Interpretive Tradition

Early commentators tended to read this text (particularly 5:7-9) through the lens of Christ's two natures, stressing how it applied to the human nature but not to the divine, which was not subject to suffering (Theodoret of Cyr, John Chrysostom). At the same time, they highly valued what this passage has to say about Jesus' subjection to every manner of trial and temptation that might afflict his followers, making him sympathetic to the plight of the human beings who seek refuge in him now and in the judgment (Theodoret of Cyr), and also about Jesus' sinlessness, making him an empowering example and a suitably blameless offering (Leo the Great).

■ The Text in Contemporary Discussion

It is important to remember, when reading material that seems at the surface to be so otherworldly and theological, that the author of Hebrews writes, essentially, to equip members of a voluntary counterculture to maintain the will to resist cultural, religious, and other forms of domination and repression. Holding on to their "confession" (4:14) is an act of resistance against the dominant culture's religious practices, against their more empowered neighbors' attempts to enforce conformity to the same, and against the prevailing mythos that legitimates power relations within the Roman Empire. It is, similarly, an act of resistance against a tolerated subculture's (Judaism's) attempts to enforce conformity among Jewish converts to the Christian movement. Keeping the original setting and challenges of the sermon firmly in our minds helps us remain attentive to how the author uses theological and traditional resources in settings where resistance is costly but necessary, if one's integrity is to remain intact.

The summons to prayer (4:14-16) and the portrait of Jesus' engaging in prayer to equip him to run his course (rather than to allow him to avoid unpleasantness) also challenges the expectations of many modern people of faith, for whom prayer and God represent ways *out* of suffering rather than ways to persevere *through* suffering. The experience of suffering is, for the author of Hebrews, neither the result of failed or unanswered prayer, nor a cause to question God's goodness or existence. Rather, Jesus' example suggests that suffering—here, particularly suffering endured as a result of responding faithfully to God's call—becomes an opportunity for deepening obedience and for discovering God's ability to provide the resources required to persevere in faithfulness so as to experience not deliverance *from* death, but deliverance *on the other side of* death.

Hebrews 5:11—6:20: Summons to Respond Honorably and Appropriately

■ The Text in Its Ancient Context

The author pauses in his exploration of Jesus as "high priest in the order of Melchizedek" (5:10) to attend to his hearers' disposition. He wants to ensure that they will listen attentively and commit to invest themselves fully in their response to Jesus' investment in them. He chides them for not having yet taken up the responsibility for keeping one another steadfast in their commitment ("becoming teachers"), acting instead like children waiting for him to come alongside and administer the needed instruction and discipline. "Milk" and "meat" (or "solid food") were common metaphors for the stages of instruction through which a person passed in any educational process. In keeping with Greco-Roman philosophical discourse, the author uses these metaphors to shame the hearers into taking responsibility for living up to their potential and to what they already knew to be true (cf. Epictetus, *Diatr.* 2.16.39; *Ench.* 51.1).

The author urges the hearers to invest themselves in persevering together toward the final goal (the "perfection" or "completion," 6:1) of the pilgrimage that began with their conversion and instruction in the fundamental tenets of the Christian worldview (6:1-2). The metaphor of growing into maturity (becoming *teleios*) in 5:11-14 is morphed into the metaphor of moving forward to the end of a journey (*teleiōtes*). This exhortation is supported with an argument from the contrary: failure to move forward amounts to desertion of one's benefactor and a trampling on his gifts (6:4-6). Repentance here refers not to the act of contrition (see on 12:15-16), but to restoration—in effect, "starting over" with God from step one (cf. the place of "repentance" in 6:1). The audience will likely accept the claim that restoration to favor is "impossible" based on their cultural knowledge of the expectations of patron-client relationships (the social context of "grace" relationships; deSilva 2000; 2012): "those who insult their benefactors will by nobody be esteemed to deserve a favor" (Dio Chrysostom, *Or.* 31.65).

The author further supports this warning with an argument from analogy taken from agricultural practice. Sowing, reaping, and quality of soil were frequently used metaphors in ancient discussions of giving benefits and responding to a benefactor's kindness (see Seneca, *Ben.* 1.1.2; 2.11.4-5; 4.8.2; 4.33.1-2; Pseudo-Phocylides, *Sentences* 152). The gifts that God has lavished on the congregation (6:4-5) ought to produce a suitable return that will please the divine Patron who has "cultivated" this relationship with them. If the hearers return insult for grace by choosing friendship with the non-Christian society over a friendship with God in which God has invested so much, they should expect fiery retribution (6:8; 10:26-31).

Up to this point, however, the hearers have largely responded well. The author recalls their investment of themselves and their resources in one another, helping one another persevere in the face of hostile neighbors. Because they have responded nobly to God's favor, God, being just, will continue to favor them (6:9-10). The warning of 6:4-8 serves, in the end, to sustain the hearers' "long obedience in the same direction" (Nietzsche), their responsiveness to God's call (6:11-12).

Abraham naturally comes to mind as an example of "those who inherited the promises through trust and perseverance" (6:12; see *Jub.* 17:17-18; 19:3, 8). Oaths are a common feature in courtrooms and other contexts where added assurances of truthfulness are called for (see Aristotle, *Rhet.* 1.15.27–32). While human beings might indeed take such oaths deceptively, they tended nevertheless to carry considerable weight (6:16; see Philo, *Dreams* 1.12). God gave such an assurance to Abraham (Gen. 22:17), but the author avers that God gave such an oath to the hearers as well. This promise and oath are both found in Ps. 110:4 and depend on reading this verse as *addressing* Jesus (like Ps. 110:1). Describing the hearers as people who have "fled" subtly reminds them of the greater dangers that they have escaped (viz., "eternal judgment," 6:2) by joining the Christian movement, and thus of the advantage of persevering. Jesus is consistently described as going where the hearers would one day enter, and thus their connection with Jesus remains an assurance of their own entrance into the divine realm (see 2:9-10; 12:2).

This brings the author back to the place from which he will resume his exploration of Jesus' priesthood (cf. 5:10 with 6:20).

The Text in the Interpretive Tradition

Interpreters have long struggled with the author's claims about the impossibility of restoration to favor through repentance after some grievous—but unspecified—sin. Tertullian (*Pud.* 20) and the Novatians (see Epiphanius, *Pan.* 59.1.1–3.5) argued that the passage barred those who, after having been baptized, committed serious sins (like apostasy and adultery) from restoration. Those who favored restoration of the penitent argued, in turn, against the authority of Hebrews on the basis of its non-Pauline authorship (e.g., Gaius the Elder; see Eusebius, *Hist. eccl.* 6.20.3).

Another stream of interpretation focused on reading this passage primarily as a warning intended to spur Christians on in their commitment to discipleship, calling them to take the consequences of willful persistence in sin seriously enough to avoid such paths and to match God's gifts with earnest striving to make progress in the new life (see Clement of Alexandria, *Strom.* 2.13; 4.20; Origen, *Hom. Jer.* 13.2; Erasmus, *Paraphrase*, 227–28). Ambrose (*Paen.* 2.2) and John Chrysostom (*Hom. Heb.* 9.5–10.1) solved the problem by reading the passage not as a prohibition against readmitting the penitent, but merely against rebaptism, essentially turning the passage *into* an exhortation to repent speedily, lest one alienate God further and further (so also Luther and Calvin). Whether a person's repentance was effective would be evident in his or her amendment of life.

Luther used the language of Heb. 6:4-6 to denounce the view that the Mass was a repetition of Christ's sacrifice, since this would amount to crucifying Jesus anew (*Misuse of the Mass, LW* 36:147), and the quest to establish one's own righteousness apart from Christ, which meant trampling Christ underfoot (cf. Heb. 10:29; *LW* 52:282), though he did not deny that such people could repent of such practices.

The Text in Contemporary Discussion

Contemporary Christian readings of Heb. 6:4-8 often continue the historical patterns of interpretation, forcing it to speak in conformity with particular theological positions. For example, the passage's meaning and challenge are frequently limited by an interpreter's adherence to the doctrine of "eternal security," the idea that once a person has trusted in Jesus and been "saved," that person cannot then fall away (Gleason; Oberholtzer). Such approaches fail to do justice to the fact that the author of Hebrew conceives of "salvation" or "deliverance" as something still ahead of himself and his audience (1:14; 9:28), thus not something already possessed so as to be "lost." Alternatively, the passage can be applied at face value where the "unpardonable sin" has been committed, usually identified as a decisive moment of apostasy (Lane 1991a:142).

Other Christian scholars are reluctant to apply the passage beyond situations analogous to the situation specifically addressed by the author and outside his own rhetorical purpose, which was to motivate perseverance in commitment to the Christian faith, practice, and community, even when such commitment carried an unwelcome price tag. Thus the passage has force as an exhortation to believers, but not as case law to be applied to those who have "fallen away," to whom the author might indeed have addressed himself differently. The author thus does not make an absolute statement about the limits of God's beneficence, but about the parameters within which recipients of God's costly gifts must act and the considerations they should keep before them as they weigh any courses of action (deSilva 2000). The author of Hebrews is thus understood to preach "costly grace," the necessity of responding nobly and justly, whatever the cost, to a God who has given so much (Bonhoeffer). If the author's real intent was to suggest that it would be unthinkable for persons who have received such great gifts from God to respond in any way that showed a lack of valuing the gifts and dishonored the giver, readers might take issue with the way he has couched this argument in terms of what God might or might not forgive.

Hebrews 7:1-28: The "Better" High Priestly Mediator

The Text in Its Ancient Context

This passage begins the "long and complicated message" about Jesus' high priesthood, which extends through 10:18. The author opens by considering the founder of the priestly "order of Melchizedek" named by Ps. 110:4. Every detail of (or silence concerning!) Melchizedek's story (see Gen. 14:17-20) is interpreted in such a way as makes this shadowy figure a prototype for Jesus, legitimating Jesus' unconventional appointment to priestly office. "Peace" and "righteousness" were attributes of the Messiah's government (e.g., Isa. 9:6-7; 11:1-9; *4 Ezra* 13:37-39; *T. Levi* 18.2–4). The silence concerning Melchizedek's genealogy established the possibility of a priesthood based not on pedigree (descent from Levi, 7:13-14), but on some other quality—here, the quality of a life without beginning or ending (7:3, 15-17, 23-25). The author finds this intimated in the phrase "a priest *forever*" (Ps. 110:4; Heb. 7:16-17)—not just made a priest permanently (i.e., for life), but a priest eternally ("forever").

Melchizedek's priestly line is not just different, however, but superior, as demonstrated from Abraham's giving the tribute of a tithe to Melchizedek. Because an ancestor was thought of as holding within himself his entire line, the author can assert that Levi and his priestly descendants paid the tithe to Melchizedek (and *his* successor, Jesus), acknowledging the latter's superiority (7:4-10). Jesus' priestly mediation, moreover, is supported by God's oath ("the Lord has sworn and will not change his mind," Ps. 110:4), giving the new covenant, of which Jesus is the guarantor, a more certain foundation than the old (Heb. 7:20-22; see 6:13-20).

The author employs another argument from chronology (Spicq, 1:365): the fact that God spoke through David about appointing a new priest (Ps. 110:4) demonstrates that the earlier priesthood and the covenant that regulated it—and that it, in turn, sustained—had been superseded (7:11-12, 18-19). Why would God set aside the former covenant? The Levitical priesthood and its covenant were not able to "perfect" the worshipers, meaning, to fit them to enter into God's presence. Indeed, these worshipers were not fitted even to enter the inner chambers of the *copy* of God's realm, the tabernacle and temple, let alone "heaven itself," by the Levitical mediators (7:11, 19; 9:1-10). The author presupposes here that God's ultimate goal for God's people was not a static situation in which the majority were kept at a safe distance from God's holy dwelling but a dynamic process by which they would be brought into God's dwelling forever, such that God would indeed "dwell in their midst" (see Ezek. 37:27; Zech. 2:11; 2 Cor. 6:16b; Rev. 21:3-4, 22; 22:3b-4).

■ The Text in the Interpretive Tradition

Melchizedek drew the attention of patristic commentators who were predisposed to such typological forays into the Hebrew Bible. Some early voices regarded Melchizedek as a divine being, but Epiphanius employed this passage to refute their position. These commentators also embraced the arguments concerning the insufficiency of the provisions of the Mosaic covenant for accomplishing God's purposes for human beings, seeing in the advent, ministry, and death of Jesus the perfection of those imperfect types that came before (Theodoret of Cyr, John Chrysostom). Discussions of Jesus' death as a sacrifice naturally occasion discussions of the Eucharist, which is seen as a remembrance and not a reenactment of Jesus' unique and all-sufficient priestly act (Theodoret of Cyr, Bede).

■ The Text in Contemporary Discussion

Particularly in a world where people make competing claims concerning how best to relate to God (or the gods), how do Christians know that they can trust what the church says about Jesus and the consequences of his mediation between human beings and God? How do Christians know that God looks on Jesus and his mediation the way the church *says* God does? The author and his congregation certainly lived in such a world, and the author's attempts to construct tightly reasoned arguments from Scripture in this chapter reflect his interest in answering these questions for his audience. Whether or not his particular arguments (or the data on which they are based, like Jesus' ascension) "work" for contemporary Christians, the question remains.

Some Christians readers have decided that they cannot trust the claims made about Jesus in Hebrews—that he was, at best, a remarkable teacher with a compelling vision for human community that still merits our attention, even commitment. His death revealed his own commitment to that vision and perpetually reminds his followers of the potential cost of pursuing that vision, but does not directly impinge on one's relationship with God. For such Christians, the author of Hebrews' arguments will not carry weight. In the end, however, such arguments were not the starting point even for the author and his audience themselves. Rather, their starting point was the experience of God opened up for people in Jesus' name (2:3-4; 6:4-5; 10:22; cf. Gal. 3:1-5; 4:6-7). Again, this raises the issue for people of all faith traditions of the importance of valuing religious experience over arguments concerning religious truth in an increasingly naturalistic environment.

Hebrews 8:1-13: The "Better" Covenant

■ The Text in Its Ancient Context

Hebrews 8:1-13 advances the discussion in two respects. First, it establishes the existence of a divinely made, heavenly tabernacle and the superiority of the same to the terrestrial, material, human-made copy, based on a widely held exegesis of Exod. 25:40 (see also Wis. 9:8; Acts 7:44; 2

Bar. 4:1-7). Jesus' ascension is interpreted as his relocation to officiate in this greater sanctuary (Heb. 8:1-5; 9:24), where God is fully present. Second, it identifies an authoritative text in which God, speaking in God's own voice, invalidates the former covenant with its arrangements in favor of a "new" covenant (Jer. 31:31-34; Heb. 8:7-13). The essential element of this new covenant is God's promise decisively to remove the worshipers' sins even from God's *own* memory, thus enabling them to approach God's holy presence without fear of being consumed on account of their defilements. The author will return to this in 10:17 after showing how Jesus is the agent through whom this decisive purification takes place.

The Text in the Interpretive Tradition

Patristic theologians read the author's interpretation of Jeremiah 31:31-34 as an authoritative declaration concerning the invalidation of the Mosaic covenant on account of its perceived limitations. This, in turn, reinforced their prejudices against Judaism in general and its sacrificial cult in particular (Bede). Nevertheless, these authors also regarded the author of Hebrews to validate the importance of the old covenant as "type" and prophetic prefiguring of what would be accomplished in Jesus, thus affirming the connection between the covenants (Theodoret of Cyr).

The Text in Contemporary Discussion

Hebrews 8 acutely raises the problem of supersessionism (the idea that Christianity has *replaced* Judaism in God's dealings with humanity, not merely grown up alongside it), particularly in a post-Holocaust environment (as in any setting in which the church is empowered and the synagogue more marginal and disempowered). This is exacerbated by the author's use of Septuagint Jeremiah, which renders the Hebrew "although I was their husband" (a clause attesting to intimate involvement and concern) as "I ceased to be concerned about them," which contrasts with other voices expressing their own and God's ongoing concern for Israel (e.g., Paul's heartfelt wrestling with the question in Romans 9–11).

Even while asserting a radical discontinuity between an old and a new covenant and priesthood, the author nevertheless grounds the new fully in, and legitimates it fully on, the old. Continuity with the earlier revelations of the God of Israel remains essential to his enterprise. In this regard, he challenges post-Holocaust Christians to continue to search out this continuity in their own attempts to extend their understanding of God's work in an ever-changing world.

Hebrews 9:1—10:18: The "Better" Sacrifice

The Text in Its Ancient Context

The author focuses now on the ritual that both inaugurates the new covenant and effects the decisive cleansing of sin's defilement from the worshipers' consciences and God's presence. While the author evokes pictures of a sequence of ritual acts ostensibly played out in the heavenly sanctuary, these pictures are meant collectively to interpret the significance for the divine-human relationship of this-worldly events: the crucifixion of Jesus and its aftermath.

The primary templates ("types") for framing the discussion are the Day of Atonement ritual (Leviticus 16, an essential chapter for understanding this section) and, less prominently, the covenant inauguration ritual (Exod. 24:1-8; see Heb. 9:15-22). The former involves ritual acts "outside the camp" (the sending of the scapegoat to die in the desert and the burning of the bodies of the sacrificial animals; Lev. 16:20-22, 27) and a ritual act involving the taking of blood into the holy of holies (Lev. 16:15-19). These acts now provide the meaning behind Jesus' crucifixion "outside the city" (Heb. 9:14; 13:12) and ascension into the heavenly holy of holies (Heb. 9:11-14, 23-26): the worshipers' consciences on earth are cleansed, and the defilement of the heavenly place of intercession by the worshipers' sins is removed, thus wiped clean as far as God is concerned (Nelson, 76–78, 148–52).

The author offers, as further evidence for the inefficacy of the sacrifices performed in the earthly tabernacle, their annual repetition (10:1-3). The layout of the earthly tabernacle/temple and the ongoing limitations of access to the inner sanctum signify the failure of the Levitical sacrifices to bring God and human beings as closely together as God intended (9:6-7), proof once again of the need for new cultic arrangements. He attributes this ineffectiveness, in part, to the reliance on the blood of animals as the medium for reconciliation and purification, drawing on popular philosophy (Thompson, 103–15) and the Jewish prophetic critiques of animal sacrifices as inadequate for any spiritual or ethical purpose (9:13; 10:4; cf. Isa. 1:11-13, 16-17; Hosea 6:6). He finds scriptural support for his claims (which contradict such key texts as Lev. 16:30; 17:11) in the Greek version of Ps. 40:6-8, read as if spoken by Jesus himself. The Hebrew original speaks of God's preferring obedience to Torah to the sin offerings that followed disobedience. While the Greek translator probably had the same intent, the author of Hebrews finds in the Greek version now a warrant for "a body"—the human body that the Son took on in his incarnation—as the sacrifice that God appointed to be offered in place of the ineffective animal sacrifices (10:5-10).

That Jesus' priestly work was decisively accomplished after his unique offering of himself is demonstrated through an inference drawn from the thematic Ps. 110:1. Priests performed their duties while standing (Deut. 10:8; 18:7); the fact that Jesus, the priest in Melchizedek's line, was invited by God to "sit" (Heb. 10:11-14) signals the successful accomplishment of reconciliation, the decisive removal of sins promised as part of the "new covenant" (10:15-18). As the final act of the Levitical high priest on the Day of Atonement was to return from the holy of holies to declare forgiveness to the people, so the author speaks once more of Jesus' forthcoming return from "heaven itself" to bring final deliverance to his followers (and subjection to his enemies; 9:28; 10:13).

■ The Text in the Interpretive Tradition

The author of Hebrews restrained himself in regard to the symbolic significance of each item in the sanctuary, but the same was not true of early Christian commentators, who interpreted the layout of the tabernacle and its accoutrements allegorically as representations of elements of the cosmos or of the human psyche (Origen, John Cassian, Bede, Luther). Again, Jesus' one-time sacrifice is related to the regular remembrance of the same in the Eucharist (John Chrysostom, Luther). This lengthy passage also served to reinforce early Christian discourse concerning the relationship of the Mosaic covenant and Hebrew Scriptures to the new covenant as type of fulfillment or shadow to the reality casting the shadow (Origen, John Chrysostom, Symeon the New Theologian, Bede). These commentators continue to embrace the author's Christocentric lens as the appropriate resource for interpreting particular Old Testament texts like Psalm 40 (John Chrysostom).

The Text in Contemporary Discussion

The author of Hebrews provides the earliest thoroughgoing interpretation of the significance of Jesus' death and ascension for humanity's relationship with the divine. Contemporary theologians have been moving away from thinking about Jesus' reconciliation of humankind with God in terms of sacrificial metaphors (with their emphasis on the spilled blood and the death of a victim). This is motivated not just by a growing distaste with images involving the actual slaughter of a victim, but also by a desire not to sanction an act of political injustice and oppression (the brutal execution of a dissenting voice) with a theological overlay and not to continue to attribute to God the desire for blood and death.

We should not lose sight, however, of the fact that the author of Hebrews was using this language figuratively as a means of helping his hearers appropriate for themselves the significance of Jesus' death for their relationship with God. He could not have imagined Jesus carrying physical blood into "heaven itself": the blood is a metonym for Jesus' absolute obedience and commitment to God, undeterred by the prospect of a bloody death. Jews reflected on the deaths of the martyrs for Torah in similar terms, positing that such extreme commitment to the covenant acted as the equivalent of an effecting atonement offering on behalf of the nation: but again it was their obedience, not their blood, that satisfied the alienated Deity and restored God's favor toward the nation (2 Macc. 7:37-38; 8:5; 4 Macc. 6:29-31; 17:21-22; see deSilva 1998, 137–41). Jesus' death can be similarly understood as an offering of representative obedience that restores God's favor—as well as redirects humanity's hearts back to God and pursuing what pleases God out of a desire to maintain this restored relationship.

Hebrews 10:19-39: Summons to Persevere in Faithful Response

The Text in Its Ancient Context

The author concludes his sermon with a climactic exhortation to persevere in the course of action that shows proper gratitude and loyalty toward God (10:19-13:25). The "long and complicated word" about Jesus' high-priestly mediation (7:1-10:18) provides the basis for an exhortation to hold on to the advantages this mediation has gained, which includes nothing less than the "boldness" to enter God's very presence when "the Day" of Christ's visitation and the eschatological removal of the visible, material creation arrives (10:25; see 9:28; 12:26-28).

This course of action involves group-sustaining practices. "Drawing near" to their destiny (10:22; the opposite of "shrinking back," 10:37-39) means continuing to meet together and engage in community- and identity-maintaining activities such as public witness to their hope and mutual encouragement and care (10:23-25). English translations since the KJV often err in regard to 10:24. The Greek does not speak of considering *how to provoke* other disciples to do good and to show love (CEB; NIV; NLT; NRSV); rather, the author urges his hearers to consider their fellow believers with the result that they themselves will be motivated by what they see to show love and do good

(NJB; Lane 1991b, 273; Ellingworth, 526). The author would have the hearers feel confidence in regard to continuing in this path.

If some are disposed to throw it all away because they have a greater concern for what they have lost in this transitory world (10:25a), what are the implications of doing so? The author answers this in 10:26-31 (strongly reminiscent of 6:4-6). By describing the alternative course of action as "sinning willfully" (10:26; see Num. 15:22-31), the author reminds the audience that there is *always* a choice to be made between bearing up under their neighbors' disapproval and hostility and giving in, thus betraying their commitments to God and one another. He employs another "lesser-to-greater" argument to propose that the fate of those who break faith with the Son will be worse than the fate of those who broke faith with the Mosaic covenant (10:28-29; cf. 2:1-4), that is, a fate worse than death (reciting Deut. 17:6). Preferring their neighbors' friendship to the continuing friendship of God means trampling God's Son (who awaits all things to be subjected under *his* feet, Heb. 1:13; 10:13) and meeting favor with insult (10:29). The stark impropriety of such images is calculated to shock the audience into seeing defection as an absurd, and ultimately more dangerous, choice with much more frightful consequences than persevering in faith (10:27, 30-31).

The author returns to topics that will arouse confidence in place of fear in 10:32-36. Like a general pointing out his troops' former victories, the author recalls the audience's former investment in and commitment to their cause (10:32-34) as the best model for them to imitate in the future (10:35-36). Their former courage in the face of their neighbor's repressive pressure exhibited *parrhēsia*—the boldness to declare one's convictions and commitments in the face of power and violence, an ancient political value. The author urges them, after giving such testimony to the value of Jesus, his gifts, and his promises, not to be cowed into silence now. Maintaining "boldness" in the face of society's hostility is intimately connected with retaining their "boldness" to enter God's presence at last (10:19, 35).

▌The Text in the Interpretive Tradition

Hebrews 10:26-31 posed many of the same problems and concerns as 6:4-8, and thus received similar attention. Most read the passage as a call to repentance (Oecumenius) and as a call to take seriously the need to turn from sin rather than continue to indulge it (Theodore of Mopsuestia). The ongoing possibility of repentance, however, was not to become an excuse for a continuous cycle of sin and repentance, which was no better than apostasy with a conscience (Clement of Alexandria, *Strom.* 2.13.56–57).

John Chrysostom recognized the rhetorical force of speaking of events meant by the Christians' neighbors to shame them into conforming once again with their former lives as a "contest" (10:32). Victims become contestants, and resisting pressures to conform becomes the path to an honorable victory in God's sight.

▌The Text in Contemporary Discussion

The theological problems concerning the place of fear in mature discipleship and the positing of unpardonable sins (10:26-31) were already discussed in regard to 4:12-13; 6:4-8. The author's use of Scripture again raises issues for the modern reader. At 10:37-38, the author combines a phrase from Isa. 26:20 with Hab. 2:3-4 in order to stress the imminence of God's visitation, and further rearranges the phrases of the Habakkuk passage in order to craft an antithesis between persevering in faith and shrinking back in fear. Eusebius, who recognized these changes, affirmed this as an appropriate correction of that which was obscure in the older text. Modern readers might be more willing to question how far one can go to shape a text to address the need of a situation before one has done violence to it and undermined the integrity of one's argument.

The author's selective introduction of Isa. 26:20 into this recitation also raises the issue of the early Christian belief in the imminent return of Jesus to dispense judgment and rewards. While Christians may still affirm that "he will come again to be our judge" (Nicene Creed), they may justifiably ask—after two millennia passing without the Day, which may still be "drawing nearer," actually arriving—what "in just a very little while" was supposed to mean and whether the author ought rather to have prepared his congregation for resistance over the long haul. This question remains relevant to Christian leaders' seeking to encourage congregations in repressive environments throughout the world.

These potential limitations, however, do not negate the force of the author's challenge to contemporary Christians to exercise "boldness" in regard to their witness in the face of modern systems of domination built on values and goals different from, and in many instances antithetical to, the values and goals for human community attested in the Scriptures. To the extent that people of any faith tradition are bound to temporal goods and enjoyments, are geared toward seeking acceptance by their neighbors, and fear hostile confrontation, they will be cowed into not bearing witness—both in speech and in living practice—to those latter values and goals. The author would consider this a gross failure in Christians' obligation to their divine Patron.

Hebrews 11:1—12:3: Encomium on Faith

■ THE TEXT IN ITS ANCIENT CONTEXT

Hebrews is probably best known for its portrait of "faith" in action, the encomium (a laudatory, celebratory speech) on the "heroes of faith" and how they responded to God's word and promise in the midst of challenging circumstances. The author shapes these examples to address the specific challenges facing the addressees (deSilva 1995, 165–208; Eisenbaum, 178–83), providing them with a model (see 6:11-12) of how to respond advantageously in light of Christ's imminent visitation (10:37-39).

One recurring theme is that people of faith respond to the challenges and circumstances of the moment with a view to God's future intervention and to the invisible realities beyond this world (11:1). Noah orients his whole activity around meeting a disaster yet to come (11:7); Abraham moves throughout his life with his eyes fixed on the promise of receiving a homeland in the future (11:8-22); Joseph gives instructions about his burial on the basis of God's future acts on behalf of the Hebrews (11:22); Moses chose his allegiances with a view to God's future acts of liberation and the future reward (11:23-27), and so forth. People of faith take their bearing in this life from the invisible Cause of the visible world (11:3), as did Moses (11:27). Looking to the future acts of

God and to the invisible realm are vitally important components of the author's program for his audience, who must conduct themselves now in such a way as to encounter future crises successfully (1:13; 2:3; 10:30-31, 37-39) and to maintain their grasp of goods as yet not seen (3:6, 14; 6:12; 10:34-35; 11:16; 12:28; 13:14).

A second recurring theme is that the person of faith accepts temporal loss and deprivation for the sake of eternal ("abiding," "lasting") gain (deSilva 2012, 64–83). Such acceptance gives the person of faith freedom to pursue this greater hope and calling. The author particularly crafts certain examples in such a way as to resonate as strongly as possible with the addressees' plight in their setting. Abraham leaves behind his place in his homeland, accepting the lower status of sojourner and alien in Canaan, mirroring the audience's loss of status within their native cities (11:9, 13). The patriarchs' rejection of being "at home" in their native land becomes a source of witness to the "better, heavenly homeland" that they seek (11:14-16). Moses relinquished his status in Pharaoh's household, choosing to identify with God's marginalized people and the reproach that befalls God's people and God's "Anointed" in this world (11:24-26; cf. 10:32-34; 13:3, 13). Prophets and martyrs (see *Liv. Pro.*; 2 Maccabees 6–7; 4 Maccabees 5–17) accepted being driven into the margins of society and even being subjected to the degradation of torture and death for the sake of loyalty to God and the "better resurrection" God would bestow on God's faithful clients (10:32-34; 11:35-38; 13:3).

Jesus crowns the list of examples as the "perfecter of faith" (not, as in many translations, the "perfecter of *our* faith"), such that one needs to read the exhortation of 12:1-3 in connection with 11:1-40. Jesus showed faith to the utmost degree by "enduring a cross, despising shame." The path of responding obediently to God and attaining the reward God set before him involved embracing the most abject humiliation (including the "verbal abuse" with which so many of the addressees could relate, 12:3) and suffering, showing that faith looks not to human approval but only to God's approval and, in so doing, attains eternal honor and place. The addressees' past behavior also falls into this commendable pattern (10:32-34), and the author shapes his exhortations simply to urge them to continue to exhibit that kind of commitment to God and to one another, deliberating with a view to holding on to God's promises, not temporal goods.

■ The Text in the Interpretive Tradition

Patristic authors give ample attention to these heroes of faith as moral examples of a foundational virtue in Christian culture, with the example of Jesus crowning the series. In dying for our sake, Jesus obligates us all the more to endure for his sake and to be willing to despise temporal honor in order to attain the lasting honor in God's sight (John Chrysostom). These authors also tend to interpret these figures as "types" prefiguring Jesus in some way, reading chapter 11 as if the author himself were continuing to appeal to Hebrew scriptural narratives typologically, as he had in regard to Moses, Joshua, and the Levitical cult and its staff. Their own penchant for a typological reading of the Hebrew Bible takes over, as it were. This is especially true in regard to Abraham's near-sacrifice of Isaac (Athanasius, Theodoret of Cyr, Augustine), Moses and the Passover (Theodoret of Cyr, John Chrysostom), and Rahab's scarlet thread (Justin Martyr, John Chrysostom). This same connection between the heroes of faith and Christ, however, assures their enjoyment of the same rewards as Christian disciples, all of whom look ahead together to Christ's second coming for the rewards of their perseverance in faith (Origen, John Chrysostom).

The Text in Contemporary Discussion

The author's descriptions of faith in action, like his description of the challenges faced by his audience throughout their existence as a faith community, may seem remote to contemporary Western Christians and to people of other faith traditions where theirs is the majority religion. However, these descriptions are quite immediately relevant to many who profess allegiance to Jesus in openly repressive societies or societies where Christians constitute a disempowered minority culture. Some Western Christians have read this text as a challenge to think and look beyond their borders and to include Christians in hostile contexts in their plans for relief and political activism.

The passage also serves as a check on the practice of making Christian faith a means to the end of the enjoyment of temporal gain, seen most egregiously in the "prosperity gospel." The promotion of Christianity as a means of tapping into God's endless supply for the sake of the material enrichment of one's life and its associated enjoyments not only is only rampant in popular culture in the United States but has been exported throughout the world and been embraced as particularly appealing in situations of significant poverty. Nothing could be more antithetical to the author's vision of faith-in-action or the attitudes toward the temporal and its rewards that he seeks to inculcate. This chapter challenges any interpretation of Christianity that makes of it a means to attain consumerist or materialist ends.

The author's choice of subjects to include in his parade of praiseworthy and exemplary persons also critiques popular fascination with the lives of celebrities, whose basic claim to hold people's attention is wealth, glamour, and notoriety. Where such people hold a prominent place in a person's focus, that person's sense of what is desirable and what is valuable will be shaped accordingly. The "heroes of faith," however, include both those who were "success stories" by temporal standards as well as abject failures who died in disgrace, and, more often than not, people who were characterized more by "downward mobility" than the reverse. Freedom from attachment or attraction to the rewards over which the domination systems of this world have control is essential to the exercise of the *parrhēsia*, the prophetic witness to alternative values and practices that the author so values in the Christian movement.

Hebrews 12:4-29: Challenge to Endure and Show Gratitude

The Text in Its Ancient Context

While separating 12:1-3 from 11:1-40 is problematic insofar as Jesus is the climactic example of faith-in-action, separating 12:1-3 from what follows is also problematic in that it is the transition back to direct exhortation. Indeed, 12:1-4 works in tandem with 12:5-11, as the author uses two powerful images to reinterpret the unpleasant experience of the Christians' neighbors' rejection and abuse in a manner that empowers and encourages continued resistance rather than abdication. Hebrews 12:1-3 used the image of the footrace, with the stadium filled with the heroes of faith who now watch how the audience will perform in the event they have successfully completed. Hebrews 12:4 shifts this to the image of the wrestling match, where the addressees are matched against "sin," the impulse to choose the temporary rewards of friendship with society over friendship with God. Both images implicitly shame the hearers into perseverance, the first by convening a court of reputation before whom failure would be truly disgraceful, the second by suggesting that the hearers have not yet begun to endure for Jesus what he endured for them (12:2), so how could they be so cowardly and faithless as to contemplate abandoning their obligations to their benefactor (Petersen 1982, 174)?

Hebrews 12:5-11 shifts further to the image of parental discipline (*paideia*, 12:5, 7-8, 11): what their neighbors inflict with a view to shaming them is interpreted as something God uses to shape them, contributing to their positive formation as committed, courageous, virtuous citizens of their heavenly country (12:10-11; see Croy). The negative experience, moreover, becomes a proof of their adoption by God as God's legitimate sons and daughters (12:7-8; cf. 5:7-8). While the author uses a quotation from Proverbs (3:11-12) to launch this exhortation, nearly every line is paralleled in Seneca's *De providentia*. Moreover, he concludes this paragraph with an expanded paraphrase of a popular classical maxim attributed to Isocrates—"the roots of education [*paideia*] are bitter, but its fruits are sweet"—showing the author to be drawing on well-established topics to reinterpret hardship and empower continued endurance of repressive measures.

Esau's example (12:16-17), like that of the exodus generation (3:7—4:11), reinforces the danger of choosing poorly between temporary relief and long-term goods—thus, in the audience's situation, between securing escape from their neighbors' disapproval (and its negative effects on their lives and psyches) and holding securely onto God's friendship and promises through perseverance (see also 2:1-4; 6:4-8; 10:26-31). Esau's story has been reshaped somewhat to conform more closely to the author's purposes in using it (cf. Gen. 25:29-34; 27:30-40; deSilva 2000, 461-63).

The author has been strategically arousing both fear and confidence throughout the sermon; his work climaxes with a pair of images that continue the alternation. Using many scriptural allusions to the event, he paints a picture of the encounter with God at Sinai that is dark, fearsome, and dangerous (12:18-21). This is the encounter with God that the hearers do *not* have to endure because of the Son's mediation, which opens up for them a festive and confident approach to God at the heavenly Zion (12:22-24).

Recalling the Sinai event leads the author to another warning, using another "lesser-to-greater" argument to suggest that greater danger awaits those who reject the message spoke in the Son (and, even more specifically, the Son's death, 12:24) than befell those who cast off the Sinai covenant (12:25; cf. 2:1-4). Similarly, the earthquake that traditionally accompanied God's appearance at Sinai (Judg. 5:4-5; Ps. 68:7-8) leads the author to consider the future, decisive shaking and removal of the entire material creation (12:26-27, reciting and interpreting Hag. 2:6), revealing the way into the (already extant) unshakable kingdom, the divine realm, which God wishes to share with the faithful (12:28). The author's cosmology and eschatology continue to suggest the lesser value of all that pertains to this present, visible world (as opposed to "the coming world," 2:5)—an estimation that is essential to his advice concerning what course of action is ultimately advantageous.

In light of God's plan to confer such a benefit on the audience, the only appropriate response is to "show gratitude" (12:28; deSilva 2000, 473-77). Gratitude toward a more powerful patron generally took on the forms of witness (increasing the patron's reputation by praising his or her generosity), loyalty (when faced with a choice between standing by and deserting one's patron), and service (that is, doing whatever the patron might ask). This well encapsulates the response the author hopes his audience will continue to make in regard to God and God's Son in their present circumstances.

The Text in the Interpretive Tradition

Patristic readers appreciated the author's discussion of trials and hardships as the exercise regimen and diet for God's athletes being trained in virtue (Basil). Basil thought the passage to apply to such experiences as illness, and not merely social opposition for the sake of one's commitment to Jesus. John Chrysostom recognized the pastoral value of this passage, since the typical human reaction to suffering or ill-fortune is to read it as a sign of divine displeasure or abandonment. On the contrary, encountering trials may still be an opportunity to experience God's love.

Early church commentators also focused on the virtue of peace extolled in 12:14, agreeing with the author that communal harmony was indeed prerequisite to enjoying the divine presence (Augustine, Gregory the Great). They understood the "all" here to denote fellow believers, since "peace" would only be made with unbelievers by defecting from the group. Once again, these authors tended to interpret the author's warnings in such a way as promoted the perpetual availability of repentance during this life (Theodoret of Cyr, Theodore of Mopsuestia); for example, suggesting reasons why Esau's repentance was rejected and describing, on that basis, what kind of repentance ought to be nurtured.

The contrast between the approach to God at Sinai and at the future, heavenly Zion in 12:18-24 fed Christian criticisms of the old covenant (for example, John Chrysostom interpreted the "darkness," "gloom," and "tempest" as indications of "the obscurity of the Old Testament and the shadowy and veiled character of the Law") and celebrations of the more positive community of angels and righteous disciples formed around the new covenant, brought together like "living stones" in the new kingdom of God (Ambrose).

The Text in Contemporary Discussion

This passage has raised disturbing questions about God's relationship to experiences of suffering. It is important to note what the text does *not* say. The author does not say that God inflicts suffering in response to something the addressees have done wrong (Croy, 196–214). He distances himself, in fact, from Prov. 3:11-12 on this point. God may *use* suffering as a crucible for character, but the suffering is still born of the "hostility of sinners" (12:3). The author also does not say that human beings are divinely sanctioned to inflict punishment on those whom they "love" in order to correct them (as some spousal-abusers will claim). In its original context, the passage speaks only of the deprivations and hardship endured from human beings who regard the Christians as deviants on account of their religious commitments. Applying the passage to suffering beyond this is risky business (Croy, 222). Within these limits, Heb. 12:5-11 still speaks a word of encouragement to many Christians across the globe, whose experience may match or outdo that of the original audience in many respects (10:32-34), empowering resistance and, therefore, the freedom and integrity of each believer in a repressive environment.

The example of Esau challenges contemporary allegiances to the values and practices of gratification, consumption, and materialism. The author would ask many Christians how often their choices reflect a hunger and love for God or a desire to serve as God's instruments in this world and how often, to the contrary, their choices reflect their obsession with this world's trivial entertainments, pursuits, and rewards. He would call such Christians to examine the folly of being rich in the moment, but bankrupt in eternity.

The portrayal of the Sinai theophany in 12:18-21 is fair enough, but it is not an adequate representation of the experience of God known by persons who approached God through the Torah prior to, or apart from, Jesus. One thinks of the rapture of the psalmists, for whom the presence of God is peace, safety, and refreshment, for whom the law is light and joy. One thinks also of the representatives of the Jewish wisdom tradition like the authors of Proverbs, Wisdom of Solomon, and Ben Sira, for whom God and God's instruction are ever-present guides to walk in secure and stable paths. The author's contrast between the approach to God at Sinai and the approach to God through the new covenant aligns too readily with the ongoing Christian assumption that the "God of the Old Testament" (a fearsome and vindictive deity) is somehow different from the "God of the New Testament" (a deity of love and acceptance), which is a gross caricature of the image of God in both.

One of the author's foundational assumptions, shared with his host society, is that costly gifts call forth costly response. This dynamic of favor and gratitude, of gift and response, potentially reconnects grace and Christian discipleship, the experience of God's favor, and the investment of one's whole self in responding. It challenges the contemporary Christian commodification of God's gift (or of "salvation") as something enjoyed independently of an ongoing, dynamic response to the Giver in the way of testimony, loyalty, and obedient service.

Hebrews 13:1-25: Specific Exhortations for Making a Grateful Response

THE TEXT IN ITS ANCIENT CONTEXT

The author concludes his sermon with practical instructions on how to "show gratitude" and live "in a manner well-pleasing to God" (12:28; cf. 13:16, 21). These focus chiefly on group-sustaining practices (13:1-6, 15-17). The willingness of Christians to open up their homes to the group for worship and study or to traveling teachers and missionaries was essential to the Christian movement (13:2). Reaching out to support those members who were most targeted by their neighbors for "corrective discipline" was similarly essential to sustaining commitment (13:3). The most intimate human relationships needed to be safeguarded against erosive behavior (13:4). Attachment to temporal goods—when deprivation of such goods is a major tool for pressuring deviants into conformity—is also assiduously to be avoided (13:5-6; see 10:32-34). High regard to leadership, both those who currently exercise their office (13:17) and those who have passed (13:7), gives a strong internal focus for the group. In every way, the author seeks to stimulate a strong sense of mutual commitment and investment—the kind that would normally be reserved for one's natural brothers and sisters—within the group, such that they will put themselves out to meet one another's need and, thus, sustain one another's commitment (13:1, 3, 16).

The declaration "Jesus Christ is yesterday and today the same—and forever" (13:8) activates a topic familiar from discussions of trust (see, notably, Dio Chrysostom, *Or.* 74.4, 21–22). This is less an ontological statement than an ethical one: the hearers can count on Jesus to be constant and reliable in their relationship. What he was for them in the past, he will yet be for them in the future. This was the basis for their departed leaders' faith (13:7) and can be for theirs as well. The author contrasts this basis for trust one final time with elements of the Levitical system of mediation (13:9-11; see Lev. 16:27), recalling in a summary way the surer mediation the hearers have in Jesus, and therefore the firmer foundation for continued trust.

The author returns to the theme of making an appropriate return to God and to Jesus for their costly favor. Since Jesus suffered "outside the camp" for the hearers, the author urges them similarly to "go out of the camp"—that is, willingly to leave behind their place in their society—to meet him in the margins of society, being willing to bear temporary disgrace for their association with him (13:12-13). Such loyalty is a component of a grateful response. But the way "out" of the camp is also the way "in" to the unshakable realm of God, into which they are being welcomed (13:14). They are also urged to continue to bear witness to the value of Jesus' mediation and God's promises (13:15) and to invest in one another's perseverance (13:16). These acts of bringing honor to the Patron and offering service are also recognized elements of gratitude toward superiors. They are painted in cultic terms: such enactments of gratitude, and not animal sacrifices, are now the language of and means of expressing their ongoing relationship with God (see also 6:9-10).

The sermon ends with the typical elements of a letter's closing (13:18-25; cf. 1 Thess. 5:23-28; 1 Pet. 5:10-14).

The Text in the Interpretive Tradition

John Chrysostom appreciated the practical guidance for disciples, particularly as regards the proper accumulation and use of property (promoting keeping oneself from superfluities and prioritizing charity). Hebrews 13:8 became a frequent text invoked in conversations about Christology, especially the divine nature of Christ that undergoes no change in the incarnation, passion, death, and ascension.

The Text in Contemporary Discussion

Hebrews 13 brings together many of the themes encountered throughout the sermon, and hence raises once again many of the issues already discussed—the state of Christians in restricted nations and the obligations of Christians in free (and often prosperous) nations toward them; the author's challenge to contemporary boundary lines between "family" and "outsiders," private and public; the notion of "grace" as a relationship of ongoing mutual exchange and obligation rather than a commodity simply to be received.

The text challenges the fundamental logic of Western economic practice, which is to amass capital and, in a sense, "build bigger barns" for the future in the form of investment portfolios and retirement accounts. The author of Hebrews would not take issue with this, were it not for the fact that many lack the daily necessities of life *this* day and are not being relieved. Allowing Heb. 13:5-6 to take deeper root in Western Christian practice would enable more "capital" to be directed toward meeting such needs (13:2-3, 16).

This closing chapter also challenges the tendency of Christian people in the West to prioritize insulating themselves against suffering or hardship, avoiding negative circumstances as if they were an absolute evil. Where do "Christ followers" in West *not* go, *not* dare to follow Christ and his call, out of this deep-rooted unwillingness to lose face or temporal advantages, or to fail to attain what our socialization has taught us to value?

Works Cited

Attridge, Harold W. 1989. *The Epistle to the Hebrews*. Hermeneia. Philadelphia: Fortress Press.
Becker, Ernst. 1973. *The Denial of Death*. New York: Free Press.
Bonhoeffer, Dietrich. 1966. *The Cost of Discipleship*. New York: Macmillan.
Bultmann, Rudolf. 1953. *Kerygma and Myth*. London: SPCK.
Croy, N. Clayton. 1998. *Endurance in Suffering: Hebrews 12:1-13 in Its Rhetorical, Religious, and Philosophical Contexts*. Cambridge: Cambridge University Press.
deSilva, David A. 1998. *4 Maccabees*. Sheffield: Sheffield Academic Press.
———. 2000. *Perseverance in Gratitude: A Socio-Rhetorical Commentary on the Epistle "to the Hebrews."* Grand Rapids: Eerdmans.
———. 2012. *The Letter to the Hebrews in Social-Scientific Perspective*. Eugene, OR: Cascade.
Eisenbaum, Pamela Michelle. 1997. *The Jewish Heroes of Christian History: Hebrews 11 in Literary Context*. SBLDS 156. Atlanta: Scholars Press.
Ellingworth, Paul. 1993. *The Epistle to the Hebrews*. NIGTC. Grand Rapids: Eerdmans.
Filson, Floyd Vivian. 1967. *"Yesterday": A Study of Hebrews in the Light of Chapter 13*. London: SCM.
Gleason, Randall C. 1998. "The Old Testament Background of the Warning in Hebrews 6:4-8." *BSac* 155:62–91.
Heen, Eric M., and Philip D. W. Krey, eds. 2005. *Hebrews*. Ancient Christian Commentary on Scripture. Downers Grove, IL: InterVarsity Press.
Lane, William L. 1991a. *Hebrews 1–8*. WBC 47A. Dallas: Word.
———. 1991b. *Hebrews 9–13*. WBC 47b. Dallas: Word.
Nelson, Richard D. 1993. *Raising Up a Faithful Priest: Community and Priesthood in a Biblical Theology*. Louisville: Westminster John Knox.
Oberholtzer, Thomas Kem. 1988. "The Thorn-Infested Ground in Hebrews 6:4-12. *BSac* 145:319–28.
Petersen, David G. 1982. *Hebrews and Perfection: An Examination of the Concept of Perfection in the "Epistle to the Hebrews."* SNTSMS. Cambridge: Cambridge University Press.
Spicq, Ceslaus. 1953. *L'Épitre aux Hébreux*. 2 vols. Paris: Gabalda.
Thompson, J. W. 1982. *The Beginnings of Christian Philosophy: The Epistle to the Hebrews*. CBQMS. Washington, DC: Catholic Biblical Association of America.
Vanhoye, Albert. 1963. *La structure littéraire de l'Épitre aux Hébreux*. Paris: Desclée de Brouwer.

JAMES

Timothy B. Cargal

Introduction

Little can be said with certainty about the origins of the Letter of James. Although there has been widespread agreement for associating the letter with James the Just, the brother of Jesus and a leader of the early church in Jerusalem (Matt. 13:55; Acts 15:13; Gal. 1:19; 2:9), there has been just as widespread disagreement over the centuries as to whether the letter was actually written by him or by someone else using his name. The argument that the literary quality of its Greek surpasses the likely ability of a Galilean laborer is just as strong as the argument that the book lacks specific biographical references such as are usually found in pseudonymous writings that establish the connection with the person named as the author. Since the name James (Greek, *Iakōbos*, from the Hebrew name Jacob; James 1:1) was common among Jews of the first century, it is as likely that the association with James the Just is a result of misidentification as it is of authentic authorship or even pseudepigraphy.

Beyond the name James/Jacob, other characteristics of the letter associate it with what has been called "early Jewish Christianity," although some of this evidence is more ambiguous than sometimes asserted. Imagery linking gentile Christians with Israel as now people of God, such as the description of this letter's recipients as the "twelve tribes in the Dispersion" (1:1), was not uncommon (see, e.g., 1 Pet. 1:1). Similarly the use of the Greek word *synagōgē* ("synagogue") to refer to the recipients' Christian "assembly" (James 2:2) is also found in such non-Jewish writers as Hermas, Justin, Origen, and Eusebius, who use *synagōgē* and *ekklēsia* ("church") interchangeably for gentile Christian communities. While the letter clearly has a positive view of "the law" (*nomos*, corresponding to Hebrew *tôrâ*; see 1:25; 2:8-12; 4:11), it does not address controversies between "Jewish Christians" and "gentile Christians" over circumcision or other aspects of Torah observance.

Evidence from literary dependence suggests the letter was written in the 60s or 70s CE. It seems likely that the assertion people are "not [justified] by faith alone" (2:24) is indirectly related to Paul's statement, "a person is justified by faith apart from works prescribed in the law" (Rom. 3:28), which would set the late 50s or early 60s as an earliest possible date. Sections of *1 Clement* are likely reliant on material in this letter (cf. *1 Clem.* 29.1; 30.1–5; 31.2 with James 2:14-26; 4:1-10), which would establish the early to mid-90s as a latest possible date. This general time period, which encompasses the run-up to and aftermath of the first Jewish War with Rome (66–73 CE), also provides a fitting historical setting to the letter's imagery of social dislocation and expectation of an imminent "coming of the Lord" (5:1-8). The economic and cultural disruption of the war might also have prompted the letter's strong interest in social justice concerns (see, e.g., 1:27; 2:5; 5:1-5). If indeed the first Jewish War provides some of its historical background, this would preclude the current form of the letter from being an authentic writing of James the Just, who was executed by the high priest Ananus II in 62 CE (Josephus, *Ant.* 20.9.1).

There has been a tendency, particularly since the Protestant Reformation, to read the Letter of James as in direct conflict with the apostle Paul's understanding of the relationship between faith and works in establishing a person's relationship with God (that is, one's "justification"). The likely literary dependence of James 2:24 on Rom. 3:28 has already been noted, and there is also the striking similarity in how the two letters employ Abraham as an example in their discussions of this issue—albeit to opposite conclusions (cf. Rom. 4:1-25 with James 2:20-24). More recently, however, many interpreters have moved toward seeing libertine Pauline enthusiasts as the more likely catalysts for James's statements about the necessity of both faith and works. Both Paul and James understand faith in terms of trust in God (rather than, say, holding certain beliefs about God; cf. Rom. 4:5 with James 1:5-6). Additionally, Paul himself had both anticipated and argued against those who might conclude that, having been justified by faithful trust in God, their actions did not matter (Rom. 2:13; 3:31; 6:1-2; Phil. 2:12-13; and cf. James 2:18). Even more beneficial has been the trend to see the doctrine of justification as an important but not all-consuming concern within the Letter of James. Read as a whole, James's primary interest centers on encouraging consistency in living out "the implanted word" (1:21) both individually (1:19-21, 26; 3:13-18) and communally (2:2-4; 4:11-12), particularly as it gives rise to the social justice themes already mentioned.

James 1:1-21: Obtaining Wisdom from God

■ THE TEXT IN ITS ANCIENT CONTEXT

James describes himself as "a servant of God and of the Lord Jesus Christ" (1:1a). The word "servant" might also be translated as "slave." Surprising as it may seem today, to describe oneself as a "slave of God" could actually be a claim of status and authority in the letter's Greco-Roman context, where slaves could be used as their masters' personal representatives and so receive a kind of ancillary authority. This social reality led to Israel's prophets also being referred to as "God's servants." Nevertheless, slaves did lose all independence to the will of their masters—and the idea that God's will should supplant our own desires and will is a recurring theme within the letter that will be firmly established in this opening section.

Before turning to that, we need to consider how James characterizes the audience to whom he is writing. He addresses the "twelve tribes in the Dispersion" (1:1b). Clearly the language is metaphorical because Israel had lost any real twelve-tribe structure since at least the Assyrian conquest of the northern kingdom in 722 BCE. The question is, then, how far does the metaphorical aspect extend? The metaphor may simply identify ethnic Jews ("the twelve tribes") living outside Roman Palestine ("in the Dispersion"). However, the fact that the author closes the letter by suggesting some "among you" have "wander[ed] from the truth" and so need to be brought back (5:19-20) opens a broader possible meaning: the recipients are people of God ("the twelve tribes") who have departed from ("in the Dispersion") a proper understanding of their relationship with God ("wandered from the truth") and so need James's correction.

Following a pattern often used in letters of this period, James lays out this purpose in a twofold introduction. This relationship between the key ideas can be illustrated by presenting the two subsections of 1:2-12 and 1:13-16 in parallel columns.

1:2-4: "trials" (*peirasmoi*) and tests   1:13-16: temptation (*perirazein*)
1:5-8: God's gift is "wisdom"   1:17-19a: God's "perfect gift" is the "word of truth"
1:9-12: culminates with a "crown of life"   1:19b-21: culminates with the salvation of the soul

Thus James identifies what he believes is the problem in the recipients' current understanding (how they view "trials" and being "tempted"), offers a correction (God's "perfect gift" of "wisdom"/"the word of truth"), and concludes with the benefit it promises ("life" for the "soul").

In order to see the corrective aspect of his opening paragraph (1:2-4), it is necessary to challenge the customary translation of the word "consider" (*hēgēsasthe*) in verse 2. Most Greek verbs have quite distinct forms and spellings when they are used as simple statements (the indicative mood) as compared to being used as commands (imperative mood). Some, however, have exactly the same forms, and the verb *hēgesthai* is one of them. Since the Letter of James has more than fifty imperative verbs in its 108 verses, most translations take it as an imperative here in 1:2; thus James is encouraging the recipients to respond to "trials of any kind" as an occasion for "nothing but joy" because "the testing of ... faith produces endurance," which in the end will make them "mature and complete, lacking in nothing" (1:3-4). This idea that trials make one's faith stronger was common in the first century (and even today).

But notice that James immediately says that if one "is lacking in wisdom," it can only be received as a gift from God (1:5); thus, at least for James, "endurance" *cannot* cure every "lack" because being "lacking in wisdom" is only resolved by God's gift. This point suggests that James makes an observation in the previous paragraph about how they have been thinking about "trials" (thus "you consider," in the indicative mood) that is in fact different from how he wants them to think about trials. That James is indeed trying to correct their views is reinforced by the parallel subsection in 1:13-18. Whereas some believe they are being "tempted by God" (using the cognate verb for the noun translated as "trials" in 1:2)—perhaps identifying these temptations as "trials" meant to strengthen faith through "endurance"—James emphatically insists God can neither be tempted nor tempts anyone else. Rather, God is the unvarying source of "every generous act of giving" and "every perfect gift" (1:17).

Trusting in God's unvarying goodness is the essence of "faith," as distinct from "doubt," which is tossed back and forth between trust and uncertainty (1:7-8) since it can never be sure whether God will provide a "perfect gift" or "trials" and temptations. It is the "implanted word" (1:21) that unifies God's wisdom and will *within* the individual that "has the power to save [one's] soul" (1:21) and bestow "life" (1:12), so that one is no longer "double-minded" (1:7-8) and "lured and enticed" by one's own improper "desire" (1:14).

The Text in the Interpretive Tradition

The Letter of James has often been described as "the New Testament's Proverbs"; that is, many have seen it as a collection of sayings expressing conventional wisdom without an overarching structure or argument. Especially in its opening chapter, the view has been that sayings have been strung together by "catchwords": the occurrence of a word in a saying calls to mind another saying with the same word, which is then placed immediately after it without developing the idea. Over the last several decades, that view has been challenged by studies employing a variety of literary-critical and linguistic approaches. Though there is variation in the details of the analysis, there is an emerging consensus that a twofold introduction sets out the key themes that will be given further development later in the letter.

The Text in Contemporary Discussion

James's insistence that "God cannot be tempted by evil and he himself tempts no one" (1:13) serves his rhetorical and theological purposes well. It clearly establishes a reason why someone could ask God for whatever they need without doubting either God's generosity or the goodness of God's response (cf. Matt. 7:9-11). But the assertion is not without its difficulties in light of the broader scriptural tradition, as James himself must have known. After all, he will later refer to one of the most important stories about God's testing someone when he says, "Abraham [was] justified by works when he offered his son Isaac on the altar" (James 2:21; notice how James avoids using the word *test* in this passage, even though it opens the story in Gen. 22:1-19). He also will allude to "the endurance of Job" (James 5:11b), a story often seen as God's testing of Job even if at the instigation of the Satan (Job 1:1—2:10). And in Exodus, Moses persuades God to take a different course of action lest the Egyptians accuse God of having acted with "evil intent" (Exod. 32:11-13). The narrator's summary comment in Exod. 32:14 goes so far as to flatly state that God not only can be but also has been tempted to do evil, leading God to repent, where (the Hebrew behind the NRSV's "the LORD changed his mind about the disaster that he planned" can be translated more bluntly, "the LORD repented of the evil").

But in a post-Holocaust world, the challenge to James's assertion goes beyond just conflicting Bible stories. Theodicy—how an all-good and all-powerful God can allow evil to exist—may well be the preeminent theological issue of our age. True, James is not engaging in a philosophical discussion of theodicy; but it is an issue that moderns cannot avoid when confronted with assurances about God's unvarying goodness. At the risk of gross oversimplification, process theologians (such as Charles Hartshorne, John Cobb, and Marjorie Suchocki, who hold that God is changed by and develops though relationship with creation) might say that God is striving to become a God worthy of James's trust/faith, but the evidence suggests that neither God nor the world has yet arrived at that point.

James 1:22—2:13: Doing the Word

■ THE TEXT IN ITS ANCIENT CONTEXT

Two concepts, one theological and the other sociological, provide the foundations for this section of the Letter of James. The "piety of the poor" was a conviction within Judaism and early Christianity, that God had "chosen the poor in the world" (2:5b)—not because they were more religiously or spiritually pious, but because "the rich" and powerful have "oppressed" and defrauded them (see 2:6b; 5:1, 4). This theological concept stood in marked contrast to the Greco-Roman cultural system rooted in honor and shame. Those cultural values provided the sociological framework for an extensive patronage system through which the rich and powerful received honor, in part, from the beneficence they showed to others. By showing honor to upper classes, the lower classes hoped to become beneficiaries of the patronage from the rich.

Having in the opening section of the letter focused on the need to receive God's "wisdom" expressed within the "word of truth" (1:5, 18, 21), James now emphasizes that his readers must become "doers of the word, and not merely hearers" (1:22). To be a "doer of the word" is to be a person who brings to reality God's will for the world. For that reason he defines "religion" not merely in holiness language ("pure and undefiled," "unstained by the world") but also in terms of acting on the basis of God's choice in favor of the poor by "car[ing] for orphans and widows in their distress" (1:27).

But to the degree that his readers had chosen anyone for special attention, James charges they have shown "favoritism" toward those "with gold rings and in fine clothes" (2:1-2). Beyond even the demands for displays of honor required by the patronage system, they have come to identify with the rich against the poor whom God has chosen. Notice how he alleges the readers would direct those "wearing the fine clothes . . . [to] 'Have a seat *here*, please'" (that is, *here among us*), whereas "to the one who is poor [they] say, 'Stand there,' or, 'Sit at my feet'" (that is, *away from us or in a place that illustrates your subordination to us*, 2:3). In a string of rhetorical questions, James expresses his amazement at their choice because their actions have not brought them the patronage they might have expected but rather further abuse (2:6b-7).

In James's view, such "partiality" is the very antithesis of the "royal law" (2:9), the "law of liberty" (2:12). And that "law" must be understood as a unified whole; a person can no more violate only one of its provisions than one can break *only* the stem of a crystal goblet.

■ THE TEXT IN THE INTERPRETIVE TRADITION

Because the Letter of James has been associated with "early Jewish Christianity," there has been a particular interest in its use of the phrase "the law of liberty" (2:12). Some have suggested that it draws on the Stoic ideal of life in accord with the rule of reason (the *Logos*), others with Jewish descriptions of the Torah as providing joy and freedom, and still others with Christian conceptions of Jesus' ethical teachings as a "new law" that either replaces or "fulfills" the mandates of Torah (cf. Matt. 5:17-48). But given the way James links the images of "law" and "word" in 1:22-25, and the image of the "implanted word" in 1:21, it may be that the best antecedent is to be found in Jeremiah's "new covenant," whereby God promises to "put my law within them, and . . . write it on their hearts" (Jer. 31:31-34). As Leonard Goppelt (2:206) described it, "For James, the Law was not an objectively prescribed norm . . . but the will of God that was written in the heart."

Keeping this "perfect law, the law of liberty" (1:25) for James required a consistency between one's speech and actions ("bridle their tongues," 1:26), and attention to what later Christian moral tradition would refer to as "sins of commission" (improper actions) and "sins of omission" (failure to do those things that God desires). Often Christian communities have tended to emphasize one or the other. James's admonition "to keep oneself unstained by the world" has been emphasized within certain holiness movements as the core of the religious life. His charge to "care for orphans and widows in their distress" has been emphasized by social gospel movements. But James calls for a "both . . . and" rather than an "either . . . or." Just as God's will/law is characterized by a unifying wholeness, James calls for "keep[ing] the whole law" (2:10) even as he also reminds his readers that "mercy triumphs over judgment" (2:13).

■ The Text in Contemporary Discussion

The discussion of "favoritism" and "partiality" in terms of economic distinctions has a special relevance in terms of modern concerns regarding classism, but also calls to mind all forms of discrimination. In some ways, though, classism has grown as a problem in our society even as more overt forms of discrimination based on gender, racial, or other physical distinctions are openly criticized. While people increasingly accept others who are physically different from them, they still tend toward "favoritism" and "partiality" for those who are like them in terms of educational attainment and socioeconomic status. And as work on the social structures of "white privilege" in Western societies and corollary forms of privilege in other cultures has demonstrated, we are often blind to the "favoritism" we both bestow on others and benefit from ourselves.

The way in which James unmasks the real allegiances of his readers is instructive. Although they would certainly have called on the "piety of the poor" to associate themselves with those whom God has "raised up" in contrast to "the rich" who are "brought low" (see 1:9-11), their actions demonstrate they strive to be "the rich" ("Have a seat *here*"; 2:3). James repeatedly reminds his readers to assess all progress toward becoming the just world that he believes God desires not by declarations about inclusivity but by concrete actions. His admonition continues to be a warning to any who speak more about God's "preferential option for the poor" than act in ways to make it a lived reality.

James 2:14-26: A Living Faith

■ The Text in Its Ancient Context

A repetition of keywords establishes the concern and the limits of this section of the letter: For "faith" to be any "good" in the sense of "sav[ing] you" it must "have works," because "without works" faith is "dead" (2:14, 26). But James structures the argument in a way that makes clear that the "good" (or "benefit") that comes from being "save[d]" will respond to material needs as well as spiritual ones.

Just as the discussion of "favoritism" (2:1), in the previous section, was rooted in values of honor and shame and the Greco-Roman patronage system, so also the discussion throughout this section presupposes cultural expectations regarding hospitality (2:15, 25). The idea that someone might refuse to assist a "brother or sister" in need of material assistance would have been shocking to everyone in that society; when almost everyone struggles at subsistence for themselves, they know in the most pragmatic ways why providing for others is a communal responsibility. But for James, hospitality is more than a social obligation. The invocation of blessing ("Go in peace") especially when joined with what are in Greek passive imperative verbs—more literally, "Be warm and be well fed" (2:16)—are indications that the speaker recognizes that it is God's will that these material needs be met (see 1:27). Jews often used passive voice verbs to avoid naming God directly. To use such constructions to tell another to "keep warm and eat your fill" was to invoke God to keep them warm and fed. Such knowledge of God's goodness ("faith"), if it produces only words ("has no works"), accomplishes no "good" and is in fact "dead" (2:16-17).

That one's knowledge about God should determine one's actions is the central point of the diatribe (a literary device involving an imagined exchange with a person holding a different view) in 2:18-26. Given a text that originally had no punctuation at all and certainly no quotation marks, it has proven difficult definitively to assign certain words to James and others to his rhetorical partner. What is clear, however, is that James insists not only that heroes of the "faith" like Abraham (2:21-23) and Rahab (2:24) act on what they believe about God, but so do "even the demons," who "shudder" (2:19). He is astounded that any sensible person (2:20), then, could think "faith" and "works" are separable in any way.

Close attention needs to be given to the word order in James's summarizing analogy: "just as the body without the spirit is dead, so faith without works is also dead" (2:26). Notice the "body" correlates to "faith," and the "spirit" to "works"—*not* "body" to "works" and "faith" to "spirit." As the "spirit" animates the "body," so "works" animate (that is, "bring to life" or "live out") "faith" (2:26).

▇ The Text in the Interpretive Tradition

During the great debates of the Protestant Reformation about the means by which people are "justified" by God (see 2:21, 24-25) and "save[d]" (2:14; see also 1:21; 5:19-20), considerable attention was given to the fact that Gen. 15:6, "[Abraham] believed the LORD; and the LORD reckoned it to him as righteousness," is employed as a proof text by both James (2:23) and Paul (Rom. 4:3; Gal. 3:6). Whereas Paul uses the Abraham example in support of the view "that a person is justified by faith apart from works prescribed by the law" (Rom. 3:28), James uses Abraham to show "that faith apart from works is barren" (2:20).

In the view of many interpreters, Paul and James held contradictory views. More traditional theologians argued that James demonstrated that both faith *and* works contribute to justification. Martin Luther and some other Reformers agreed that James contradicted Paul, but held that Paul was correct in insisting that works contribute nothing to justification. Luther went so far as to state that James's letter had "nothing of the nature of the Gospel about it" (Luther, 362).

John Calvin, however, was not convinced that James and Paul truly contradicted one another. He argued Paul was concerned exclusively with "the ground on which our hope of salvation ought to rest," whereas James was concerned only with "the manifestation of righteousness by conduct" that follows from having been "justified" by God. For Calvin, this distinction was seen clearly in James's statement, "faith was brought to completion by the works" (2:22), about which he commented, "the question here is not respecting the cause of our salvation, but whether works necessarily accompany faith" (Calvin, 314–15).

■ The Text in Contemporary Discussion

The common tendency among interpreters to construe Abraham and Rahab as examples for us to follow can create problems. If Abraham is said to *epitomize* faith in "offer[ing] his son Isaac on the altar" (perhaps, as Heb. 11:19 suggests, trusting "God could even raise him from the dead") and "Rahab the prostitute" to *embody* hospitality that spares others from destruction (see also Heb. 11:31), then emphasizing Abraham's *faith* and Rahab's *work of hospitality* serves to reinscribe her primarily as "the prostitute." Too easily, Abraham and Rahab come to exemplify two extremes: God justifies not only the venerated Abraham but also the lowest of sinners, the prostitute Rahab.

It is possible to read this letter, however, in a way that resists debasing Rahab. James states she not only "welcomed the messengers" but also "sent them out by another road" or "way" (the word used in 1:6-8 and in 5:20 of one's manner of life [the NRSV's "wandering" is more literally "error of one's way"]). Her story in Joshua 2 relates how she encouraged the spies and, through them, all the Israelites to adopt a manner of life that ended their wilderness wanderings by believing in God's promises (especially Josh. 2:8-11). As distinguished from the so-called hospitality of a harlot, Rahab can exemplify those whom James describes as "bringing back" others who "wander from the truth" and so "will save" them "from death" (5:19-20).

James 3:1—4:12: Humbly Preparing for Judgment

■ The Text in Its Ancient Context

The central theme of this third section in the letter is expressed through the contrast between the readers' desire to obtain for themselves power and high social standing—the reason for James's warning, "Not many of you should become teachers" (3:1; see the earlier discussion of 1:22—2:13)—and what is for James a proper attitude of humility: "Humble yourselves before the Lord, [so that] he will exalt you" (4:10). Such humility is required because of the coming judgment, which is again explicitly mentioned at the beginning and end of the section—teachers "will be judged with greater strictness" (3:1) by the "one lawgiver and judge who is able to save and to destroy" (4:12a).

James believes that his readers perceive the role of teachers as being to exercise authority over errant members of the community (possibly punitively: "So who, then, are you to judge your neighbor?" 4:12b). Rather than being dispensers of punitive "judgment," he argues, "teachers" will be the recipients of "stricter judgment." Within the overall context of the letter, James considers teachers "servant[s] of God and of the Lord Jesus Christ" (1:1) who "save the sinner's soul from death and will cover a multitude of sins" (5:19-20), thereby sparing errant members of the community from harsh judgment rather than inflicting judgment on them.

The question of proper and improper speech plays an important role in the development of this section. In 3:2, James describes the "perfect" person as one who "makes no mistakes in speaking"; such a person stands in stark contrast to one who "speaks evil against or judges another" and so "speaks evil against the law" (4:11). But improper speech is only a symptom, one of "many" ways in which people sin (3:2). The origins of evil behavior and speech, James argues, reside in the "cravings that are at war within you" (4:1; cf. 1:14-15). The true problem, in his view, is desire for social status (3:1), "envy and selfish ambition" (3:16), and arrogance (4:6).

James contrasts the fact that "all of us make many mistakes" (3:2; see 3:14-16 for some of his examples) with the many things that should typify one "who is wise and understanding" (3:13) in terms of "the wisdom from above [that] is pure, then peaceable, gentle, willing to yield, full of mercy and good fruits, without a trace of partiality or hypocrisy" (3:17). True "wisdom" is demonstrated not by what one says but by "works" that display "gentleness born of wisdom" (3:13).

What is true of individuals is also true of communities. "Conflicts and disputes" arise between members of the community because of their covetous "cravings" that James alleges have even led to "murder" (4:1-3). While some argue James is alluding here to Jesus' saying that links anger with "murder" (see Matt. 5:21-22), it is possible James uses the word in a more literal sense. If a failure "to care for orphans and widows" (James 1:27) and other indigent members of the community (2:15-16) results in unnecessary deaths, then the evil desire to "spend what you get on your pleasures" (4:3) would be a kind of murder.

The promise in the proverb that God "gives grace to the humble" (4:6; see Prov. 3:34) provides the basis for James's call to "submit yourselves . . . to God" (James 4:7) and to "humble yourselves before the Lord, and he will exalt you" (4: 10; cf. 1:9-10). The "laughter" and "joy" that come from "friendship with the world" must be replaced with the grief, mourning, and gloom of realizing that one has "become an enemy of God" (4: 4, 9). Genuine humility and repentance—both turning away from evil and turning to God—is the only way to prepare oneself to come before the "one lawgiver and judge" (4:12).

THE TEXT IN THE INTERPRETIVE TRADITION

Some commentators have argued that James uses his metaphors about bridles and ship rudders (3:2b-4) to illustrate the influence of teachers over the "body" of the community. Ralph Martin (103–7) went so far as to argue that not just these particular metaphors but all of 3:1-12 presents "a discussion where (i) 'the body' [see 3:2b] in question is the ecclesial one, not the anatomical one, and (ii) the tongue is used in a setting of the congregation at worship" where "'praising God' is the chief component" (see 3:9-10). This communal reading seeks to resolve the difficulty that the human tongue does not actually control human actions in the way that a bit does a horse or a rudder does a ship. Others argue that the allegorical relationship is more general, perhaps even alluding to Jesus' statement, "out of the abundance of the heart the mouth speaks" (Matt. 12:34;

Luke 6:45). One's speech is a clear indicator of the internal desires that control all one's actions (notice James explicitly mentions that "ships . . . are guided by a very small rudder *wherever the will of the pilot directs*" [3:4]).

■ The Text in Contemporary Discussion

How does one square the view of God as "the one lawgiver and judge," able both to "save" or "exalt" (4:10) and to "destroy" (4:12), with James's conviction that God is the source of "every perfect gift" and nothing bad or evil (1:17)? Could recognizing God as such a "judge" lead to "doubt" and "double-mindedness" (1:7-8), since one does not know whether to expect salvation or destruction from God? It seems likely that James would respond that while "judgment" is clearly a bad thing for those who will be destroyed, that does not mean God's destructive judgment is a bad thing in itself. Moreover, no one should have any "doubt" about what awaits them (even the demons "shudder" in their certain knowledge of God's judgment, 2:19). Those who have asked for, received, and lived out God's gift of wisdom can trust they will be saved (see 1:21-22).

But theologies—whether Christian or of another tradition—that depend on the destruction not only of evil but also of those caught under its control and who do its bidding have had terrible effects in the world. Those who are sure they know whom God will ultimately "destroy" in judgment often have little regard for James's admonition that they should not judge their neighbors (cf. 4:12). James will himself later advise patience while God's harvest is reaped (5:7; cf. Matt. 9:37-38; 13:24-30), but if God were to show a bit more patience—tending the fields for as long as it might take—could it be possible to "save" the whole crop? Perhaps James, like Moses, should have worked harder at persuading God to turn aside from any "evil intent" to destroy as an act of judgment (see discussion of James 1:1-21 in "The Text in Contemporary Discussion" above).

James 4:13—5:20: Restoring One's Neighbor—and Self

■ The Text in Its Ancient Context

James concluded the previous section of the letter by calling his readers to repentance (4:7-10). As he draws the letter itself to a close, he challenges them to follow his example by bringing back others within their community who may be "wander[ing] from the truth" (5:19-20). He again reminds them that the standard of judgment will be whether they have accepted the divine will as their own (see especially 4:13-17), and creates a sense of urgency by asserting, "the Judge is standing at the doors!" (5:9b). He insists that they cannot restore others by "grumbl[ing] against one another" (5:9a); rather, they must encourage "patience" and "endurance" (5:10-11) by directing the attention of those who are "suffering" to God's goodness and provision through communal prayer, praise, and confession (5:13-18).

In the midst of this summons to his readers to bring back anyone who "wanders from the truth," James once more calls "the rich" to account (5:1-6) and encourages "patience" on the part of those who suffer at their hands (5:7-11). The unmistakable harshness of the imagery he employs against the rich (the corrosion that consumes their hoarded goods will likewise "eat [their] flesh like fire,"

5:3) may on the one hand seem justified since their abuse of others (5:4) is once again said to have resulted in deaths (5:6) but on the other hand seems overly strident from one who advises against judging others (4:11-12). Notice, however, that James calls on the rich to "weep and wail for the miseries that are coming" (5:1). James has earlier associated weeping with repentance (4:9), and the decay of their possessions calls to mind the demise of their way of life in 1:11. It is likely that rather than taking joy in their "miseries," James hopes these events will awaken the rich to their dependence on God and lead them to repent of their past sins. The prospect that they too might yet be "brought back" is the only reason to counsel patience.

Although we have seen that 5:19-20 provides a key insight into how James understands his purpose for writing the letter, there is an ambiguity that lies at the heart of these verses. The NRSV flags the issue with its textual note in 5:20 that the word translated as "sinner's" is in Greek simply "his" (*autou*). The problem resides in identifying the antecedent of "his." Is it the "sinner's soul" that is saved (as the NRSV has it), or is it the soul of "whoever brings back a sinner"? Perhaps James intends the ambiguity because it is in doing such things consistent with God's will that people are "blessed" (1:22-25) and that their "faith" is able to save them from spiritual death (2:14, 26).

THE TEXT IN THE INTERPRETIVE TRADITION

James 5:14-16 has been a key passage in the development of the Catholic "sacrament of the sick," commonly referred to as "the last rites." While the "call[ing] for the elders of the church," prayer, "anointing ... with oil," and confession and forgiveness of sins mentioned in those verses are widely recognized aspects of that liturgical practice, some may be surprised that a ritual so closely associated with death (at least in the popular imagination) is rooted in a passage that holds out the hope of healing.

A deeper insight into this relationship between the "last rites" and "healing" can be found by carefully considering the specific words James uses for God's response to the act of anointing the sick with oil: "The prayer of faith will *save* the sick, and the Lord will *raise* them up" (5:15). While the Greek verbs *sōzein* and *egeirein* were commonly used to refer to healing and restoration to wholeness, they also have specialized uses within Christian theology. All the other uses of "save" (*sōzein*) in the Letter of James (1:21; 2:14; 4:12; 5:20) have the sense of salvation and eternal life. Although "raise" (*egeirein*) is not used elsewhere in this letter, it is widely used in reference to resurrection, and specifically of Jesus being "raised" from the dead (see, e.g., 1 Cor. 15:12-14). Thus the "sacrament of the sick" holds out the hope that even if physical healing does not come, there remains God's promise of wholeness in the life to come.

THE TEXT IN CONTEMPORARY DISCUSSION

Two aspects of James's discussion of prayers for healing open possibilities for abuse. First, relating healing and forgiveness reflects a traditional view that connected sin and sickness (cf. John 9:1-2) and leads some to conclude that every disease is a result of sin, either as a natural consequence or even as an act of divine judgment (but see John 9:3). Second, James's assertion, "The prayer of the righteous is powerful and effective" (James 5:16), leads some to affix blame for unanswered prayers by impugning the righteousness either of the sick person or of those who pray on her or his behalf.

To the degree that James offers any explanation as to why some prayers for healing do not result in physical restoration, it is that the elders are to pray "in the name of the Lord" (5:14). The invocation of "the name of the Lord" is both an appeal to the power and authority of God, and a recognition that our desires—even in prayer—must be conformed to God's will (cf. 4:3). But once again it seems that James is sidestepping the problem of theodicy that we in the twenty-first century cannot so easily avoid (see the discussion on 1:1-21). Therein may lie the single greatest theological challenge for the Letter of James in contemporary discussion.

Works Cited

Calvin, John. 1855. *Commentaries on the Catholic Epistles.* Translated and edited by John Owen. Edinburgh: The Calvin Translation Society.

Goppelt, Leonard. 1982. *Theology of the New Testament.* 2 vols. Translated by John E. Alsup. Grand Rapids: Eerdmans.

Luther, Martin. 1960. "Preface to the New Testament of 1552." In *LW* 35.

Martin, Ralph P. 1988. *The Epistle of James.* WBC 48. Dallas: Word.

1 PETER

David L. Bartlett

Introduction

The First Epistle of Peter claims to be written by the apostle Peter to a group of churches in Asia Minor. Some scholars believe that the letter was written, as claimed, by Simon, one of Jesus' first four disciples, whose nickname, given by Jesus, was Peter. Others, including this author, believe that the letter was written after Peter's death, in the sixties of the common era, by another Christian writing in Peter's name and trying to apply the principles of apostolic faith to a new generation.

There are several reasons why many doubt that this letter was originally written by Peter. First, the letter is written in quite sophisticated Greek, and when it quotes Scripture it quotes from the Greek Old Testament, the Septuagint. From what we know of Peter, that he was an Aramaic-speaking fisherman, it seems unlikely that he would have written in this language and this style.

Second, the letter seems to be appropriate to the situation of the churches in the later part of the first century, after Peter would have been martyred. The sense that the church is undergoing widespread opposition from society looks more appropriate to the latter part of the century than to the fifties and sixties. While such judgments are always a matter of guesswork, it is a plausible guess that the kind of church order that 1 Peter implies, with a group of leaders designated as elders, was a development as the original apostles were passing away. Indeed, 1 Peter 5 is in many ways most reminiscent of Acts 20, probably also a late first-century composition, where Paul gives orders to the elders of Ephesus concerning their leadership of the church after he has departed.

Third, there are enough hints that the author of 1 Peter knows Paul's writings, and in particular the letter to the Romans, to suggest that our letter is written after Paul's letters have already begun to circulate among the churches.

Because the author says in 5:12 that he has written this letter "though Silvanus [Silas]," some have thought that the letter was written in its final form by Silas, either as he took instructions from Peter or on the basis of Peter's notes. This is not impossible, but seems like a stretch in order to preserve the conviction that Peter wrote the letter himself.

The letter is written from "Babylon," almost certainly a code name for Rome. We know that from early in the church's history, Peter was especially associated with Rome. So perhaps the letter comes from leaders of the Roman church writing in the name of their favorite apostle.

The letter is directed to the churches in seven communities in Asia Minor. The list of areas may represent the order in which a courier would have carried this circular letter through Asia Minor. A glance at a map will indicate that such a route would have been a plausible way to make such a journey.

We will see the themes of the letter as we go through its claims. Clearly there is concern for rebirth, regeneration. The letter claims that the church has become Israel: that all the promises of the Old Testament were really promises for the church. There is considerable concern with the conduct of new Christians in the midst of their pagan neighbors, but also considerable encouragement for living with opposition—whether that consists of actual persecution or constant disrespect, it is hard to know. The author expresses a strong belief that the end of the ages is at hand and that God in Christ will come to judge the living and the dead and to reward those who have proved faithful to the end.

1 Peter 1:1-12: The Foundation of Christian Hope

■ The Text in Its Ancient Context

This letter begins, as do other letters written in the first century, with the simple formula: From _____ To _____. The letter purports to be from Peter the apostle, and it is written to a group of churches in Asia Minor. I suggested above that the letter is probably written by a later follower of Peter, in Peter's name.

The information in the address goes far beyond the simple listing of the churches to which the letter is sent. Those who are to receive the letter are called "exiles of the Dispersion." This reference to exile compares the churches to the people of Israel and Judah who were exiled from their homelands in the eighth and sixth centuries BCE. As they are cut off from their homeland, so the Christians who receive this letter are cut off from a homeland too. The reference also compares the recipients to the Jewish people of the late first century CE who have been exiled from the Holy City, Jerusalem, which was destroyed by the Roman armies in 70 CE. It is likely that the Christians who receive this letter were not historically Jewish at all. We see this especially in the references to the readers' pre-Christian life in 1 Pet. 1:14, 18; 2:10, 35; 4:3-4. We will need to ask, therefore, why they are to identify with Jewish exiles far from home. Our letter will give us some clues. In addition to the kind of imaginative description of the letter's audience, we have a theologically rich description of who they are. They are a people entirely defined by their relationship to God in Jesus Christ. That relationship has both a present and a future dimension. In the present, these Christians hope in the care of God. For the future, they hope for God's glory to be revealed. What they now know in part they will then know entirely.

Some students of this letter think part of it was originally a sermon for a baptism service. Certainly the references to a "new birth into a living hope" fit the theme of baptism, now as much as in the first century. As Christians await what is hoped for, they need to choose how to live in the meantime, even though that time may be filled with tests and tribulations. The way the Christians are to live is by loving God and hoping for God's future.

We do not know for sure what kind of tribulations these people were facing, but we do know that the author sees those tribulations as a test and as a strengthening. He uses the analogy of gold being refined by fire to suggest the way in which trouble can refine the faith of these early Christians (1:6-7).

A major theme of 1 Peter is that it is Christians who are the true inheritors of the promises of Scripture (what Christians now call the Old Testament). Contemporary scholars tend to believe that when the prophets of Israel and Judah wrote, they wrote of promises fairly close at hand. From the beginning, however, Christians have read those promises as pointing to their own situation: prophecies about the people of God are read as foreshadowings of the church; prophecies of a Messiah or of a greater prophet are read as pointing to Jesus Christ. So for 1 Peter, promises to Abraham and his descendants are not so much a witness to the story of Israel as a witness to the story of Jesus Christ. We shall see throughout this letter that because the Scripture he inherits is always looking ahead, Peter can affirm that the church is now the real Israel: not just Israel-like, but Israel itself, Israel in the flesh.

The Text in the Interpretive Tradition

This letter grows out of an interpretive tradition at least as much as it funds one. The authority of the letter may originally have depended on the identification of the author with Simon, traditionally one of the first four disciples called by Jesus (Mark 1:16-20). Simon is renamed "Peter" (Cephas in Aramaic; see Gal. 2:11-14), "the Rock." In the book of Acts, he is the interpreter of the events of Pentecost and therefore the homiletical father of the emerging church. In both Acts and the Letters of Paul, we discover that Peter was designated the apostle to the Jews as Paul was to the gentiles. This is one of the reasons John Calvin assumed Peter writes this letter to Jewish exiles.

Catherine Gunsalus González helpfully points out that though the full doctrine of the Trinity was a later development of the church, these early verses of 1 Peter help give us an insight into a very early emerging affirmation about the way in which the one God is evident in Father, Son, and Holy Spirit. These three are all affirmed in verse 2, and then in succeeding verses the author testifies that the Father gives new birth through the Son; that the Father and the Son will judge the world; and that the Spirit inspired the prophets and now inspires the church (González, 15).

The Text in Contemporary Discussion

Much of the discussion of these verses still focuses on the question of authorship and in a related question, the date of the letter. (For a thorough presentation of the details see Achtemeier, 1–43; more briefly, Bartlett, 234–36.)

Contemporary readers are appropriately concerned about the ethical implications of a letter written in someone else's name. While our ethical queasiness has some rationale, it seems unlikely that the readers of this letter thought it had actually been written by Peter. By the time the letter was written, he had been martyred. More likely they read it as a kind of tribute to him, written by someone trying to bring faithful understanding to new and challenging circumstances. If "Babylon" is a code word for "Rome" in this text, it seems likely that the letter was written from Roman churches early associated with Peter. (For a much fuller discussion, see Achtemeier, 42–43.)

1 Peter 1:13-25: The Shape of New Christian Life

The Text in Its Ancient Context

Again in verse 17, the author refers to the time of the Christians' "exile." It may be helpful to try to understand what that exile might mean.

Some scholars have thought that this letter was written with a particular socioeconomic group in mind, those resident aliens who were not citizens of the lands in which they live but were there on a kind of green card. The letter is written to help them live in a land where they, under an emperor far away, have little power (see Elliott). Other scholars think these people are exiles because they are exiled from their heavenly home, and that when Christ comes in his glory, the Christians will be returned to their rightful destination, with God in Christ. While both these insights may be valid, it is also fairly clear that the people who received this letter are exiled from their own former lives as pagans. "You know that you were ransomed from the futile ways inherited from your ancestors" (1:18; on the options for exiles, see Achtemeier, 125). We will see time and again that 1 Peter distinguishes the Christians from the world around them, which is also the world where they used to live. They are in the world of pagan values and practices, but they are not of that world: they are exiles.

Like the apostle Paul, 1 Peter emphasizes again and again that the central act which redeems people from their past in idolatry is the death and resurrection of Jesus Christ. Here Christ's death is seen as comparable to the sacrifice of a lamb in the Old Testament; it brings the curtain down on past sins and opens a future for redemption. Christ's resurrection is the ground of Christian faith for now and of Christian hope for the future, when God will consummate God's will.

But as we might expect for an author who thinks that Israel's Scripture points entirely to Christ, this sacrifice and triumph of Jesus Christ was not a second thought on God's part. It was the plan from before the foundation of the world. "He was destined before the foundation of the world but was revealed at the end of the ages for your sake" (1:20). One could almost say that for the author, as the purpose of Israel's Scripture is to reveal Christ, the purpose of creation is to make possible the new creation.

When in 1:16 the author quotes from Lev. 4:44, "You shall be holy, for I am holy," he seems to understand that both Moses and God had the early Christian church in mind. For our author (at 1:24-25), when the book of Isaiah says that "the word of the Lord endures forever" (Isa. 40:6-8), the text refers to the Christian gospel, the word that these early Christians have heard and that they now read in this letter.

■ THE TEXT IN THE INTERPRETIVE TRADITION

In his discussion of 1:17, Richard Vinson quotes at some length from a sermon John Donne preached on this text to seventeenth-century British magistrates. While Donne's talk about "judgment" is clearly particularly pertinent to judges, it is also a word for all Christians, who have to make judgments daily. Our life in the world, says Donne, is not just a passing through, "but such a stay as upon it our everlasting dwelling depends." And Donne tells the magistrates to live in such a way that they can pray: "'God be such to me at the last day, as I am to his people this day,' and for that day's justice in thy public calling, God may be pleased to cover many sins of infirmity" (Donne, sermon number 13, quoted in Vinson, 81–82).

■ THE TEXT IN CONTEMPORARY DISCUSSION

Catherine González finds in these verses the ancient but always contemporary discussion of the relationship between faith and works.

> "Therefore."... *Because* these Christians have been chosen by God the Father, *because* by baptism they have been joined to Jesus Christ the Son and redeemed by him, and *because* they have been strengthened by the Holy Spirit, *therefore* they are to be holy. On their own, by their own strength, without the involvement of the triune God, they could not be holy. (González, 33)

For our author as for Paul, the first mark of holiness is belonging in the community of the holy, the community of saints. It is the church in its entirety that is a royal priesthood and a holy people (2:9). At the same time, individual Christians now live a life that is different from the life they lived in their "pagan" years; in particular, they move away from idolatry to faithful worship of the one God revealed in Jesus Christ.

1 Peter 2:1-10: The Royal Priesthood

■ THE TEXT IN ITS ANCIENT CONTEXT

In this section of the letter, the author reminds his readers of the radical newness of their lives in Christ. This is yet another instance of the emphasis on rebirth and regeneration that has led some scholars to believe that at least the first portion of 1 Peter may have been a baptismal homily.

As individuals, Christians are called to their new identity. But they find that identity in part by looking back—by becoming like infants, trusting in God as an infant trusts a parent. They are to drink spiritual milk, the formula for beginnings, first things.

Of course, new beginnings require re-formation, so readers are encouraged to give up the trappings of what seemed like maturity in their pagan days: guile, malice, insincerity, envy, slander. Though he does not explicitly say so, the author calls his hearers away from those particular vices and sins that might destroy Christian community. Again, as is so often the case, he has a scriptural citation to underline this call to newness: "O taste and see that the Lord is good" (Ps. 34:8).

Being born anew does not mean simply adding a belief in Jesus to one's established patterns of thought and action. Being born anew means giving up a whole host of comfortable habits, including guile, malice, insincerity, envy, and slander: the ways of the world. No wonder these Christians seem like exiles.

Notice, too, that while these Christians have been born again, born anew, their pilgrimage as Christians has not yet reached its goal. The milk of the childlike Christian is the beginning of a process of maturity—"so that by it you may grow to salvation."

The call for a new life is a call for a new community as well, but again Peter looks ahead by looking back. Now he looks not to the images of childhood but to the images of Israel—the covenant with God's people now extended to God's new people, the Christians.

The mélange of images is also a mélange of biblical texts. The image of the stone is applied both to Jesus and to the believers. Jesus is the stone who is chosen, the stone who provides the foundation for the new household of faith, the stone on which unbelievers will stumble. The richness of the image depends on the combination of scriptural texts: Isaiah 28, Psalm 118, Isaiah 8. All these texts are cited elsewhere by Christian writers (see Matt. 21:32; Acts 4:11; Rom. 9:33).

The image of the stone is also applied to believers: Christ is a living stone, but so are believers living stones. Christ is the cornerstone of the new building, but all the faithful are built into that new edifice. The edifice is a new temple, and references to temple, priesthood, race, nation now affirm what Peter has already insisted on. The Church is now Israel. God's promises to Israel are fulfilled in the life of the church. "But you are a chosen race, a royal priesthood, a holy nation, God's own people" (2:9). As the Christian moves from unbelief to belief, from the old life to the new, so the whole community moves out of darkness to light.

The author ends this section by recalling one of the most moving narratives of the Old Testament—Hosea's reconciliation with his wife and with his children (see Hosea 2:23). Hosea gives his children new names when their new lives begin. The author gives the Christian community new names as well: "a chosen race, a royal priesthood, a holy nation, God's own people."

The Text in the Interpretive Tradition

Not surprisingly, pietistic Christianity has played down the heavily apocalyptic theme in 1 Peter and, to some extent, the radically communal theme as well. Charles Spurgeon, in a sermon on this text, talks about "coming to Jesus" and about the Christian hope in ways that are probably more individualistic and less eschatological than Peter had in mind: "Coming to Christ . . . is, in one word, a trusting in and upon him. He who believes Jesus Christ to be God and to be the appointed atonement for sin, and relies upon him as such, has come to him, and it is this coming which saves the soul."

Every interpretation of a text is of course also a reinterpretation, but we can see Spurgeon's sermon a move away from the strongly communal and future-oriented themes of 1 Peter. For our author, people come to Christ by coming to the community, and Christ comes to them on the last day. For Spurgeon, people come to Christ by trusting in him, and in that moment, Christ also comes to the believer.

The Text in Contemporary Discussion

It is striking that in 2:9-10, the language traditionally applied to Israel is now applied to Christians. But there is no claim here that this represents any revocation of the Old Testament promises. Rather, the author simply reads the words as applicable to the church (too?).

> There is no trace of polemic in this practice, however, but only a curious appearance of naiveté. Nowhere in 1 Peter are the readers addressed as a new Israel or a new people of God as if to displace the Jewish community.... If there is an "anti-Jewish" polemic here, it is a polemic that comes to expression simply by pretending that the "other" Israel does not exist. (Michaels, 197)

1 Peter 2:11-17: Living Honorably among the Gentiles

The Text in Its Ancient Context

When the author calls the Christians to become a new temple for God, he also calls them to be part of a new house, and a new household. In the portions of the letter that we now discuss, Peter talks about what life in that new household looks like. We will see that much of the discussion assumes a kind of hierarchical society, ordered from the top-down, which is difficult for twenty-first-century Christians to affirm—often with good reason.

Note, however, that the author, like many other first-century Christian writers, has two main concerns. First is that the church should be ordered according to the will of God. The author interprets that will in ways more highly structured and even authoritarian than some would affirm, but nonetheless he thinks that his orderliness reflects the orderliness of God.

Second, the church should be a peaceful and respected part of the larger community in which it lives. Already our author's people must seem like "exiles" to the very friends, families, and institutions that they have left behind to become part of the church. This letter is concerned that Christians be respected as good citizens, good householders, orderly family members. If they are to be immigrants and aliens, at least let the larger community admire them for their exemplary behavior.

Such behavior starts with the civil authorities. The emperor is both the pinnacle of civil authority and its most visible symbol. Included in the injunctions to honor the emperor is the injunction to honor local and provincial officials as well.

Yet even in this fairly staid view of a submissive community, there are important distinctions to be drawn—distinctions that in other circumstances might well lead Christians to other, less polite behavior.

First of all, though Christians are under government authority, that authority does not take away from their freedom, which is grounded in God. Christians should be good citizens only because they choose freely to do so; they are under no compulsion to obedience save obedience to God.

Second, notice how the last sentence makes a kind of rhetorical, almost poetic point. There are four injunctions for Christians. The first and last injunction go together and so do the middle two. (The technical word for this device is *chiasmus*.) The first and last injunctions tell Christians how to get along as members of the community. They urge a kind of prudence: "Honor everyone.... Honor the emperor." In the world of the first century, "honor" is a kind of social convention in which one promotes civic harmony by giving honor to those to whom honor is due.

The second and third injunctions tell Christians who they are as a new community, a royal priesthood. "Love one another" instructs regarding how to attend to the fellow Christian. "Fear God, reverence God" tells how to attend to the Creator. Notice that these Christians, who face some kind of persecution or slander, are *not* told either to fear the emperor and his deputies, or to reverence them (see, e.g., Kelly, 113).

The Text in the Interpretive Tradition

John Calvin writes about honoring the ruler in ways that reflect his situation in Reformation-era Geneva and have influenced a good deal of theology since.

> We ought to respect the civil authority because it has been appointed by the Lord for the common good of mankind, for we must be utterly barbarous and brutal, if the public good is not close to our hearts. This, in short is what Peter means, that since God keeps the world in order by the ministry of magistrates, all those who detract from their authority are the enemies of mankind. (Calvin, 12:270)

Of course the situation becomes more complicated if the magistrate is not devoted to the common good. Both our letter and the Reformers tend to assume that rulers promote good order. For 1 Peter, any thought of overturning the governmental order would have seemed impracticable, and in the face of the coming end of the age, pointless. Calvin sought to establish good order where magistrates ruled according to Christian principles.

The struggle of the contemporary church has often been how to be faithful when the civil authority seems to contradict the precepts of the faith. Dietrich Bonhoeffer finally turned to plot against the authorities; Martin Luther King Jr. was willing to break the laws in the hope of changing them.

The Text in Contemporary Discussion

These verses have provided crucial resources both for contemporary biblical studies and in the United States, especially, for contemporary theological reflection.

John Elliott is among the American scholars who has paid special attention to the social location of New Testament writings, and he has argued that 1 Peter was written for Christians who were legally and socially—and not simply metaphorically—exiles in their place and time. Much recent discussion of the text has been in response to Elliott's claim (see Elliott; Bartlett).

Stanley Hauerwas and William Willimon have argued that the picture of the church as a community of "resident aliens" provides a proper description for the church in America. The influence of the church has waned as Christendom has given way to a more diverse and secular society. For them, the claims and values of Christian faithful are now not those of the culture but of a counterculture. Church is and should be less an institution and more a movement.

Other Christians, often inspired by Calvin, see a more complicated relationship between the society and the church. For them, Christians live both as citizens of this world and as citizens of God's rule, and faithfulness consists in balancing those demands.

1 Peter 2:18—3:7: Living Honorably in the Household

The Text in Its Ancient Context

In these verses, the author continues to present his version of good order. The standards he suggests for Christians are not very different from the standards that upstanding "pagan" citizens of Asia Minor would have suggested for the right ordering of a household. (See Bartlett, 278; I use "pagan" as a shorthand for those who were neither Jews nor Christians.) Here a powerful christological formulation is drawn in to buttress a widespread social practice and institution. The more general exhortation to endure suffering that follows is finally in the service of the instructions to slaves. "Slaves, accept the authority of your masters with all deference, not only those who are kind and gentle but also those who are harsh" (2:18).

The christological passage powerfully provides one reading of Christ's suffering and death, which are rightly designated by the church's theology as both essential and mysterious. Not surprisingly, 1 Peter looks at the mystery through the lens of the Old Testament. First Peter 2:22-25 is in many ways a Christian commentary on the meaning of Isaiah 53.

In 3:1, the author shifts the focus from slaves to wives, but makes clear by his sentence structure that the obedience of wives is another example of his vision of right order for a Christian household. "In the same way"—in the same way as slaves, that is—"wives, accept the authority of your husbands" (NRSV). In fact, in both the instance of slaves and wives, the Greek imperative would better be translated: "Be obedient" or "be subject."

Appropriate wifely conduct includes a kind of dress code. Most likely the standards for appropriate dress are the standards that right-thinking non-Christians would also uphold. If Christians are to stand out, it is for the beauty of their lives, not the luxury of their attire. We notice that the description of the obedient Sarah is a considerably sanitized version of the Sarah we meet in Genesis, where her wifely obedience is considerably more ambiguous (see Kittredge, 618).

Strikingly, in 3:7 husbands are not told to live in mutual obedience or subjection to their wives but to "show [them] consideration . . . as the weaker sex" (NRSV). (See Eph. 6:21 for a somewhat more egalitarian alternative.) However, there is no license given here for a husband to harm a wife, physically or psychologically. Husbands are enjoined to honor their wives.

The Text in the Interpretive Tradition

Calvin provides the kind of reading that has informed much Christian understanding of this passage from the first century until today.

> [Peter] proceeds now to another instance of subjection, and bids wives to be subject to their husbands. Since those who are married to men who are unbelievers seem to have more reason for shaking off the yoke, he expressly reminds them of their duty, and shows particular reason why they ought to obey more faithfully, so that by their honesty they may attract their husbands for faith. If wives ought to obey ungodly husbands, those who have believing husbands ought to obey even more readily. (Calvin, 12:280)

The Text in Contemporary Discussion

While considerable helpful scholarship has suggested some of the differences between slavery in the Roman Empire and slavery in pre–Civil War America, the appropriate consensus among Christians in our time is that slavery is an unacceptable human practice and that the defense of slavery is an unacceptable use of Scripture. It would simply be unethical and unfaithful for people to live in the twenty-first century as Peter enjoined Christians to live in the first.

For some Christians, this discrepancy leads them to reinterpret the text to try to soften its impact. For many Christians, this involves arguing against the text, acknowledging that other parts of Scripture read slavery far less favorably (e.g., Philemon), or arguing that we must sometimes distinguish the gospel for our time from the Scripture of another.

In understanding the relationship between men and women, too, this is a difficult chapter. Cynthia Kittredge reminds us how problematic this portion of 1 Peter is for Christians who want to move toward an egalitarian vision both of marriage and of the church.

> [First] Peter presents difficult interpretive issues for women today because its rhetoric constructs the female gender as the "weaker sex" (3:7) and both assumes and reinforces the social structures of masters and slaves. Its injunctions . . . have inflicted harm when perceived as universal instruction to the weak to endure injustice and abuse. (Kittredge, 616)

Many Christians would argue both from a theological and from a humane point of view that the center of Christian practice should be Gal. 3:28: "[in Christ] there is no longer Jew nor Greek, there is no longer slave nor free, there is no longer male and female" (NRSV).

1 Peter 3:8-22: Faithful Suffering

The Text in Its Ancient Context

Now the exhortations for right Christian conduct move from the household to the church and then to the larger community. Verse 8 seems to be directed toward the Christian community itself and seems almost a mirror image of 1 Pet. 2:1. There, new Christians are called to reject "malice, guile, insincerity, envy, slander." Here, new Christians are called to embrace "unity of spirit, sympathy, love for one another, a tender heart, and a humble mind."

With verse 9, we move to the question of the conduct of Christians in the larger society and especially Christian interaction with nonbelievers who may abuse them. These verses may provide some insight into the circumstances of these first-century churches. The issue does not (yet at least) seem to be persecution and martyrdom, but slander and abuse.

The proper Christian response to evil is good, and the proper Christian response to abuse is blessing (see also Matt. 6:38-42; Rom. 12:17-18). The author seems here to draw on a widespread Christian ethic of nonretaliation. His own addition to this tradition is his citation of Ps. 34:12-16.

As in previous exhortations, the author gives two reasons for such peaceful behavior. The first is that Christians want to have a good reputation in the larger community. The second reason is that Christians are to live their lives according to the shape of Jesus' own passion, resurrection, and ascension. It is not only that Christ's sacrificial acts are worthy of imitation but also that these acts are atoning. "For Christ also suffered . . . in order to bring you to God" (3:18).

There follows a description of the passion and resurrection of Christ that has puzzled Christian commentators through the ages. The first part is clear enough. Jesus was "put to death in the flesh but made alive in the spirit" (3:19). The claim is not strikingly different from that in Rom. 1:3-4. Peter is not arguing that only Jesus' spirit was made alive, but that he was made alive in the power of the Spirit.

Now comes the particularly puzzling description of what the living Jesus did after his resurrection: "he went and made a proclamation to the spirits in prison" (v. 19). The connection of these spirits with the flood (Genesis 6–9) suggests one of two possibilities. Perhaps these spirits are those of the disobedient people who perished in the flood. Or perhaps these spirits are the offspring of the "sons of God" and mortal women described in the puzzling passage Gen. 6:1-4. William Joseph Dalton argues persuasively that this passage fits with other first-century texts that speculate on the fate of these human/divine offspring. He further suggests that when the risen Christ preaches to these spirits, they are imprisoned in a kind of holding place located between earth and the upper heaven, where God the Father dwells. Jesus preaches to the spirits as part of his ascent.

The author now uses the reference to the ark and the flood to remind the readers of their own baptism. The flood prefigures baptism, but of course only in a kind of striking reversal. Noah and his family were actually saved from water; Christians are saved through water.

■ The Text in the Interpretive Tradition

Karl Barth drew on 1 Peter 3 along with other texts in his discussion of Christian suffering and Christian hope.

> The true analogy of the resurrection of Jesus Christ in the existence of oppressed Christians, the true might and power of the future which already in their present is appointed for them in their fellowship with Jesus Christ . . . simply consists in the fact that the Christian in affliction is a man who is absolutely secured by the goal appointed for him in Christ. (*CD* IV/3, 644–45)

■ The Text in Contemporary Discussion

Catherine González reads the text in ways that are clear and pertinent for contemporary North American and Western European Christians.

> Christians in the ancient world were at risk of being persecuted for their faith. In the midst of such suffering, they gave witness to the power of that faith. The same is true of Christians in some parts of our world today. . . . But that is not usually our situation. . . . What is it that Christians do in our culture that makes them stand out enough that others ask what is the source of their strength and joy? (González, 102)

For those who live in countries where Christian faith is perfectly acceptable and sometimes even assumed, there may be a temptation to use the dangerous situation of first-century Christians in

Asia Minor as an inappropriate analogy for the so-called War on Christmas, for example, or for the anxiety Christians may feel at having soccer practice compete with Sunday school. We would do well to distinguish the diminution of cultural hegemony in our era with genuine persecution and shunning in that earlier era.

Furthermore, the text reminds us that there are still many parts of the world where being a Christian is not only unpopular but also dangerous. In churchly concerns and with regard to national foreign policy alike, we should continue to oppose any genuine religious persecution of Christians (and, it goes without saying, *by* Christians, too).

1 Peter 4:1-11: Christ's Suffering as Example

■ The Text in Its Ancient Context

The author continues to reflect on Christ's suffering as a guide to the current situation of those who hear his letter. Now, however, Christ's suffering "in the flesh" becomes a paradigm for first-century Christians to understand their new conduct as Christian believers.

For the author of 1 Peter, as for Paul, the distinction between "flesh" and "spirit" does not relate to two different aspects of the personality but to two different ages in God's dealing with humankind. In the time of the flesh, people live selfishly, competitively; in the time of the spirit, people live selflessly and cooperatively. Until their baptism, these Christians of Asia Minor have lived according to the flesh—in licentiousness and idolatry. In these behaviors, they have linked their lives not only to the old age of the flesh, which is passing away, but also to the environment around them of "gentiles," pagans, those who have not become part of God's Israel, God's true people.

The consequences of citizenship, whether people choose to live in the time and community of the flesh or in the time and community of the Spirit, will be judgment. Again, as so often, we realize that 1 Peter is written with the impending end of the world very much in mind.

Yet in a somewhat mysterious verse, our author seems to hint that at least for those who have gone before and lived lives according to the flesh, it is not too late to repent and become part of the community of the Spirit. "For this is the reason the gospel was proclaimed even to the dead, so that, though they have been judged in the flesh as everyone is judged, they might live in the spirit as God does" (4:6). It is unclear whether the "dead" are those who preceded Christ and are now included in the proclamation of the gospel, or believers who have died between Christ's resurrection and his return, or perhaps even those unbelievers who have died more recently. It is not even clear that it is Christ who preached the gospel in this passage. What is clear is that not even the dead are separated from the love of God, forever.

The reference to the glory of God leads the author to move into a kind of doxology, a poem that might almost be better sung than read: "To God be the power and the glory forever and ever. Amen." Not only does this hymn of praise end this part of the letter's exhortation, but also some have thought that it marks an end to an earlier, shorter writing that was basically a sermon on baptism.

The Text in the Interpretive Tradition

Some early Christian theologians (including Clement of Alexandria and Augustine) allegorically understood the dead to whom the gospel was preached to be the spiritually dead (see Kelly, 173). Calvin understood the preaching to the dead as a word of comfort to the (already) faithful who die in Christ: "It is a remarkable consolation to the godly that death itself brings no loss to their salvation. Even if Christ does not appear as deliverer in this life, yet His redemption is not void, or without effect, for His power extends even to the dead" (Calvin, 12:302).

The Text in Contemporary Discussion

Catherine González, while acknowledging the obscurity of the reference to preaching to the dead, has a more generous view of what the text might imply than Calvin's. "There is some hope at the end of verse 6 that those who had been judged and condemned at the end of their earthly lives might be given the ability to live in the spirit just as God lives.... The former companions of these converts have been judged on the basis of their earthly life, but there is hope that they will be able to live a new life, just as these Gentile converts have begun to do" (González, 118).

We might wish that we could use this text answer the question, which goes back at least to the third century, whether God intends finally to redeem everyone. There are passages in the New Testament that suggest the hope of universal salvation (see Rom. 5:18, for instance). The meaning of this text, however, is too uncertain for the text to be of much help in discussing this disputed issue.

1 Peter 4:12-19: The Coming Crisis

The Text in Its Ancient Context

Partly because our letter seems to come to a kind of full stop at 4:11 and partly because the mood of the letter shifts and intensifies with 4:12, some have thought that from 4:12 to the end of the epistle we have a real and urgent letter appended to what was originally some kind of sermon. We notice, however, that in other letters like Paul's Letter to the Romans, an author is perfectly capable of moving into a doxological hymn right in the middle of things and then moving on to the next part of his argument (see, e.g., Rom. 11:34-36). And it may be that the injunctions of 1 Pet. 4:12 do not indicate a new situation but a new perspective on the situation in view throughout the letter—where Christians are subject to some kind of slander and abuse from the very gentile communities they have left behind.

In this passage, the exemplary behavior is particularly straightforward. We can paraphrase: "do not be a criminal or a busybody" (4:15). Whether this injunction represents a real danger or a rhetorical flourish we cannot know. What is clear is that here the question of the law is not about idolatry or emperor worship. Christians are commanded not to be murderers or thieves.

Furthermore, in this passage the sufferings of the present time are explicitly linked to the final judgment. It is not just that judgment is coming but also that these very sufferings are themselves the firstfruits of that judgment, the small tribulation that points toward the great and fearful Day of the Lord, when the faithful will be redeemed and the unfaithful will suffer desolation greater than these passing trials.

The Text in the Interpretive Tradition

In commenting on this (and several similar texts), Karl Barth writes:

> Thus those who, like Christians, suffer something corresponding in their little passions as a reflection and likeness of His great passion, may rest assured that their suffering takes place in the light of the Easter revelation toward which He moved in His great passion. . . . Hence they can and may expect no other than their existence in fellowship with the One who rose again and lives as the crucified and slain. (*CD* IV/3, 372)

The Text in Contemporary Discussion

J. Ramsey Michaels resists the claim that the tone and focus of the letter change radically with 1 Pet. 4:12. Rather, he suggests that these verses provide a kind of retrospective look at the claims about the difficulty of Christian life that have preceded these verses in our epistle.

> Although it has often been suggested that there is an intensification or a heightening of the urgency between 4:11 and 4:12 (as if Peter had just heard of a sudden crisis or disaster) there is no real evidence of this. . . . The difference in tone between 1:6-8 and 4:12-19 on the one hand, and most of 2:11—4:6 on the other, is the difference between a rhetorical summary of the Christian community's position in a hostile world and a series of directives on how to respond to specific aggravations or challenges. (Michaels, 258)

1 Peter 5:1-11: Instructions for Community Order

The Text in Its Ancient Context

With 5:1, the author shifts from addressing the congregations at large to devote particular attention to church leaders. Whether the "elders" of the church are to be understood as designated offices or as more informal leaders is impossible to tell. What we do know is that from the beginning of the church, the different gifts of members suggested different functions. The issue becomes even murkier with the reference to those Christians who are younger (5:5). Are the "elders" always older members of the church? Or is the distinction between those who have been Christians for a time and those who are younger in faith? In any case, whatever their age and however they are chosen, the pastoral and ethical responsibilities of the elders are clear enough. Their pastoral responsibility is to provide oversight for the congregation and to do so with proper humility. Their ethical responsibility is not to do so for personal gain. (For similar injunctions to church elders, see Paul's address to the elders of Ephesus in Acts 20). The author puts before the elders of Asia Minor two examples of the right exercise of the pastoral, shepherdly role. The first example is the person whose identity he takes on for the writing of this letter—Peter, who knew Christ's glory. The second example is Christ, the great shepherd of all the flock—including the elders.

In 5:5b-11, the author turns from the distinction between elders and younger to address again all the members of the congregations, returning to the theme of suffering and distress but elaborating on his portrayal of this stressful situation in two ways. First of all, the present tribulations are not simply the consequence of human opposition to the believers, they are signs of the continuing devouring strategies of Satan. It is a general feature of Christian and Jewish apocalyptic expectation for the future that the present time is an age of warfare between God and God's great enemy. God of course will emerge victorious, but in the present moment the battle is joined.

Second, it is made clear to each of the congregations that what they suffer is not their unique and local difficulty but part of the ongoing tribulation of the whole church. This is presented not only to provide the comfort of community but also as one more reminder that all the world is caught up in the struggle between Satan and God—a further sign that the end must be near.

The good news is that the end will be God's gracious end. First Peter 5:1-10 is not only a prophecy but also a benediction. And as with the first part of this letter (4:11), this second section of the letter ends with doxology: "To him be the power forever and ever. Amen."

■ The Text in the Interpretive Tradition

Augustine of Hippo of course assumed that 1 Peter was written by the apostle Peter, and he therefore connects this passage with Jesus' dialogue with Peter in John 21, where Peter is commanded by Jesus to "feed his sheep" (*Homily on the Feast of St. Peter and St. Paul*). Here, as Augustine reads our text, Peter, himself a shepherd and elder, tells other elders that they are to be good shepherds too.

■ The Text in Contemporary Discussion

In 1973, a group of Lutheran and Roman Catholic scholars completed a series of discussions of the apostle Peter by publishing a book called *Peter in the New Testament*. The hope was that by better understanding the biblical portrait of Peter, Catholics and Lutherans—and presumably other Protestants as well—might come to a more nuanced and even ecumenical understanding of the relationship of Peter to the bishopric and especially to the bishopric of Rome. In their discussion of 1 Peter, the authors present both sides of the discussion about authorship, but in looking at these verses from 1 Peter 5 they come to a kind of consensus.

> In 5:1 the author of 1 Peter, introducing himself to the presbyters (elders) of the communities of Asia Minor assumes the title of "fellow presbyter" or "co-presbyter." We should not be deceived by this modest stance as if the author were presenting himself as their equal. He has already identified his authority as "apostolic" (1:1); and so the use of "fellow presbyter" is a polite stratagem of benevolence, somewhat as when a modern bishop of a diocese addresses his "fellow priests." (Brown, Donfried, and Reumann, 152–53)

1 Peter 5:12-14: Final Greetings

■ The Text in Its Ancient Context

We have discussed in the introduction the issue of who wrote this letter and where it was written. What becomes clearer at the letter's end is that the purpose of the letter is not finally instruction about morals or warnings about last things, but encouragement. If the Christians have heard this letter right, they have found courage (though the Greek word translated as "encourage" [*parakalein*] is rich enough that it can mean that they have found exhortation and instruction as well).

Whether the author of our letter knew a Christian named Mark, or uses the name "Mark" (and perhaps, Silvanus, Silas) to connect "Peter" with other another first-generation Christian, we cannot know.

The exhortation for the holy kiss strengthens our conviction of the importance of communal love and fellowship for the first churches and probably gives us a glimpse into a liturgical practice common to their assemblies. The final word of this sometimes tumultuous discourse is, blessedly, "Peace."

The Text in the Interpretive Tradition

These last verses have not been at the center of any basic theological discussion over the centuries, nor are their themes subject to much debate even now.

What they provide is a hint or two of church life toward the end of the first century. The church in Babylon/Rome is sufficiently connected to these churches in Asia Minor to join in greeting.

The Text in Contemporary Discussion

The citation of "Silvanus/Silas" and Mark provides fuel for the ongoing discussion of authorship and, in recent years, the tricky question of pseudonymity. Some scholars have tried to hold to Peter's authorship of this letter by suggesting that his work was edited and presumably improved literarily by his companion Silvanus.

Certainly for centuries—certainly as early as Polycarp's *Letter to the Philippians* in the early second century CE—Christians assumed this was written by Jesus' companion Peter. Early on, it was treated as part of the canon, as part of Sacred Scripture, probably in part because of its assumed apostolic authorship.

From at least the beginning of the twentieth century, many scholars have suspected that 1 Peter was written in Peter's name. Perhaps it was written by late first-century Christians devoted to Peter and hoping to provide the kind of perspective he might have offered for the new situations of their own age.

In any case, 1 Peter has continued through the centuries to provide, above all, a word of encouragement for Christians suffering for their faith, and a thoughtful attempt to wrestle with the relationship between the church and the world that is sometimes both its opponent and its home.

Works Cited

Achtemeier, Paul. 1996. *First Peter*. Hermeneia. Minneapolis: Fortress Press.
Augustine. *Homily on the Feasts of St. Peter and St. Paul*. www.onbehalfofall.org/2013/06/29.
Barth, Karl. 1963. *Church Dogmatics*, trans. G.W. Bromiley et al., Edinburgh: T&T Clark.
Bartlett, David. 1998. "First Peter." In *The New Interpreter's Bible*. Vol. 12, *Hebrews–Revelation*, edited by Leander E. Keck, 229–301. Nashville: Abingdon.

Brown, Raymond A., Karl Donfried, and John Reumann. 1973. *Peter in the New Testament: A Collaborative Assessment by Protestant and Roman Catholic Scholars.* Minneapolis: Augsburg, 1973.

Calvin, John. 1970. *Commentaries.* 12 volumes. Translated by William B. Johnson. Grand Rapids: Eerdmans.

Dalton, William Joseph. 1989. *Christ's Proclamation to the Spirits: A Study of 1 Peter 3:18—4:6.* 2nd ed. Rome: Pontifical Biblical Institute.

Elliott, John H. 1990. *A Home for the Homeless: A Social-Scientific Criticism of 1 Peter, Its Situation, and Strategy, with a New Introduction.* Minneapolis: Fortress Press.

Gonzáles, Catherine Gunsalus. 2010. *First and Second Peter and Jude.* Louisville: Westminster John Knox.

Hauerwas, Stanley, and William Willimon. 1989. *Resident Aliens.* Nashville: Abingdon.

Kelly, J. N. D. 1976. *Epistles of Peter and of Jude.* London: Black.

Kittredge, Cynthia Briggs. 2012. *1 Peter* in *The Women's Bible Commentary* 3rd edition, pp. 616–19. C. Newsome, S. Ringe, and J. Lapsley, eds. Louisville: Westminster John Knox,

Michaels, J. Ramsey. 1998. *First Peter.* WBC. Waco, TX: Word.

Spurgeon, Charles H. 1916. "Coming to Christ: A Sermon." The Spurgeon Archive. April 27. www.spurgeon.org/sermons/3509.htm.

Vinson, Richard B., with Richard F. Wilson and E. Mills Watson. 2010. *First and Second Peter and Jude.* Macon, GA: Smyth & Helwys.

2 PETER

Pheme Perkins

Introduction

Faced with growing skepticism over belief in the second coming of Christ and the consequences of that view for the ethical conduct of believers, a pseudonymous author invoked the authority of the apostle Peter to confirm established teaching. The transfiguration of Jesus (2 Pet. 1:16-18), establishes both Jesus' divine identity and belief in his parousia. This focus on Jesus as God is reflected in the opening verse (1:1) of the letter as well as its concluding doxology (3:18). Since Jesus is their benefactor and divine Savior (1:11; 2:20; 3:2), Christians must hold fast to the true knowledge of the Lord (Kistemaker, 221–26). The divine power and goodness of the Savior enables the faithful to participate in the divine nature (1:4; Craddock, 88).

The author reinforces the Petrine voice by employing a Semitic version of the apostle's name, "Simeon" instead of "Simon" (v. 1), and referring back to an earlier epistle written in Peter's name, our 1 Peter (3:1). By suggesting that in this letter one also possesses Peter's "testament," his final teaching at the point of death (1:12-15), the author invokes the authority of a revered figure delivering final instructions and warnings as Moses does in Deuteronomy. The reference to Jesus' prediction of Peter's death in 1:14 reflects a tradition attested in John 21:18-19. In addition to these Petrine echoes, 2 Peter also insists that "our beloved brother Paul" presented the same teaching, despite the attempt by false teachers to use the complexity of his letters in support of their theological innovations (3:15-16).

Although the reference to the transfiguration does not quote any one of our written Gospels, it seems reasonable to conclude that 2 Peter expects Christians to know one or more of the Gospels and a collection of apostolic letters that includes several from Paul as well as 1 Peter. When we compare the Old Testament examples used to support the teaching of divine judgment in 2 Peter 2 with Jude 4-13, it becomes clear that the author has employed that writing as well without appealing to Jude as apostolic. Although 2 Peter does not identify either its place of origin or the locale of its audience, several features of the work suggest that it may have been composed in Rome in the early second century CE. In addition to the traditional association of Peter with that city, 1 Peter was dispatched from Rome to believers in Asia Minor. Toward the end of the first century, *1 Clement* invoked the authority of both apostles, Peter and Paul, in writing to Corinth (*1 Clem.* 5.4-5). In addition to the traditional link between Peter and the city, some scholars find a clue in the ethical teaching of 2 Peter. Christian faith as commitment to purity and holiness of life that distinguishes believers from their pagan surroundings is characteristic of Roman Christianity (Bauckham, 158–61).

Though it is difficult to untangle the logic of an opponent's argument from a well-crafted polemical response, scholars have detected traits of Epicurean philosophy that could have supported the false teaching opposed here (Neyrey, 122–25). Epicureans argued against any belief in intervention by or punishment from the gods and held that the universe reflects the eternal, random interactions of various sorts of atoms moving in a void. Death is the dissolution of the atoms that make up the person. Therefore there is no such thing as a divine providence in the world or divine punishment and reward. By following this philosophy, humans liberate themselves from fear of the gods, the future, or death. Exactly how the false teachers adapted Epicurean principles to distort Christian faith is unclear. Presumably the opposition must have held out some view of salvation, perhaps a divinization of the soul similar to that envisioned in 2 Peter. At the same time, they may have used Epicurean cosmology to reject as mythology all teaching about an end-time judgment. Perhaps they also adopted an ethic of the pleasant life, which 2 Peter interprets as freedom for immorality or caving in to the passions (2:2, 10a, 13-14, 18).

2 Peter follows the structure of a letter.

> Greeting (1:1-2)
> Opening, purpose for writing (1:3-15)
> Summary of the faith shared by believers (vv. 3-11)
> Peter's testament to endure beyond his death (vv. 12-15)
> Body of the letter; the certainty of divine judgment (1:16—3:13)
> The transfiguration confirms the truth of the Lord's coming in glory (1:16-18)
> True prophecy is inspired by God (1:19-21)
> False teachers are comparable to false prophets (2:1-3)
> Examples of divine punishment and rescue of the righteous (2:4-10a)
> Application to the false teachers and their followers (2:10b-22)
> Exhortation to the readers (3:1-13)
> Body closing (3:14-18a)
> Final doxology (3:18b)

2 Peter 1:1-15: Christ's Calling

■ The Text in Its Ancient Context

The greeting and opening of 2 Peter adopt the voice of the apostle Peter in defense of a shared faith that is summarized in verses 3-11. By casting this work as a testament of the apostle intended to enable future believers to recall Peter's teaching after his death, the author has crafted a piece intended to transcend the historical particulars of Peter's life (Harrington and Senior, 250–52). Verses 3-11 summarize the faith shared by believers, which forms the basis of "entry into the eternal kingdom of our Lord and Savior" (v. 11). "Knowledge of our Lord Jesus" refers to the moral goodness, separation from the passions, and mutual love appropriate to persons who will share the divine nature.

The Text in the Interpretive Tradition

Doubts about its Petrine authorship based on the obvious difference in style between 1 and 2 Peter led fourth-century authors to treat it as marginal to the canon (Eusebius, *Hist. eccl.* 3.3.1; Jerome, *Vir. ill.* 1). John Calvin defends reading this letter despite such doubts by suggesting that even if written by another it reflects Peter's teaching.

The Text in Contemporary Discussion

Though 2 Peter does not develop the reference to sharing divine nature in 1:4, divinization would become the centerpiece of Christ's saving work in the fourth-century-CE Greek fathers. The Son of God became man so that we might become God. This transformation could be expressed as participating in divine immortality (Novatian, *Trin.* 15.1) or linked with receiving a divine nature by participating in the Eucharist (Cyril of Jerusalem, *Cat. Lect.* 4.3). Contemporary theologians look to the insights of the Greek fathers in formulating a soteriology of human transformation into the new being envisaged by God.

2 Peter 1:16—2:3: The Example of the Prophets

The Text in Its Ancient Context

An indirect reference to John's Gospel may have been intended by the comment that Jesus had predicted Peter's death (v. 14). This section makes a more explicit allusion to the story of Jesus' transfiguration in the Synoptic Gospels (Matt. 17:1-8; Mark 9:2-13; Luke 9:28-36) by referring to a group of apostolic witnesses ("we"), the glory of Jesus, and the words of God's voice. Most of the details of the Gospel stories have been omitted from this précis. The divine words are closest to Matt. 17:5.

The transition to a discussion of authentic prophecy points to a specific crisis behind the composition of 2 Peter. How affirming the validity of Old Testament prophecy as it points forward to Christ in verse 19a relates to the transfiguration is not entirely clear. Perhaps 2 Peter expects readers to treat the presence of Moses and Elijah as prophetic witnesses. The metaphor of a shining lamp and the morning star rising in the heart recalls such earlier Christian language about awaiting the day of judgment as 1 Thess. 5:5-8 (Neyrey, 183). Second Peter insists that the prophets neither invented their oracles nor fabricated interpretations of their visions, since they spoke under the guidance of the Holy Spirit (vv. 20-21). This argument could be directed against an Epicurean skepticism concerning all oracles or against claims on the part of the false teachers to divine inspiration.

Since biblical prophecy is divinely inspired, the author will connect ancient examples of divine punishment with the fate that awaits false teachers who delude believers and corrupt their morals (2:1-3). Greed is often invoked as a motive in polemical rhetoric along with the standard items of moral depravity. Second Peter employs the polemic of Jude 4 in depicting the false teachers, but it adds an ironical turn. Though they point to the apparent delay as evidence against a day of judgment, the condemnation of these false teachers has been fixed in God's plan, and is not suspended (v. 3b; Kraftchick, 121–23).

The Text in the Interpretive Tradition

Justin Martyr may be alluding to 2 Pet. 2:1 when he compares the false prophets of the Old Testament to the many false teachers of his own day (*Dial.* 82.1).

The Text in Contemporary Discussion

Although Christians reaffirm their belief in the Hebrew prophets as witnesses to Christ and in the Lord's coming in judgment whenever they recite the creed, many consider that language a mythological or poetic holdover from a more naive time. The transfiguration story presents the presence of God in the Son as the culmination of a story of God's saving presence with humanity that began with creation. To use the language of end-time judgment as a way of underlining the moral seriousness required of believers (1:3-11) is one way of holding on to a biblical heritage that no longer matches scientific or popular media scenarios for the end of planet earth. Since 2 Peter clearly retains the early Christian tradition that this world will come to a cataclysmic end when the divine Christ appears as judge, its explanation of the delay (3:5-10) does not imply that the phrase "until he comes again" should be dropped from the creed.

2 Peter 2:4-22: Lessons from the Biblical Past

Second Peter 2:4-10a has modified the language and content of Jude 4-13. It omits Jude's references to Jewish apocryphal material, such as the contest between Satan and Michael over the body of Moses in Jude 9 or the citation of Enoch as an authoritative prophet in Jude 14-16. These omissions may reflect an awareness that such apocrypha are not inspired Scripture. However, the author might simply have dropped material unfamiliar to the intended audience (Bauckham, 260). In another striking modification, the author adds the dimension of salvation to the judgment and punishment motif in the examples of the flood ("Noah, a herald of righteousness, with seven others") and Sodom and Gomorrah ("Lot, a righteous man"). This shift helps readers to view their own situation in these ancient stories. Second Peter even stresses the distress of a righteous man like Lot faced while living among the ungodly (vv. 7-8). Therefore the lesson that his audience is to learn includes God's ability to rescue the righteous who suffer trials (v. 9a; Bauckham, 257).

Second Peter harangues the opposition (vv. 10b-22) under two heads, the depravity of persons driven by fleshly desires and their arrogant disregard for authority. The latter is picked up first in an ambiguous charge that they engage in some form of slander against heavenly beings that not even angels would attempt (vv. 10b-11). Subjection to fleshly passions reduces the opponents to the level of irrational animals, destined to be the hunter's prey (v. 12). This section culminates in two proverbial sayings about the filth of irrational animals: dogs that lick their own vomit and pigs that go from water to rolling in mud (v. 22). Disgusting animalistic behavior reflects the dissipation that characterizes the life of the opponents and their followers (vv. 13-14, 18).

With characteristic irony, the invective points out that the freedom promised by the opposition is nothing less than slavery. To adopt false moral teaching is worse than living as the unbelievers do because it undermines the liberating power of Christ (vv. 18-21).

The Text in the Interpretive Tradition

First Clement 11.1–2 also uses the rescue of Lot to drive home the point that God never abandons the godly. Lot's wife becomes a warning to believers who might begin to doubt God's power.

The Text in Contemporary Discussion

Second Peter 2:5-9 emphasizes God's power to preserve the moral character of the faithful even when they live in situations that are shot through with evil. It acknowledges the spiritual suffering that causes righteous people to keep themselves apart from the wicked but does not advocate sectarian isolation. Christians can bear witness to the gospel in such a world by refusing to accept its moral relativism.

2 Peter 3:1-18: Salvation and Judgment

Second Peter invites the audience to apply two sources of insight to their situation: the holy prophets and the commandment of the Lord handed on through the apostles (vv. 1-3; cf. Jude 17-18). The author then defends Christian belief in divine judgment. Those who deny it ignore the truth that the same power by which God created all things preserves them until the day of judgment (vv. 5-7). Another argument points to the psalm text that distinguishes the human and divine perceptions of time (v. 8; Ps. 90:4). Once again, 2 Peter includes God's saving power in the discussion, since new creation follows judgment (vv. 11-13). To account for the delayed end-time, verse 9 invokes a familiar Jewish treatment of the question of divine punishment. God withholds it to provide opportunity for the wicked to repent (Exod. 34:6; Joel 2:12-13; Sir. 5:4-7; Bauckham, 312). God's merciful forbearance does not mean that judgment has been canceled. The traditional Christian conviction that the Day of the Lord will come suddenly remains true (v. 10; cf. 1 Thess. 5:2-6).

Therefore Christians should appreciate the delayed judgment as an opportunity for salvation, not license (vv. 14-15). Second Peter insists that the letters of Paul teach the same understanding of the Christian life despite the use false teachers make of them and other Scriptures. A final exhortation to remain steadfast in faith concludes with a doxology to Jesus as Lord and Savior rather than God, as in Jude 25, "to the only God our Savior, through Jesus Christ." Praising Jesus in this fashion suggests that at least in its worship, the community perceives him as fully divine.

The Text in the Interpretive Tradition

A rabbinic tradition that the arrival of the end time is somehow correlated with Israel's repentance (*b. Sanh.* 97b–98a) raises an interesting possibility for verse 9b (". . . is patient with you, not wanting any to perish"). The delay could reflect a lack of repentance among Christians. Bede reads this passage with Rev. 6:11 as indicating the time for God to gather all those elect predestined before creation.

The Text in Contemporary Discussion

The balance 2 Peter exhibits in revising the apocalyptic traditions adapted from Jude—namely, incorporating salvation of the faithful along with condemnation of the wicked—highlights the deficiency of our secular apocalypses. Unlike the postapocalyptic world in contemporary films, which leaves a few humans wandering amid the ruins of civilization, the Christian hope extends beyond judgment to the new creation no longer marred by evil (v. 13; Rom. 8:21; Rev. 21:1).

However, the methodological problem still engages Christian theology. How can traditional Christian belief address the skepticism generated by scientific descriptions of the universe? Though cast as a form of polemic that most Christians today find distasteful, the ethical emphasis in 2 Peter points to the key area of dispute. Scientific theories about the world are not a threat. It is the moral consequences that opponents of religion such as the "new atheists" attach to them that believers must resist.

Works Cited

Bauckham, Richard J. 1983. *Jude, 2 Peter.* WBC 50. Waco, TX: Word.
Craddock, Fred. 1995. *First and Second Peter and Jude.* Louisville: Westminster John Knox.
Kistemaker, Simon. 1996. *Exposition of James, Epistles of John, Peter, and Jude.* Grand Rapids: Baker.
Kraftchick, Steven J. 2002. *Jude, 2 Peter.* Nashville: Abingdon.
Neyrey, Jerome H. 1993. *2 Peter, Jude.* AB 37C. New York: Doubleday.
Senior, Donald, and Daniel J. Harrington. 2008. *1 Peter, Jude and 2 Peter.* Sacra Pagina 15. Collegeville, MN: Liturgical Press.

1, 2, 3 JOHN

Jaime Clark-Soles

Introduction

The Johannine Epistles, along with the Gospel of John, occupy a substantial position in the canon, constituting "The Johannine literature" and perhaps indicating a "Johannine school of thought" from which they all emerged, akin to the notion of a "Pauline school of thought." Certainly 1 John has provided the church ample liturgical material with its insistence on confession of sin and assurance of pardon (1:8-9); the call to prayer (4:14-15), especially intercessory prayer (4:16); and its proclamation that "God is love." The epistles raise and inform the following issues:

- *Ecclesiology*: How is the group to form and maintain a cohesive communal identity? How should it handle church discipline when conflict arises? Who has the authority to instruct the church in matters of theology and praxis? Does the "elder"? On what is this authority based?
- *Hospitality*: Who deserves hospitality from Christians and who does not? On what basis is this decision made?
- *Ethics*: What is the shape of a Christian praxis based on the preeminent commandment from Jesus to "love one another"? How does this cohere with denying hospitality to certain individuals? How should the Christian interact with "the world"?
- *Theology*: What is the nature of sin? Who is Jesus and how has his blood cleansed the Johannine Christian?

Unlike 2 and 3 John, the author of 1 John remains entirely unnamed, but claims to be an eyewitness to the earthly Jesus (1:1-4). Due to apparent knowledge of and dependence on the traditions evinced by the Fourth Gospel, some assume that the same author penned both texts. Based on differences in theology and style, however, others attribute 1 John to a different author, perhaps the "elder" referred to in 2 John 1 and 3 John 1 (though the epistles may well come from different hands). The composition history of the Fourth Gospel itself is quite complex and probably reflects various stages of the community in which it arose (see the entry on the Gospel), and more than one authorial or editorial hand. As a result, theories concerning the authorship and dating of the Gospel and each epistle abound. If, as seems likely, the epistles were composed after the Gospel, they should be dated to around 100 CE. (For a thorough treatment of the composition history of the Johannine material, see von Wahlde.)

Also unlike 2 and 3 John, 1 John is more a hortatory address or essay than an epistle. It lacks the conventional features of a letter, including the names of the sender and recipient, opening and closing greetings, or a thanksgiving. Second John is written to "the elect lady and her children" and 3 John, to Gaius. First John does not designate its audience, but its rhetoric, allusions, and assumptions indicate that the audience is part of the same community from which the Fourth Gospel arose. In each case, the author is concerned with both the theology and the ethics of the community. Whereas the Gospel of John devotes much attention to the relationship between the Johannine community and other entities outside of it (the parent Jewish tradition, Rome, other Christian groups: Clark-Soles), the Johannine Epistles focus internally. The letters share a common language, outlook, and social setting. They instruct their readers regarding how to deal with those who have abandoned the community (and thereby apostatized) as well as those who espouse false teachings. The tensions felt in the community with respect to those members who have become a problem raise questions about the nature of Christian hospitality and inclusivity. In addition to building up the faithful who remain by demonizing those who departed, the epistles also reiterate the importance of binding the community together through active, sacrificial love.

"God is love [*agapē*]." This central, climactic assertion provides shape to the Johannine Epistles. Inseparable from this main theme are two others: proper Christology and the avoidance of sin, especially the sin that leads to death (5:16). As an act of love, God sent Jesus (1) to reveal the nature of love, which is always concrete and other-oriented (if sectarian), and (2) to free people from the power of sin by his sacrificial act through his blood (1:6—2:2; 4:10).

First John appears concerned to combat what historians call docetic Christology. The term *docetism* derives from the Greek verb *dokeō*, "to seem." Broadly speaking, it refers to a form of Christianity, known to us chiefly from the writings of other Christians who condemned it, that maintained Jesus was not really human but only appeared to be. He was not truly subject to the vicissitudes of embodied fleshly existence and therefore only "appeared" to suffer physically. Docetism is usually described as related to Gnosticism, another modern name for a number of early Christian movements that until the mid-twentieth century were also known only through the writings of polemicists like Irenaeus. Bishop of Lyons in the late second century, Irenaeus mocked certain other Christian teachers as "falsely so-called 'knowers' [*gnōstikoi*]." As conventionally understood, both docetism and Gnosticism malign the material order and denigrate the usefulness of the flesh; both were declared heresies in the early centuries of the church.

Curiously, "gnostic" thinkers such as Valentinus drew heavily on the Gospel of John. Indeed, the renowned theologian Ernst Käsemann detected what he called a "naïve docetism" in the Fourth Gospel, generated by the author's heavy emphasis on Jesus' divinity, not to mention the aplomb with which Jesus manages his passion as compared to the Synoptic Gospels. But the author of 1

John castigates docetic Christologies, and was followed by numerous subsequent theologians (see Ignatius's *Letter to the Smyrnaeans* 1–7; *Letter to the Trallians* 9.1–2; Irenaeus's *Against Heresies*).

Although the authors of the epistles remain anonymous, all three became associated with "John" in the early church, whether that John was identified as the son of Zebedee or "John the Elder." Eventually, Revelation, the one text that actually names its author as John (but does not give any more identifying details), becomes associated with the Gospel and the three epistles. From the outset there were doubts about the authenticity of the material, especially of 2 and 3 John (Eusebius, *Hist. eccl.* 6.25.9–10). The letters are cited unevenly among the church fathers, and the reception of each varies geographically (Lieu 2008, 25–28). While 1 John appealed widely early, 2 and 3 John experienced rockier paths to canonization. Their survival and final inclusion in the canon signifies that, regardless of their authorship or original audience, the contents of the letters were and are useful to the wider Christian church.

1 John

1 John 1:1-4: The Prologue

No two commentaries agree on the structure of 1 John. The epistle does not present a clear thesis that drives forward to a compelling conclusion. Rather, it is marked by repetition, a spiral-like collection of themes, and self-referential habits (e.g., 1 John 3:24 and 4:13 make the same statement; 4:1-6 picks up on 2:18-28). Like the Fourth Gospel, 1 John begins with a prologue that introduces key themes and terms: word, life, revealed, testify, declare, fellowship, and the relationship between God and Jesus as Father and Son. Authority is justified by a claim to eyewitness status. The prologue also anticipates a major theme of the epistle, namely, the incarnation, the embodiedness of the Messiah, such that he could be perceived by the senses: he was seen, heard, and touched. In addition, the transmission of the Gospel involves attending to the embodiedness of one's brothers and sisters (3:16-18) and abiding with another in love; as the text demonstrates, this ideal can be elusive.

1 John 1:5—2:17: Walk in the Light

■ The Text in Its Ancient Context

After declaring that "God is light" (v. 5), the author continues to solidify bonds with the listeners by drawing them into "we" rhetoric and indicating what behavior and beliefs they should espouse and what they should eschew. The audience is to walk in the light. The language of walking (Greek *peripatein*) as a metaphor for ethical behavior is common in the Hebrew Bible and stems from the Hebrew verb *halak*, to walk. Hence, even today the collection of rabbinical ethical teachings is called the halakah.

First John 1:6-10 enjoins the audience to walk in the light, for those who do so testify to truth; enjoy fellowship with one another; confess that they have sin; and have been forgiven their sin and cleansed from all unrighteousness by the blood of Jesus, God's Son. Those who walk in the darkness can enjoy none of these benefits. As parents assume the role of moral formation in their children, so the author addresses them as "my little children" (note that the "we" language has receded here). With respect to sin, one must confess that one has sin in order to receive forgiveness (1:9). Although the author wants the audience to behave ethically and avoid sin (indeed, this is a main point of the sermon as indicated in 2:1), he makes allowance for it by noting that if anyone does sin, Jesus Christ provides the solution. How?

First John 2:2 deserves further explication. The sentence reads: "And he himself is a *hilasmos* on behalf of our sins, but not only on behalf of our [sins] but also on behalf of the whole cosmos." It is difficult to translate *hilasmos* because apart from here and 1 John 4:10, it appears nowhere else in the New Testament. The NRSV translates it as "atoning sacrifice"; Judith Lieu (2008, 64) as "forgiveness"; and John Painter (146) and D. Moody Smith (52) as "expiation." Unfortunately, the word appears only six times in the Septuagint (Lev. 25:9; Num. 5:8; 2 Macc. 3:33; Ps. 129:4; Amos 8:14; Ezek. 44:27; Dan. 9:9) and does not always have the same meaning. It can refer to the effects of cultic (or sacrificial) action, such as expiation (which emphasizes the subjective agency of God in removing sin) or propitiation (which emphasizes the human action in appeasing God's wrath); or it can refer to the action itself, specifically a sin offering; or it can simply refer to forgiveness. Those who argue for a cultic meaning in 1 John point to Lev. 25:9 and the context of the Day of Atonement. They also note the phrase "on behalf of our sins" in 2:2 and link this verse with 1:7-9, which refers to Jesus' blood and cleansing. Lieu 64 disagrees with this approach and argues that the scant evidence does not bear out such specificity as a translation such as "atoning sacrifice" would imply. Those Christian scholars who do see a cultic meaning are careful to translate *hilasmos* as "expiation," not "propitiation," because God and Jesus the just (*dikaios*) are the actors and agents in dealing with sin.

A connection is sometimes made between 2:2 and the martyr traditions found in 4 Maccabees and the Suffering Servant of Isa. 52:13—53:11. The servant is just (*dikaios*; Isa. 53:11); his death is "on behalf of sin" (Isa. 53:10); and he "bore the sins of many and was handed over on account of their sins" (Isa. 53:12 LXX; Lieu 2008, 63–64). The Maccabees, as just martyrs, may present a parallel: "the tyrant was punished, and the homeland purified—they having become, as it were, a ransom [*antipsychon*] for the sin of our nation. And through the blood of those devout ones and their death as an atoning sacrifice [*hilastērion*], divine Providence preserved Israel that previously had been mistreated" (4 Macc. 17:21-22). If martyrdom is the notion the author has in mind, it raises doubts about 1 John's containing a developed doctrine of atonement at all.

Whatever one decides, it is important to be clear that (1) God and Jesus provide the solution for sin; (2) Jesus continues to solve sin in the present as a living, active agent; and (3) Jesus' action was and is part of God's original plan, not, so to speak, an improvisation. That is, we should not imagine that in the author's view, God had devised a plan A for the Jews, through the Torah and covenants, which failed so that God was forced to scramble to initiate a plan B in the form of Jesus. Jesus' work implements God's initial plan. There are at least three problems with imagining that atonement in Jesus is in any way an innovation or improvisation. First, it divorces Jesus from his own Jewish identity and tradition. Second, it postulates Christianity as a solution to the failure of atonement in Judaism and is therefore supersessionist and, potentially, antisemitic. Third, it appears gnostic; that is, it seems to see the Old Testament as evidence of a lesser God of a lesser religion and the New Testament as evidence of Jesus who frees the believer from the gnostic demiurge.

The proclamation that Jesus' justifying work is on behalf of "the whole cosmos" is noteworthy and, when combined with 4:14, where Jesus is denoted "the savior of the world," sounds quite hopeful and expansive. As it turns out, however, this is probably the exception to the general rule of 1 John (and the Gospel of John); the world represents opposition to God and God's children. In this way, 1 John may be described as sectarian and dualistic.

It is not surprising in a hortatory address to find the author moving from a discussion of sin to that of obeying Jesus' commandments and imitating Jesus' behavior. Though the author speaks of commandments in the plural at 2:3-4, he really has only one commandment in mind: "Love your brother [*adelphos*]." This commandment may well allude to John 13:34: "I give you a new commandment, that you love one another. Just as I have loved you, you also should love one another." In both cases, the author calls the audience to love fellow believers (this use of sibling language for church relationships is typical for early Christians). Those familiar with the Synoptic Gospels will miss the charge to "love your enemies" (Matt. 5:44; Luke 6:27, 35) or "love your neighbor as yourself" (Matt. 19:19; 22:39; Mark 12:31; Luke 10:27), neither of which appears in the Gospel of John. Instead, Johannine Christians are to love the other members of the group, but they are to do so specifically by imitating Jesus' own way of loving. The author is trying to create a household of love where the family ties are strong enough to maintain group cohesion: note the familial language in 2:12-14—fathers, children (*teknia*), young people (*paidia*), and that the family ties that bind also liberate (1 John 3:17-18).

At 2:15, the author warns the listeners that one can either love the world or love God; the two are mutually exclusive. Scholars debate extensively the meaning of the triad presented in 2:16, which the NRSV translates: "the desire [*epithymia*] of the flesh [*sarx*], the desire [*epithymia*] of the eyes [*ophthalmōn*], the pride [*alazoneia*] of riches [*tou biou*]." Some consider the first two to refer specifically to sexual issues; others consider all three to relate to greed, a lust for wealth. Desire in and of itself may not be problematic, but deformed desire always is. William Loader suggests that the author signifies "the depraved excesses of the rich at their often pretentious banquets" where money, drunkenness, and sexual immorality inevitably coalesce (forthcoming, 6). This passage relates to a fundamental ethical concern that runs throughout the epistle: the care of the poor. The Roman Empire in the first century had nothing like "the middle class" of today; the vast majority of people lived in poverty at a bare subsistence level and depended on handouts from the state or wealthy persons. The passage immediately preceding demands that the Christians love one another, referring not to a mere feeling but to concrete action as defined in 3:16-18. Faithful Christians will resist greed and exploitation of others, both of which are tantamount to "hate" and even "murder." In 2:14, the author declares that true Christians have "overcome the evil one."

■ THE TEXT IN THE INTERPRETIVE TRADITION

First John 2:1-2 has given rise to christological debates about the work accomplished by Jesus in solving the problem of sin. This includes attention to various hotly debated theories of atonement.

Many Christians unjustifiably assume penal substitutionary atonement theories when reading any New Testament texts. In this view, God's justice demands a legal payment as the penalty for human sin. Rather than each sinful person having to pay that price, Jesus is substituted. First John should challenge that assumption. In fact, the issue already arises in the Gospel of John itself, when Jesus is referred to as "the Lamb of God who takes away the sin of the world" (John 1:29), and where Jesus dies a day earlier in the Gospel of John than in the Synoptics, at the time when the sacrifice of the Passover lambs occurred in the temple. Technically speaking, the Passover lamb was not a sacrifice *for sin* (so no particular theory of atonement is in view), but symbolized deliverance from death. Most likely, the Gospel's language of the "Lamb of God" represents a merger of Passover-lamb symbolism with imagery of the Suffering Servant in Isaiah 53. Rather than presenting a notion of penal substitutionary atonement, John depicts Jesus as dying to reconcile an alienated world to its God by overcoming the world's hostility through belief. "*When the love of God, conveyed through the death of Jesus, overcomes the sin of unbelief by evoking faith, it delivers people from the judgment of God by bringing them into true relationship with God.* This is atonement in the Johannine sense. . . . There is no suggestion that dying 'for' the people equals paying the legal penalty for sin. The Fourth Gospel has a different understanding of sacrifice" (Koester 2008, 115–16). This understanding is probably what the author of 1 John also has in mind.

Others debate whether *hilasmos* means expiation or propitiation (see above). Still others argue that 1 John may have both expiation and propitiation in mind (Painter, 146–47).

■ The Text in Contemporary Discussion

From purely academic contexts to popular Christianity today (e.g., Rob Bell, Brian McClaren, Emergent Christianity), atonement theology has recently come under scrutiny. Feminists and others raise deep concerns about the marriage of religion and violence in sacrificial language. Did God will the death of God's own child? Is child sacrifice ever warranted? Does God ever perpetrate violence and demand it as an act of faith from God's followers? If so, by what standards does one judge a violent act done in the name of God as faithful or evil? How does voluntary or involuntary martyrdom relate to these themes, if at all? If Jesus' act was performed on behalf of the whole world, does this imply that, finally, the whole world will be saved?

Though nuances inhere, there are currently five primary views of atonement in play in modern Christianity.

1. The first is *Christus Victor* or "Ransom." Human beings used their free will to rupture their relationship with God, and Satan used this opportunity to imprison us in sin and death. Sinless Jesus was sent as a "ransom" and won the victory over sin, death, and Satan.
2. The "satisfaction theory of atonement" was championed most famously in the eleventh century by Anselm the archbishop of Canterbury in his book *Cur Deus Homo* ("Why did God become human?"), and furthered by Thomas Aquinas in the thirteenth century. God created the universe in an orderly manner in which human beings are meant to honor and obey God. In the Garden of Eden episode, God's honor was offended and the universe was thrown off balance. Someone must satisfy the debt due God's offended honor. That someone has to be

infinite since God is infinite. Enter Jesus, the one who is both human and infinite. "By dying on the cross, Jesus, as a man, satisfied God's honor. As God, he provided the infinite payment necessary to satisfy an infinite debt" (Baker, 57).

3. The third model of atonement, Jesus as moral example, is associated with Peter Abelard (1079–1142) and employs the metaphor of courtly love. "Abelard wanted his listeners to think about God as loving, compassionate, and merciful. Consequently, Jesus lived, died, and rose again in order to reveal God's love to us. Everything Jesus said or did served as an example not only of how God behaves, but how we should behave too" (Baker, 60).

4. The model popularized by John Calvin (1509–1564), and the one probably most familiar to contemporary Christians, is penal substitution. Those familiar with or committed to the so-called Romans Road to Salvation will consider it the singular version of atonement theology: (a) "All have sinned and fall short of the glory of God" (Rom. 3:23); (b) the wages of sin is death (Rom. 6:23); (c) though all deserve eternal punishment, Jesus "acts as our substitute, taking on our sin and suffering our punishment so we don't have to" (Baker, 63).

5. Finally, the model of atonement made popular by authors such as Sharon Baker and Raquel St. Clair may be called an "antiviolent atonement theory." It lays the blame of Jesus' violent, unjust death at the feet of all of us human beings (rather than God or Satan) who are addicted to violence in the name not only of barbarous entertainment but also of political expediency. The salient features of this view of atonement (as enumerated by Baker) are as follows:
    a. "Jesus emptied himself of the right to live selfishly and gave his life in service to all creation" (Baker, 158).
    b. Jesus died as a consequence of human sin.
    c. Jesus asked God to forgive that sin, and God complied with Jesus' prayer.
    d. Jesus' salvific work undoes the sin of Adam and brings salvation on a cosmic level (Baker, 159).
    e. "Through his life, death, and resurrection, Jesus reveals to us the incomprehensible love of God . . . toward all creation. . . . God forgave all people universally, without condition and without exception" (Baker, 159). When human beings embrace this forgiveness, reconciliation and justice abound.

The evidence in 1 John (and the Gospel itself) probably cannot bear the weight imposed on it by those who would argue for a "theory of atonement," and certainly not a singular one. Lieu is wise to warn against overinterpreting the *hilasmos* language. Of the five models mentioned above, the Johannine Epistles (and Gospel) may have most in common with the fifth. "In 1 John, however, there is nothing to demand a sacrificial understanding . . . particularly as not only did God *send* (aorist) Jesus as a *hilasmos* (4:10), but he *is* (present) one (2:2)—past act and present reality. In all the emphasis is probably on the reconciliation thus made possible and not on any precise model of its method" (Lieu 1991, 64).

First John 2:15-17 may be less about asceticism than it is about care for the poor. Though readers are often tempted to focus on sexual lust in the passage, the better question is, how do sex and greed and lust combine to promote injustice? As Philo already noted: "For strong drink and gross eating accompanied by wine-bibbing, while they awaken the insatiable lusts of the belly, inflame also the lusts seated below it" (*Spec. Laws* 1.192). In our world as well, insatiable sexual lust and economic injustice are intertwined. Loader's depiction of the gluttonous banquets of the rich relates directly to the staggering enormity of human slavery and sex trafficking worldwide at present. The text lends urgency to our consideration of such issues by setting it in an eschatological context, noting that one's choices have ultimate consequences before God.

1 John 2:18—3:24: Love in Action

The Text in Its Ancient Context

Those who have left the community are antichrists and liars and do not love God. While they are not directly equated with "the world," by denying God they show that they love the world. What makes these apostates antichrists? Their Christology. Not only do they deny the Father and the Son and that Jesus is the Messiah (2:22), but they also deny the flesh of Jesus. For the author, it appears to be a short step from denying the importance of Christ's fleshly embodiedness to denying the importance of a fellow Christian's bodily needs. When one does this, one walks in the footsteps of Cain, who is associated with the evil one and traffics in fratricide (3:12-15). Wealthy Christians are to care for poorer Christians.

The ethical exhortation is set in an eschatological context. It is "the last hour" (2:18). The faithful community is able to do right because they are "christs" (2:20; 27), having been anointed by the Holy One. They know everything they need to know to abide and love; even more will be revealed to them when Jesus comes again (2:28; 3:2; cf. 1 Corinthians 13). They are on an ethical journey that has not yet been brought to fruition; in the end, they will be like Jesus. Jesus is pure, holy, and just (2:20; 3:3, 7).

It is clear, however, that the author of 1 John holds an apocalyptic worldview (like most New Testament authors). Like Paul, he understands that Christians live in a "middle period," the time between Christ's effective work on the cross and the full unveiling of the eschaton. There is a cosmic battle being waged between the forces of good and evil. Human beings can enlist with one or the other, but they cannot remain neutral. While the devil's days are numbered, he still wanders to and fro about the earth causing trouble for the faithful (cf. the figure of "the adversary," *ha-Satan*, in Job, and the devil in 1 Pet. 5:8). Even Christians must be on guard lest they inadvertently lend their energies to the work of the devil. When they slip up, they confess and are righted; this distinguishes them from those who have departed and abandoned Jesus entirely.

The leitmotif of 1 John is love. God loves us, as shown through the way Jesus has loved us (by laying down his life) and continues to love us (including advocating for us in our weakness). This love commandment dominates as it has "from the beginning." The latter is a favorite phrase of the author and is multivalent. Surely it means, at least, from the beginning of everything, since it defines God's character (1 John 4:16); from the beginning of creation; from the beginning of humanity's story (Cain and Abel are representative of the fruits of love and hate); from the beginning of the Son's particular work in the incarnation (cf. the Gospel of John); and quite possibly, from the beginning of the Johannine community, likely in Palestine, and continuing in the author's day: in Ephesus, according to some traditions. Love is foundational. It is also generative: note both the mention of God's seed (*sperma*) in 1 John 3:9 as well as the language of birth, children, and life throughout. Love is eternal and abiding. As noted earlier, the practical expression of love involves trusting in the name of Jesus and loving one another (3:23).

■ The Text in the Interpretive Tradition

First John 3:2 has been beloved by the mystics who longed to attain illumination and the beatific vision (Murphy, 59–60), while 1 John 3:3 (sometimes in concert with 2:16) has inspired asceticism among many church fathers, such as Tertullian and Augustine (Greer, 21–26).

First John 3:4-10 is one of the most difficult passages in 1 John. Verses 4-6 have appeared in debates both about the doctrine of the sinlessness of Jesus and about the doctrine of original sin. Furthermore, in it the author declares that Christians do not do sin (*ou poiei hamartian*) and cannot sin (*ou dynatai harmatanein*). Those who sin are children of the devil, do not do justice, and do not love. This proclamation is puzzling, given the author's insistence that one must not deny having sin (1:5-10) and his assurance that if they sin, Jesus will advocate for them (2:1-2). How is this apparent contradiction to be explained? Some suggest that the earlier discussion refers to a person's pre-Christian life as if that were in the past tense, whereas 3:4-10 refers to a person who has become a Christian. This fails to convince, however, because both the having sin in 1:8 and the doing sin in 3:4 are in the present tense. Another proposed solution depends on the language of abiding (*menō*). As long as one abides, one does not sin; when one does not abide, one sins. This notion of moving in and out of the state of abiding, however, does not make sense in Johannine terms. The word "abide" denotes stability and something God and Jesus are said to do as well. A third suggestion is to consider that, while the abiding might be stable, it is incomplete until the eschaton. Others find this explanation wanting, arguing that it applies to the cosmic level but not the individual (Lieu 2008, 132).

■ The Text in Contemporary Discussion

The emphasis on care for those in poverty draws the contemporary reader's attention to gender, race, and disability concerns. Who is poor and why? Faith and love belong together and coalesce in a concern for economic justice. While the author may have only the Christian poor in mind, doesn't morality compel modern readers to both acknowledge the sectarian impulse in the text and move to universalizing the principle of concern for the poor? Johannes Beutler declares: "Christians living in affluence must share their material goods with their brothers and sisters beyond the boundaries of their Christian communities on a worldwide scale and challenge unjust social structures. . . . For the nations of the northern hemisphere, this responsibility means sharing their wealth with the nations of the south. But this commandment also applies to the developing nations that are characterized by vast inequality in material wealth. A rich ruling class often exploits the masses of the poor" (556–58).

1 John 4:1-6: Incarnation and Antichrists

■ The Text in Its Ancient Context

First John 4:1-6 returns to the theme of 2:18-28. There the subjects were the last hour and the antichrists associated with it, who deny that Jesus is the Messiah and deny the Father and Son;

those who went out (from the Greek verb *exerchomai*) from the community (19); and a warning to abide and not fall under the spell of deceivers. Likewise, 1 John 4 depicts an urgent eschatological scenario (4:3) characterized by the activity of false prophets (4:1) who have "gone out [from *exerchomai* again] into the world." (Recall that in 1 John, "the world" represents a sphere where God's values are not regnant.) There are antichrists who apparently deny that Jesus has come in the flesh and do not confess Jesus (4:2-3). For this author, having the right Christology is not merely an academic exercise but is essential for acting justly, which is to say, loving in the way that God loves (*agapē* language occurs forty-eight times in 1 John). The denial of Jesus' fleshly existence along with the overwhelming use of "knowing" language (*ginōskō*, twenty-five times; *oida*, fifteen times) immediately raises the specter of docetic or gnostic Christology among opponents. It is no accident that the noun "knowledge" never appears in 1 John; the emphasis is on action. Knowing is doing, and knowing rightly is tied to acting rightly. Those who disembody Jesus easily disembody their neighbor. Certain ways of "knowing" cause arrogance and disdain of others in the community.

The Text in the Interpretive Tradition

The insistence on proclaiming that Jesus came in the "flesh" (*sarx*; 1 John 4:2; 2 John 7) indicates that the opponents deny Jesus' flesh or separate the human Jesus from his role as the Christ.

Not surprisingly, docetic Christology also has implications for eucharistic theology, with its emphasis, in some traditions, on consuming Jesus' flesh and blood. First John 4:2 (and 2 John 7) also appear in debates about the virgin birth, the doctrine that Jesus was miraculously conceived by the Holy Spirit and that Mary remained a virgin until after he was born. In 1 John, the emphasis is on the fact of Jesus' physical birth, not on Mary's virginity (which is never mentioned). That is to say, docetic Christologies, with their disparagement of the flesh, would not tolerate a literal incarnation; clearly the author of 1 John insists on it and, therefore, lends support to those who argue for an actual human birth (if by miraculous conception: Sweeney).

The Text in Contemporary Discussion

First John's focus on the incarnation implies that Christians ought to be concerned with ecological matters (Lee). The prologue to John proclaims: "The Word became flesh [*sarx*] and tabernacled among us." Though Jesus is the unique Son of God, he is related to us insofar as we have become children of God through his blood. As the Son, he has authority over all flesh (*pas sarx*; 17:2). Since the prologue narrates the Word's participation in the creation of everything (John 1:3), "all flesh" presumably includes the whole created order, not just human beings (cf. Romans 8). First John eschews docetist theologies that denigrate the material order. Do we? Should human beings relate to the earth in a hierarchical, dominating fashion by which the earth exists merely as an object to be used in the gratification of human greed and gluttony as described in 1 John 2:16?

Ecofeminists argue that denigration of creation is usually connected to denigration of female bodies. The power dynamic of patriarchy involves a system of hierarchy where the male rules as lord (Latin *dominus*, tied to the word "dominate") and the female (and children) are subjects (objects, really) to be used as the male sees fit. Rape, of the earth or of people, is inherent in such a system. Postcolonialism extends the conversation to other bodies, colonized bodies.

The Gospel of John draws heavily from creation language in Genesis. There God created the first earth creature ('adam) from the ground ('adamah). The fall points to the tragic disruption of the synergistic relationship between humans with each other and humans with the earth (Trible). Jesus redeems this problematic situation from the prologue to the Garden, where Jesus and Mary become a new Adam and Eve. Given 1 John's apparent frustration with "the world," some might argue that ecological concerns are not in its purview. On the contrary, since the "world" signifies those ignorant of or in opposition to God's values, then

> this attitude of the world, to find its own answers and to create its own security outside the realm of light and truth, is the real cause for the exploitation of the earth in a manner that shows no concern for the commandment of neighbourly love. The endless ravaging of the earth for economic progress, and the consequential pollution of the earth, the atmosphere and the oceans, are all symptoms of the world's blindness, its mindless quest to establish a security of its own, to erect its own modern Tower of Babel.... Neighbourly love must take on a concrete form, and there is no way that people can continue to ravage their neighbour's environment and pollute the air that they must breathe and still say that they are walking in the light, that they are keeping the commandment of neighbourly love. (Pretorius, 273, 277)

1 John 4:7—5:12: The Church Defined by Love

THE TEXT IN ITS ANCIENT CONTEXT

This section of 1 John repeats numerous themes and images from earlier:

- The mark of being a child of God is to love one another.
- To love God is to obey God; to obey God is to love one another.
- God's love was "revealed" (1:2; 2:28; 3:2, 5, 8, 10) by sending his son Jesus to provide life (*zōē*) for God's children.
- Jesus is an "atoning sacrifice" (4:10; cf. 2:2).
- The ability to love depends on the abiding relationship that involves the believer, the Holy Spirit, God, and Jesus (4:13-15).
- God's love precedes and is the basis for the love that Christians manifest for one another (4:19).
- God is not visible to the human eye at this point in history except through acts of love (4:20); until the eschaton (and the full unveiling of God's face), the only way to surely connect to God is to practice loving with the expectation that practice will make perfect, eventually.
- Love and God go together; hate and God do not (20); fear and God do not (18).
- Proper christological confession is important and entails these beliefs about Jesus:
- He is the Messiah (5:1).
- He is the Son of God (5:5).
- He came in the flesh (5:6-7).
- Proper belief empowers one to overcome "the world" (5:4).

Thus no new topics are introduced except perhaps the water and blood (5:6-7). This may refer to John 19:34, where Jesus was stabbed in his side with the spear and water and blood came out. Even apart from that possible allusion, the language fits well in 1 John, where all the "begetting" language implies birth language, which involves both blood and water (cf. the woman in labor in John 16:21 and the womb [*koilia*] and water language in John 3:4; 7:38). Furthermore, the blood of Jesus has already been mentioned in chapter 1 in relation to his salvific death. By insisting on this earthy, earthly, wet, and bloody reality that Jesus experienced, the author may be emphasizing his actual death, thus countering once again a docetic Christology that insists that Jesus only "seemed" human. As often happens with the passage in John 19, some find baptismal and eucharistic allusions in the language. While this is possible, 1 John does not mention either ritual explicitly.

The Text in the Interpretive Tradition

As noted earlier, many over the centuries have interpreted the Gospel of John docetically. It may be that some in the community of 1 John already made this docetic move, thereby provoking the vitriol of the elder who considers these docetic Christians to be opponents and even antichrists.

Study Bibles note that some early Latin manuscripts insert the following just before the phrase "and these three are one": "There are three that testify in heaven, the Father, the Word, and the Holy Spirit." This is referred to as "The Johannine Comma" and reflects a later stage in textual transmission in which a scribe, familiar with trinitarian debates, makes a marginal note that subsequently enters the body of the text in some later Greek manuscripts and thus into the Authorized Version of the English Bible of 1611. It does not appear in most ancient texts and should not be considered original. Martin Luther dismissed it as an addition by "an ignoramus," by which he meant to refer to an early Catholic Christian who opposed Arianism (Posset, 247).

The capacious proclamation at 4:16 complexifies the epistle because, on the one hand, it has been interpreted as highly sectarian and dualistic, but now it appears to be the most expansive and universal of all New Testament literature. The latter accounts for its appeal over the centuries to Indians and its repeated translation into Sanskrit. Commenting on a new "presentation of the first letter of St. John in Sanskrit poetry and Indian symbolic idiom," G. Gispert-Sauch declares: "The text has a clear mystical resonance that cannot but appeal to all religious people specifically those nurtured in Indian religions, and the nature of its teaching has a certain universality that can be applied to different doctrinal contexts" (422).

The Text in Contemporary Discussion

First John 4:16 may be the most famous verse in the epistles, if not the New Testament: "God is Love." As such, it touches on everything, from the individual-psychological to the radically communal. Writing from the perspective of a therapist, William Clough draws on 1 John 4. He concludes:

> 1 John 4:19 is the ultimate summation of the process of sanctification, and, one might suggest, the best possible outcome of counseling, therapy, or spiritual direction. We love because he first loved us. . . . The Logos shows itself therapeutically as love: the deep energy that motivates us to

seek spiritual direction, therapy, counseling, mentoring, education, advice, sermons, worship, and community. It lives in our affection for our children; our debt to our parents; our concern for one another; and our responsibility to the earth, to other species, and to God. Love challenges and convicts us. It is the living reality that drives and can ground "discourse" and "meaning-making" in existential psychotherapy and post-modernist psychology: It is the basic motivation which must be addressed in counseling. (Clough, 30)

Throughout this study, I have noted the author's tendencies toward dualistic, binary categories. This philosophical habit typically quickly degenerates into systems of hierarchies where one element is valued and empowered at the expense of the other: male versus female; white versus black; rich versus poor; this culture versus that culture; this religion versus that religion. Many contemporary thinkers (e.g., Fr. Richard Rohr of The Rohr Institute) are calling for unitive ways of thinking, replacing either/or modalities with both/and. Such approaches have great potential for addressing oppressive divisions of all kinds and invite readers to contemplate the challenging tension that Miroslav Volf has identified between "Johannine Dualism and Contemporary Pluralism."

1 John 5:13-21: Final Verses

■ The Text in Its Ancient Context

First John 5:13 echoes the thesis statement of John 20:31 and connects back to 1:4. The author writes to engender belief, knowledge, and eternal life. He reminds the readers to be confident, even bold in prayer (cf. 3:21-22) and to pray for any fellow Christian who is sinning, but not "sinning to death." What is the difference? The author indicates that all injustice (*adikia*) is sin. When a Christian does not "do justice," does not love a brother or sister, she is not acting in accordance with God's will or loving the way God loves. That person needs to recognize that she is out of step with God and the community and is thereby affecting the whole group negatively. She needs to recognize her sin, rely on Christ's advocacy (2:2), and move back into harmonious relationship with God and neighbor. The result will be, as usual, life.

But there is a different kind of sin that leads to death: apostasy. Those who leave the Johannine community abandon their church and enlist with the world, which lies under the power of the evil one (5:19). They have not simply faltered momentarily but have severed their connection to life; their end is destruction. Those who abide with the community by definition do not sin in this way. As long as one abides, life is inevitable; as soon as one apostatizes, death is inevitable. The same distinction is made in 3:9. Again, there is a cosmic battle going on between God and Satan; as long as the readers remain in the Johannine community, they are protected by Jesus.

First John 5:21 may seem like a strange way to close the epistle, but it aptly concludes not only what immediately precedes it but also the whole letter. The readers have a choice: serve the true God or serve idols. This is reminiscent of the Old Testament, when Israelites were tempted to worship the gods of other nations or apostatize. The language is a trope and is often described in the metaphorical imagery of sexual immorality ("play the harlot," "commit adultery"). It is clear throughout 1 John that those who remain in the Johannine community do serve the true God (5:20), which leads to life and to "conquering the world"—a typically Johannine phrase that is never defined but that points to the Johannine understanding of the world as oppositional. In contrast, those who go out from the community serve Satan. Since he has power over the whole world (5:19), those who leave oppose Christ (i.e., they are antichrists) and instead adopt the values of Satan and his world: desire of the flesh, desire of the eyes, the pride in riches (2:16). The author closes by asking the readers: "Whom will you serve?"

■ The Text in the Interpretive Tradition

The textual transmission of 5:18 reveals that it has caused some consternation: Who is protecting whom? It makes the most sense to argue that Jesus, the Son of God, does the protecting. He is like those he is protecting because he is born of God as they are (both are described using a participle of the verb *gennaō ek tou theou*), but he is unique in that he is the only Son of God, whereas they are children. The concept that Jesus was "born of God" offended some thinkers as the christological debates of the later centuries developed, so one finds glosses in some manuscripts that make the text say that the believer protects himself (*heauton*); but that obviates the essential role played by Jesus in 1 John. A third option suggests that God is the protector: "This connection with John 17:15 seems close enough to lead to the conclusion that somehow 1 John 5:18 means that God keeps the believer" (Painter, 324).

Due to later trinitarian debates, some have tried to distinguish between Jesus' birth from God and the believer's birth from God by noting that the perfect participle of the verb is used for believers (*gegennēmenos*) and the aorist tense (*gennētheis*) for Jesus. That is, the perfect tense, on the one hand, is used for an action that occurred in the past but has continuing effect in the present (those who have been begotten, the effects of which are continuing). The aorist tense, on the other hand, refers to a single completed action in the past, without reference to an ongoing process. Centuries later, post-Nicene Christianity would resolve the debate by using the phrases "eternally begotten" and "begotten not made" to refer to the Son.

The reference to mortal sins calls Christians to serious reflection about sin, confession, and repentance, both individually and corporately. The later church distinguished between "mortal" sins (pride, covetousness, lust, envy, gluttony, anger, and sloth) and "venial" sins. Tertullian claims that John refers to murder, idolatry, injustice, apostasy, adultery, and fornication (Smith, 134).

■ The Text in Contemporary Discussion

A number of important questions for contemporary Christians arise from this passage. Does the contemporary church adhere to a notion of mortal sin? If so, what should be added or deleted from the lists above, if anything?

How vital is intercessory prayer? "How seriously does the Church take its responsibility to intercede on behalf of a sinning brother or sister? What formal means of reconciliation and forgiveness are available and utilized with the Church?" (Thomas, 281–82).

Finally, what constitute idols in our contemporary context? Do wealth, status, power, ego, vanity, and nationalism qualify? Are there other false teachings or gods that tempt people away from God?

2 John

Introduction

This short book follows some of the themes addressed in 1 John (see the introduction to 1 John). For example, the call to love one another is an ancient command present from the beginning. It also warns of practicing this love with some caution; receiving or welcoming those who deceive can compromise the faith of both individuals and the community. The whole of this epistle is treated as a single sense unit.

■ THE TEXT IN ITS ANCIENT CONTEXT

Written in letter form, 2 John opens with the identification of the sender and receiver followed by a greeting that, in this case, appears as a benediction. But the atypical immediately captivates: Who is the "elder"? The author never names himself but assumes authority of some kind on the basis of advanced age or, perhaps, by virtue of an office. Verse 12 indicates that he plans to educate them more deeply in person (cf. Paul).

And what of the recipients, the *eklektē kyria* and her "children"? *Eklektē* (whence we derive the word "eclectic") means "chosen" or "elect." *Kyria* is the feminine form of *kyrios*, which means "sir" or "lord" or "master." Usually *eklektē kyria* is translated "elect lady" and assumed to refer metaphorically to the gathered church receiving the letter (as opposed to being addressed to a woman named Eclecta or Kyria), particularly because the letter closes with reference to "your elect sister," likely a reference to the author's own church community. The "children" of the elect lady probably refers to church members. The intimate, relational, familial language, quite typical of the Johannine literature, strikes the reader immediately. Furthermore, the personal tone, signified especially by the abundance of first-person constructions, is remarkable and lends a sense of immediacy to the letter.

The immediate preoccupation with truth looms large, as the word *alētheia* ("truth") appears five times in the first four verses. This author links truth and love together from the start (1, 3, 5-6) and assumes that these attributes tie Christians together into a cord that cannot be easily broken. To love one another is to walk in the commandment(s) (cf. John 15:12; 1 John 1:7). This does not imply a generalized love but rather a choosy love that embraces only those who agree with the author's vision of truth. Based on the author's language, one can delineate the characteristics of the two opposing groups: those who abide (who believe correctly) and those who are antichrists (those who oppose truth and promote falsehood).

Led by figures such as Irenaeus and Hippolytus, subsequent readers of the Johannine Epistles have expressed consistent fascination with the antichrist language, identifying characters from the historical to the fantastic and mythical as "*the* Antichrist." For the elder, however, "the antichrist" was not an individual character; rather, it described anyone who expressed a Christology incommensurate with the elder's own. Specifically, it denoted "those who do not confess that Jesus Christ has come in the flesh" (v. 7; cf. 1 John 2:18, 22; 4:3). These antichrists are deceivers; they are "many" (v. 7); and they are former members of this very community, known personally by the readers and elder (cf. 2:18, 22). Antichrists are probably Christian, since non-Christians are unlikely to deal in the details of various Christologies. Any Christian, then, can remain a christ (2:20, 27) or become an antichrist at any time (Koester forthcoming).

To summarize this dualistic picture: the elder and his sympathizers abide with the community and the inherited tradition, are marked by truth and love and obedience, have the Father and the Son, and deny hospitality to those deemed unorthodox in their Christology. The opponents are deceivers and antichrists who depart and who "go beyond" the christological tradition (v. 9) and try to tempt others to do the same; they do not have God.

The elder forbids the readers to extend hospitality to anyone espousing an alternative Christology. To receive that person is to become an antichrist; it has eschatological ramifications, namely, the loss of all heretofore accumulated rewards.

The Text in the Interpretive Tradition

Although Polycarp (*Phil.* 1 34) followed the elder's lead in construing the antichrist as pluriform (using the term to refer to docetists, for example), the habit of envisioning a single political or religious figure as *the* Antichrist began early in Christian history and continues today. By combining traditions such as "the lawless one" of 2 Thessalonians and the beast described in Revelation 13, Christians have imagined a single person who represents pure evil, serving in the army of Satan in an apocalyptic eschatological battle between God and Satan. Sometimes the figure is Jewish (Hippolytus), sometimes Muslim, sometimes this or that Roman emperor. The pope as antichrist has enjoyed a long tenure beginning in the fourth century. Indeed, in the Middle Ages, Emperor Frederick II Hohenstaufen's publicists "gained an advantage by showing how the numerical value of the name *Innocencius papa* was 666, concluding that there can be no doubt that Innocent IV is the 'true Antichrist!'" (McGinn, 154). Luther, Calvin, Increase and Cotton Mather, and Jonathan Edwards all capitalized on this tradition. Those named as the Antichrist throughout history are too many to list, but include Hitler, Reagan, Elvis, and Saddam Hussein (Nichols, 81–83). The impetus of the original text, whose purpose was to insist on the humanity of Jesus and to emphasize the incarnation, has largely been eclipsed by the construction of the later Antichrist myth and rapture theology.

The insistence on embodiedness described in verse 7 has also fueled enduring and sometimes vociferous debates in Christian tradition about the virgin birth, the incarnation, and the real presence of Christ in the Eucharist (Painter, 350).

The Text in Contemporary Discussion

The phrase identifying the addressee, *eklektē kyria*, may refer to a church leader named either Kyria ("lady") or Eclecta ("the elect"). If either word is a proper name, this would show the importance of female leadership in the early church. More likely, however, the phrase is a metaphor imaging the church as a lady (*kyria*) in relationship with her lord Jesus (*kyrios*). This image may offer a liberating trajectory regarding women, their value, and their experience. However, such language might simply entrench patriarchy where the male elder becomes "lord" over "lady church" (O'Day, 467).

The insistence on incarnation is important. Womanists and feminists know that theologies that view the body and soul as binary categories (as in docetism and Gnosticism) are always detrimental to women. The soul is valued and the body is denigrated as a hindrance to the soul (summarized in the pithy saying, *sōma sēma*—"the body is a tomb"). Women are associated with the bodily, which is to be controlled and subdued.

Second John's injunction against hospitality and his promotion of exclusionary practices toward opponents raise deep concern regarding current ethno-religious conflicts, whether it is the Catholic-Protestant conflict in Northern Ireland or Catholic-Muslim-Orthodox fighting in Yugoslavia (Slater, 511). However, our reading of 2 John today may evoke important questions about how to maintain group cohesion and draw healthy boundaries when destructive persons are allowed to wreak havoc on a community with impunity.

3 John

Introduction

See the introduction to 1 John for additional commentary regarding the connection of the three Johannine Epistles. Here again, the theme of discerning truth and being coworkers with the truth is emphasized. Gaias and Demetrius are commended for walking in the truth, while Diotrephes is accused of spreading false rumors. Again, the whole of this brief letter is treated as one sense unit.

THE TEXT IN ITS ANCIENT CONTEXT

If one were to title this letter, it might be "Good Gaius, Dastardly Diotrephes, and Devoted Demetrius." Like 2 John, 3 John is a letter written by "the elder," but in this case to an individual, Gaius, "whom I love in truth" (cf. 2 John 1, where the same language is used of "the elect lady and her children"). The elder uses *agapē* language twice in the opening sentence. It is almost as if "Beloved" were the author's nickname for Gaius (1, 2, 5, 11) since he begins the next sentence with it as well.

As is customary in an epistle, the author follows the introduction with a prayer on behalf of Gaius and words of praise about his "walking in truth" (3, 4). The language of "walking" as a metaphor for ethical behavior is typical for the Johannine Epistles (cf. 1 John 1:6, 7; 2:6, 11; 2 John 4, 6). As in all of the epistles bearing the name of John and in the Gospel of John, concern for *truth* predominates (1, 3, 4, 8, and 12).

The body of the letter comprises verses 5-12. Immediately we learn that just as Gaius is beloved, he also loves fellow believers (v. 6), in accordance with the commandment of Christ so fundamental to the Johannine community (John 13:34; 1 John 3:11). Thus walking in truth is synonymous with loving. Gaius expresses his love in practical terms by showing hospitality to Christian missionaries: feeding, housing, and financially supporting them. This model was common in the early church.

Third John testifies to a power struggle in the church between the elder and Diotrephes. The elder has written to the church requesting that the church receive the missionaries and show them hospitality as Gaius has previously done. Diotrephes, however, does not recognize the elder's authority;

instead, he commands the community to reject hospitality to the missionaries or be expelled. Many details remain obscure, including whether or not Gaius is subject to Diotrephes' power. Since he implies that Gaius is his child (v. 4), one wonders if the elder converted him. No specific church offices are mentioned in the letter, but it attests to the struggle regarding the best way to structure Christian communities both locally and at a broader level.

Unlike 1 and 2 John, 3 John does not refer to false teachings or particular christological claims. In fact, neither the word *Jesus* nor *Christ* appears in the letter (NRSV fills it in at v. 7, but the Greek word *Christos* is not there). The author exhorts Gaius not to imitate evil (associated with Diotrephes), but good (modeled by Demetrius, who may be the bearer of the letter).

The letter concludes with almost identical words as 2 John 12 about not writing more but meeting in person. This is followed by a word of peace, greetings from the elder's church, and a request that Gaius share the elder's greetings with those whom he knows personally.

■ The Text in the Interpretive Tradition

Citations of 3 John are rare, though verse 2 has appeared occasionally. Some imagine in verse 2 a distinction between the prosperity of the body and the prosperity of the soul and quickly move to asceticism (Tertullian and Augustine). The Benedictine Bede saw prosperity as a communal category so that prosperity was a way to gift others in need. Debates arise about the relationship between spiritual health and physical health, in some cases leading to the founding of medical institutions or healing movements, as in the case of Carrie Judd Montgomery. Montgomery (1858–1946), was a leader in the Divine Healing movement and an influence in Pentecostalism. She began opening healing homes in the 1880s. The translation of the phrase *peri pantōn* leads to different stances. Those who translate it as "above all things" see God as supporting an emphasis on financial prosperity (Oral Roberts); those who translate it as "with respect to all things" do not (Landrus).

■ The Text in Contemporary Discussion

Third John addresses questions about hospitality as an ethical imperative for Christians. Christians are called to love not only those whom they know but also those who are "strangers" to them. It also raises questions about how Christians are to support financially those who are called to teach and preach the gospel near and far.

Third John also demands that individual Christians and communities guard against those who have a "passion for preeminence" (Jones, 272), who "love being first" (*philoprōteuō*) in church leadership. Conflict is inevitable, but is there a better way to address it than the elder's strategy of vituperation (v. 10, "talking nonsense about us with evil words," author translation).

Finally, the interpretation of verse 2 raises questions about the relationship between faith and physical well-being as well as faith and financial well-being. Those committed to the "prosperity gospel" (also known as "the health and wealth gospel") suggest that faithful believers should expect physical and financial deliverance. Others link holiness with poverty. Are Christians free or even obligated to succeed financially? Does wealth necessarily cause spiritual injury? Is poverty a sign of a lack of faith or a sign of blessedness?

The field of disability studies has taught us to ask these questions about physical health as well. Should those who have physical or mental disabilities seek physical healing to conform to "normal" bodies, or does physical suffering bring holiness (cf. 2 Corinthians 12)?

Works Cited

Baker, Sharon. 2013. *Executing God: Rethinking Everything You've Been Taught about Salvation and the Cross.* Louisville: Westminster John Knox.

Beutler, Johannes, SJ. 2004. "1, 2, and 3 John." In *Global Bible Commentary*, edited by Daniel Patte, 553–58. Nashville: Abingdon.

Clark-Soles, Jaime. 2003. *Scripture Cannot Be Broken: The Social Function of the Use of Scripture in the Fourth Gospel.* Leiden: Brill.

Clough, William R. 2006. "To Be Loved and to Love." *Journal of Psychology and Theology* 34, no. 1:23–31.

Gispert-Sauch, G., S.J. 1987. "St John's Nectar in Indian Flavour." *Vidyajyoti* 51:421–24.

Greer, Rowan A. 2005. "Sighing for the Love of Truth: Augustine's Quest." In *God, Truth, and Witness: Engaging Stanley Hauerwas*, edited by L. Gregory Jones, Reinhard Hütter, and C. Rosalee Velloso Ewell, 13–34. Grand Rapids: Brazos.

Hill, Charles E. 2004. *The Johannine Corpus in the Early Church.* Oxford: Oxford University Press.

Jones, Peter Rhea. 2009. *1, 2 & 3 John.* Macon, GA: Smith & Helwys.

Koester, Craig R. 2008. *The Word of Life: A Theology of John's Gospel.* Grand Rapids: Eerdmans.

———. Forthcoming. "The Antichrist Theme in the Johannine Epistles and Its Role in Christian Tradition." In *Communities in Dispute: Current Scholarship on the Johannine Epistles*, edited by R. Alan Culpepper and Paul N. Anderson. Atlanta: Society of Biblical Literature.

Landrus, Heather L. 2002. "Hearing 3 John 2 in the Voices of History." *Journal of Pentecostal Theology* 11, no. 1:70–88.

Lee, Dorothy. 2010. "Ecology and the Johannine Literature." *St. Mark's Review* 212, no. 2:39–50.

Lieu, Judith. 1991. *The Theology of the Johannine Epistles.* New Testament Theology. Cambridge: Cambridge University Press.

———. 2008. *1, 2, and 3 John: A Commentary.* Louisville: Westminster John Knox.

Loader, William. 1992. *The Johannine Epistles.* London: Epworth.

———. Forthcoming. "The Significance of 2:15-17 for Understanding the Ethics of 1 John." In *Communities in Dispute: Current Scholarship on the Johannine Epistles*, edited by R. Alan Culpepper and Paul N. Anderson. Atlanta: Society of Biblical Literature.

McGinn, Bernard. 1994. *Antichrist: Two Thousand Years of the Human Fascination with Evil.* San Francisco: HarperSanFrancisco.

Murphy, Francis X. 1984. "The Patristic Origins of Orthodox Mysticism." *Mystics Quarterly* 10, no. 2:59–63.

Nichols, Stephen J. 2001. "Prophecy Makes Strange Bedfellows." *JETS* 44, no. 1:75–85.

O'Day, Gail. 2012. "1, 2, and 3 John." In *Women's Bible Commentary*, edited by Carol A. Newsom, Sharon H. Ringe, and Jacqueline Lapsley, 622–24. 2nd ed. Louisville: Westminster John Knox.

Painter, John. 2002. *1, 2, and 3 John.* Sacra Pagina. Collegeville, MN: Liturgical Press.

Posset, Franz. 1985. "John Bugenhagen and the *Comma Johanneum*." *CTQ* 49, no. 4:245–51.

Pretorius, N. F. 1998. "Redemption of the Earth or from the Earth? The Gospel of John and the Johannine Epistles." *Scriptura* 66:269–78.

Rensberger, David. 2001. *The Epistles of John*. Louisville: Westminster John Knox.
Slater, Thomas B. 2007. "1–3 John." In *True to Our Native Land: An African American New Testament Commentary*, edited by Brian K. Blount, Cain Hope Felder, Clarice J. Martin, and Emerson B. Powery, 496–517. Minneapolis: Fortress Press.
Smith, D. Moody. 1991. *First, Second, and Third John*. IBC. Louisville: Westminster John Knox.
St. Clair, Raquel. 2008. *Call and Consequences: A Womanist Reading of Mark*. Minneapolis: Fortress Press.
Sweeney, James P. 2003. "Modern and Ancient Controversies over the Virgin Birth of Jesus." *BSac* 160:142–58.
Thomas, John Christopher. 2004. *Pentecostal Commentary on 1 John, 2 John, 3 John*. Cleveland: Pilgrim.
Trible, Phyllis. 1986. "A Love Story Gone Awry." In *God and the Rhetoric of Sexuality*, 72–143. Minneapolis: Fortress Press.
Volf, Miroslav. 2005. "Johannine Dualism and Contemporary Pluralism." *Modern Theology* 21:189–217.
Von Wahlde, Urban C. 2010. *The Gospel and Letters of John*. 3 vols. Grand Rapids: Eerdmans.

JUDE

Pheme Perkins

Introduction

A warning against the false teachers who would arise at the end of days concludes the collection of seven letters in the Christian canon attributed to Peter, James, the brother of the Lord, John, the son of Zebedee, and Jude, the brother of James (Mark 6:3). Though the author of 2 Peter employed its material, Jude is rarely mentioned in early Christian authors or read in worship services today. Unlike the Pauline Epistles, which are targeted to specific churches or individuals, the so-called Catholic Epistles are addressed to churches in a broad region. Those attributed to brothers of Jesus give voice to a Greek-speaking Jewish Christianity that had become marginalized by the second century (Perkins, 1–2, 141–45).

Visions of the end of days connected with the figure of Enoch (Gen. 5:22) circulated widely among first-century Jews, so it is not surprising that Jude adopts a prophecy from Enoch (v. 15; *1 En.* 1:9). The author also knows popular Jewish legends about the fallen angels responsible for the evils of the preflood generation, as well as a tale that the devil attempted to wrest the body of Moses from the archangel Michael (v. 9). In that episode, Satan, acting out his role as prosecutor (Job 1:6-7), apparently charged Moses with the murder of the Egyptian (Exod. 2:12). No murderer should enjoy divine burial (Deut. 34:5-6). By using these dramatic stories, Jude underlines the serious evil at work in the false teachers (vv. 8, 10, 12, 16; Painter and deSilva, 208–17). This polemical rhetoric (vv. 5-16) makes it difficult to determine what the specific points of dispute were (Thurén). Certainly, Jude's demand that readers exclude false teachers from the communal meal (*agapē*) because their presence defiles indicates that the opponents are part of the local church (v. 12). Matthew 18:15-17 has such a ban on sinners who will not listen to the voice of the community, as does 1 Cor. 5:3-5, 11, in a case of extreme immorality. Therefore most interpreters conclude that the false teaching more likely involved Christian conduct than points of doctrine (Painter and deSilva, 183–84).

Several phrases in the letter's appeal to the audience envisage the difficulty that a postapostolic generation may have in preserving a tradition ("faith") entrusted to them (vv. 3, 20; Kraftchick, 62–65). In addition to the warnings embedded in familiar stories from the Torah, Jude reminds readers that "the apostles of our Lord Jesus Christ" had predicted the rise of such scoffers at the end of days (vv. 17-18). By presenting this exhortation in the form of an apostolic letter, the author suggests that its message enjoys comparable authority. The concluding doxology (vv. 24-25) follows a familiar liturgical pattern already employed in the Pauline Epistles (Rom. 16:25-27; Phil. 4:20; 1 Tim. 1:17; 6:15-16). However, Jude lacks the concluding greetings that ordinarily precede the liturgical-sounding phrases that conclude those letters. That omission suggests that this piece was intended for general circulation.

Jude follows a standard pattern (Bauckham, 3).
Greeting (vv. 1-2)
Opening stating the occasion for writing (vv. 3-4)
Body of the letter, establishing judgment awaiting the impious (vv. 5-19)
Three examples: wilderness generation, Sodom and Gomorrah, death of Moses
Three additional examples: Cain, Balaam, Korah
Two prophecies of judgment against false teachers: Enoch, the apostles
Conclusion, exhortation to the recipients (vv. 20-23)
Doxology (vv. 24-25)

Jude 1-25

Because the book of Jude is just one chapter, all verses will be dealt with as a single sense unit.

■ The Text in Its Ancient Context

The greeting of the letter (vv. 1-2) identifies the sender as "brother of James" rather than "brother of the Lord," as James was commonly known (Gal. 1:19), suggesting that this work is directed to Jewish Christian churches that revered James (Mark 6:3). Instead of the familiar "grace and peace" of the Pauline letter, Jude has an augmented Jewish formula, "mercy, peace, and love," but retains the two-part reference to the Father and Jesus Christ. The expression "kept safe" in Jesus Christ strikes the ominous note that believers must be protected against the end-time ravages of the wicked (Fuchs and Reymond, 155).

In verses 3-4, the author suggests that the danger of false teachers infiltrating the community has forced him to break off an exposition of Christian salvation to compose this warning. He telegraphs the two sections that follow: (a) evidence from ancient Scripture and prophecy for the condemnation of such persons; and (b) appeal to the recipients to resist their influence. The charges, turning grace into the occasion for immorality and denial of "the only Master," probably meaning God (v. 25), and the Lord Jesus, reflect a general disdain for God's commandments (cf. Titus 1:16).

Verses 5-8 describe divine judgment against the rebellious. The first three examples of destruction employ a schema in which those who had experienced God's salvation rebel and are destroyed: the

Israelites in the wilderness, through lack of faith (Num. 14); the fallen angels, who desert their proper place (Gen. 6:1-4) out of lust for human women; and the people of Sodom and Gomorrah, who are punished for unnatural sexuality. Imprisonment of the angels prior to judgment belongs to the Enoch material (*1 En.* 6–19). Verse 8 applies the examples to the present by providing three corresponding vices, though not in the same order, "defile flesh" (= fallen angels); "reject authority" (= that of Moses), and "slander glorious ones" (= the demand that Lot turn over his angelic visitors; Bauckham, 48–55).

In verses 9-11, the woe against those who are acting like irrational beasts and who are primed to reap the consequences that befell those led astray by Balaam (Deut. 23:3-6), or the rebellious Israelites at Korah (Num. 16:1-3), invokes an apocryphal tradition concerning the burial of Moses. Satan attempts to snatch the body of this murderer (Exod. 2:11-15) from the archangel Michael. Patristic sources (Clement of Alexandria, Didymus the Blind, Origen) attribute the story to a *Testament of Moses* that is no longer extant. Michael's response, a phrase from Zech. 3:2 (LXX), charges Satan with blasphemy for putting himself forward as judge against the Lord (Bauckham, 60–67).

Verses 12-13 include a warning to guard against false teachers, whose presence in the community corrupts its most sacred ritual, the "love feasts" or communal meal. A catalog of striking images builds to the rhetorical climax, eternal confinement in darkness for such brazen individuals.

Readers should not be taken off guard, according to verses 14-19, since God's judgment against such impiety has been prophesied from the earliest days, from "the seventh from Adam, Enoch," up to the apostles themselves. The rhetorical climax, which declares this wickedness evidence of the end-time and describes the schismatics as "without Spirit," suggests that Jude is not an appeal for their conversion.

However, all are not lost. The final words of encouragement and ethical advice to the community in verses 20-23 include the possibility that some can be rescued from the fiery judgment, which otherwise awaits them. Ancient scribes found verses 22-23a problematic: the three-clause exhortation to "convince, save, and have mercy" found in some manuscripts appears to be a clarification of a problematic two-clause sentence, "saving from fire, having mercy," that alluded to Zech. 3:1-5 (LXX).

Jude 24-25 concludes with a traditional doxology (cf. Rom. 16:25) that has been modified to underline the author's concern that his audience remain firm in their faith until the Lord's coming in judgment.

■ The Text in the Interpretive Tradition

Both its attribution to a little-known figure and the treatment of Jewish Christianity as heretical by later church fathers may explain why Jude plays no role in later Christian worship or theology. Doubts about its place in the canon focused on the appeals to the legend about the death of Moses and to the authority of Enoch. John Calvin bolstered the apostolic authority of Jude by identifying its author as the apostle mentioned in Luke 6:16 and Acts 1:13.

■ The Text in Contemporary Discussion

The theological emphasis on a "deposit of faith" received from the apostles coupled with polemic invective against "false teachers" whose views are never directly confronted makes Jude problematic for modern readers who seek churches that welcome diversity. Some respond by highlighting comparable positions in Paul's Epistles and emphasizing the need for Christians to retain an ethical holiness that could be undermined by pluralism (e.g., Bauckham). Jude also provides an opening to the Jewish matrix in which Christianity was born. Instruction in piety does not stop with the Jewish canon but extends to the apocryphal Jewish traditions concerning Moses and Enoch.

Works Cited

Bauckham, Richard J. 1983. *Jude, 2 Peter.* WBC 50; Waco, TX: Word.
Fuchs, Eric, and Pierre Reymond. 1980 *Le deuxième épître de Saint Pierre. L' épître de Saint Jude.* Commentaire du Nouveau Testament Deuxième série XIIIb. Neuchâtel: Delachaux et Niestlé.
Kraftchick, Steven J. 2002. *Jude, 2 Peter.* Nashville: Abingdon.
Painter, John, and David deSilva. 2012. *James and Jude.* Grand Rapids: Baker Academic.
Perkins, Pheme. 1995. *First and Second Peter, James, and Jude.* Louisville: Westminster John Knox.
Thurén, Lauri. 1997. "Hey Jude! Asking for the Original Situation and Message of a Catholic Epistle." *NTS* 43:451–65.

Revelation

Barbara R. Rossing

Introduction

The apocalyptic book of Revelation is one of the most disputed books of the Bible. Full of mysterious and bizarre symbolism, its visions have inspired artists and musicians as well as doomsday prophets and activists. Revelation was one of the latest books to be included in the biblical canon.

The book consists of a series of visions experienced by a prophetic leader, John, while he was on the island of Patmos, off the coast of western Turkey. Early tradition dates this book to the end of the first century, late in the reign of the emperor Domitian (95 CE; Irenaeus, *Against Heresies* 5.30.3). This was a time when other Jewish apocalypses such as *2 Baruch* and *4 Ezra* were also being written, in response to the trauma of Rome's destruction of Jerusalem in 70 CE. Revelation's label of "Babylon" for Rome—invoking the ancient empire that had destroyed Jerusalem six hundred years earlier—offers the strongest internal evidence, albeit implicit, for a date later than 70 CE (Collins 1984, 85).

The author's name, John, is the same as that of several other New Testament figures. In later Christian tradition he came to be identified with the apostle John as a way of affirming the book's place in the canon. From early times, however, interpreters realized he was likely not the same person as the author of the Gospel of John, since his Greek style of writing is so different. He makes no claim to be an apostle; his references to the apostles (18:20, 21:14) do not include himself. He is certainly Jewish, as evidenced by his hundreds of scriptural allusions and his advocacy of strict observance of Jewish purity laws (Frankfurter 2011). John's idiosyncratic Greek leads some scholars to suggest Greek may not be his first language. He may have been a Jewish refugee from Palestine who settled in Asia Minor in the aftermath of the Roman-Jewish war.

Writing at the height of imperial prosperity in Asia Minor, John proclaims the message of hope that Rome's unjust reign would last only a little while longer, and that Rome had already been defeated by the nonviolent victory of Jesus the Lamb. Unlike other ancient apocalypses, John's message is not a secret to be sealed up until the end (in contrast to the apocalyptic book of Daniel; see Dan 12:4). Rather, as a public prophetic letter, Revelation is to be "read aloud" in the communities to which it is addressed (Rev. 1:3).

Several literary genres characterize Revelation. The first word of the book, "apocalypse," literally means revealing, or pulling back a curtain. Apocalypses were a popular type of literature for Jews and others in the ancient world. Apocalypses communicate their message not by logical proofs or arguments but by means of visionary journeys and pictures, creating an alternative "world of vision" (Schüssler Fiorenza 1991, 22). They typically use exaggerated imagery in order to heighten a sense of urgency and call readers to commitment and action.

The book also calls itself "prophecy," a second genre, which may reflect a circle of itinerant or resident Christian prophets in the cities of Asia Minor (as evidenced by other early Christian texts such as the *Ascension of Isaiah*; Bauckham 1993a, 84–85). Like other biblical prophets, John's primary purpose in writing prophecy was not to predict future events but rather to wake people up to the peril of their present situation. In John's view, faithfulness to God necessitated uncompromising resistance in the midst of the Roman Empire. Rival Christian prophets in these same communities apparently preached a very different message, permitting greater participation in Roman culture. John wants the audience to accept his prophetic interpretation of their situation.

A third genre is that of epistle or letter. John employs the format of a letter to communicate his prophetic message, much like the letters of the apostle Paul. From the island isolation of Patmos, John could not visit Christian communities in cities of Asia Minor (Turkey). So he communicates by writing a letter to them. The epistolary framework at the beginning and end (Rev 1:4-6; 22:10-12) underscores the book's character as a prophetic letter.

Because Revelation does not unfold in linear fashion, it can be difficult to outline. Numbered sequences of seven seals, seven trumpets, and seven bowls, as well as messages to seven churches, may have provided a structure helpful for those listening to the oral performance of the book. The book may follow a concentric or chiastic structure, a model popular in antiquity, in which the end of the book reprises the beginning (Schüssler Fiorenza 1998, 175). The book's chronology includes flashbacks to earlier events, such as the battle in heaven narrated in chapter 12. Revelation unfolds in cyclical or spiral fashion, often showing the same series of judgments from different angles, rather like a kaleidoscope. Each cycle of visions includes warnings as well as hymns, blessings, and promises.

Like other apocalypses, the book has a narrative framework. It tells a story (Barr 1998, 1)—the story of the Lamb Jesus who defeats evil and leads the community on a great exodus out of the unjust empire, personified as a dragon. The narrative journey ends in a utopic new city, the bridal new Jerusalem, with a river of life and a healing tree in a renewed creation. The entire book draws on prophetic cadences from the Hebrew Bible, without ever quoting Scripture directly. Stories of the exodus plagues, Danielic beasts, exile in Babylon, and other biblical narratives are remapped onto John's own time.

Creation and the earth play a central role in the dramatic conflict. In one of the most spectacular scenes in chapter 12, earth itself becomes a hero—coming to the aid of a mythic woman who represents God's people. Revelation's plagues of bloody oceans, giant hailstones, and other ecological catastrophes can give the impression that the book condemns the earth to destruction at the hands of a wrathful God. Such destruction has been the focus of many interpretations, including the recent best-selling *Left Behind* novels. But Revelation is clear that God created the world and everything in it. The book describes not the destruction of the earth but earth's liberation and renewal, with the proclamation that "the time has come ... for destroying those who destroy the earth" (Rev. 11:18; my translation, here and throughout, unless otherwise noted).

Interpretive History

No other book of the Bible has had such a profound and wide-ranging impact on literature, art, music, theology, liturgy, politics, psychology, spirituality, and popular culture. Throughout the centuries, interpreters have disagreed about whether the visions refer to John's own time or to future ages, or whether they are timeless truths for all ages.

From earliest times, many have attempted to "figure out" the mysterious symbols of Revelation as if they were a timetable of future events. Beginning in the second century, followers of the New Prophecy, or Montanist movement, predicted the descent of the new Jerusalem in their own area of Asia Minor, while other early interpreters expected a future millennial paradise on earth.

Augustine and others critiqued such movements as "chiliast" (from the Greek word for one thousand, a reference to the millennium) and successfully shifted interpretations in a more timeless, spiritual direction. Allegorical readings predominated for the next five hundred years, with the understanding that the church was already living in the millennium.

Futurist interpreters resurfaced again in the Middle Ages and Reformation. Some even predicted specific dates when Christ would return. The landscape of futurist interpreters included Joachim of Fiore, followers of St. Francis of Assisi, Anabaptists, and even Martin Luther, who correlated specific images of Revelation with enemies in his own time. Two recent American denominations have origins tied to futurist interpretations of Revelation: the Seventh-Day Adventists (founded by William Miller, who predicted the return of Christ in the 1840s) and the Jehovah's Witnesses.

The premillennialist dispensationalist line of interpretation was developed in the nineteenth century by British preacher John Nelson Darby and popularized by the *Scofield Reference Bible*. Premillennialists view the millennium as a literal event still to happen in the future (disagreeing with Augustine and others who view the church as already living in the millennium); they view history as divided into distinct dispensations or epochs, with the present time a "parenthesis" between dispensations that will end with the so-called rapture of Christians up to heaven.

One of the key tenets of premillennialists since 1948 has been that the nation of Israel plays a pivotal role in what they view as God's prophetic plan. Revelation's suggestion of a battle of

Armageddon provides the playbook for their understanding of a future World War III, read through zealously nationalistic and sometimes violent lenses. Today's radio preachers, televangelists, prophecy novels, and rapture websites correlate current political events with Revelation according to Darby's system, based also on his reading of Daniel 9.

Most scholars reject premillennialism. They point out that the book's images have multiple meanings, and were not intended as a futurist script or timetable for geopolitical events in this century. The Greek word for what Revelation "shows" or "makes known" in the very first verse of the book is the same as the word for "signs" in John's Gospel. The whole book may be intended to be read at a deeper sign level, more like poetry or art than any predictive script. Essayist Kathleen Norris makes the case for poetic interpretation.

> This is a poet's book, which is probably the best argument for reclaiming it from fundamentalists. It doesn't tell, it shows, over and over again, its images unfolding, pushing hard against the limits of language and metaphor, engaging the listener in a tale that has the satisfying yet unsettling logic of a dream. (Norris, ix)

Among the many poets, artists, liturgists, and musicians who have loved Revelation and whose interpretations continue to be influential are Hildegard of Bingen, Emily Dickinson, Christina Rossetti, William Blake, George Friedrich Handel, Charles Wesley, as well as Thomas Dorsey and many anonymous composers of African American spirituals and blues music. Some interpreters critique pietistic and poetic interpretations as collapsing Revelation into nothing but a privatistic message of personal salvation. But the book's power as public liturgy also resonates in churches and communities through their work, especially in situations of suffering. The liberationist poetry of Guatemalan Julia Esquivel and others shows that poetic interpretations can also foster liberation. Liberationist voices have turned to Revelation as a message of hope for justice overcoming oppression, as evidenced by the African American and feminist interpretations, and voices from South Africa and Latin America.

Triumphalistic, even violent readings have also played a role in history. Again and again, the book has proved irresistible to those in power, sometimes providing biblical justification for attacks on their enemies. After 2001, for example, Revelation's critique of "Babylon" was used by some to make the case for the United States' invasion of Iraq, noting that ancient Babylon is located in today's Iraq. Fanatical self-proclaimed prophets such as David Koresh of the Branch Davidians and others have also laid claim to the book.

No single interpretive strategy can encompass the richness of Revelation. Rhetorical readings of Revelation that investigate its persuasive power in its original first-century context may provide the most promising criteria for interpretive communities adjudicating competing readings today. Seeking analogies to John's rhetorical situation can bring certain readings to the fore while problematizing others. I especially encourage reading from the perspective of marginalized people, and with communities and movements who have found in this book a profound message of hope—including ecological hope for our life together on this earth. John's emphasis that God is the one who creates the world—and who will not leave the world behind—makes a hermeneutics of hope appropriate for reading the book today.

Revelation 1:1-8: Prologue

■ THE TEXT IN ITS ANCIENT CONTEXT

John writes as a visionary. The book gives testimony to "what he saw" (1:2). The literary prologue of 1:1-8 has strong echoes in the epilogue of 22:6-21.

John sets up a chain of authority that validates the book. He claims he is not writing for himself but on behalf of God, who gave the revelation to Jesus Christ. An angel delivers the revelation to God's "slaves," or servants—perhaps a reference to early Christian prophets (Schüssler Fiorenza 2001, 40), among whom John names himself.

John intends his apocalypse to be read aloud to the community, as a prophetic letter. The blessing for the person who "reads aloud" (1:3) underscores the oral character of Revelation. Revelation contains seven such blessings (1:3; 14:13; 16:15; 19:9; 20:6; 22:7, 14). "How fortunate" may be a better translation than "blessed." Blessings were prophetic forms familiar from the Hebrew Scriptures, with the power to enact what they describe. Together, "the seven beatitudes comprise a kind of summary of Revelation's message" (Bauckham 1993a, 30).

The characterization of the book as "prophecy" (1:3) situates it in the tradition of Hebrew Bible prophets. John may also be contrasting his message with that of Rome's official political prophets, such as Virgil and Horace, who prophesied about the Roman Empire's eternal destiny and divine favor (Georgi 1986). John in effect says no to the claim by Roman prophets that Emperor Augustus's reign had already ushered in a new eschatological age of peace for the whole world.

Beginning in 1:4-6, John follows the typical letter format used also by the apostle Paul, marking the entire book as a letter. The sender first identifies himself (John), then names the recipients (the seven churches that are in Asia), and then gives a greeting, followed by a doxology. "Grace and peace" is the typical Pauline greeting. The greeting is threefold: from God, the seven spirits, and Jesus.

John's use of peculiar Greek grammar in 1:4 is probably deliberate. Literally translated, the greeting from God is "from He the Is and He the Was" (incorrectly using a nominative case following the preposition *apo*). John often defies grammatical rules in ways that would have sounded strange to Greek ears (see also Rev. 1:11, 13, 15; 2:13, 20; 3:12; 4:1; 8:9; 14:7, 19; 19:6, 20). English translations that smooth out his Greek may do John a disservice, since his use of nonstandard Greek appears intentional. He may be calling attention to scriptural allusions to create a "biblical effect" (Beale, 103), or he may be subverting grammar rules of the dominant culture as a form of protest or resistance (Callahan 1995).

Jesus is the faithful "witness" (1:5), a term of crucial importance throughout the book. The Greek word "witness" (*martys*) can also mean "martyr." John aims to inspire hearers themselves to become witnesses, even to the point of martyrdom. Jesus was martyred ("by his blood," 1:5). John may expect martyrdom for his followers, although he is able to name only one actual martyr, Antipas, in the church of Pergamum (2:13).

Jesus also is "the one ruling the kings of the earth" (1:5)—a daring claim in the face of the Roman Empire's hegemonic rule, and expressed already in the present tense. John also ascribes political values of "glory" and "dominion" (1:6) to Jesus, values ascribed to Rome in imperial hymns and celebrations.

Throughout the book, John continually shapes the Christian community as a countercultural community. God's people are called a "kingdom of priests" (1:6; a theme that will recur in 5:10 and 20:6; see also 1 Pet. 2:5, 9). John draws this imagery from the exodus story in which God liberates Israel from Egypt to be a "priestly kingdom" (Exod. 19:6), and from Isaiah's description of God's people as priests in the return from exile in Babylon (Isa. 61:6).

Two liturgical exclamations of "Amen!" bracket a description of Jesus' coming with the clouds (based on Dan. 7:13). "Look! He is coming" is present tense, suggesting a coming already underway.

Only twice in Revelation does God speak directly (1:8; 21:5-7). "I am the Alpha and Omega" uses the first and last letters of the Greek alphabet to underscore God's all-encompassing presence. God is the first and the last, the beginning and the end (see also 1:17; 21:6; 22:13).

The Text in the Interpretive Tradition

In the sixteenth century, Reformer Martin Luther drew his doctrine of the priesthood of all the baptized from the proclamation of God's people as a "kingdom of priests" (Rev. 1:6), similar to the "royal priesthood" of 1 Pet. 2:5 and 2:9. Luther's notion that "we are all priests" (*Babylonian Captivity of the Churches*) became a central tenet for Protestants, countering the medieval Catholic division of Christians into separate estates of clergy (the "religious") and laity.

The Alpha and Omega of Rev. 1:8 have inspired visionary art and music throughout Christian history. The fourth-century Latin hymn "Of the Father's Love Begotten" describes Christ as "Alpha and Omega," the source, the ending. The prevalence of the Alpha and Omega in earliest Christian art, including catacomb art, may reflect its use as an anti-Arian symbol in christological controversies (Kinney, 202). A mosaic of Christ as the Alpha and Omega adorns the late fourth-century Church of St. Pudenziana in Rome, along with other images from Revelation (Klein, 160). In the twelfth century, the most influential medieval interpreter of Revelation, Joachim of Fiore, used the Alpha and Omega in the "psaltery with ten strings," a figure that came to him in a mystical vision (Kovacs and Rowland). Methodist hymnist Charles Wesley used the Alpha and Omega image in his "Love Divine, All Loves Excelling" ("Take away the love of sinning / Alpha and Omega be").

The Text in Contemporary Discussion

Scholars differ on how Revelation understands Jesus' "coming" (1:7). John switches freely among past, present, and future tenses throughout the book in a manner typical of the visionary language of apocalypses.

A traditional view has seen Revelation as primarily referring to Jesus' "second coming" (a term never used in Revelation), an eschatological future event when Jesus will come to judge. The apocalyptic vision of the figure coming on the clouds lends support to such a view, drawing on traditional Jewish eschatology from Daniel.

Recent scholars also emphasize Jesus' sacramental coming—as evidenced by numerous "Amens" and other liturgical acclamations, as well as the setting of the book within the Sunday worship service ("on the Lord's day," 1:10). The antiphonal call-and-response invitations to "come" in Rev.

22:17 may be part of a eucharistic dialogue between lector and hearers (Vanni, 363; Ruiz 1992). Some even argue that the book's "eschatology is realized" in the worship setting, via the book's journey into another reality (Barr 1984, 46). The book sweeps hearers up into a dramatic experience of apocalyptic transformation, leading to a new way of life (Rhoads). The ritual setting enables worshipers' experience of the coming of Jesus in a way that "brings the future into the present" (Barr 1998, 174).

Most scholars reject a fully "realized eschatology" that collapses Jesus' coming primarily into a liturgical event, however, since this would leave in place the unjust Roman system. Revelation is unquestionably anti-Roman—and this may shed light also on the book's eschatology, if John is critiquing Rome's own eschatology embodied in slogans such a *Roma Aeterna*. References to Jesus' future coming in judgment may herald God's judgment against the unjust Roman Empire much more than the end of the world. Increasingly, scholars think the comment that the "time is near" (1:3) may proclaim the impending end of Rome, not the end of the cosmos itself.

Revelation 1:9-16: Introducing John of Patmos

The Text in Its Ancient Context

Revelation 1:9 sets the narrative context for the entire book. John does not claim authority as an apostle. Instead, he introduces himself by expressing solidarity with his hearers, calling himself a "brother" and a "partner" (*synkoinōnos*).

Three key words in 1:9 describe the situation John shares with the communities. The first word, "tribulation" or "persecution" (*thlipsis*), can have a wide range of meanings. We know of no historical evidence of state-sponsored persecution at the time of the emperor Domitian, the time Irenaeus assigns for the book's writing and the consensus of most scholars. The "persecution" (*thlipsis*) of Revelation's audience was likely the local harassment or social marginalization experienced by a few of John's communities for refusing to participate in the Roman imperial economic system or imperial cult worship. John anticipates that if the communities are faithful to Jesus, their witness may provoke some kind of persecution in the future.

"Kingdom," or *basileia*, the second term John says he shares with his communities in 1:9, likely refers to both the kingdom of God and the kingdom of Rome. "Kingdom" is a political term used frequently in Revelation with profound religious power.

The third term, *hypomonē*, becomes a core ethical imperative for Revelation's strategy of resistance (2:2, 3, 19; 3:10; 13:10; 14:12). Translations as "patient endurance" (RSV, NRSV) are too passive for this word. John champions a more active engagement, rooted in the radical Jewish apocalyptic tradition of nonviolent resistance to idolatrous empires. A better translation might be "nonviolent resistance" (Blount 2009, 42), or "resistance" (Richard 1995).

John gives his location: the island of Patmos, about sixty miles off the coast of modern Turkey. He is on the island "because of the word of God and the testimony of Jesus" (1:9). There is no historical evidence for the Roman use of Patmos as a place of banishment or exile, although that became the understanding of John's situation in later Christian tradition (Eusebius, *Hist. eccl.* 3.18;

Boxall). "Because of the word of God" could have a range of meanings. What is important is that John identifies himself as unable to visit his communities in person. So he writes to them. Like the apostle Paul, he wants his letter to embody his physical presence.

John dates his letter "on the Lord's day" (1:10), anchoring it in the church's gathering for liturgy and the sacraments. Revelation was written to be read aloud in the worship service on Sunday. John wants hearers to join in the "Amens" and "Alleluias" of the book.

John "turned to see the voice" (1:12), an example of the Apocalypse's mixing of hearing and seeing. John had never seen Jesus in the flesh, but he saw Jesus as "one like a son of humanity," drawing on images from Daniel that combine the heavenly Ancient of Days with the human "son of humanity" figure. With hair "as white as white wool" (Dan. 7:9) and feet "like burnished bronze" (Dan. 10:6), Jesus looks African (Blount). The two-edged sword issuing from his mouth is the word of God (Isa. 49:2). Jesus' all-seeing eyes "like a flame of fire" (1:14; 2:18; 19:12) alert hearers to Jesus' power to scrutinize them.

This vision, like John's other visions, is beyond description in words. John uses the words "as" and "like" (*hōs, homoios*) more than seventy times in this book, a reminder that the images are metaphorical. John "gropes to find the language to convey adequately" what he sees (Rowland, 566), appealing to readers' imaginations more than to logic or literal representation.

John falls down when he sees Jesus, almost terrified to death. But Jesus stoops to touch him, telling him not to be afraid. This scene is modeled on Daniel's call story in Dan. 8:15-18.

In addition to allusions from Hebrew Scripture, John also situates Jesus in terms of Greco-Roman imagery familiar to his first-century audience, as a way of underscoring Jesus' sovereignty. The seven stars may challenge the emperor Domitian's own use of astral imagery, as depicted on a coin from 83 CE commemorating his son's death, showing seven stars and proclaiming the "Divine Caesar" (Barr 1998, 47; Kraybill). The image of Jesus holding the keys to death and Hades may reference the Greek goddess Hecate, often depicted as holding the keys to Hades. John's point is that Jesus—not Roman emperors or deities—holds power over life and death, and over the cosmos itself.

John is called to communicate the vital message that the risen Jesus is alive and present, personally walking among the seven churches (2:1, depicted as seven lampstands), with a message for each one.

■ The Text in the Interpretive Tradition

From earliest times, readers longing for more information about John have filled in additional information not found in the text itself. Some imagined John sentenced to hard labor in the mines of Patmos. Tertullian (*Praescr.* 36) and subsequent interpreters (including Albrecht Dürer) depicted John as being boiled in oil, unscathed, before his exile to Patmos (see Smith; Boxall).

John provides the only physical description of Jesus in the Bible, a description that has inspired many artists through the centuries. Yet the Jesus of Revelation is impossible to depict. If Jesus has a sword literally coming from his mouth—as in illuminated manuscripts such as the eleventh-century Bamberg Apocalypse, as well as Albrecht Dürer's late-fifteenth-century woodcut—he would not be able to speak. In some artistic depictions, the two-edged sword becomes two swords.

The command to "write" has inspired many Christian mystics and visionaries. Hildegard of Bingen's twelfth-century *Scivias* is introduced by a voice from heaven telling her to "write what you see and hear" (Huber, 98). John's apocalyptic vision inspired William Blake's visionary world during England's Industrial Revolution, furnishing a template for both artistic appropriation and social critique (Blake's hymn "Jerusalem" from *Milton* critiqued the "Satanic Mills" of industry). Hildegard and Blake encourage their audience themselves to "envision," in part to encourage reform in their own times (Huber).

■ The Text in Contemporary Discussion

Did John really see things? John's statement that he was "in the spirit" (1:10; 4:2; 17:3; 21:10) has generated much debate. Did his visions occur in an altered state of consciousness, in an ecstatic trance of divine possession? Or are his visions more interior hallucinations brought on by mental illness, or even hallucinogens?

Visionary experiences were understood to be a genuine channel for divine revelation in the ancient Greco-Roman context, in contrast to our post-Freudian understandings of dreams as private phenomena (Aune 1983; Flannery, 105). John's visionary claims situate him in a Jewish visionary tradition with other prophets who are described as experiencing heavenly revelations, including Ezekiel and Daniel, and even the apostle Paul. The question whether these depictions are literary motifs or based on visionary experiences—or both—is raised concerning other writings as well, including *1 Enoch*, the *Sibylline Oracles*, *4 Ezra*, *2 Baruch*, and the *Testament of Levi*. John is deeply immersed in the Scriptures, yet his visions are more than simply a mosaic of scriptural images (deSilva, 121–24). Speaking in the spirit, John claims to represent the voice of Jesus (Barr 1998, 36).

In 2 Cor. 12:1-4, the apostle Paul himself narrates an experience of visionary travel to the third layer of heaven, a description that gives important details even if Paul's intention in this passage is to be ironic. In 1 Corinthians 12–14, Paul makes clear that many early Christians experienced a mantic state of prophetic speech, and that prophetic gifts were both revered and contested in the community. Richard Bauckham compares John's experiences narrated in Revelation with the *Ascension of Isaiah*, another early Christian apocalypse that was also influenced by Jewish Merkabah mysticism, where a circle of prophets gather to experience inspiration and then interpret visionary experiences through the Scriptures (Bauckham 1993b, 89, 141). Falling into a trance, the prophet Isaiah is invited up through an open door into seven heavens, where "the mind in his body was taken up from him. But his breath was in him, for he was seeing a vision.... And the vision which he saw was not from this world, but from the world which is hidden from the flesh" (*Ascension of Isaiah* 6:10-15).

Early Christian prophecy was also influenced by Hellenistic oracular and revelatory traditions (Aune 1983). Visionary travel into the underworld or the realm of the divine was a familiar vehicle for receiving divine revelations, as described in literary sources such as Cicero's *Dream of Scipio* (Flannery). The presence of two well-known oracular sanctuaries of the Greek god Apollo in the same region of Asia Minor as John's cities, in Claros and Didyma, as well as a sanctuary of Asclepius at Pergamum, where people went for dream incubation, make it likely that John's communities would have known traditions about revelatory experiences.

What is important is that John does not want to undertake the transformative apocalyptic journey alone. His visions are not private. He takes readers along with him on his time-travel journey (Maier, 56), conducting his audience also into an altered state of consciousness, a new reality (Barr 2002, 35). His first-person narrative is like on-the-scene reporting, inviting hearers into the journey in the spirit. Through this shared experience, the audience itself, "by subtle degrees, is brought around to a new way of seeing and understanding" (Maier, 58).

John's goal in sharing "in the spirit" is to recount not an ecstatic experience but rather a prophetic experience. The visionary journey is meant to be transformative, both for John and for his communities. John's primary focus in narrating his visionary experiences is "not spiritual fervor but ethical awareness" (Blount 2009, 42).

Revelation 2–3: Seven Churches on Earth; Seven Messages

The Text in Its Ancient Context

The so-called letters to the seven churches function as prophetic messages, similar to imperial edicts (Aune 1990). All seven messages are intended to be heard by all the churches—a point made explicit in the message to Thyatira (2:23), the longest of the seven messages. The messages give the risen Christ's assessment of each church's situation.

The seven messages furnish our most detailed historical information about each church in late first-century Asia Minor. These seven churches were quite different from one another, economically and socially, some with leaders who did not agree with John's uncompromising perspective. Most of the cities named had official Roman imperial altars or temples, promoting worship and allegiance to the empire and emperors (Thompson). The seven cities form a geographical circuit northward and inland from the port city of Ephesus on the Aegean coast.

All seven messages are addressed to the "angel" or "messenger" of the church—probably the corporate spirit of the congregation (Wink, 3). The seven messages follow a similar pattern, in differing order: Each begins with a description of Jesus, echoing some aspect of the inaugural vision (2:1, 8, 12, 18; 3:1, 7, 14). Next comes a performance review, introduced by "I know"—a reminder of the all-seeing eye of Christ, who walks among the churches (imaged as seven golden lampstands, 2:1). "Works" (*erga*) set a standard by which the churches are measured. Four churches are told to repent, and five churches experience sharp rebuke. John uses rhetoric of innuendo to vilify rival prophetic leaders with biblical labels ("Jezebel," "Balaam"), criticizing what he considers overly assimilationist practices such as eating food that has been sacrificed to pagan deities. The call to "hear" resembles Jesus' call in the Gospels (Matt. 11:15; Mark 4:9, 23; Luke 8:8). Finally comes a wondrous promise from the Spirit to the "conquerors" (from the Greek verb *nikaō*), motivating hearers to remain faithful so they can "conquer" as Jesus conquered.

A promise-fulfillment compositional structure ties the seven messages to the final vision of the book in a concentric pattern (Schüssler Fiorenza 1998). The promises will be fulfilled in the final vision of the new Jerusalem, in chapters 21–22.

Ephesus, the largest city and closest to the island of Patmos, receives high praise for its "resistance" (*hypomonē*, 2:2) and for its strict standards in judging of false teachers, including the "Nicolaitans," a group whose identity and "works" are uncertain. But the church has forgotten to love. The tree of life (2:7; 22:2, 14, 19), the most famous of the promises of future blessing, draws on the paradise traditions from Gen. 2:9.

The messages to Smyrna and Philadelphia introduce the difficult question of the relationship of the churches to Judaism. We cannot know why John labels opponents in both cities the "synagogue of Satan" (2:9; 3:9). Since John is clearly a Jew himself who identifies strongly with the traditions of Israel, his criticism should be viewed as a sibling dispute within the Jewish family rather than as anti-Judaism. Given the great diversity of first-century Christian communities in Asia Minor, it is even possible that John is critiquing not Jews at all, but Christian gentiles in the same cities who followed the teachings of Paul—those who think they can inherit the promises of Israel without following Jewish dietary law (Pagels). Alternately, if the word "synagogue" refers to actual Jews, then these two churches may have been experiencing separation from local Jewish communities—thereby risking loss of official legitimacy negotiated by Jewish communities within the empire. Within the diverse landscape of early Christianity and Judaism in the cities of late first century Asia Minor, multiple scenarios are possible for reconstructing the history of Revelation's seven churches.

The message to Pergamum (2:12-17) brings up two issues that also concern Thyatira: eating food offered to idols and participating in "fornication" (*porneia*), probably a metaphor for participation in the imperial cult (2:14, 20). Food was a divisive issue for early Christians, as evidenced by the many New Testament debates about eating meat offered to idols (Rom. 14:13-23; 1 Cor. 10:23-33). John's strict vegetarian line prohibiting all meat sacrificed to pagan gods in the city markets would have meant social marginalization, especially for wealthier Christians seeking to move up socially by participating in civic banquets.

John's polemic reveals intense theological debate within the churches. John labels a leader in Pergamum who was apparently advocating a more lenient position as "Balaam," the name of a notorious false prophet (Numbers 22; 31:16). Similarly, in Thyatira, John labels a rival prophet who permits Christians to eat meat as "Jezebel"—a pejorative link to the queen of Israel who promoted pagan worship (1 Kgs. 18:19). The woman prophet in Thyatira is clearly influential, with many followers whom John calls her "children." Accusation of "deceit" (2:20) links her to Roman figures who practice deceit later in the book (the whore of Babylon, 17:23; the two beasts, 12:9; 13:14; 14:17).

The sixth church, Philadelphia, receives only praise. This church will be kept from the "hour of trial coming upon the whole empire [*oikoumenē*]"—probably a reference to God's impending judgment against the whole Roman Empire rather than to general end-times tribulation (Rossing 2003; Richard 1995). That judgment or legal trial will happen in the Babylon vision of chapter 18.

The Laodiceans receive the harshest critique. Prosperous Laodicean church members who may feel secure in their wealth do not "see" that their situation nauseates God. To persuade the church to repent of its complacency, John gives the image of Jesus knocking at the door and promising to eat with the church—possibly a reference to the Lord's Supper. The "conqueror" receives the promise of sharing a throne with Jesus, as Jesus shares a throne with God.

The Text in the Interpretive Tradition

Although addressed to the Laodicean community corporately, the image of Jesus knocking at the door in 3:20 is frequently interpreted by mystics and pietists as the door of the individual's heart. Hildegard of Bingen heard 3:20 as an invitation to the spiritual life. For St. John of the Cross (1542–1591), when Christ knocks on the soul's door he brings the supper of "his own sweetness" (Wainwright, 203). Warner Sallman's nineteenth-century painting *Christ at the Heart's Door*, displayed in many churches, exemplifies the popularity of this understanding.

Premillennial dispensationalists use Rev. 3:10 as proof of the so-called rapture, a word not mentioned in Revelation. Their interpretive system, developed by John Nelson Darby in the nineteenth century, undergirds modern fundamentalist "prophecy" writings such as Tim LaHaye and Jerry Jenkins's *Left Behind* (1995) and Hal Lindsey's *The Late Great Planet Earth* (1970). Proponents claim that being saved "from the hour of trial coming upon the whole world" (3:10) means that born-again Christians will be snatched up to heaven for seven years while others suffer a period of tribulation (Boyer; Rossing 2004).

Elaborate dispensationalist charts interpret Revelation 2–3 as depicting seven stages, or "dispensations," of church history "from AD 96 to the end" (the *Old Scofield Reference Bible*).

In these charts, Ephesus is viewed as the apostolic church of the first century; Smyrna as the persecuted church until the time of Emperor Constantine; Pergamum as the church "where Satan's throne is," after the conversion of Constantine; Thyatira as the church of the Roman Catholic papacy; and Sardis as the Protestant Reformation that became "the Dead Church" when it retained rituals such as infant baptism (LaHaye, 50). Laodicea is viewed as the present lukewarm, mainline church.

Contrary to such "futurist" interpretations, most scholars consider it highly unlikely that John wrote the seven letters with any predictive system of future church history in mind. To claim that Revelation was written in order to predict events hundreds or thousands of years later in the United States or the Middle East detracts from its original meaning to communities in the first century.

The Text in Contemporary Discussion

Scholars debate whether the intra-Christian polemic against rival prophetic leaders is primary or secondary to the overall anti-imperial polemic of the book. John fights on multiple fronts at once, using innuendo and even death threats ("I will strike her children dead," 2:23) to discredit fellow leaders with whom he disagrees. The question is whether it is this rivalry among Christian prophets, rather than the critique of Rome, that constitutes John's principal purpose in writing (Thompson; Duff). Recent consensus among scholars that there was no systemic persecution of Christians may lend support to this perspective, although other scholars point to the all-pervasive pressure to participate in Roman imperial cult (Friesen).

John clearly views Roman imperial cults and Rome's military and economic hegemony as demonic. But aspects of the rhetoric of Revelation complicate the perception that we might read the book today as supporting a straightforward anti-imperial agenda. The book's rhetoric of gender further complicates the issue, as does the antisemitic legacy of the phrase "synagogue of Satan" (2:9;

3:9) in Christian history. John's violent polemic against the woman he labels "Jezebel" and other scenes of violence against women (17:16) may make any liberating reading impossible for women today (Pippin). On the other hand, John critiques "Jezebel" not because she is a woman per se, but because John disagrees with her teachings (Schüssler Fiorenza 1998). We know that other women prophets were revered in nearby Christian communities in Asia Minor in the first and second centuries. (The historian Eusebius lauds the four prophesying daughters of Philip [Acts 21:9] in Hierapolis, as well as later women prophets Quadratus and Ammia, *Hist. eccl.* 5.17). What John seems to be advocating is a "rigorous priestly purity" of Jewish dietary practices (Frankfurter 2011, 468) over against those who permit intermingling with Greco-Roman culture. It may even be that all John's attacks concern the same issue: his "synagogue of Satan" label for Pergamum and Smyrna, as well as his "Balaam" and "Jezebel" labels for leaders in Pergamum and Thyatira, may all represent thinly veiled attacks on Christian communities that abandoned Jewish dietary law, perhaps the heirs of Paul's gentile-Christian churches (Pagels; for history of this view see Rowland, 545).

Revelation 4–5: Heavenly Throne Room, the Lamb, All Creation's Worship

THE TEXT IN ITS ANCIENT CONTEXT

A voice summons John to "come up" to heaven. The vision takes place "in the spirit" (the same terminology as in 1:10; 17:3; 21:10). Many ancient apocalypses contain such visionary journeys involving travel into layers of heaven or time travel into the future. The seer returns from the transformative journey with an urgent message for readers, typically calling for repentance and faithfulness.

John borrows imagery from the prophets Ezekiel and Isaiah to describe what he sees in heaven. The divine throne looks as the prophets saw it (Isa. 6:2; Ezek. 1:4-28), with concentric circles of worshipers including Ezekiel's four mysterious living creatures. Too holy to be named, God is simply the "One seated on the throne." Peals of lightning and thunder recall God's theophany at Sinai. John adds a rainbow, connecting the throne to God's covenant with Noah and all creation (Gen. 9:20-21).

Power is the key to this scene. The throne is the central symbol of power in Revelation. The central questions addressed by Revelation are questions of power: "Who is the true Lord of this world?" "To whom does this earth belong?" (Schüssler Fiorenza 1991, 58, 120). Dueling thrones throughout Revelation represent the struggle between God's agents and evil that is at the heart of the book. Satan (2:13), represented as the dragon (13:2), and his agent the beast (16:10) are both portrayed symbolically as having thrones. As representatives of imperial evil, they must be dethroned, giving way to the final vision of God's throne from which flows the river of life at the center of the renewed earth (22:1).

As political imagery, the heavenly throne-room scene evokes comparisons with the Roman emperor's throne-room ceremonies (Aune 1983). In Roman imperial throne rooms, worshipers threw their crowns before the emperor as a sign of allegiance, singing hymns and liturgies of praise. With the image of the elders casting their crowns before God's magnificent throne (4:10), John in effect trumps Roman court liturgies. The message is that only God, not the emperor or the empire, is worthy of worshipers' allegiance.

More than fifteen hymns or hymnlike compositions occur throughout Revelation, all giving encouragement to God's people on earth from the perspective of heaven. In the book's three-tiered cosmology (heaven, earth, and the Abyss or underworld), events in heaven give direction for how things should be on earth. Revelation's frequent use of hymns, doxologies, and descriptions of heavenly liturgies is "not for the sake of persuading his audience to participate in the daily or weekly liturgy," but rather "for the sake of moving the audience to political resistance" (Schüssler Fiorenza 1991, 103).

Revelation 5:5 introduces Jesus into the throne-room scene via a surprising plot development. The sealed scroll God holds must be opened. But no one can be found worthy to open the scroll's seals and learn its secrets. John invites readers to "weep much" (5:4) with him, employing pathos as part of his persuasive strategy (Maier, 57). One of the elders tells John not to weep because "the Lion of the tribe of Judah, the Root of David, has conquered" (5:5). Two words—"lion" and "conquer"—lead us to expect a fierce animal to open the scroll, like the fierce animals of other apocalypses (compare the lion that conquers the Roman eagle in 2 Esdras 12).

Yet John delivers an amazing surprise. In place of the expected lion comes a Lamb: "Then I saw . . . a Lamb standing as if it had been slaughtered" (5:6). The Greek word John uses for "lamb" (*arnion*) actually is a diminutive form, suggesting vulnerability. This is one of a number of passages where hearing and seeing reveal two different and paradoxical dimensions of the same reality. John "hears" a lion but "sees" a Lamb.

This powerful image of Jesus as "the Lamb that was slaughtered" (Rev. 5:12) becomes the central symbol of Jesus for all of Revelation. No other apocalypse portrays its divine hero as a lamb (Johns). This depiction reveals Jesus in the most vulnerable way possible, as a victim who is slaughtered but standing upright—crucified, yet risen to life. The image links Jesus to the Passover lamb that saved the Israelites in the exodus story. Reminiscent also of the servant-lamb of Isaiah 53 who "is led to the slaughter," the Lamb of Revelation becomes the victor not by militaristic power and bloodshed but rather through being slaughtered. Evil has been conquered not by overwhelming force or violence, but by the Lamb's victory on the cross.

Singing breaks out in heaven for a second time when the Lamb is introduced. John of Patmos envisions a liturgy where animals and all creatures in heaven, on earth, and under the earth join in exuberant singing. The four living creatures and twenty-four elders now take up their harps to sing a "new song," this time praising Jesus, the Lamb (Rev. 5:8-14). The emphasis on "new" hints at the way everything will be renewed at the end of Revelation, in the vision of the new heaven and the new earth (Revelation 21–22).

The Text in the Interpretive Tradition

Since the second century (Irenaeus, *Against Heresies* 3.11.8), Christian tradition has associated the four living creatures with the four Evangelists, identified by Jerome (*Preface to the Commentary on Matthew*) as Matthew (the human); Mark (the lion); Luke (the ox); John (the eagle).

The Lamb, the most important image of Jesus in Revelation, figures prominently in Christian imagery from the time of the catacombs. The Moravian church's emblem is the Lamb carrying a flag of victory, held in its right foreleg and resting on its shoulder. The church's motto is "Our Lamb has conquered; let us follow him." Liturgically, the Lamb of Revelation became combined with Jesus as "Lamb of God who takes away the sin of the world" from John's Gospel, although the words for lamb differ (*arnion* in Revelation, *amnos* in John 1:29, 36) and Revelation's Lamb is not described as "Lamb of God." The most notable difference between the lamb Christologies of the two books is that Revelation lacks the Gospel of John's expiation model of the Lamb "taking away" or atoning for sin (Schüssler Fiorenza 1998, 95–97; Johns; Blount 2005, 78).

No book of the Bible has had more influence on Western music and art than Revelation. The hymns of Revelation are familiar to Christian worshipers from the liturgy (the Sanctus, "Holy, Holy, Holy"; "This is the Feast of Victory for Our God") and choral works such as Handel's *Messiah* ("Worthy Is the Lamb Who Was Slain"). Alfred Lord Tennyson acclaimed Reginald Heber's hymn "Holy, Holy, Holy," based on Rev. 4:8-11, as "the world's greatest hymn."

The hymns are not intended to be understood literally. Their symbolic dimension is precisely what gives these songs their power. Songs connect God's people to something deeper. Songs serve to "unbind a people from their fear" (Blount 2005). That is why so many African American spirituals are based on Revelation ("Shall We Gather at the River?," "I Want to Be Ready to Walk in Jerusalem Just like John," "Down by the Riverside"). Often using a call-and-response format, they evoke hearers' capacity for solidarity and resistance. They give courage and hope.

The Text in Contemporary Discussion

"Does the Lion lie down with the Lamb?" asks one scholar (Moyise 2001). The question is important because of implications for the representation of divine violence. Scholars differ regarding the extent to which the figure of Jesus as "Lamb" supersedes that of "Lion" in 5:5 or what relationship is intended between lionlike and lamblike elements in Revelation's Christology. In biblical and apocalyptic tradition, the lion symbolized ferocity and destructive strength (Bauckham 1993a, 183). The lion was interpreted messianically as a devouring lion at Qumran (1QSb 5:29) and in *4 Ezra* 11-12, where the lion destroys the Roman eagle.

John hears of a Lion but sees a Lamb. For many scholars, this means the nonviolent Lamb image has replaced the violent Lion (Caird 1966, 75; Johns; Barr 1997, 161; Kraybill). Even a scholar who argues that hearing normally interprets seeing in Revelation, not vice versa (Resseguie), thinks that seeing reinterprets hearing in Rev. 5:5. Yet Steve Moyise and others make the case that the Lion/Lamb juxtaposition may instead necessitate the two images mutually interpreting each other (Moyise 2001, 194).

All scholars agree there is no textual basis for dispensationalist claims, like those made by San Antonio preacher John Hagee and others, that Jesus will return the second time as a violent "Lion of the tribe of Judah, who will trample His enemies until their blood stains His garments," replacing Jesus' first Lamblike incarnation (Hagee 1999, 239).

The hymn of 4:8 also raises an ecological question for scholars. The hymn draws closely on the "Holy, Holy, Holy" of Isa. 6:3. But why does John omit the line of Isaiah, "The whole earth is full of God's glory"? This change suggests John does not yet consider earth to be filled with God's glory (Bauckham 2011, 179; Stephens, 178). God does not intend to destroy the creation, however; the repeated emphasis in Revelation's hymns on God as creator and allusions to the rainbow of the flood narrative (4:3; 11:8) make that clear. Yet the earth must be liberated from the "destroyers of the earth" (11:8) before it can be filled with God's glory. In this way, John's change in the use of Isaiah reveals an earth-focused dimension of his eschatology.

Revelation 6: The Seven Seals: Diagnosing the Crises of Empire

■ The Text in Its Ancient Context

The journey up into heaven (begun in Rev. 4:1) continues with the opening of the seven seals. The seals interpret events on earth from a heavenly perspective, giving John an apocalyptic view of causality and consequences. The four living creatures represent the whole cosmos (Bauckham 2011). One by one, the living creatures call out "Come," unleashing scenes of destruction rampaging across the world. The command "Come," addressed to the four horses and riders, may also be addressed to John himself. ("Come and see" is the sense in a few later manuscripts that add the word "see" in verses 1, 3 5, and 7.)

Like an urgent wake-up call, the first four seal visions deliver God's exposé of the evils of the Roman imperial system. John sees vivid pictures of war, famine, and the pathologies of empire, drawing on the prophet Zechariah's visions of horses of different colors patrolling the earth's four directions (Zech. 1:7-11; 6:1-8).

As a quartet, the four horsemen most likely portray the imperial system gone awry. The first horseman who "conquers" mimics Christ in appearance, leading some interpreters to identify him as Christ. But the resemblance to the figure of Christ on the white horse in Rev. 19:11 is more mimicry, not identification. The Lamb Jesus and his followers conquer only nonviolently, whereas this rider on a white horse conquers with killing.

The second horseman represents a critique of Rome's own internal "peace," the *Pax Romana*. This rider of the red horse wields a sword to instigate civil war so that people slaughter "one another." This verse also introduces the difficult image of these calamities being "permitted," a passive verb used frequently in the book. The presumed subject who permits these disasters is God.

The third horseman brings food insecurity and inflation, symbolized by the commercial scales (literally, "yoke") that he carries for measuring. An unidentified voice uses irony to underscore the pointedly economic critique: Grain has become so expensive that a whole day's wage buys only a measure of staple food. Cropland is used to grow export crops of wine and oil, which must not be harmed. Rome's predatory economy causes food insecurity for the poor.

The fourth horse, the color of grass and vegetation, represents the consequences of the first three calamities for the whole creation. Personified figures of Pestilence (Death) and Hades follow war, bringing power to kill and devour one fourth of the world with a lethal mix of natural and human-caused calamities.

With the fifth and sixth seals, the pattern shifts. John sees an altar in heaven, sheltering Rome's victims who had been "slaughtered." (The same word as was used to refer to Jesus' death in 5:12.) "Souls" (*psychai*) can also be translated as "lives," with slaughtered victims including even the creation itself (see 8:9 for the "souls" of sea creatures among those killed). The altar signifies the promise of restoration to life for those who, like Jesus, have been slaughtered for their active witness (see 20:4; Blount 2005).

"How long, O Lord?" is the cry of ancient Israel throughout the Hebrew Bible, especially in the Psalms (Pss. 13:1; 35:17). This prayer for vindication underscores Revelation's call to readers to identify with those who have suffered for their testimony. "Just a little longer" assures victims of the nearness of Rome's end, in contrast to Rome's own claims of eternal rule. God's justice will soon be "fulfilled" or made "complete" (*plērōthēnai*) by the community's defiant witness.

The whole cosmos undergoes cataclysms with the opening of the sixth seal, unleashing terrifying visions of the sun darkening, stars falling, and the moon turning to blood. Such imagery is conventional, recalling the Hebrew prophets' descriptions of the "Day of the Lord" (Isa. 13:6, 10; Joel 2:31). It also resembles the Synoptic Gospels' apocalypses (Matt. 24:29; Mark 13:24). The imagery is hyperbolic, not literal. The cosmic Day-of-the-Lord cataclysms envelop everyone, from rich to poor. All seek to hide from God's judgment. The attribution of the earthquake to the "wrath of the Lamb" (6:16) is the only reference in Revelation to the Lamb's wrath. The sixth seal concludes with the ominous question, "Who is able to stand?"

The Text in the Interpretive Tradition

From earliest times, interpreters have debated the meaning of the seals, as well as the two other numbered sequences of sevens, the seven trumpets (Revelation 8–9) and seven bowls (Revelation 16). Those who interpret the sequences as providing a detailed map of history or ages of the church tend to view themselves as living in the time between the fifth and sixth seals. During the Crusades of the twelfth century, Joachim of Fiore believed the opening of the sixth seal was imminent (Daniel). A similar perspective has been taken by others, such as David Koresh and his Branch Davidian sect at the end of the twentieth century. Some contemporary fundamentalists read the series of numbered sevens as a step-by-step chronology of twenty-one future calamities, all scheduled to happen after a supposed rapture. Most interpreters, however, have recognized that attempts to make sense of these visions in a strict linear chronology do not work logically. For example, the stars fall from heaven after the sixth seal is opened (6:13), yet the stars are back in the sky again for the trumpet visions (8:12). Since the time of Joachim, most interpreters have recognized that the visions of the seven seals, trumpets, and bowls recapitulate one another in spiral-like fashion, diagnosing deeper and deeper aspects of the same structures of evil in the world.

The four horsemen figure prominently in interpretive history. Albrecht Dürer's 1517 woodcuts of the four horsemen rampaging across the earth furnished a pattern for many subsequent artists and interpreters, including Lucas Cranach and William Blake. Dürer's portrayal of the third horseman swinging his scale like a weapon against the poor in the center of the scene, and the huge sword and bow of his other three horsemen, have engendered reinterpretation in many contexts, especially in times of war (Smith).

The Text in Contemporary Discussion

Most contemporary scholarship seeks the meaning of the seals not by attempting to figure out a chronology but by analyzing the literary and rhetorical structure. Rhetorically, the seals, trumpets, and bowls all function as warnings, with the aim of strengthening an ethic of resistance on the part of the audience. The warnings intensify with each sequence. The trumpets and bowls are modeled on the Exodus plagues of the Hebrew Scriptures, whereas the seal sequence does not follow one specific biblical pattern.

The violence of the seal sequence poses troubling ethical questions for contemporary interpreters. Most scholars argue that the violence of the seals represents Rome's own violence, not God's violence. John is not glorifying war, but rather unmasking structural violence and the consequences of militarism. The sixth seal becomes harder to explain in terms of such Roman imperial violence, however, since it seems to portray natural calamities as divinely authorized. Recent comparative scholarship on the Jewish apocalypses of Daniel and *1 Enoch* makes the case that even such "cosmic catastrophe" imagery of earthquakes functions politically, as a critique of imperial terror and brutality so severe that the very ordering of the world is "de-created" (Portier-Young, xxiii).

Liberation scholars read Revelation's seals as proclaiming a judgment against empires and a vision for justice for all victims. God's assurance that it will be "just a little while" before oppression ends has brought hope to marginalized peoples throughout history. In the 1980s, Allan Boesak interpreted the cry of the souls under the altar, "How long, O Lord," as a voice of protest to bring hope for liberation to South Africans, while in the 1990s Pablo Richard drew on the seals to expose violence of the rich against the poor in Latin America. The four horsemen elicit rich analogies among scholars and commentators. Employing the methodology of ecological hermeneutics, some scholars find analogies to the seals in environmental-justice crises today. One classical historian likens the four horsemen to "climate change, famine, state failure and disease" (Morris). If the seals function to diagnose crises today, Harry Maier and others underscore that in the logic of Revelation's sense of urgency, there is still time for repentance and hope.

Revelation 7: First Interlude: The People of God

■ The Text in Its Ancient Context

Instead of the expected seventh seal, there is now a delay. The scene shifts. Four angels stand at the four corners of the earth, holding back destructive winds of judgment until God's people can be "sealed" (7:1-8).

Even in the most difficult sections of Revelation, judgment is not unrelenting. A similar interlude will interrupt the trumpet sequence, between the sixth and seventh trumpets (Revelation 10–11). These interludes employ the ancient rhetorical model of a "digression," presenting material that is set apart from—and even sometimes more urgent than—the body of the narrative. Revelation's interludes function rhetorically to shape the identity of God's people as "protected, separated, praising, persecuted, and vindicated" (Perry 2009, 217), preparing the community to persevere in its prophetic witness even in the midst of hardship.

The "sealing" that marks God's people on their foreheads is the same word used to identify the seven seals on the scroll in chapter 6. Sealing may be baptismal imagery (as in 2 Cor. 1:22; Eph.

1:13; 4:30), though there is no actual mention of baptism in Revelation. "Sealing" recalls Ezekiel's description of the mark on the forehead that saved a remnant from judgment (Ezek. 9:4) as well as the Passover story in Exodus, when the angel seals the Israelites' doorposts with the blood of the Passover lamb so their children will be spared (Exodus 12). The seal on God's people's foreheads suggests ownership, like a brand. It contrasts with the symbol of the imperial "mark" followers of the beast receive on their foreheads or right hands (representing some aspect of Roman economic participation) in 13:16-17; 14:9.

Two visions describe the community of followers of Jesus. The first vision, introduced with "I heard" (Rev. 7:4), gives the number of 144,000 Israelites, consisting of 12,000 people from each of twelve tribes. The second vision, introduced with "I saw" (7:9), describes a gentile multitude that no one can count. Since hearing and seeing often show the same thing in different ways in Revelation (In 5:5–6, for example, John "heard" about a Lion but "saw" a Lamb—both referencing Jesus), both visions probably depict the same group of people. As in 5:5–6, the second vision reinterprets the first.

At a time when followers of Jesus were few in number, the huge symbolic number 144,000 would have encouraged an expansive vision for the people of God. The number 144,000 will recur in Revelation 14, as a description of those who "follow the Lamb wherever he goes" (14:4).

The second vision (7:9-16) portrays the multiethnic multitude standing before the throne of God. Variations of the phrase "from every nation, from all tribes and peoples and tongues" (Rev. 7:9) occur seven times in Revelation (5:9; 7:9; 10:11; 11:9; 13:7; 14:6-7; 17:15; González 1999), underscoring the multiethnic character of God's people. The white-robed multitude sings songs and waves palm branches. "Salvation," "blessing," "glory," and "power" were imperial terms common in Roman propaganda, used in the songs here to make counterimperial claims for God alone. Palm branches in the hands of these worshipers allude to the Feast of Tabernacles, one of Revelation's many exodus links (Lev. 23:40-43). For Revelation, a dramatic new exodus is being undertaken "not in Egypt but in the heart of the Roman Empire" (Richard 1995, 77).

After the vision, one of the elders gives its interpretation. The question-and-answer section also helps cement John's identity with his community. Like them, he has to ask for interpretive help. People who belong to the Lamb's multitude are those who have come out of the great *thlipsis* ("persecution," "tribulation"; see the discussion of 1:9).

In an incongruous combination of colors, the multicultural multitude wash their robes in the Lamb's blood to make them white. This may be a reference to the washing away of sin commanded in Isa. 1:16-18 ("though your sins are like scarlet, / they shall be like snow").

God tenderly cares for the people. The verb "shelter" (*skēnōsei*) invokes tabernacle imagery, the sense of God's radiant presence or dwelling (see Ezek. 37:27) as a canopy or tent over the community. The Lamb Jesus now becomes also the shepherd, tending the flock, leading people to springs of water, and wiping away all their tears (a quotation from Isa. 25:8, cited again in 21:4).

"Who is able to stand?" was the ominous question at the end of the dreaded sixth seal (Rev. 6:17). The interlude of Revelation 7 gives God's people their answer to that question by depicting their identity as a redeemed community. By the end of the interlude of Revelation 7, God's people can confidently answer: "With God's help, *we* are those who are able to stand."

The Text in the Interpretive Tradition

The question of the identity of the 144,000 has had a lively interpretive history. The Jehovah's Witnesses, founded in the late nineteenth century, argue that the 144,000 form the new nation who will rule with Christ in the millennium (Wainwright), while the larger multitude of 7:9—a different group of people—will not rule but will share in a blessed life on earth. Most interpreters agree that since those who belong to the Lamb are said to be a multitude "that no one could count" (Rev. 7:9), any literalistic fixation on the number 144,000 in the earlier vision of twelve tribes (Rev 7:4) is thus undermined.

When Revelation 7 is read at funerals and on All Saints' Day, the white-robed host of saints waving palms and praising God becomes a consoling vision of the heavenly afterlife. In her devotional commentary, poet Christina Rossetti interpreted the tribulation out of which the saints have come in 7:14 as the chastening or "sifting" that believers experience in their daily life (Rossetti, 236). The imagery of God wiping away all tears (from Isa. 25:8, also read for All Saints' Day), as well as the tabernacling God and springs of water, comforts believers with the assurance of God's living presence.

The Text in Contemporary Discussion

Rhetorical critics point to the importance in Revelation's interludes of the use of pathos or emotion to shape the confidence and identity of God's people (deSilva, 217; Perry 2009). The interludes of chapters 7 and 10–11 give the audience strong, positive characters with whom to identify. After the wrath of the sixth seal, hearers are drawn to see themselves in the great multitude in white robes, as those who have courage to endure further tribulation and follow the Lamb. The interlude also develops John's own ethos in relation to the audience.

The multitude is strikingly multicultural, from many tribes and nations. Cuban scholar Justo González compares the multicultural perspective of Revelation to mestizo literature, addressed to people of a mixed cultural heritage. John may have been a recent refugee to Asia Minor from Palestine following the trauma of the Roman-Jewish War. For González, John's dual identity as a Jew writing to Greek-speaking people in Asia Minor, in a land and language not his own, places him in a situation similar to those of people with hybrid identities today (González 1999, 59).

Revelation 8–9: Woes, Seven Trumpets: Alas for the Earth

The Text in Its Ancient Context

At the end of the interlude, the Lamb opens the seventh seal. The result brings silence in heaven for half an hour (8:1), like the silence of the seventh day of creation (Aune 1988). The foreboding silence does not last long. More calamities will follow, as seven angels receive seven trumpets that unleash seven more terrifying visions of judgment.

But first, an opening scene in heaven functions to give assurance to the community, identified with the "saints" (8:3). The altar in heaven connects the trumpet sequence back to the fifth seal of

6:10 and the cry of "How long, O Lord?" The urgent prayers of the saints that rise before God serve as a catalyst to set in motion the series of trumpet judgments on earth (Talbert). This message is that prayers matter, and that God hears their prayers.

The seven trumpets follow a pattern similar to that of the seven seals (Revelation 6): the first four elements form a quartet, followed by the fifth and sixth elements intensifying the destruction, and then an interlude of hope (Revelation 10-11) before the seventh element. The first four elements reflect a fourfold division of creation: earth, sea, rivers and springs, and heaven (Bauckham 2011).

John models the trumpets of Revelation on trumpet passages from the Hebrew Scriptures. In Ezekiel 33, the primary model, the prophet blows the trumpet to warn people so that the wicked "turn from their ways and live" (Ezek. 33:11). Trumpets can also function militarily (Joshua 6; 2 Chron. 13:12), as priestly announcements of festivals (Num. 10:1-10), or eschatologically to announce the Day of the Lord (Joel 2:1; Zeph. 1:16).

The calamities announced by trumpet borrow their imagery primarily from the Exodus plagues, although the word "plague" is not used until the sixth trumpet (9:18, 20). The trumpet visions will be closely paralleled by the seven bowls in Revelation 15-16, where each calamity is called a "plague." Together, the trumpet and bowl sequences function to evoke a sense of a new exodus for God's people, this time from the Roman Empire. Like the plague sequence leading up to the exodus of Israel from Egypt, the judgments announced by the trumpets elicit both hope and terror—enacting a cosmic judgment that brings justice and liberation. The trumpet and bowl sequences recapitulate the seal sequence, with ever-increasing intensity of destruction.

The first trumpet's rain of hail and fire on the earth, mixed with blood, is modeled on the seventh Exodus plague (Exod. 9:22-26). Narration of the action in the passive voice suggests God as the one permitting the calamity. The destruction of one-third of the earth and its trees intensifies the one-fourth destruction of the seal visions (6:8)—yet, two-thirds of the creation is still spared. John may even be critiquing Rome's destructive practices of over-logging the forests of conquered nations, a practice lauded by Rome's own propagandists (see Aelius Aristides, *Orations* 26.12).

The second trumpet's killing of one-third of the sea creatures echoes the first Exodus plague (Exod. 7:20-21; cf. Ps. 105:29). John also weaves in creation motifs with the description of the sea creatures as "having souls" (8:9, another example of John's defying grammatical rules, similar to 1:4). He alludes to Gen. 1:20-21, where sea creatures and mammals also are called "living souls" (Perry 2010). John adds a sharp element of economic critique of Roman maritime trade by stating that one-third of the ships are also destroyed. Judgment on Roman maritime trade will be taken up in chapter 18, the Babylon vision.

The poisoning of one-third of the springs and rivers sounded by the third trumpet, caused by a falling star named Wormwood, has no Exodus antecedent. John likely draws imagery from the prophet Jeremiah ("Because they have forsaken my law . . . Behold I will feed this people with wormwood and give them poisonous water to drink," Jer. 9:13-18; cf. Lam. 3:15). In Hebrew Scriptures, a falling star heralds the death of a tyrant (Isa. 14:12; Richard 1995).

The fourth trumpet resumes the reworking of the Exodus calamities with darkness wiping out one-third of the sunlight, moon, and stars, similar to the darkness brought on Egypt in the ninth plague (Exod. 10:21; cf. Ps. 105:28).

While the first four trumpets are broadly modeled on Exodus plagues, John also makes important changes. Absent from Revelation is any element similar to the hardening of Pharaoh's heart in Exodus, thus keeping open the possibility for repentance—a theme underscored in 9:20-21, albeit negatively (in actuality "they did not repent"). The consequences of the trumpets are more cosmic than the Exodus plagues, falling on the entire creation rather than on a specific nation, Egypt. In effect, the trumpets' destruction functions as a cosmic "de-creation," reversing the order of Gen. 1:1-25, where stars, sun, moon, sea creatures, and plants are created in sequence (Maier, 106).

After the fourth trumpet, the imagery shifts. An eagle flies through mid-heaven crying out, "Woe, woe to the inhabitants of the earth" (8:13). The eagle was a familiar symbol of the Roman Empire, ironically used here to proclaim the empire's demise. The Greek word translated "woe" (*ouai*) voices an untranslatable sound expressing lamentation or mourning as well as horror (Alexiou). In chapter 18, the same word is usually translated "Alas, alas, alas," 18:10, 16, 19 NRSV, RSV). The translation "alas" rather than "woe" may be better here as well, in which case the "woes" declare not so much a curse or woe *against* the inhabitants and the earth as God's grief-stricken lament *on behalf of* the earth and its inhabitants (Rossing 2002, 181–83). These verses also introduce the peculiar use of *ouai* as a noun in 9:12, constituting the final three blasts of the trumpets ("the first woe/alas," 9:12; "the second woe/alas," 11:14). Although the third woe is never identified, it is likely the seventh trumpet, blown in 11:14-15.

With the fifth and sixth trumpets, Exodus imagery gives way to more sinister destruction, magnifying the horror of de-creation. A falling star (see also 8:10) breaks the locked boundaries between heaven and the underworld, resulting in smoke that darkens the cosmos. The underworld is allowed to invade the realm of earth with mutant creatures worse than any biblical plague. Monstrous locusts recall the locusts of the Exodus story (Exod. 10:1-20), but now with the supernatural power of scorpions and the military appearance of war horses (Joel 2:4).

Yet a word of assurance is given to the audience in 9:4, in the midst of the locusts: God's people who received the seal on their foreheads will continue to be protected (9:4), as will the grass and trees. This verse reminds the audience that longs for justice to view the trumpets with hope rather than dread, since they herald the collapse of the unjust imperial system.

Apollyon, the name of the commander of the locusts (literally, "the destroyer"), likely alludes to the Greek god Apollo, whose identity was claimed by some Roman emperors. The Euphrates River was both the boundary of ancient Israel and the boundary of the Roman Empire, from where the dreaded Parthians threatened invasion. The sixth trumpet's demonic cavalries, of 200,000 surreal horses that kill one-third of the world's population (9:13–19), evoke potent anti-Roman overtones (similar also to the anti-Kittim or anti-Roman polemic in the Habakkuk pesher among the Dead Sea Scrolls).

The verses about repentance immediately following the description of this sixth deadly plague (9:20-21) underscore that the goal of the entire sequence is repentance: The rest of humanity "did not repent of the works of their hands." A similar warning about the lack of repentance will be noted in the bowl plagues (Rev. 16:11). These verses suggest the purpose of such horrific imagery is not to inflict cruelty but to "shock the audience" into changing their lives (Schüssler Fiorenza 1991, 73).

Suspense builds as hearers await the seventh trumpet.

The Text in the Interpretive Tradition

The series of horrible plagues (trumpets, bowls) that constitute the middle chapters of the book are unquestionably the most difficult section, giving rise to highly problematic interpretations.

For Martin Luther, the trumpets correlated to spiritual tribulations—encompassing the history of heresies in the church. Unlike the seals, which to him represented persecution and injustice on earth, Luther related the trumpet angels to doctrinal heretics such as Marcion, the Manicheans, Montanists, the medieval Cathars, and even Thomas Müntzer "and the fanatics" in his own time. Luther viewed the fifth angel, or first woe, as Arius. The sixth angel, or second woe, was "the shameful Mohammed, with his companions, the Saracens, who inflicted a great plague on the church."

Others who have tried to understand Revelation as a code with one-to-one correspondences to contemporary events likewise "discover" in the trumpets and woes almost limitless possibilities for correlations. One contemporary blogger interpreted the burning Deepwater Horizon oil rig in the Gulf of Mexico as the "great mountain" that was thrown, burning, into the sea in Rev. 8:8 (Miller). Today's dispensationalists interpret the trumpets militaristically, likening the monstrous locusts with scorpion-like powers to attack helicopters and other military vehicles. Since they plan to be in heaven, watching the destruction from a safe distance, adherents of the so-called rapture have little to fear from the ghoulish violence.

The Text in Contemporary Discussion

Scholars debate whether the primary purpose of the trumpets is to elicit repentance, or whether they serve more to inaugurate end-times calamities. Those who emphasize repentance see the closest analogy to the trumpet of Ezekiel 33, whereas those who see predictions of judgment call attention to other trumpets in the Hebrew Scriptures. Liberation scholars view the trumpets and bowls as calling for a new exodus on the part of the Christian community, an exodus out of participation in the Roman imperial system.

Some scholars who emphasize repentance note that the strategy of using plagues and threats in the sequences of the trumpets ultimately resulted in failure, because it did not elicit the desired response of repentance (Koester, 101). In light of the trumpets' failure to persuade people to repent, God will now change strategies in the interlude of chapters 10–11, turning to the two witnesses—a strategy that will prove to be more persuasive than the plagues in eliciting repentance.

Revelation 10–11: Second Prophetic Interlude; the People of God

The Text in Its Ancient Context

Before the expected seventh trumpet, an interlude interrupts the narrative. The seventh trumpet will be delayed until 11:15.

This interlude's many images can be confusing, combining descriptions from the book of Daniel and other texts. The overall goal is to encourage prophetic witness. John's hearers are not just passive spectators in the cosmic drama. Two witnesses show the audience its urgent prophetic role. Like the interlude between the sixth and seventh seals (chapter 7), this interlude uses delay to strengthen the audience for prophetic testimony and resistance.

The interlude consists of two parts: renewal of John's call to prophecy (chapter 10) and the story of two witnesses (chapter 11). Both together make up a single vision introduced by "I saw" in 10:1.

A mighty angel, wrapped in cloud and rainbow, straddles sea and earth, indicating God's dominion over both realms. The rainbow recalls the promise to Noah that God will not destroy creation. The angel holds a little scroll, representing the prophetic call. Amid thunder, the angel swears a solemn oath by God the Creator: There shall be no more delay, no more time for repentance. The focus is on the present moment, announcing (*euangelizein*) the mystery of God's judgment as "good news" that will now be "fulfilled" or completed (*telesthēnai*). Yet John is told *not* to write down the prophecy—a departure from the book's many commands to "write."

John's authority is underscored through the renewal of his own prophetic call, symbolized in three actions: swallowing, prophesying, and measuring. By swallowing the scroll, John internalizes its message into his own life, in the tradition of Ezekiel (Ezek. 2:8—3:3). His prophecy is to be "concerning many peoples, nations, tongues, and kings" (10:11).

Measuring the temple, a symbolic action, recalls the prophet Ezekiel (Ezek 40:3). Since the physical temple in Jerusalem had long since been destroyed by the Romans, "temple" and "holy city" probably refer not to the former Jerusalem temple or to a heavenly temple, but rather to John's own community. "Temple" recalls the promise to the Philadelphian community that they would become pillars in the temple (3:12). Measuring symbolizes divine protection (Zech. 2:1-5; *1 En.* 61:1-5).

The story of the two witnesses (11:3) serves as a kind of parable (Bauckham 1993b). Described as two "lampstands" (the same name given to the churches in 1:20), the two witnesses likely represent the community as it is called to engage in prophetic confrontation with the idolatry of Rome. John models the two witnesses on Elijah and Moses. Like Elijah confronting Jezebel, they exercise power over fire and rain (1 Kings 17:1); and like Moses confronting Pharaoh and his magicians (Exodus 8–12), they can turn water to blood and strike the earth with plagues.

The symbolic period of time for the two witnesses' prophetic testimony, 1,260 days, is the same finite period in which the holy city is to be trampled (forty-two months, 11:2). This "Danielic time-period" of three and a half years (Bauckham 1993b, 284) occurs in different forms in 11:2, 3; 12:6, 14; and 13:5, drawing on Dan. 9:25-27. It represents the present time in which the community is now living. It is a time of limited duration, "the period just before the destruction of the empire" (Friesen, 159).

The monstrous beast from the bottomless pit, introduced here for the first time, represents Rome's power to kill. The community's prophetic testimony may lead to martyrdom, as portrayed in the beast's killing the two witnesses. But God's breath of life raises the two witnesses to stand again on their feet (see Ezek. 37:5), vindicating their testimony.

An earthquake accompanying the two witnesses' resuscitation decimates one-tenth of the great city, killing seven thousand people. The symbolism of this city is debated. Most important is that the earthquake now persuades the other nine-tenths of the city's people (presumably more than sixty thousand) to give glory to God (11:13). Nine-tenths of the city is saved. The story of the two witnesses thus assures John's churches that their prophetic testimony will succeed where the trumpets' violent plagues failed: namely, in converting the world to give glory to God. The vision of 11:3 anticipates the announcement of 15:4 that "all nations" will worship God (Schüssler Fiorenza 1991).

The seventh trumpet finally sounds at the end of the interlude. The third "woe" is most likely the seventh trumpet (11:14). Unlike the first six trumpets that brought disaster, this trumpet brings rejoicing, celebrating the reign of God.

The antiphonal victory song of the elders praises God that the "time" (*kairos*) has finally come. The time is not for destroying the earth but for destroying earth's destroyers (11:18)—that is, the Roman imperial system of military conquests and client kings that enslaves lands and peoples. God's will is for the fulfillment of creation, not its destruction.

More destruction is still to come in the second half of the book, as Satan and his agents continue to stalk the earth. But the hymn celebrates in advance that "the kingdom of this world has become the kingdom of our Lord" (11:15).

A theophany in 11:19, with lightning and thunder and a vision of God's temple in heaven, underscores the solemnity of this moment.

The Text in the Interpretive Tradition

Many throughout Christian history have identified themselves and their communities with the two witnesses. Early interpretations of the two witnesses expand on the expected return of Elijah (Mal. 4:5) combined with Enoch, who had never experienced death (Gen 5:24).

The beast from the abyss became a potent symbol, especially as it coalesced with legends of the "Antichrist" (a word not found in Revelation). Illustrations of the two witnesses preaching to the Antichrist were common in medieval illuminated manuscripts. In the twelfth century, Franciscans and other fraternal orders identified themselves and their leaders as the two witnesses. Medieval interpreters often used the image of the beast to critique popes and church practices they viewed as illegitimate.

During the Reformation, Protestants and Catholics traded polemics back and forth, using the two witnesses of Revelation 11. In one of the most famous woodcuts from Luther's 1522 September Bible, artist Lucas Cranach depicted the beast of Revelation 11 wearing the three-tiered crown of the pope—a visibly anti-Catholic polemic. Cranach softened the anti-Catholic image in the December reprint of the Bible by eliminating the two upper levels of the tiara. In both depictions, however, the temple sanctuary being measured is clearly Luther's Wittenberg Castle Church, and the two witnesses tormented by the beast are Reformers.

In the eighteenth century, William Blake identified the two witnesses as founders of Methodism, John Wesley and George Whitefield (*Milton* 22.52–62; Jeffrey, 231), praising them for their social concern as well as their signs and miracles.

The time span of 42 months, or 1,260 days, and the reference to the temple have given rise to elaborate timetables for supposed end-times events. Dispensationalist proponents of the rapture theology of Darby argue that the temple in Jerusalem must be rebuilt in modern times for a period of 42 months, so that it can then be desecrated by an "Antichrist," fulfilling their interpretation of the seventieth week in Dan. 9:27 and precipitating a final battle of Armageddon. In this view, time periods of Revelation 11 spell out a predictive chronology of violent geopolitical events in the Middle East that must happen before Jesus is able to return to earth.

The Text in Contemporary Discussion

Scholars discuss whether the open little scroll of Revelation 10 is the same scroll as the sealed scroll in 5:2. Although different words describe the two scrolls (*biblion* in 5:2; *biblidarion* in 10:2, 8) and the little scroll is "open," contrasting with the "sealed" scroll of 5:2, John may understand them as the same scroll (Bauckham 1993b, 243; Blount 2009, 190; contra Schüssler Fiorenza 1991, 73).

The phrase in 10:11, "peoples, nations, languages, and kings," can be understood positively or negatively, depending on whether the preposition *epi* means "against" these nations or "about" these nations. The addition of "kings"—not found in previous listings of peoples, tongues, and nations (5:10; 7:9)—suggests the negative connotation of "against" (Schüssler Fiorenza 1991, 76; Aune 1998, 571). González, however, makes the grammatical argument on the basis of the dative case that John is to speak positively to his own communities "about" God's multicultural mission that includes Gentiles—a task he finds bitter to the taste (González 1999, 91).

A related question is whether John truly envisions the repentance and conversion of the nations in 11:13. Bauckham makes a convincing case that the terms "fear God" and "give glory to God" are always positive in Revelation, and that the conversion of the nations is at the center of John's prophetic message (1993b, 238). Others caution that the nations' worship is motivated only by fear. "Nothing about coming and worshiping implies conversion or redemption" (Carey 1999, 161–62).

Recent ecological scholarship underscores the centrality of God's declaration to "destroy the destroyers of the earth" (11:18). The term "destroyers" (*diaphtheirontes*) also refers to "corruption," a likely allusion to the flood story of Genesis 6–9, applied to the Roman Empire's violence also in 19:2. John makes an important change from the original flood story. Whereas in Genesis the intent was to destroy the earth along with evildoers (Gen 6:13), John underscores that only the destroyers themselves—not the earth—will be destroyed. The declaration of Rev. 11:18 sets the program for the entire second half of the book (Stephens, 197–98). The judgment that will subsequently unfold in chapters 12–20 is the judgment God pronounces on the violent systems that destroy peoples and the earth.

Revelation 12: Witness to Hope: The Woman, the Dragon, and Earth's Daring Rescue

The Text in Its Ancient Context

Beginning with chapter 12, the second half of the book is about the defeat of evil. Different aspects of the unjust Roman imperial system—personified as Satan and his agents—are defeated in reverse order of their introduction (Bauckham 1993a, 20; Koester). Satan is introduced in chapter 12 and defeated in chapter 20. The beast from the sea and the beast from the earth, together representing Rome's military/political system and its local collaborators, are introduced in chapter 13 and then defeated in chapter 19. The whore of Babylon, representing Rome's predatory economic system, is introduced and defeated in chapters 17–18.

Revelation 12 takes the form of an inclusion, with a central story of the war in heaven (Rev. 12:7-12) sandwiched between two stories about the cosmic woman and the dragon (12:1-6 and 12:13-17; Schüssler Fiorenza 1991, 80). These deeply symbolic stories represent the life-and-death struggle against evil that is at the heart of the book. They give hearers hope and courage to persevere in witness.

Revelation does not proceed chronologically. Even though these stories come in the middle of the book, they are most likely flashbacks to the past—to Jesus' victory on the cross—in which Satan and evil were already defeated. Revelation uses highly pictorial and visionary language to communicate spiritual truths.

In the first story (Rev. 12:1-6 and 12:13-17), a pregnant woman in the throes of labor gives birth to a son, then acquires two wings of a great eagle to escape the dragon. Both the woman and the dragon are called "signs" (*sēmeia*, 12:1, 3), underscoring the symbolic character of the stories.

John borrows and subverts a popular mythological story of his day, familiar from multiple Roman, Egyptian, and Hellenistic variations (Collins 1976 and 1993). The story of the birth of the god Apollo to the goddess Leto, and their escape from the dragon Python, was a favorite of Roman emperors who identified themselves with Apollo. By scripting the emperor as the dragon, John used the story to assert Jesus' lordship rather than the emperor's.

John reworks the story to make it a story about Jesus. The child is depicted as the Messiah of Psalm 2, who will "rule all the nations with a rod of iron" (Rev. 12:5; see also 2:27; 19:15). The heavenly woman probably does not represent the Virgin Mary (since John does not appeal to other stories of Jesus' mother or family) but is a larger symbolic depiction of Israel, the whole people of God, imaged in cosmic terms. Jesus is born of the people of God.

John models the dragon on earlier political references to foreign nations as "dragons" (Egypt as a dragon, Ezek. 32:2; the Roman general Pompey who conquered Jerusalem as an "arrogant dragon," *Pss. Sol.* 2:25), combined with the deceptive serpent from Genesis 3 and the ten horns from Daniel's fourth beast (Dan. 7:7). The woman flees from the dragon into the wilderness, a familiar biblical place of refuge for the Israelites as well as for Hagar (Gen. 21:14-21).

Into this story of the woman's childbirth and rescue in the wilderness, John sandwiches the epic heavenly battle of the "dragon-slayer" (Sánchez), with overtones of a legal courtroom trial (Schüssler Fiorenza 1991, 81). The angel Michael is familiar from Daniel (Dan. 10:21; 12:1). Satan is familiar as a biblical name given to the personification of evil and deceit as an "accuser," especially in Job. In 12:9, John lists other names for the dragon, culminating in "deceiver of the whole empire [*oikoumenē*]." Michael and his angels defeat the dragon and his angels, throwing them down from heaven to earth. But although heaven is now become a "Satan-free zone" (Smith, 65), Satan still temporarily prowls the earth. Readers live in the in-between time, symbolically pictured as the time and space between Satan's expulsion from heaven and his being thrown down into the abyss (20:3, 10).

Even though earth cannot yet rejoice, a voice calls out in heaven, celebrating Satan's defeat. The victory hymn (12:10-12) makes the surprising declaration that it is God's people themselves who have "conquered" Satan, both by the blood of the Lamb (underscoring nonviolent resistance) and by the power of their witness or martyrdom (two possible translations of the same Greek word, *martyria*). "Conquer" recalls the promises to the churches in Revelation 2–3 that they would become "conquerors," just as Jesus conquered. The victory song concludes with a lament ("Alas" or "woe," 12:12) on behalf of the earth and sea, similar to 8:13.

Earth plays a heroic role as the mythic story resumes. Personified as a feminine figure (the feminine noun *gē*) with a mouth, the earth rescues the heavenly woman by swallowing the dragon's river. Heroic swallowing by Earth is a motif found also in the anti-Roman apocalypse *2 Baruch* (2 Bar. 6:6-10). Earth's heroic swallowing recalls the Exodus victory song after the crossing of the Red Sea, when the Israelites gave thanks that the earth "swallowed" up the Egyptians (Exod. 15:12).

Chapter 12 closes on an ominous and deeply symbolic note. The woman and child have been rescued, but the dragon is angry that he has been thrown out of heaven. Since he cannot devour Jesus, he goes off to make war against the "rest of [the woman's] children, those who keep the commandments of God and hold the testimony of Jesus" (12:17). Things will get worse under Rome's rule before they get better. During the time visualized by the sequence of the seven bowls (Revelation 16), the suffering will be twice as intense as it was during the seven trumpets sequence.

The Text in the Interpretive Tradition

Battles and characters from Revelation 12 feature prominently in interpretive history and art. In some Western churches the Feast of the archangel Michael and All Angels is celebrated on September 29 (with lectionary readings from Dan. 12:1; Rev. 12:7-9). The Feast of the Virgin of Guadalupe on December 12, celebrated by many throughout Latin America and North America, also assigns Revelation 12 as the lectionary reading.

The woman clothed with the sun has shaped the self-understanding of many Christian women prophets, beginning with Maximilla and Priscilla, the leaders of the New Prophecy ("Montanist") movement popular in Asia Minor and North Africa in the late second century. Mother Ann Lee (1736–1784), founder of the Shakers, also saw herself in the woman of Revelation 12 (Wainwright, 96). Women mystics such as Hildegard of Bingen and Hadewijch of Brabant drew on imagery of the heavenly woman to narrate their own visionary experiences (Huber).

The Virgin Mary became associated with the woman of Revelation 12. Sixth-century commentator Oecumenius interpreted the woman's flight into the desert as the flight into Egypt to escape Herod's plot and the "wings of the great eagle . . . given to the all-holy Virgin" as the angel who exhorted Joseph to take the child and his mother to Egypt (Suggit 2006, 116). Pope Sixtus IV's approval of the Feast of the Immaculate Conception of Mary in the fifteenth century further strengthened the identification of Mary, as the Queen of Heaven, with the woman of Revelation 12 (Kovacs and Rowland, 135).

The Virgin of Guadalupe, who appeared to indigenous Mexican peasant Juan Diego Cuauhtlatoatzin on December 12, 1531, took the form of the woman of Revelation 12, with the moon and stars around her head. Indigenous resistance to Spanish conquest both appropriated and subverted apparition accounts of the Virgin—drawing on traditions brought to the Americas by the Spaniards, who were themselves steeped in Franciscan apocalyptic spirituality (Sánchez).

Protestants view the woman of Revelation 12 either as the church or as Israel. Martin Luther's hymn "My Bride, the Church, Is Dear To Me" (trans. Samuel Janzow [St. Louis: Concordia, 2004]) sings a love song about the church portrayed as the woman of Revelation 12. The bridal church wears a crown of gold with twelve stars, and "brings forth her noble Son."

Many artists have illustrated the woman of Revelation 12. Inspired by the fourteenth-century Angers Apocalypse Tapestry, French artist Jean Lurcat's huge 1950 tapestry in the church in Plateau d'Assy depicts the woman and dragon facing each other, in red, black, and white. The worshiper's eye is drawn to the victorious woman enclosed in the sun's flaming orb, her arm raised in triumph. Red and green panels on either side show the tree of life and the Jesse tree of Christ's genealogy.

The Text in Contemporary Discussion

Feminist scholars debate the feminine symbolism of Revelation, including whether the heavenly woman of Revelation 12 is the same figure as the bridal new Jerusalem of Revelation 21 (Humphrey 1995). From a history of religions approach, the woman is portrayed as a strong goddess figure, in contrast to the imperial goddess Roma (Collins 1993). Yet both of Revelation's positive feminine figures—the woman of Revelation 12, who is exiled, and the bride of 19:17, who is transformed into a city—can become overshadowed by the stereotypically evil feminine portraits. Elisabeth Schüssler Fiorenza cautions against a reading approach that focuses single-mindedly on a dualistic gender framework, since gendered language is symbolic, not natural (Schüssler Fiorenza 1998). The legacy of Revelation's gendered imagery, including its bride/whore polarity, is ambiguous at best (Pippin).

"Earth," another positive personified feminine character well-known from Greek mythology, should not be overlooked (Friesen, 186). Earth plays a heroic role in Revelation's cosmic drama. While Revelation's ecological "texts of terror" (Stephens, 216) can give the impression that the book predicts destruction for the earth, the rescuer role given to the earth in 12:16 underscores a positive valuation for it.

Revelation 13: Sea Beast and Earth Beast: Allies of the Dragon

The Text in Its Ancient Context

In chapter 13, John critiques a "web of empire-worship institutions" (Kraybill, 53) by portraying the Roman Empire as a tool of Satan—a bold portrayal, since Rome was still very much in power. Specifically, John links the leaders of the empire with the images of two monstrous beasts in order to critique Rome's ideology of power.

Daniel 7 provides the model for the beasts, with its succession of four world empires. John's beast from the sea incorporates aspects of all four of Daniel's beasts. Its seven heads and ten horns are identical to those of the dragon in 12:3. The head that has suffered a mortal wound (13:3) should probably be identified with the emperor Nero. After Nero's death in 69 CE, the Roman Empire had fallen into chaos but then recovered, becoming even more invincible with the Flavian emperors, including Domitian. People became enthralled by Rome's power; thus John depicts them crying out, "who is like the beast?" (13:4).

Imagery of the throne and worship is central to John's critique of Rome. The whole earth now follows the monstrous beast and "worships" (*proskynei*, 13:4, 8) its imperial system, along with the dragon whose throne is given to the beast. The beast's throne and worship constitute a direct affront to God's throne and the worship scene of chapter 4. Imagery of the beast mimics that of the Lamb, with the same word group (*esphagmenon*, "wounded"; *sphazein*, "to slaughter") used for the mortal "wound" marking the deathblow of both the beast and the Lamb (5:6, 9, 12; 13:3, 8). A demonic "trinity" of Satan, the beast from the sea, and the beast from the earth (the false prophet) is a hideous distortion, parodying the divine trinity of God, the Lamb Jesus, and the spirit (Koester).

Rome rules through military power and also through deception. The first beast, representing the government of Rome and its military and political system of conquest, "is allowed to make war on the saints and to conquer them" (13:7). The second beast likely represents Asia's elite local leadership that "deceives" (13:14). Imperialism requires indigenous collaboration (Carey). The second beast is able to perform prophetic signs to deceive people (13:13), perhaps a reference to the cult statues of emperors and divinities that could be made to speak. The beast from the earth is also called the false prophet (16:13; 19:20; 20:10).

The "mark of the beast" (13:17) probably refers to the image of the emperor on Roman coins, or to some other economic aspect of empire. Rome's predatory economic system will be critiqued as the whore of Babylon in chapters 17–18. The numerical reference to the satanic dragon as "666" (13:18; 616 in some manuscripts) is a riddle that may have multiple meanings, including that of imperfection. (Since seven was considered the number of perfection, six would have implied imperfection.). However, a Hebrew practice of assigning numerical value to transliterated letters of the alphabet, called gematria, may be intended to calculate the sum of numbers to refer to a specific emperor's name—most likely Nero Caesar. (The Latin transliteration for Nero would explain the variant 616; Aune 1998, 769–71).

The Text in the Interpretive Tradition

The two beasts of Revelation fueled interpretive imagination, especially as they became associated with the "Antichrist" (a figure not found in Revelation or Daniel). In the tradition of Augustine, most interpreters understood the beasts as general manifestations of evil (Reeves). Joachim of Fiore broke from tradition, however, labeling each of the beast's heads as specific historical tyrants, including the Muslim Saladin and a final Antichrist still to come. Influenced by Joachim, radical Franciscan Peter Olivi correlated the first beast to Islamic power and the second beast to false prophets and a false pope within the Christian church (McGinn 1994). Many reformers in subsequent centuries, including John Wycliffe and Jan Hus, seized on Olivi's identification of the papacy with the beasts, a tradition that had intensified during the fourteenth-century split of the papacy between Avignon and Rome. Reformer Martin Luther simply appropriated this already-existing critique and applied it to the papacy of his own time in the sixteenth century.

Various interpreters today claim to have "figured out" the symbolism of 666, whether in universal product bar codes, credit cards, or in world leaders whom they detest. Mary Stewart Relfe's

When Your Money Fails: The "666 System" Is Here, published in 1981, sold more than 600,000 copies (Boyer). Fears of the number 666 remain widespread in popular culture.

■ The Text in Contemporary Discussion

Scholarly debates have focused on particular issues such as the meaning of 666 as an anti-Roman economic symbol, and the critique of the local imperial cult leadership in Asia Minor as the second beast.

Revelation 13 has played an important role in liberation movements and their contribution to New Testament scholarship. In John's view, the Roman government was satanic; it must not be honored or obeyed. Revelation 13 gives a different view of government from Paul's counsel in Romans 13 that government is "God's servant for your good" (Rom. 13:4), and from 1 Pet. 2:13-17 and other passages that exhort Christians to honor government. The 1985 South African "Kairos Document" critiqued the use of Rom. 13:1-7 to justify the apartheid system, instead lifting up Revelation 13, where "the State becomes the servant of the dragon (the devil) and takes on the appearance of a horrible beast. Its days are numbered." In Brazil, a landless peasants' protest encampment was inspired by the depiction in Revelation 13 of the state as the beast (Westhelle).

Recent New Testament scholarship on Paul's epistles and the Gospels has moved in major anti-imperial directions (Horsley 1997; 2003), in part thanks to Revelation 13. In John's view, Rome itself was the primary perpetrator of satanic violence in the world—and that is why the entire Roman Empire must come to an end.

Revelation 14: Followers of the Lamb, Harvest of the Earth: The Alternative Community

■ The Text in Its Ancient Context

Revelation 14's vision of the people of God constitutes a bold response to the realities depicted in chapter 13. Satan's two agents—the beast from the earth and beast from the sea—may seem to have the upper hand. But on Mount Zion, "the Lamb of God holds the high ground" (Koester, 136).

This chapter shapes the identity of the people of God as an alternative community of followers of the Lamb, in contrast to the community of the beast. Like the interludes after the sixth seal and sixth trumpet, Revelation 14 functions to encourage the churches to see their role in God's spiritual battle of salvation and judgment. This chapter may even be viewed as the literary and theological center of Revelation (Richard 1995, 117).

Several images draw on Joel 3, including Mount Zion, the imagery of holy war, and a two-stage harvest. In biblical tradition, Zion evokes a place of safety and protection (Isa. 24:23; Joel 3:21), where the remnant is gathered. It is not clear whether John envisions Mount Zion as a gathering on earth (Richard 1995, 117) or in heaven (Talbert, 59; Koester, 136). The Lamb "standing" (resurrected) hearkens back to 5:6. John depicts the Lamb's community as "standing strong" (Blount 2009, 265) against the community of the beast.

John uses multiple metaphors to depict the community. The number 144,000 is familiar from Revelation 7 as the 12,000 sealed from each of Israel's twelve tribes. Now this same group of 144,000 is imaged as "those who follow the Lamb wherever he goes" (14:4)—that is, those who resisted Roman assimilation and obeyed the call for endurance and faith (13:9-10). As in Revelation 7, the number 144,000 is not meant literally. That the community is imaged as an army is suggested by the word "thousands" (*chiliades*), a military term. This army's weapons are not violence but endurance and faithfulness (14:12).

The "new song" represents the spirituality of resistance on earth that God's people learn from heaven (5:9). Only followers of the Lamb can learn to sing the new song, in contrast to worshipers of the beast who "cannot sing" (Richard 1995, 119).

To further shape the identity of the alternative community as a spiritual army, John draws on holy war metaphors of purity and virginity (Deut. 23:9-10; 1 Sam. 21:5), as well as a Sinai holiness tradition requiring men not to defile themselves with women (Exod. 19:5). "Defile" is figurative language for idolatry, as in the message to Sardis (3:4), perhaps alluding to Enoch's Watchers who "defiled" themselves (*1 En.* 7:1; 9:9; 10:11; Stenstrom). Holy war imagery is employed metaphorically to portray a war of religious commitments—the Lamb's community versus the army of the beast.

In 14:4, John draws on additional metaphors to portray the Lamb's followers as an alternative community: They are "first fruits," dedicated to God (Exod. 23:19), the first offering without blemish. Harvest metaphors for the community will be used again in 14:14-16. The community is "redeemed" or "purchased," a metaphor for buying a slave's freedom (recalling 5:9).

Three angels with messages fly through the air in quick succession, similar to the eagle of 8:13. The angels' exhortations and threats summarize Revelation's entire argument (deSilva, 258). The first angel proclaims the "gospel" that the hour of God's judgment has come. This judgment is good news: God is the one "who made the earth," and God's desire is for the whole world to give God glory and worship.

The second angel announces the fall of "Babylon the great" (Isa. 21:9), using a prophetic funerary dirge to preview the portrayal of Babylon's destruction in Revelation 17–18. The label "Babylon" links Rome and its recent destruction of Jerusalem to the hated empire that destroyed Jerusalem six centuries earlier, in 587 BCE.

The third angel's proclamation brings terrifying threats. Those tempted to worship the beast are threatened with God's cup of wrath, a contrast to Babylon's wine of wrath (*thymos*, the same word in 14:8 and 10, drawing on Jer. 25:15). The message to readers is that neutrality is not possible. People must worship either God or the beast. Graphic threats of eternal torment in the presence of the Lamb and God's angels function as warnings, shocking the audience.

Exhortation is also the goal of the next two prophetic utterances. Revelation 14:12 calls for hearers' resistance (*hypomonē*) and faithfulness, similar to 13:18. The beatitude for those who die (14:13) is the second of Revelation's seven beatitudes. Deeds (*erga*) are the crucial measure of faith, underscored in 20:12 with the image of books recording the deeds of the dead.

The two-stage harvest (grain harvest followed by grapes) draws on Joel 3:13. The first stage—the grain "harvest of the earth" (14:15)—is likely a positive image for the community's ingathering, similar to Mark 4:29 and John 4:35-37, recalling the Lamb's community as "first fruits" of the harvest (14:4). John reflects the positive, even joyful, usage of the term "harvest" (*therismos*). The vision of one "like a Son of Humanity" (14:14) hearkens back to 1:13 and Dan. 7:13. John adds the sickle as a positive image of harvest, not an image of destruction (Bauckham 1993a, 96–98).

By contrast, the second stage of grape harvest and grape-pressing inaugurated by a different angel brings terrifying judgment. The image of treading the winepress of the fury of God's wrath draws on Isa. 63:3-6. The judgment is executed not by God but by an angel—thus tempering the Isaiah imagery. The bloodbath up to the horse's bridle is a standard apocalyptic image (*1 En.* 100:1-3; *4 Ezra* 15:35).

The Text in the Interpretive Tradition

The identity of the Lamb's followers as 144,000 "virgins" (a number mentioned also in 7:4) evokes diverse interpretation. The virgins were sometimes understood literally as Christian virgins (Tertullian), or as Jewish Christians (Victorinus; Wainwright, 28). Drawing on the "first fruits" imagery, some Roman Catholics interpreted them as a special group of celibates within the larger group of the church (Murphy, 314). Protestants understood them symbolically as the whole church, imagined as a priestly people. For Jehovah's Witnesses, founded in the late nineteenth century, a literal interpretation of Rev. 14:1-4 means that a special class of exactly 144,000 people will rule with Christ in the millennium (Wainwright)—although their identity as "virgins" is not literal.

During the Civil War, Julia Ward Howe applied the violent imagery of the trampling of the grapes of wrath in 14:17-20 to what she viewed as God's judgment on citizens of the United States for their tolerance of slavery. Her 1862 abolitionist hymn "The Battle Hymn of the Republic" interpreted the bloody Civil War as a loosing of God's "terrible swift sword" against a bloody institution of her day—slavery. In majestic cadences, she portrayed the imagery of grape harvest as bringing justice and liberation. John Steinbeck drew on her imagery in *The Grapes of Wrath* to critique the economic injustice of the effects of the Dust Bowl in the 1930s.

The image of the blood flowing as high as horses' bridles is prominent in the *Left Behind* novels. Authors Tim LaHaye and Jerry B. Jenkins, like other premillennialists, understand the image literally, as the bloody future battle in Israel after Christ's "glorious appearing" when Christ and his forces return to earth to kill his enemies with the sword of his mouth (19:15).

In his *German Requiem*, composed in 1865, Johannes Brahms gives one of the most moving and beautiful musical interpretations of the beatitude in 14:13, "Blessed are those who die . . . their works follow them" ("Selig sind die Toten").

The Text in Contemporary Discussion

Many interpreters grapple with the misogyny implicit in the description of the followers of the Lamb as 144,000 male "virgins who have not defiled themselves with women." Taken literally, the language depicts a community of only celibate males—no women or married men. Such a misogynist view that all women are defiling is not likely John's intent, however, since elsewhere he uses positive feminine metaphors for marriage and the community (the mother, Revelation 12; the bride's marriage, 19:7; 21:2; Schüssler Fiorenza 1991). If John intends the celibacy language literally, he may mean a temporary or priestly celibacy, perhaps analogous to the Essenes (Collins 1984).

The language of defilement makes this gendered metaphor especially problematic, with its legacy of excluding women as "defiled" throughout Christian history (Pippin).

Chapter 14 also raises ethical questions about divine violence. The scene of eternal torture (14:9-11), carried out "in the presence of the Lamb," furnishes some of the most graphic imagery of the book. Even if John uses imagery of fire and sulfur hyperbolically, for the purpose of exhortation rather than prediction—effectively shocking the audience into repentance (Schüssler Fiorenza 1991, 91; Koester, 139)—the language is terrifying. Its function may also be cathartic, preventing Christians from engaging in any actual violence themselves (Collins 1984, 156–75).

Revelation 15: The Song of Moses and the Lamb

■ The Text in Its Ancient Context

John introduces a new vision by the word "sign" or "portent" (*sēmeion*, 15:1), the same word used for the heavenly woman and the dragon in 12:1, 3. Seven angels with seven bowls containing plagues are the "last," after which the wrath of God will end. But first, as with the seven trumpets, John lifts the community's eyes to the heavenly throne room to give assurance, in advance of the terrifying plagues to come.

The Exodus link is now made explicit: Those singing the Song of the Lamb in heaven also sing the "Song of Moses" (15:3). John remaps the story of the Exodus onto his own community. Those who have refused to participate in Roman worship are metaphorically likened to the Israelites who crossed through to the other side of the Red Sea. The community stands at the shore of the sea of glass (4:6), like the Israelites standing on the shore of the Red Sea. Jesus the Lamb is scripted in the role of Moses. Bestial Rome becomes the new Egypt, from which God's people escape. Their "new song" of victory hearkens back to the song Moses and Miriam taught the Israelites (Exodus 15), combined with imagery from the Psalms (Pss. 86:8-10; 98:1-2).

The reference to those who "conquered" the beast makes a bold claim for God's people, as does their "standing." In contrast to Rome's violent conquest, God's people have conquered by their faith and endurance.

This song, like the other heavenly songs of Revelation, functions to give direction and interpretation to the community, "like the chorus in a Greek drama" (Schüssler Fiorenza 1991, 92).

Judgment means justice for victims. "All nations" will worship god, a universalizing of the Exodus song (Bauckham 1993a, 100–101).

The reference to the heavenly temple as the tent of witness (15:5) constitutes another Exodus link, corresponding to the tent sanctuary or tabernacle on Mount Sinai (Exod. 25:9). A living creature holds golden bowls, as in 5:8. Here the bowls contain not the prayers of the saints but the wrath of God that will be poured out upon the earth.

■ The Text in the Interpretive Tradition

The richness of the worship scene is reflected in Christian hymnody drawing on imagery from the scene of the worshipers singing beside the sea of glass, often combined with imagery from worship before God's throne in chapters 4–5. Most famous is "Holy, Holy, Holy," written by Reginald Heber, with the image of the saints "casting down their golden crowns upon the glassy sea." Isaac Watts's hymn "Babylon Falling" includes the line "The Christian church unites the songs of Moses and the Lamb." Activist and war protester Daniel Berrigan titled his 1978 book of prayers *Beside the Sea of Glass: The Song of the Lamb*, drawing on imagery from this chapter.

The earliest artistic representation of the glassy sea of 15:2 (also 4:6) is in the apse mosaic in the Church of Sts. Cosmas and Damian, from the sixth or seventh century (McGinn 1992, 207, and 105 fig. 1).

■ The Text in Contemporary Discussion

What is the function of heavenly liturgies and hymns in Revelation such as 15:3-4? Older scholarship saw Revelation's hymns as reflecting the church's actual liturgies. Most scholars now agree that John composed the hymns himself, as part of his rhetorical program.

The hymns of Revelation, including the hymns of chapter 15, likely function as correctives against praise offered to gods and emperors, more than as forming a new cultic liturgical experience for Christians (Schüssler Fiorenza 1976; Ruiz 2001). The cities of Asia Minor were replete with imperial cult liturgies and celebrations including hymns, liturgical processions, altars, and other cultic features, all fostering patriotic allegiance to the empire (Friesen; Thompson). Revelation challenges the imperial cult's liturgies and claims to allegiance by hearkening back to the Psalms and hymns of liberation from Israel's past.

John does not simply adopt biblical hymns but transforms them. By juxtaposing the "Divine Warrior" victory hymn of Exodus 15 with the song of the Lamb, John may be underscoring that God's people conquer nonviolently, through the Lamb's death rather than by divine acts of aggression (Friesen, 190). John calls it the Song of Moses, but the words of the song in fact draw more from Psalms 96 and 98 than Exodus 15. John's intertextuality sets the hymns in "dialogical tension" (Moyise 2004). Perhaps most importantly, John shifts the focus of the hymn from praising God for victory over enemies (Exodus 15) to celebrating the universal worship and praise of God by all nations, thereby developing "the most universalistic form of the hope of the Old Testament" (Bauckham 1993a, 306, 311; contra Beale, 799).

Revelation 16: Seven Bowls, Seven Plagues, and the Angel of the Waters

■ The Text in Its Ancient Context

The seven bowl plagues recapitulate the seven trumpets of Revelation 8–9, with even more destructive intensity. Their effects target the four elements of the cosmos, including earth, sea, rivers and springs, and air. Their destruction is double that signaled by the trumpets. Yet it is important to note that these are not universal plagues against all of humankind, but only targeted against the beast and its followers (Richard 1995, 84).

Like the seven trumpets, the bowl plagues come from the heavenly temple. They follow the same 4-2-1 pattern as the seals and trumpets, but with a much shorter interlude (or no interlude at all) between the sixth and seventh element.

The word "plague" (Greek *plēgē*) literally means "strike" or "blow." The parallel use of the same verb "pour out, shed" (*ekchein*) to refer to both a crime and its consequences underscores the logic of reciprocity, using legal language. The "pouring out" of each bowl's contents of judgment (16:1, 2, 3, 4, 8, 10, 12, 17) reciprocates Rome's own "shedding" of blood (16:6), both described by the same verb. Measure for measure, God's judgments against evildoers match their offense (Blount 2009, 293).

The first bowl plague of boils reflects a brutal symmetry: Those who accepted the mark of the beast are now branded with gruesome sores by God (Blount 2009, 295). The second bowl poured out on the seas recalls the Exodus plagues, turning the water to blood and killing every creature. As in 8:9, sea creatures are described as "souls" (*psychai*), hearkening back to Genesis.

With the third bowl, the logic of consequences is made explicit in a lengthy liturgical doxology about blood by the angel of the waters (16:6). The angel explains that it is precisely because oppressors "shed" the blood of saints and prophets that the waters have turned to blood, and God now gives them blood to drink. As in Isa. 49:26, the bloodthirsty are made to choke on the very blood they shed (Blount 2009, 97). These consequences are "worthy" or appropriate (*axios*; compare "axiomatic," in the sense "self-evident")—reflecting the logic of the action itself. Antiphonal liturgy breaks in at this point in the narrative "so that the community can be actively present" (Richard 1995, 83). A personified talking altar responds to affirm the just judgments of God.

The fourth plague darkens the sun, similar to the fourth trumpet. The function of the plagues to elicit repentance is made clear, by noting that people should have repented (16:9). Instead of acknowledging their Creator and giving God glory, however, recipients curse God. The case is similar with the fifth bowl, poured onto the "throne" of the beast, the seat of the monstrous empire's power. Reminiscent of the Exodus plagues, the beast's kingdom is plunged into darkness. Still, the people curse God and again refuse to repent (16:11).

The sixth bowl, like the sixth trumpet, affects the River Euphrates, the eastern border of the Roman Empire. The Euphrates was familiar from the biblical traditions of enemy nations amassing from the East. The river dries up, facilitating the invasion of demonic foreign nations. Frog-like evil spirits represent the demonic evil trinity of the dragon, the beast, and the false prophet. The false prophet lures kings of the earth into attacking, using "deception" to bring about the collapse of the dragon's entire political system.

Interjected into this scene is the prophetic warning of the third beatitude, urging readers to keep awake (16:15). There is no lengthy interlude between the sixth and seventh elements as in the sequences of seals and trumpets. The brief interjection of Jesus in 16:15, "Behold, I am coming soon! Blessed is the one who stays awake and is clothed," fits the pattern of interludes, although much briefer. Like the other interludes, it shapes the identity of the community. This interlude is so short because the emphasis is now on the imminence of the end, rather than its delay.

"Armageddon" is probably a reference to the ancient site of Megiddo in Israel, where a number of battles in the Hebrew Scriptures were fought (Judg. 5:19; 2 Kgs. 23:29–30; *har* means "mountain" in Hebrew, so *Har-Megiddo* would mean "mountain of Megiddo"). While Armageddon is popularly imagined as a battle, it is striking that no battle is described in 16:16. Instead, the battle is delayed—most likely until 19:19-21—although even there, no battle is narrated. This is typical of John's use of delay, to allow time for repentance, and to temper the threats of violence. The armies amass at the mountain of Megiddo. But instead of a battle, the scene shifts to the judgment of Babylon (16:19).

When the seventh bowl is poured out, the voice from God's throne pronounces the end, accompanied by a theophany and earthquake greater than at any previous time (Dan. 12:1). The seventh bowl targets the air, one of the four elements of creation. God "remembers" Babylon, and forces the unjust city to drink the hated cup of wrath (recalling 14:8 and Jeremiah 25). Even in the face of huge hailstones and cosmic destruction of mountains and islands, people still refuse to repent.

The Text in the Interpretive Tradition

Those who view Revelation as a road map for world history tend to see themselves as living between the fifth and sixth bowl. In the eighteenth century, Jonathan Edwards viewed Revelation's sixth bowl as coming to fulfillment in the decline of Catholicism, with the "drying up" of the Euphrates (16:12) referring to the evaporation of financial revenue to the Vatican (Thuesen, 47).

Armageddon has engendered more focus than any image of Revelation, even though the word appears only once (16:16) and, as we have seen, no battle is actually narrated there. Some have assumed it is a battle already past (the siege of Masada in 70 CE: Wainwright, 132). For today's premillennialists, it will be a future World War III, centered on the plains of northern Israel, where Christ will defeat the Antichrist and establish a literal thousand-year kingdom in Jerusalem. Ronald Reagan famously speculated about Armageddon in a 1971 dinner speech, pointing to a coup in Libya: "that's a sign Armageddon isn't far off. . . . It can't be long now." For Reagan, the fire and brimstone of Ezekiel and Revelation referred to nuclear weapons (Boyer, 142).

The Text in Contemporary Discussion

The angel of the waters and the extended judgment doxology of 16:16 raise the question of how Revelation understands the solidarity between humans and the natural world. John understands natural elements to be represented by messengers or angels (see also the angel of fire in 14:18) who speak out on their behalf against oppressors. John may be drawing on an older tradition that represents the four Hellenistic "elements of the cosmos" (earth, air, fire, and water: Betz, 1969), here made to speak out against human oppression, similar to Enochic literature and to the Egyptian *Kore Kosmou* from the *Corpus Hermeticum*. The angel interprets the plague sequence in a way that can also be understood ecologically: oppressors who commit acts of violence will unleash their own destructive consequences against themselves. A similar ecological logic of consequences can be seen in the Exodus plagues (Fretheim, 1991), the antecedent for John's bowls. The response from the personified altar affirms the judgment as the just consequence, engaging the community in active liturgical response to the empire's own violence that de-creates the very fabric of the world.

Liberation scholar Pablo Richard likens the bowl plagues to multiple forms of contemporary imperial oppression, identifying the plagues of Revelation today as "the disastrous results of ecological destruction, the arms race, irrational consumerism, the idolatrous logic of the market" (Richard 1995, 86).

Revelation 17:1—19:8: Courtroom Trial, Judgment, and Funeral for Babylon/Rome

■ The Text in Its Ancient Context

Revelation culminates in a tale of two cities, with a call to make a choice between them. Like a tour guide, John leads the audience on contrasting tours of the two rival political economies. The same angel issues the invitation, "Come, I will show you," and carries John "in the spirit" to a location where he is shown each city (cf. 17:1 and 21:9). Readers must make the urgent choice to "come out" of the imperial system of Babylon (18:4), so that they can "come in" to God's new Jerusalem, the city of blessing and promise (22:14).

Both cities are personified metaphorically as feminine figures, reflecting the grammatically feminine gender of the noun "city" (*polis*) in Greek, a trait of the Hebrew Bible as well. The city of Babylon is labeled a "whore" or "prostitute," whereas new Jerusalem is called a "bride" (Rev. 17:1; 21:2). John may be structuring the ethical contrast according to the binary structure of two feminine figures, good and evil, from Proverbs 5–9, or from the familiar story of the choice between Pleasure and Virtue posed to Heracles (Rossing 1998). He applies feminine personifications of cities, as we find in the Hebrew prophets, to political economies.

The first tour shows the judgment of the evil city, Babylon (Revelation 17–18), representing Rome's seductive economic system. Babylon is clad in luxurious jewelry and scarlet, riding astride the seven-headed Roman beast (familiar from Revelation 12–13). The refrain of "purple and scarlet," gold, and "jewels and pearls" unites the entire Babylon vision (17:4; 18:12; 18:16).

The label "Babylon" triggers biblical memories of the hated Babylonian empire that destroyed Jerusalem in 587 BCE, analogous to Rome's destruction of Jerusalem in 70 CE. Other Jewish and Christian texts also call Rome "Babylon" (1 Pet. 5:13; *2 Bar.* 11:1; *Sib. Or.* 5.143, 158–59; *4 Ezra* 2:36-40).

The charge of "fornication" against Babylon/Rome is metaphorical; the offense is economic exploitation, modeled on biblical critiques of the ancient maritime empire of Tyre. Isaiah labeled Tyre's trade and economic gain as "fornication" (Isa. 23:15–18); John attacks Rome's trading alliances.

Rome's golden cup, modeled on the biblical cup of wrath (Jeremiah 25), contains an intoxicating poison—symbolizing "desire" that is at the heart of the entire Babylon vision (Callahan 1999). Nations have become drunk on Rome's wine of fornication (17:4; 18:3). John even uses the imagery of "sorcery" (*pharmakeia*, 18:23) to describe the "deceptive" spell cast by Rome's economic system, linking Babylon to Jezebel, the beast, and other deceitful characters in Revelation.

The image of "mother" of whores (17:5) refers to Rome as a "mother city" or metropolis, capable of founding daughter colonies. The beast's seven horns are to be identified as the famed seven hills of Rome (17:9).

Babylon/Rome's downfall is launched by its own client kings who turn against the empire in 17:16. Taken literally, the punishment of Babylon in 17:16 can sound like a horrific scene of gang rape (Pippin). A better translation of 17:16 may be "they will make it a wasteland and denuded," to emphasize the language primarily as imagery of a city besieged rather than of torture of a woman's body (Rossing 1998, 87–97). That Babylon is an empire, not a woman, is made explicit in 17:18: "The woman you saw is the great city that rules over the kings of the earth."

With powerful Exodus language, echoing Jer. 51:45, John calls on the community to "come out" (Rev. 18:4) of the empire before it is too late. Their exodus is not to be a physical departure but rather an economic and social departure, as a call to "create alternatives" (Richard 1995, 135). The punishments of 18:4-6 are carefully structured to show that the judgments against the empire are what it brought on itself by its own violence against others. "Double" restitution is a biblical principle (Isa. 40:2; 47:9; 51:19), now extended into international relations.

The arrogant boast, "I rule as a queen ... I will never see grief" (18:7), reflects Rome's idolatrous claims of eternal dominance; John also draws on Isaiah's satire of Babylon (see Isa. 47:8).

John portrays the fall of Rome's unbridled economic system through a series of funeral dirges voiced by three groups who profited from Babylon's wealth: kings, merchants, and seafarers. Each group cries "Alas! Alas!" (or "Woe," *ouai*, 18:9, 16, 19), lamenting their fallen city. The central dirge is that of the merchants, lamenting the loss of shipments of cargo they can no longer buy and sell (Rev. 18:9, 16, 19).

The cargo list of Revelation 18:12-13 encompasses the span of Rome's extractions from the land and sea: gold, precious stones, pearls, exotic hardwoods and wooden products, ivory, metals, marble, luxury spices, food, armaments and war horses, and "slaves—even human lives" (18:13). The list draws from Ezekiel's critique of Tyre (Ezek. 27:12-22), updated to critique Rome's economy (Bauckham 1993a). The final two items in the cargo list—"slaves, even human lives" (18:13)—furnish the most explicit critique of slavery and slave trade in the New Testament. John denounces the lucrative slave trade that was the economic backbone of the Roman Empire (Martin). John underscores that slaves are not just "bodies" (*sōmata*) but living people, "human souls" (*psychai*).

Rome's crimes extended beyond crimes against humanity even into crimes against creation. Deforestation, erosion, the silting of rivers, and extinctions of animals and habitats were significant problems caused by the Roman extractive economy, as evidenced by archaeology and by numerous ancient sources (Hughes, 1996). With the cargo list of 18:12-13, John connects the overconsumption of the empire with ecological devastation of lands and peoples.

John portrays the final defeat of Babylon/Rome not on a battlefield but in a court scene, as of a legal class action (Schüssler Fiorenza 1991; Richard 1995, 134). The plaintiffs are the saints, representing all Rome's victims who have been killed on earth. The charge is murder: "In you was found the blood of prophets and of saints, and of all who have been slaughtered on earth" (Rev. 18:24). The cargo list of 18:12-13 serves as the list of exhibits in the lawsuit (Callahan 1999, 60). The judge is God. An angelic voice explains the verdict and sentence, pronouncing Babylon guilty on all charges, and sentencing the empire to receive a like measure of its own unjust medicine at the hands of its victims (18:6–8).

The vision culminates with a dramatization of Babylon's fall (18:21), modeled on a similar scene from Jer. 51:63-64. An angel takes up a large millstone and throws it into the sea, proclaiming Babylon's destruction.

Joy breaks out in heaven and on earth when the sentence is announced, with the posttrial celebration of plaintiffs extending to the celebration of God's angels in heaven (18:20).

The judgment scene closes with a heavenly liturgy, 19:1-8. Four hallelujah choruses and acclamations praise God for bringing the great harlot city to justice. Salvation, glory, and power (19:1) are Roman political terms, now reclaimed by God. The saints' cry from under the altar for recompense or "vindication" (6:9-11) is finally fulfilled in 19:2.

After the judgment of Babylon/Rome, a brief preview introduces the bride of the Lamb (19:7), wearing the righteous deeds of the saints. As with the brief preview of Babylon in 14:7, a beatitude follows ("Blessed are those invited to the marriage supper of the Lamb," 19:9). The invitation to the Lamb's marriage feast will be fulfilled in the new Jerusalem vision of Revelation 21–22, when the bride is transformed into a city.

The Text in the Interpretive Tradition

The image of Rome as the garish "whore of Babylon," wearing gold jewelry and a scarlet dress, and seducing victims with her cup of fornication (17:3-6), is one of the most unforgettable images of Revelation. Throughout the history of art and literature, the whore of Babylon has become the ultimate evil woman in cultural imagination—linked also to "Jezebel" of Rev. 2:20 via the vocabulary of "deception" (2:20; 18:23). Nathaniel Hawthorne's *The Scarlet Letter* speaks of Hester Prynne as "a scarlet woman and worthy type of her of Babylon" (Bond).

Both the violence and incongruity of interpreting the whore and bride as literal human women, and the Lamb as a literal sheep, can be seen in the sixteenth-century Brussels tapestry *The Marriage of the Lamb*, depicting Rev. 19:7-10. On his hind legs, the lamb stands on the dining table, being cradled by a beautiful woman, his bride, who "looks adoringly at him" (Pippin, 14). Above their heads another woman—Babylon the whore—is consumed by flames as she is being burned alive.

Elizabeth Cady Stanton critiqued the image of the whore of Babylon in her 1902 *Women's Bible*, lamenting Revelation's "painfully vivid" pictures and including much of Revelation 17–18 among texts that should "no longer be read in churches" (Callahan 1999, 54).

Novelist D. H. Lawrence critiqued the "endless envy" embodied in the cargo list of the Babylon vision of 18:12-13, embodying the "Christian desire to destroy the universe" that he saw reflected throughout Revelation (Lawrence, 48).

Yet Revelation's anti-empire critique is vital to liberation theology, especially the condemnation of the Roman economic system. Classicist Ramsay MacMullen sees Revelation 18 as the most daring anti-Roman polemic written by any ancient author during the empire's rule. Most important has been Revelation's critique of the slave trade, the clearest articulation of slave trading as evil in the New Testament. In the nineteenth century, abolitionists, including the Reverend Uzziah C. Burnap and others, lifted up Rev. 18:13 in denouncing slavery and the slave trade in the United States (Callahan 1999, 60n45).

During twentieth-century liberation struggles in Latin America and South Africa, Revelation's analysis and critique of the violent Roman economic system inspired analyses and critiques of modern-day empires and economic systems. In the Caribbean, an indigenized Rastafarian reading of the

Bible developed in response to the brutality of conquest, depicting Babylon as the colonial system of oppression (Murrell). The practice of "chanting down" Babylon is reflected in the lyrics of songs by Bob Marley and others: "Get up! Stand up!" "Let's get together to fight this Holy Armageddon" ("One Love") and "We're leaving Babylon, we're going to our Father's land" ("Exodus").

The Text in Contemporary Discussion

Feminist liberationist scholars debate how to interpret the destruction of Babylon/Rome in 17:16, since it is presented as the destruction both of a city and of the metaphorical body of a woman. In chapter 17, imagery of the feminine figure is foregrounded, whereas in chapter 18 the emphasis shifts primarily to the metaphorical description of a city. Whether the pronouns for Babylon are translated as "she" or "it" and whether translations are applied consistently to both the Babylon and new Jerusalem visions, affect how the balance between woman and city are interpreted. Unfortunately, English translations typically use "she" for most references to Babylon but "it" for the new Jerusalem (RSV, NRSV), effectively inscribing the duality as that of an evil woman versus a good city, rather than a pair of cities.

What does it look like to "come out" of Babylon? Part of the answer depends on whether the addressees of all the imperatives of 18:6-7 are "my people." The first command to "come out" is clearly addressed to the audience ("my people"). But there has been a reluctance to see the audience as the addressee of the four additional plural commands to "give back" and "double" the punishment Babylon gave to others, and to "mix" and "give" to Babylon a dose of its own torture and grief. To solve the problem, some scholars have introduced hypothetical divine "ministers of justice" (Swete 1911), "heavenly beings" (Collins 1984, 193), or even God (Talbert) as the addressee. The question is important for understanding how the audience (of "my people") plays an active role—not only in coming out of empire but also in "divesting" itself of Babylon/Rome's cup, and even participating in the empire's demise. A few later manuscripts added "to you" to make clear the identification as "my people" for all the imperatives of 18:4-7. The audience's role is "vindication," not vengeance (Callahan 1999, 63; deSilva, 266), actively handing back Babylon's cup in order to divest themselves of all participation in empire. If so, this poses interesting questions for churches and communities of faith today about how to actively "come out" of empire.

Revelation 19:11—20:15: Satan Bound: The Millennium Interlude

The Text in Its Ancient Context

Revelation 19–20 presents multiple visions of the defeat of evil. The purpose of these scenes is to show that God's justice wins in the end. Systems of oppression must be brought to judgment. Babylon/Rome's economic system has already been tried and sentenced in the divine courtroom (Revelation 18). Other aspects of Rome and its systemic oppression, represented as Satan and his other agents, must also be defeated. Each different vision begins with "I saw" (19:11, 17; 20:1, 4, 11; 21:1). The multiple visions are symbolic, defying any literal chronology.

Heaven is opened and Jesus comes out, riding on a white horse, to "judge with justice and make war." The imagery may draw from the Wisdom of Solomon, where the personified Word of God is imaged as a mighty warrior, wielding God's commandment as a sword (Wis. 18:15). The sword from Christ's mouth symbolizes the power of his word (Isa. 11:4; 49:2).

A number of features make this scene highly unusual. The garment Jesus wears is already stained with blood before the battle even starts (19:11-13). The source is Isa. 63:1-3, a battle scene in which the blood on the rider's garments is that of Israel's enemies. John changes the imagery so that the blood on the rider's robe most likely is Jesus' *own* blood, shed on the cross—not the blood of his enemies (Caird, 243–44; Boring, 196; Metzger 1993, 91). For Revelation, the key battle was already won in the crucifixion, not some future battle of "Armageddon."

A heavenly army on horses accompanies Jesus, but they have no weapons. Robed in white linen garments, they do not fight. This is different from other texts' image of eschatological battles, as in the Qumran *War Scroll* (1QM 1). In Revelation, the saints do not participate in the final battle.

The picture of the return of Jesus as a heavenly warrior has led to the idea of Christ's second coming, or *parousia*. But "second coming" is not a biblical phrase, nor does Revelation use the word *parousia*. The picture of Christ's arrival on a white horse, wearing diadems and inscription of his titles, resembles a post-battle "triumph," a well-known Roman celebration after a victory in which the victorious general and his army parade home with the spoils of war (Aune 1998, 1050–51). If this is the model, the triumph may celebrate the judgment and defeat of Babylon that already took place in chapter 18, or the defeat of Satan that happened in chapter 12, rather than a future end-times return of Christ for war.

No actual battle is ever narrated. Instead, preparation for war leads immediately to the aftermath: the grisly supper of God's enemies (19:17-21). On the menu are the defeated military leaders and nations, modeled on Ezekiel's portrait of the mythical warrior nations of Gog and Magog being eaten by wild animals (Ezek. 39:17-20). This meal serves as the revolting counterpart to the Lamb's marriage supper, to which readers were invited in 19:7-9. If the angel calling the birds from "mid-heaven" (19:17) is the same as the angel of mid-heaven in 14:16, then this scene has a similar function of "urgent warning" (Schüssler Fiorenza 1991, 106).

The defeat of evil continues with the capture and imprisonment of Satan's two beasts (20:1-3), familiar from chapter 13. "False prophet" is another name for the second beast, which "deceived" people (13:14; 19:20), probably representing local imperial elites in Asia Minor. John makes clear that the lies and deceptions by which the empire dominates the world must come to an end (20:3, 10). The lake of fire represents the threat of punishment (20:14; 21:8).

The defeat of oppression and evil culminates when Satan himself is tied up and imprisoned in the underworld, completing the expulsion from heaven begun in chapter 12. Satan symbolizes all the forces of evil in the world, represented by his many names—"the dragon, that ancient serpent, who is the Devil and Satan" (20:2)—the same list as 12:3. The image of shutting up evil in a pit echoes Isa. 24:22 (cf. *1 En.* 10:4-6; 53–54). The point is to remove imperial evil from any further deceiving of the nations. But for reasons that are not made clear, Satan's defeat happens in two steps, with an interlude between them. Satan must be released one more time before his final defeat.

In the interlude, between the first binding of Satan for one thousand years and his final capture and judgment, John introduces the notion of the "first resurrection" (20:4-6), in which those martyred are raised to life to sit on thrones and reign with God. This scene functions as an answer to 6:9, where the souls of the slaughtered cried out from under the altar for vindication (Blount 2005, 59). Now they get their vindication by being raised to life to reign with Christ.

Other Jewish apocalypses such as *2 Baruch* and *4 Ezra* similarly depict a temporary messianic kingdom between the destruction of the Roman Empire and the final judgment, with a duration of four hundred years specified in *4 Ezra* 7:28.

The symbolic millennium is not meant to furnish a literal chronology of linear time. The entire book follows a kind of journey-like "vision time" (Friesen, 158) in which the thousand years represents "vindication time" for the victims of Roman imperial rule. Although the location is not specified as earth or heaven, most likely this picture is intended as a vision of hope for life on earth after the fall of the Roman Empire. The scene ends with the fourth of Revelation's beatitudes, calling "blessed and holy" those who share in the first resurrection (20:6). They are priests of God (reprising the priestly image for the community from 1:6 and 5:10; drawing on Isa. 61:6; Exod. 19:6).

After the thousand years, Satan is released from the Abyss to deceive the mythical nations of Gog and Magog (from Ezekiel 38–39). That these nations apparently survived the previous destruction of hostile nations in 19:11-21 underscores that these visions are not to be understood chronologically. Fire from heaven defeats them, and Satan is thrown into the same lake of fire as the two beasts.

Only the final scene of judgment, 20:11-15, focuses on the judgment of individuals rather than judgment of systems of oppression. God is seated on a great white throne, with all the dead standing before the throne. Books are opened, including the book of life inscribed with people's names from the foundation of the world (13:8; 17:8; 21:27). Each person is judged according to the ledger of his or her "deeds" (*erga*). The last enemy to be destroyed is the personified figure of Death, thrown into the lake of fire along with Hades, to join the rest of Satan's agents. No actual humans are depicted as being thrown into the lake of fire.

Earth and heaven flee from God's presence (20:11)—presumably because they represent the world corrupted by life-destroying forces and imperial oppression (see 21:1).

The Text in the Interpretive Tradition

Disputes about the millennial reign of a thousand years almost kept the book of Revelation out of the Bible, and continue to play an inordinate role in discussions about Revelation. No other New Testament passage mentions a temporary messianic reign before the last judgment, nor is the millennium part of any of the early church's creeds. The brevity of the millennium passage makes clear that it is not the center of Revelation (Murphy).

Early interpreters such as Papias, Justin Martyr, and Irenaeus understood the millennium as a literal time of earthly bliss, combining it with Isaiah 65 and other Scriptures about the renewal of the earth, even though John himself does not make such paradisiacal connections. Irenaeus's hyperbole included descriptions that "vines will grow, each having ten thousand shoots . . . and in each cluster ten thousand grapes, and each grape when crushed will yield twenty-five measures of wine" (*Against Heresies* 5.33.3). Such earthly interpretations came about in part as a way of counteracting gnostic anti-earth tendencies. The thousand years were not necessarily literal years, however, since "the day of the Lord is as a thousand years" (Ps. 90:4; cited by Justin, *Dialogue with Trypho* 80).

Tyconius and Jerome shifted the millennium in a timeless, spiritual direction. The battle depicted in Revelation became the spiritual battle within the individual soul. Augustine completed the turn by claiming Christians are already living symbolically in the millennial age, in the church. The binding of Satan had happened in the first coming of Christ, embodied in Jesus' exorcisms when Satan was bound, and it would last until Jesus' second coming. The first resurrection happened in baptism, with the second resurrection being identified with the final raising of the dead for the judgment at the end of the age.

Augustine's became the dominant interpretation until Joachim of Fiore (1132–1202), when futurist interpretations once again emerged. Today's premillennial dispensationalists continue to critique Augustine's symbolic interpretation of the church as living already in the millennium.

Throughout history, social movements have drawn on Revelation's idea of an earthly millennium in order to promote reform. From the People's Crusade of 1095 (Cohn, 61–68) to the Taborites in fifteenth-century Bohemia to the attempt to establish new Jerusalem in Münster, Germany, in the 1530s (Moore, 298) to the nonviolent communal life of sixteenth-century Anabaptists to Franciscan and Jesuit missionaries pursuing millennial dreams in the New World to the "Diggers" movement advocating for restructuring land ownership in England in the seventeenth century or the Shakers and their Millennial Laws in early nineteenth-century New England, popular movements throughout the centuries have read their own history in light of the millennial vision of Rev. 20:4-6 (Reeves). Even Sir Isaac Newton, a prolific commentator on Daniel and Revelation, gave extensive interpretations of the millennium.

The great white throne of judgment from Revelation 20, combined with the judgment of the sheep and goats from Matt. 25:31-46, has shaped Christian imagination about the last judgment. Medieval cathedrals portrayed this scene over the entrance tympanum, threatening worshipers with judgment as they entered. The twelfth-century sculpture at the Cathedral of St. Lazare in Autun, France, by Giselbertus shows a terrified crowd waiting for the weighing of souls, with tiers of graphic punishments for the damned on Christ's left side, and the blessings of eternal life for those on his right side. Dante Alighieri's late-thirteenth-century Italian poem *The Inferno* depicts the last judgment as one of the church's teachings of "four last things" (death, judgment, hell, and heaven), detailing tortures far surpassing Revelation's lake of fire. Michelangelo's painting of the last judgment before the great white throne, influenced by Dante, occupies the most prominent wall in the Sistine Chapel in Rome. William Blake's allegorical painting *The Day of Judgment* (1808) retains the traditional right/left division between heaven and hell, including vivid rewards and punishments, with the great white throne in the center. He adds the element of earth convulsed with the resurrection life of the dead rising up from their graves.

The mysterious nations of Gog and Magog (Rev. 20:8; Ezekiel 38–39), prevalent in Jewish apocalypticism (cf. *3 En.* 45.5; *Sib. Or.* 3.319), have fueled multiple attempts to correlate Revelation with geopolitical events unfolding in interpreters' own times. Josephus (*Ant.* 1.6.1) identified Gog with the Scythians. Some medieval maps such as the thirteenth-century "Psalter" even pictured a wall in northeastern Europe behind which Gog and Magog were imprisoned (Boyer). Joachim of Fiore identified them as the Saracens; Martin Luther identified them as the Turks (Kovacs and Roland, 213). One British legend combined them into a single figure of a giant named Gogmagog (Jeffrey of Monmouth's *History of Britain*; Emmerson and McGinn, 312).

Twentieth-century premillennial dispensationalists identified Russia as Magog, an identification made popular by Cyrus Scofield's best-selling 1909 *Scofield Reference Bible*. Hal Lindsay's original *The Late Great Planet Earth* includes an entire chapter titled "Russia Is Gog," expanded more recently to include Islamic nations (*Planet Earth: The Final Chapter*, 1998, 280). John Hagee in 2014 interpreted the crisis in Ukraine as a signal that biblical prophecies about Gog and Magog will be fulfilled in an imminent invasion of Israel by Russia, along with Iran, Libya, and other Muslim nations.

The Text in Contemporary Discussion

Much scholarly debate focuses on how to interpret the violence and judgment of these final scenes. Whereas Jesus has been depicted as a Lamb since chapter 5, here he is depicted as a warrior, wielding the sword of his word as a weapon. The question is whether Jesus now uses violence to kill his enemies—a departure from the nonviolent Lamb—and how John employs the violent imagery of Isaiah 63. Liberation scholars do not all agree. Brian Blount has changed his position from understanding the blood on his garments to be Jesus' own blood to understanding it now as the blood of his enemies (Blount 2009, 352; contra Blount 2005, 82), although he still underscores that "John depicts the Lamb as a nonviolent resister." In Blount's view, John closely follows Isaiah, working with the imagery of a warrior and the trodden winepress (Isa. 63:1–6; Rev. 20:15), including Isaiah's depiction of the robe dipped in enemies' blood. Other liberation scholars such as Pablo Richard counter that John radically changes the imagery of Isaiah so that the blood is Jesus' own (Richard 1995, 147).

Justice is the focus of all the scenes in Revelation 19–20. When the victims of Rome's injustice are raised to sit on thrones, Richard translates their role as "doing justice" (20:4), with "justice" as a preferred translation rather than "judgment" for the Greek word *krisis* throughout the book. For Richard, the millennium must be reclaimed from the two poles of a fundamentalist literalist interpretation on the one hand or a "spiritualizing" ecclesiastical approach on the other hand that collapses the millennium into the church. The millennial vision's importance for mobilizing poor and oppressed people throughout history needs to be reclaimed as a vision for justice for victims on earth.

The location of the thousand-year reign of the resurrected martyrs is also an important question. While the location has sometimes been understood as heaven (Beale, 998), if it is on earth, as liberation scholars argue, then Revelation gives one of the most important visions for helping us imagine life after empire, on earth—an important element also for ecological hermeneutics.

Revelation 21:1—22:5: New Jerusalem and the Renewed Earth

■ The Text in Its Ancient Context

The promise of a "new heaven and new earth" offers the most earth-centered eschatological picture of the entire Bible, a countervision to Babylon/Rome. Contrary to the escapism or "heavenism" of some interpretations today, the picture of Revelation promises God's future dwelling with people in a radiant, thriving cityscape located on a renewed earth. Heaven is not mentioned again after 21:2.

The entire book leads up to this wondrous vision of renewal and joy. The Lamb's bride (introduced in 19:7) now becomes transformed into a magnificent bridal "city" (*polis*). Images of radiance and beauty persuade readers who have "come out" of empire (18:4) to "enter in" (22:14) as citizens of this landscape of blessing and healing.

Repetition of the word "new" (21:1-2) underscores the distinction between God's renewed world and the Roman imperial world that has gone before. The first earth and the sea have "passed away" (*apēlthon*, 21:1). The identity of the "first earth" that passes away is debated. It likely represents the earth as dominated by Roman imperial violence and exploitation. While some scholars interpret the word "new" (*kainos*) as implying cosmic catastrophe and discontinuity of the new earth from the present earth, similar to 2 Pet. 3:10 (Roloff; Adams), John's point is probably not that the whole cosmos will be annihilated and then replaced (Stephens). Rather, it is the Roman imperial world and the world of sin that must be replaced.

Belief in a heavenly Jerusalem was widespread in biblical times (see Gal. 4:26, "Jerusalem above . . . is our mother"; Heb. 12:22; *2 Bar.* 3:1; 5Q15). Isaiah 54 imagines the renewed Jerusalem as made of precious stones and "married" to God in covenantal love. What is so striking in Revelation—unlike any other Jewish apocalypse—is that this heavenly city descends from heaven to earth.

The radiant new city that descends to earth fulfills Isaiah's promises of newness (Isa. 43:19, 65:17) as well as covenantal promises from Ezekiel and Zechariah, and promises from Revelation's seven letters (Schüssler Fiorenza 1991, 111). Greco-Roman utopian hopes about the ideal city are also fulfilled in the vision's majestic processional street and verdant green space (Georgi 1980).

The repeated phrase "no more" (*ouk eti*, Rev. 21:1, 4) underscores new Jerusalem's contrasts with the toxic city of Babylon/Rome (Revelation 17–18). Mourning, pain, and death—all found in Babylon—come to an end in God's holy city. With great tenderness, God wipes away people's tears. The most pointed contrast between the political economies of Babylon and new Jerusalem is John's declaration that "the sea was no more" (21:1). Although this declaration may reflect biblical chaos traditions associated with the sea (Boring), more likely it serves as part of the political critique of Rome (Wengst), a perspective shared also by the *Sibylline Oracles* 5.447–49. The Mediterranean Sea was the location of Rome's unjust trade, condemned in the cargo list of Rev. 18:12-13. Therefore, in God's new Jerusalem, there will be no more sea trade.

God's presence will have its "dwelling" or will "tabernacle" (*skēnē*, *skēnoō*, Rev. 21:3) in the midst of the bridal city, recalling God's "tabernacling" with Israel in the wilderness (Lev. 26:11-12; Ezek. 37:27; Zech. 2:10-11). The descent of God's dwelling to earth draws on the descent of the personified feminine figure of Wisdom in Sir. 24:4-8, 10-11.

Readers who have come out of Babylon/Rome now are named "victors" or "conquerors" who will inherit all the promises of God (Rev. 21:7). The designation brings to fulfillment the promise to each of the seven churches in Revelation 2-3 ("to the one who conquers," 2:7, 11, 17, 26; 3:5, 12, 21).

God speaks for the first time since Rev. 1:8, not through angelic intermediaries but directly, "Behold, I make all things new." God promises water of life for all who thirst, free of charge. This twice-repeated promise of the water of life *dorean*, "without price" (Rev. 21:6; 22:17), underscores the economic contrast between God's political economy and Rome's. Unlike the unjust commerce of Babylon/Rome, in God's new Jerusalem the essentials of life are given to all who thirst as a free gift, "without money" (Isa. 55:1; Sir. 51:25), even to the poor who cannot pay for them.

The city's descent is narrated a second time, this time as an architectural tour of new Jerusalem (21:9—22:5). The same angelic guide who showed John the judgment of Babylon (17:1) now takes him to a high mountain to "show" him features of God's radiant city. The city is huge (1,500 miles in each direction), shaped as a cube, with golden streets, twelve pearly gates, and foundations of precious stones.

The tour is modeled on the angel's tour of the new temple in Ezekiel 40-48. Revelation makes important changes to open up Ezekiel's priestly vision to everyone. One striking modification is that the new Jerusalem has "no temple" (21:22). God's presence now extends to the entire city's landscape, with all of God's people serving as priests (Rev. 1:6; 5:10; 20:6; 22:3, 5). New Jerusalem is a welcoming city, not a gated community. Ezekiel's temple gate was shut so that "no one shall enter by it" (Ezek. 44:1-2), but the gates into new Jerusalem are perpetually open (21:26). Even foreigners are invited to enter into this radiant city, whose lamp is the Lamb, Jesus. Nations will walk by its light, streaming in through its open gates (21:24, 26).

The bridal city represents the entire renewed world, not just the church (Schüssler Fiorenza 1991, 112; Richard 1995, 164; Krodel, 359). Whereas in the Pauline tradition the bride is the church (2 Cor. 11:2; Eph. 5:25), in Revelation the bride is much more. The city's walls, whose twelve foundations are the twelve apostles, likely represent the church. But the size of the city itself is much larger than the walls and foundations.

Only those whose names are written in Jesus' book of life may enter as citizens into God's new Jerusalem. A lengthy vice list (21:27), similar to other vice lists (21:8, 22:15), warns those excluded from the city. The function of such threats is exhortation, in the tradition of a prophetic wake-up call. John's goal is to persuade readers to be faithful, so that their names will be written in God's book of life.

The final section of this city vision (22:1-6) features paradise-like images of nature and healing. God, nature, and human beings all become reconciled (Georgi 1980).

The image of the "throne" recurs twice in this section (Rev. 22:1, 3). Although it is not explicitly stated, Rev. 22:1, 3 suggests that God's throne will now move down from heaven to earth, in the midst of the city. God's river of life and green space fill out the final description of the city. Revelation 22:1-5 recreates the Garden of Eden in the center of a thriving urban landscape, drawing on Ezekiel's vision of a river flowing out from the temple (Ezek. 47:1-12). In Revelation the river of life flows not from the temple but from the throne of God and the Lamb, through the center of the processional street of the city. Ezekiel's fruit trees on both banks become the wondrous "tree of life" in Revelation (Rev. 22:2), invoking paradise traditions. The fruit of the ever-bearing tree of life satisfies the hunger of all in need, overcoming the prohibition of Gen. 3:22.

Most importantly, the tree's leaves provide healing. In contrast to the toxic *pharmakeia* ("sorcery," Rev. 18:23) of Babylon, God's tree of life gives medicine—*therapeia*—for the world. Healing for the earth is an important apocalyptic theme also in *1 Enoch* ("Heal the earth, announce the healing of the earth," *1 En.* 10:7). The prophet Ezekiel described trees with leaves for healing; Revelation universalizes Ezekiel's vision by adding the "healing of the *nations*" to the tree's healing leaves (Rev. 22:2; cf. Ezek. 47:12). Revelation's medicinal leaves offer a vision of a political economy that heals the entire world. Healing comes not directly from God but through the creation, from a tree.

The tour of the city concludes with reference to God's servants who offer service and worship (*latreusousin*) before the throne (Rev. 22:3). God's servants shall reign forever and ever. At a time when Rome claimed to reign forever, Revelation boldly proclaimed that it is God who reigns—not the empire—and that God's servants will also reign with God. There is no object of the verb "reign." God's servants do not reign over anyone else.

■ The Text in the Interpretive Tradition

The vision of the city with the gleaming golden street and pearly gates, where death and tears are no more, has given form and voice to the dreams of God's people through the ages. From Augustine's *City of God* through William Blake's "Jerusalem" and Martin Luther King's "I Have a Dream," Revelation's holy city has promised life and healing, reconciliation and justice.

A prophet of the New Prophecy ("Montanist") movement in the second century, Priscilla, taught that the new Jerusalem would descend in rural Pepuza in Asia Minor (Epiphanius, *Pan.* 49.1.2–3). Partly in reaction to such apocalyptic speculation, Augustine and Tyconius identified the church itself as the new Jerusalem, and baptism as the water of life.

Many have looked for the new Jerusalem as an actual city of hope within history, overturning injustice. African American spirituals and gospel songs inspire hope by evoking imagery of the golden holy city and its river of life. "Blow Your Trumpet, Gabriel" longs for the trumpet to "blow me home" to the new Jerusalem, with its tree of life:

> Blow your trumpet, Gabriel
> Blow louder, louder
> And I hope dat trumpet might blow me home
> To the new Jerusalem.

For Martin Luther King Jr., the new Jerusalem was an ethical vision, offering a view of "what we have to do." King appealed to this vision in his 1968 speech "I See the Promised Land."

> It's all right to talk about "streets flowing with milk and honey," but God has commanded us to be concerned about the slums down here, and his children who can't eat three square meals a day. It's all right to talk about the new Jerusalem, but one day, God's preacher must talk about the new New York, the new Atlanta, the new Philadelphia, the new Los Angeles, the new Memphis, Tennessee. This is what we have to do. (Washington, 282)

Revelation's tree of life gave rise to a rich interpretive history, especially in art. The twelfth-century apse mosaic of the basilica of San Clemente in Rome depicts Christ's crucifix as a life-giving tree for nesting birds and other creatures, from which flows a stream of water giving drink to two deer. The foliage of the tree is portrayed as a new Jerusalem cityscape, with vignettes of people's vocations in daily life encapsulated in the branches of the tree. The tree of life tradition is also present in the "green cross" of the stained glass windows at Chartres cathedral.

Revelation's healing tree inspired the Nobel Peace Prize–winning Green Belt work of Wangaari Maathai in Kenya. She situated her work of planting hundreds of thousands of trees in the tradition of John and other biblical prophets who ask "why we do this to the earth," and she responded that "they are commanding us to heal and replenish it now" (Maathai, 125). Revelation's tree and river also inspired US poet laureate Maya Angelou's poem "On the Pulse of the Morning," invoking the invitation of "a rock, a river, and a tree," read at President Bill Clinton's inauguration in 1993.

The new earth imagery of Revelation 21 became Christopher Columbus's inspiration for his explorations in the vision of the new earth of Revelation 21: "Of the new heaven and earth which our Lord made, as St John writes in the Apocalypse . . . he made me the messenger thereof and showed me where to go" (Kovacs and Rowland, 226).

C. S. Lewis based his "New Narnia" image on Revelation 21, envisioning "new" in terms of both continuity and transformation. In *The Last Battle*, the New Narnia where Lucy and her companions find themselves at the end of their journey is not an escape from old Narnia, but rather an entry more deeply into the very same place. Everything is more radiant. It is "deeper country." New Narnia is "world within world," where "no good thing is destroyed" (Lewis, 181).

■ The Text in Contemporary Discussion

Continuity or discontinuity between the present earth and the eschatological future is a subject of scholarly debate. Traditionally, scholars thought of apocalyptic literature as reflecting a pessimistic outlook of "cosmic dissolution and annihilation" of the present world as a precondition for any new creation (Adams). But recent scholarship has made the convincing case that what was viewed as "cosmic catastrophe" may in fact be more political than cosmic. Apocalypses are resistance literature (Portier-Young, xxii). In times of imperial oppression, Jewish apocalyptic authors employed hyperbolic imagery of the earth rent asunder, followed by a "new heaven" (*1 En.* 91:16), as a way of assuring the audience that oppressive rule will be terminated. The new heaven of *1 Enoch* "consists in the restoration of divine governance" and renewal for the people (Horsley, 2003, 76, 79). Similarly, Revelation's language of the new heaven and the new earth reflects renewal and radical transformation, not replacement or annihilation of the present earth (Stephens; Bauckham 2010, 175).

For ecological hermeneutics, Revelation 21–22 is the most important vision of the book. Revelation suggests that our future dwelling with God will be on a radiant earth. Revelation's declaration of water given "without cost" (*dorean*) can be an important corrective to modern capitalist tendencies to commodify or "festishize" everything (Richard 1995, 130), where even water must be bought and sold. The world's rivers of life and trees of life are not for sale.

As a biblical image common also to many other religions, the tree of life can be an important resource for interreligious dialogue, including "the menorah of Judaism, the tree pattern on an Islamic prayer carpet, the kadamba tree of Krishna in Hinduism, the bodhi tree in Buddhism . . . and the Lakota tree of life at the center of the world" (Ramshaw, 118; Rasmussen, 195–207). Revelation's nation-healing tree of life can invite us into interreligious dialogue with people of other faiths.

Scholars disagree as to the function of the threats of 21:8 and 21:27, and whether John envisions the possibility of universal salvation. If these threats are modeled on Ezekiel 44, they may delineate those forbidden to enter the new Jerusalem. Yet Revelation makes numerous changes to open up the city, especially the proclamation in 22:3 that nothing shall be accursed any longer—perhaps even intending an end to the lake of fire. John depicts a "radically inclusive city" (Boring, 221). Even kings, previously condemned, contribute positively to the splendor of the city in 21:24. These and other verses lead a few scholars (Georgi 1980, 183; Rissi, 80–81) to suggest that Revelation implies the salvation of all. The new Jerusalem vision's proclamation of healing for the nations "brings to fulfillment the conversion of the nations" (Bauckham 1993a, 318). Possibly, what John hopes for is the conversion and salvation of everyone—although most scholars stop short of claiming that John envisions such universalism.

Revelation 22:6-21: Epilogue: Closing Blessings and Exhortations

The Text in Its Ancient Context

Revelation 22 concludes the prophetic letter with formulaic blessings, warnings, and exhortations. Frequent changes in speaker between the sayings make it difficult to know whether an angel, or John, or the risen Christ is speaking.

Eschatological and ethical urgency underlie this chapter, with the repeated proclamation that Christ will come "soon" (*tachy*, Rev. 22:6, 7, 12, 20) and the declaration that he is the first and the "last" (*eschatos*), the Alpha and Omega (22:13). These themes parallel the opening verses, 1:1-8. The proclamation that Christ would come soon was good news for those who cried out "How long, O Lord?" (Rev. 6:10).

Revelation's journey ends as it began, pronouncing as blessed everyone who "keeps" what is written. Two references to "keeping" (22:7, 9; recalling 1:3) underscore a sense of ethical urgency. The two blessings or beatitudes in verses 7 and 14 are the last of Revelation's seven beatitudes, a typical form of speech used by Christian prophets (see Rev. 1:3; 14:13; 16:15; 19:9; 20:6; 22:7, 14). Recalling the promises to Ephesus and Philadelphia (2:7; 3:12), the beatitude of Rev. 22:14 promises the tree of life and citizenship in the holy city as a reward ("so that they may have the right to come into the city by the gates"). The beatitude assures those who have come out of Babylon (18:4) that they will "come into" God's city of blessing as citizens and heirs. Repetition of imagery of the tree of life and holy city both in this beatitude and in the closing threat of 22:19 underscores their centrality. John invites readers to desire a share (*meros*, 22:19) in the holy city and its tree of life rather than a share (*meros*) in the lake of fire (21:8).

Authentication is one function of the entire closing section. John establishes the book's authority by his claims to have seen the visions (22:8). Even here (as in 19:10), he has to be corrected to worship God alone. The directive not to seal up the vision contrasts with 10:4, where John was directed to seal up the vision (echoing Dan. 8:26).

Multiple threats and warnings also underscore a sense of urgency in this final section. The vice list of 22:15, listing those "outside" the city, like the other vice lists (21:8, 27), may be read as exhortation rather than prediction. It is harder to know what is meant by the imperatives of 22:11. They may indicate that it is too late for repentance—although the beatitude of 22:14 suggests otherwise (Harrington 1993, 222).

Jesus is the bright morning star of Balaam's oracle in Num. 24:17, a text that was already interpreted messianically by the time of the New Testament. "Washing their robes" recalls the vision of the community in 7:14.

Revelation concludes with a liturgical dialogue (Vanni). The entire book has brought hearers on a transformative journey, through hearing the book read aloud in the worship service. This final scene is the homecoming. The antiphonal "Come" (Rev. 22:17) may be part of a eucharistic liturgy in which the Spirit and the bridal new Jerusalem call the community to participate. The reference to "manna" in 2:17 also hints at Eucharist, as does the gift of water for those who thirst—perhaps analogous to some early churches' Eucharists that included water along with wine (Hippolytus, *Apostolic Tradition* 23; Daly-Denton). The invitation to "take the water of life" (Rev. 22:17) draws the new Jerusalem vision to a sacramental close. Drinking and eating at the eucharistic table transport readers in some measure into God's future holy city, to glimpse the throne of God and taste its life-giving water. As in Rev. 21:6, God gives the water of life *dorean* ("without cost"), contrasting the Lamb's gift-economy once again to the ruthless economies of all of Babylon/Rome.

The threats in verses 18-19 against "anyone who adds to" or "takes away from" the words of this book may reflect the prophetic dispute between John and other Christian leaders evidenced in the seven letters of chapters 2–3. Distinguishing true and false prophets was a concern also in other early Christian texts such as the *Didache*.

The closing invocation of 22:20, "Come, Lord Jesus," translates the Aramaic expression *maranatha*, which also appears in *Didache* 10.6 and 1 Cor. 16:22. The letter closing, like the opening, resembles a Pauline letter, with a final announcement of grace (22:21; cf. Gal. 6:18). Ancient manuscripts of Revelation differ by one word as to whether this is a final grace given to "all" or simply to "all the saints"—again raising the question of how far Revelation pushes toward universalism (Boring, 226).

■ THE TEXT IN THE INTERPRETIVE TRADITION

The threats of chapter 22 led Martin Luther, in his 1522 preface to Revelation, to criticize Revelation as "neither apostolic nor prophetic." John "seems to be going much too far when he commends his own books so highly ... and threatens that if anyone takes anything from it, God will take away from him." By the time of his second preface (1530), Luther had come to see more value in the book.

Many other interpreters have found resonances in this concluding section of Revelation. Hildegard of Bingen appealed to John's threats and pronouncements of authority in order to claim authority for her own book of mystical interpretations, *Scivias* (Kovacs and Rowland, 243). Johnny Cash quoted 22:11 in his 2002 song "The Man Comes Around," the title track of the album. In addition to the pessimistic "let the filthy still be filthy," other images from Revelation fill Cash's song about the Christ's coming in judgment, including Armageddon, the white horse, "It's Alpha and Omega's kingdom come" (21:6; 22:13), and the elders' casting of golden crowns. Cash's song is deeply personal and also dark, perhaps reflecting the sense of his own approaching death.

The Text in Contemporary Discussion

Four times in this chapter, Jesus says he is coming "soon." His coming means not a terrible final battle at Armageddon or inevitable doomsday for the world, but rather an end to oppression—a radical apocalyptic hope that still resonates today.

Revelation's apocalyptic hope can be read in multiple ways, evoking a broad range of ethical responses. In the area of public policy, for example, when Interior Secretary James Watt was asked by the US House of Representatives in 1981 about the importance of preserving the environment for future generations, he qualified his "yes" with the now-famous remark, "I do not know how many future generations we can count on before the Lord returns." Belief in Christ's imminent coming can lead some people to a disregard for environmental issues and denial of global warming (Northcott; Barker and Bearce). For many others, however, the hope of Christ's coming empowers their commitment to stewardship of God's earth, and even their nonviolent resistance against systems of domination.

Revelation's sense of time can sound threatening. But hope, not threat, is the book's central message. When musician Olivier Messiaen composed his *Quartet for the End of Time* from a Nazi prison camp in 1941, he inscribed the score with words borrowed from Rev. 10:6: "In homage to the Angel of the Apocalypse, who lifts his hand toward heaven, saying, 'There shall be time no longer.'" Revelation's sense of time can sound threatening. But hope, not threat, is the book's central message. Messiaen, like many before him, was able to articulate the radical eschatological hope of Revelation that has been proclaimed through centuries by artists, musicians, poets, reformers, activists, prophets, mystics, and many others.

John's Apocalypse has led hearers through 22 chapters, including dire diagnosis of their situation. His mission has been to help communities see the inevitable end that lies ahead, and then to give them the courage and hope to follow the Lamb, to "come out" of empire before it is too late (Rev. 18:4).

The hope John proclaims is that unjust empires and systems will soon come to an end—in fact, they have already been defeated. The message of hope assures communities thirsting for justice that God hears their cries and that God dwells with them. The hope of Revelation centers on a slain Lamb and a radiant city with gates open to all, with a river of life and a tree that gives healing for the whole world, and healing for each one of us. It is this hope that John intends in the final, summative words, "Amen. Come, Lord Jesus."

Works Cited

Adams, Edward. 2007. *The Stars Will Fall From Heaven: Cosmic Catastrophe in the New Testament and Its World.* New York. T&T Clark.

Alexiou, Margaret. 1974. *The Ritual Lament in Greek Tradition.* Cambridge: Cambridge University Press.

Aune, David E. 1983. "The Influence of Roman Imperial Court Ceremonial on the Apocalypse of John." *BR* 18:5–26.

———. 1990. "The Form and Function of the Proclamations to the Seven Churches (Rev 2-3)." *NTS* 36:182–204.

———. 1997–1998. *Revelation.* 3 vols. WBC 52. Dallas: Word.

Barker, David, and David H. Bearce. 2012. "End-Times Theology, the Shadow of the Future, and Public Resistance to Addressing Global Climate Change." *Political Research Quarterly* 66:267–79.

Barr, David L. 1984. "The Apocalypse as Symbolic Transformation of the World." *Int* 38:39–50.

———. 1997. "Towards an Ethical Reading of the Apocalypse." *SBLSP*, 358–73. Atlanta: Scholars Press.

———. 1998. *Tales of the End: A Narrative Commentary on the Book of Revelation.* Santa Rosa, CA: Polebridge.

Bauckham, Richard. 1977. "The Eschatological Earthquake in the Apocalypse of John," *NovT* 19:216–25.

———. 1993a. *The Theology of the Book of Revelation.* New Testament Theology. Cambridge: Cambridge University Press.

———. 1993b. *The Climax of Prophecy: Studies on the Book of Revelation.* Edinburgh: T&T Clark.

———. 2010. *The Bible and Ecology: Rediscovering the Community of Creation.* Waco: Baylor University Press.

———. 2011. *Living with Other Creatures: Green Exegesis and Theology.* Waco: Baylor University Press.

Beale, G. K. 1999. *The Book of Revelation: A Commentary on the Greek Text.* NIGTC. Grand Rapids: Eerdmans.

Betz, Hans Dieter. 1969. "On the Problem of the Religio-Historical Understanding of Apocalypticism." *Journal of Theology and Church* 6:134–56.

Blount, Brian. 2005. *Can I Get A Witness? Reading Revelation through African American Culture.* Louisville: Westminster John Knox.

———. 2009. *Revelation: A Commentary.* NTL. Louisville: Westminster John Knox.

Boesak, Allan A. 1987. *Comfort and Protest: Reflections on the Apocalypse of John of Patmos.* Philadelphia: Westminster.

Bond, Ronald. 1992. "Whore of Babylon." In *A Dictionary of Biblical Tradition in English Literature*, edited by David Lyle Jeffrey, 26-28. Grand Rapids: Eerdmans.

Boring, M. Eugene. 1989. *Revelation.* IBC. Louisville: Westminster John Knox.

Boyer, Paul. 1992. *When Time Shall Be No More: Prophecy Belief in Modern American Culture.* Studies in Cultural History. Cambridge, MA: Harvard University Press.

Boxall, Ian. 2013. *Patmos in the Reception History of the Apocalypse.* Oxford: Oxford University Press.

Caird, G. B. 1966. *The Revelation of Saint John.* Black's New Testament Commentaries. London: A. & C. Black.

Callahan, Allen. 1995. "The Language of Apocalypse." *HTR* 88:453–70.

———. 1999. "Apocalypse as Critique of Political Economy: Some Notes on Revelation 18." *HBT* 21:46–65.

Carey, Greg. 1999. *Elusive Apocalypse: Reading Authority in the Revelation to John.* StABH 15. Macon, GA: Mercer University Press.

———. 2008. "The Book of Revelation as Counter-Imperial Script." In *In the Shadow of Empire: Reclaiming the Bible as a History of Faithful Resistance*, edited by Richard A. Horsley, 157-75. Louisville: Westminster John Knox.

Cohn, Norman. 1970. *The Pursuit of the Millennium: Revolutionary Millenarians and Mystical Anarchists of the Middle Ages.* Oxford: Oxford University Press.

Collins, Adela Yarbro. 1976 *The Combat Myth in the Book of Revelation.* HDR 9; Missoula, MT: Scholars Press.

———. 1980. "Revelation 18: Taunt-Song or Dirge?" in Jan Lambrecht (ed.) *L'Apocalypse johannique et l'apocalyptique dans le Nouveau Testament.* Gembloux: J. Duculot.

———. 1984. *Crisis and Catharsis: The Power of the Apocalypse.* Philadelphia: Westminster.

———. 1993. "Feminine Symbolism in the Book of Revelation." *BibInt* 1:20–33.

Daniel, E. Randolph. 1992. "Joachim of Fiore: Patterns of History in the Apocalypse." In *The Apocalypse in the Middle Ages*, edited by Richard Emmerson and Bernard McGinn, 72–88. Ithaca, NY: Cornell University Press.

Daly-Denton, Margaret. 2011. "To Hear What Water Is Saying to the Churches." In *Water: A Matter of Life and Death*, edited by Norman Habel and Peter Trudinger, 111–25. Interface 14, no. 1. Hindmarsh, Australia: ATF Press.

DeSilva, David. 2009. *Seeing Things John's Way: The Rhetoric of the Book of Revelation.* Louisville: Westminster John Knox.

Duff, Paul B. 2001. *Who Rides the Beast? Prophetic Rivalry and the Rhetoric of Crisis in the Churches of the Apocalypse.* Oxford: Oxford University Press.

Emmerson, Richard Kenneth, and Bernard McGinn, eds. 1992. *The Apocalypse in the Middle Ages.* Ithaca, NY: Cornell University Press.

Flannery, Frances. 2014. "Dreams and Visions in Early Jewish and Early Christian Apocalypses and Apocalypticism." In *Oxford Handbook of Apocalyptic Literature*, edited by John J. Collins, 104–20. Oxford: Oxford University Press.

Frankfurter, David. 2001. "Jews or Not? Reconstructing the 'Other' in Rev 2:9 and 3:9." *HTR* 94:403–25.

———. 2011. "Revelation to John." In *The Jewish Annotated New Testament*, edited by Amy-Jill Levine and Marc Zvi Brettler, 463–98. Oxford: Oxford University Press.

Fretheim, Terrence. 1991. "The Plagues as Ecological Sign of Historical Disaster." *JBL* 110:385–96.

Friesen, Steven J. 2001. *Imperial Cults and the Apocalypse of John: Reading Revelation in the Ruins.* Oxford: Oxford University Press.

Georgi, Dieter. 1980. "Die Visionen vom himmlischen Jerusalem in Apk 21 und 22." In *Kirche: Festschrift fur Gunther Bornkamm*, edited by Dieter Luhrmann and Georg Strecker, 351–72. Tübingen: Mohr Siebeck. ET: "John's Heavenly Jerusalem." In *The City in the Valley: Biblical Interpretation and Urban Theology.* Atlanta: Society of Biblical Literature, 2005.

———. 1986. "Who Is the True Prophet?" *HTR* 79:100–126.

González, Justo L. 1999. *For the Healing of the Nations: The Book of Revelation in an Age of Cultural Conflict.* Maryknoll, NY: Orbis.

Hagee, John. 1999. *From Daniel to Doomsday: The Countdown Has Begun.* Nashville. Thomas Nelson.

Harrington, Wilfrid J. 1993. *Revelation.* Sacra Pagina 16. Collegeville, MN: Liturgical Press.

Horsley, Richard A. 2003. *Jesus and Empire: The Kingdom of God and the New World Disorder.* Minneapolis: Fortress Press.

———, 2010. *Revolt of the Scribes: Resistance and Apocalyptic Origins.* Minneapolis: Fortress Press.

———, ed. 1997. *Paul and Empire: Religion and Power in Roman Imperial Society.* Harrisburg, PA: Trinity Press International.

Huber, Lynn R. 2013. *Thinking and Seeing with Women in Revelation.* New York: T&T Clark.

Hughes, Donald. 1996. *Pan's Travail: Environmental Problems of the Greeks and Romans.* Baltimore: Johns Hopkins University Press.

Humphrey, Edith M. 1995. *The Ladies and the Cities: Transformation and Apocalyptic Identity in Joseph and Aseneth, 4 Ezra, the Apocalypse, and the Shepherd of Hermas.* Sheffield: Sheffield Academic Press.

Jeffrey, David Lyle, ed. 1992. *Dictionary of Biblical Tradition in English Literature.* Grand Rapids. Eerdmans.

Johns, Loren. 2003. *The Lamb Christology of the Apocalypse of John: An Investigation into Its Origins and Rhetorical Force.* WUNT. Tübingen: Mohr Siebeck.

Keller, Catherine. 1996. *Apocalypse Now and Then.* Boston: Beacon.

Kinney, Dale. 1992. "The Apocalypse in Early Christian Monumental Decoration." In *The Apocalypse in the Middle Ages*, edited by Richard Kenneth Emmerson and Bernard McGinn, 200–216. Ithaca, NY: Cornell University Press.

Klauck, Hans-Joseph. 2001. "Do They Never Come Back? Nero Redivivus and the Revelation of John." *CBQ* 63:683–98.

Klein, Peter K. 1992. "The Apocalypse in Medieval Art." In *The Apocalypse in the Middle Ages*, edited by Richard Kenneth Emmerson and Bernard McGinn, 159-99. Ithaca, NY: Cornell University Press.

Koester, Craig R. 2001. *Revelation and the End of All Things.* Grand Rapids: Eerdmans.

Kovacs, Judith, and Christopher Rowland. 2004. *Revelation: The Apocalypse of Jesus Christ.* Oxford: Blackwell.

Kraybill, J. Nelson. 2010. *Apocalypse and Allegiance: Worship, Politics, and Devotion in the Book of Revelation.* Grand Rapids: Brazos.

Krodel, Gerhard. 1989. *Revelation.* ACNT. Minneapolis: Augsburg.

LaHaye, Tim. 1973. *Revelation Illustrated and Made Plain.* Rev. ed. Grand Rapids: Zondervan.

Lawrence, D. H. 1988. "Apocalypse." In *The Revelation of Saint John the Divine*, edited by Harold Bloom, 45–53. Modern Critical Interpretations. New York: Chelsea House.

Lewis, C. S. 1956. *The Last Battle.* New York: MacMillan.

Luther, Martin. 1530. "Preface to the Revelation of St. John." In *LW* 35:398–99.

———. 1972. *Luther's "September Bible" In Facsimile. Part I. Das Newe Testament Deutzsch. Part II. Brief Historical Introduction by Kenneth A. Strand.* Ann Arbor, MI: Ann Arbor Publishers.

Maathai, Wangari. 2010. *Replenishing the Earth: Spiritual Values for Healing Ourselves and the World.* New York: Doubleday.

Maier, Harry O. 2002. *Apocalypse Recalled: The Book of Revelation after Christendom.* Minneapolis: Fortress Press.

Martin, Clarice. 2005. "Polishing the Unclouded Mirror: A Womanist Reading of Revelation 18:13," in David Rhoads, ed., *From Every People and Nation: The Book of Revelation in Intercultural Perspective.* Minneapolis: Fortress Press. 82-109.

McGinn, Bernard. 1994. *Antichrist: Two Thousand Years of the Human Fascination with Evil.* San Francisco: HarperSanFrancisco.

———, ed. 1998. *The Encyclopedia of Apocalypticism.* Vol. 2, *Apocalypticism in Western History and Culture.* New York: Continuum.

Metzger, Bruce M. 1993. *Breaking the Code: Understanding the Book of Revelation.* Abingdon.

Miller, Lisa. 2010. "Some Say BP's Oil Spill Heralds the Apocalypse." *Newsweek* June 3, 2010. http://www.newsweek.com/some-say-bps-oil-spill-heralds-apocalypse-73117.

Moore, Rebecca. 2011. "European Millennialism." In *The Oxford Handbook of Millennialism*, editd by Catherine Wessinger, 284–303. Oxford: Oxford University Press.

Morris, Ian. 2010. *Why the West Rules—for Now: The Patterns of History, and What They Reveal about the Future.* New York: Farrar, Straus and Giroux.

Moyise, Steve. 2001. "Does the Lion Lie Down with the Lamb?" In *Studies in the Book of Revelation*, edited by Steve Moyise, 181–94. New York: T&T Clark.

———. 2004 "Singing the Song of Moses and the Lamb: John's Dialogical Use of Scripture," *Andrews University Seminary Studies* 42: 347–60.

Murphy, Frederick. 1998. *Fallen Is Babylon: The Revelation to John.* Harrisburg, PA: Trinity Press International.

Murrell, Nathaniel. 2001. "Wresting the Message from the Messenger: the Rastafari as a Case Study in the Caribbean Indigenization of the Bible." In *African Americans and the Bible*, edited by Vincent Wimbush, 558–76. New York: Continuum.

Norris, Kathleen. 1999. *Introduction to Revelation.* Pocket Canon Series. New York: Grove.

Northcott, Michael. 2009. "Earth Left Behind? Ecological Readings of the Apocalypse of John in Contemporary America." In *The Way the World Ends? The Apocalypse of John in Culture and Ideology*, edited by William John Lyons and Jorunn Økland, 227–39. Sheffield: Sheffield Phoenix.

Pagels, Elaine. 2012. *Revelations: Visions, Prophecy, and Politics in the book of Revelation.* New York: Viking.

Perry, Peter Soren. 2009. *The Rhetoric of Digressions: Revelation 7:1-17 and 10:1–11:13 and Ancient Communication.* WUNT 2/268. Tübingen: Mohr Siebeck.

———. 2010. "Things Having Lives: Ecology, Allusion and Performance in Revelation." *CurTM* 37: 105–33.

Pippin, Tina. 1992. *Death and Desire: The Rhetoric of Gender in the Apocalypse of John.* Literary Currents in Biblical Interpretation. Louisville: Westminster John Knox.

Portier-Young, Anathea. 2011. *Apocalypse against Empire: Theologies of Resistance in Early Judaism.* Grand Rapids: Eerdmans.

Ramshaw, Gail. 1995. *God beyond Gender.* Minneapolis: Fortress Press.

Rasmussen, Larry. 1996. *Earth Community, Earth Ethics.* Maryknoll, NY: Orbis.

Reeves, Marjorie. 2008. "Dragon of the Apocalypse." In *A Dictionary of Biblical Tradition in English Literature*, edited by David Lyle Jeffrey, 210–13. Grand Rapids. Eerdmans.

Resseguie, J. L. 1998. *Revelation Unsealed: A Narrative Critical Approach to John's Apocalyptic.* Leiden: Brill.

Rhoads, David, ed. 2005. *From Every People and Nation: The Book of Revelation in Intercultural Perspective.* Minneapolis: Fortress Press.

Richard, Pablo. 1995. *Apocalypse: A People's Commentary on the Book of Revelation.* Maryknoll, NY: Orbis.

Rissi, Matthias. 1972. *The Future of the World: An Exegetical Study of Revelation 19:11—22:15.* SBT 23. London: SCM.

Roloff, Jürgen. 1993. *Revelation.* CC. Minneapolis: Fortress Press.

Rossetti, Christina. 1892. *The Face of the Deep: A Devotional Commentary on the Apocalypse.* London: SPCK.

Rossing, Barbara. 1999. *The Choice Between Two Cities: Whore, Bride and Empire in the Apocalypse.* HTS 48. Harrisburg, PA: Trinity Press International.

———. 2002. "Alas for the Earth: Lament and Resistance in Revelation 12." In *The Earth Bible.* Vol. 5, *The Earth Story in the New Testament*, edited by Norman Habel and Shirley Wurst, 180–92. Sheffield: Sheffield Academic Press.

———. 2003. "(Re)Claiming *Oikoumene*? Empire, Ecumenism and the Discipleship of Equals." In *Walk in the Ways of Wisdom: Essays in Honor of Elisabeth Schüssler Fiorenza*, edited by Shelly Matthews, Cynthia Briggs Kittredge, and Melanie Johnson-DeBaufre, 74–87. Harrisburg, PA: Trinity Press International.

———. 2004. *The Rapture Exposed: The Message of Hope in the Book of Revelation.* Boulder, CO: Westview.

Rowland, Christopher C. 1998. "Revelation: Introduction, Commentary, and Reflections." In *Hebrews–Revelation*. Vol. 12, *The New Interpreter's Bible*, edited by Leander E. Keck, 503–736. Nashville: Abingdon.

Ruiz, Jean-Pierre. 1992. "Betwixt and Between on the Lord's Day: Liturgy and the Apocalypse." *SBLSP* 31. Ed. Eugene H. Lovering. 654–72.

———. 2001. "Praise and Politics in Revelation 19:1-10." In *Studies in the Book of Revelation*, edited by Steve Moyise, 69–84. New York: T&T Clark.

Sánchez, David. 2008. *From Patmos to the Barrio: Subverting Imperial Myths*. Minneapolis: Fortress Press.

Schüssler Fiorenza, Elisabeth. 1991. *Revelation: Vision of a Just World*. Proclamation Commentaries. Minneapolis: Fortress Press.

———. 1998. *The Book of Revelation: Justice and Judgment*. 2nd ed. Minneapolis: Fortress Press.

———. 2001. "The Words of Prophecy: Reading the Apocalypse Theologically." In *Studies in the Book of Revelation*, edited by Steve Moyise, 1–20. New York: T&T Clark.

Smith, Robert H. 2000. *Apocalypse: A Commentary on Revelation in Words and Images*. Collegeville, MN: Liturgical Press.

Stenstrom, Hanna. 2013. "'They Have Not Defiled Themselves with Women …': Christian Identity According to the Book of Revelation." In *A Feminist Companion to the Apocalypse of John*, edited by Amy-Jill Levine. New York: T&T Clark.

Stephens, Mark B. 2011. *Annihilation or Renewal? The Meaning and Function of New Creation in the Book of Revelation*. WUNT 2/307. Tübingen: Mohr Siebeck.

Suggit, John N. 2006. *Oecumenius: Commentary on the Apocalypse*. Fathers of the Church. Washington, DC: Catholic University of America Press.

Swete, Henry B. 1911. *The Apocalypse of St. John*. 3d ed. London: MacMillan.

Talbert, Charles H. 1994. *The Apocalypse: A Reading of the Revelation of John*. Louisville: Westminster John Knox.

Thompson, Leonard L. 1990. *The Book of Revelation: Apocalypse and Empire*. Oxford: Oxford University Press.

Thuesen, Peter, ed. 2008. *The Works of Jonathan Edwards*. Vol. 26, *Catalogues of Books*. New Haven: Yale University Press.

Vanni, Ugo. 1991. "Liturgical Dialogue as a Literary Form in the Book of Revelation." *NTS* 37:348–72.

Wainwright, Arthur W. 1993. *Mysterious Apocalypse: Interpreting the Book of Revelation*. Nashville: Abingdon.

Washington, James M., ed. 1986. *Testament of Hope: The Essential Writings and Speeches of Martin Luther King, Jr*. New York: HarperCollins.

Wengst, Klaus. 1987. *Pax Romana and the Peace of Jesus Christ*. Philadelphia: Fortress Press.

Westhelle, Vitor. 2005. "Revelation 13: Between the Colonial and the Postcolonial, a Reading from Brazil," in David Rhoads, ed., *From Every People and Nation: The Book of Revelation in Intercultural Perspective*. Minneapolis: Fortress Press, 183–99.

Wink, Walter. 1998. *The Powers That Be: Theology for a New Millennium*. New York: Doubleday.